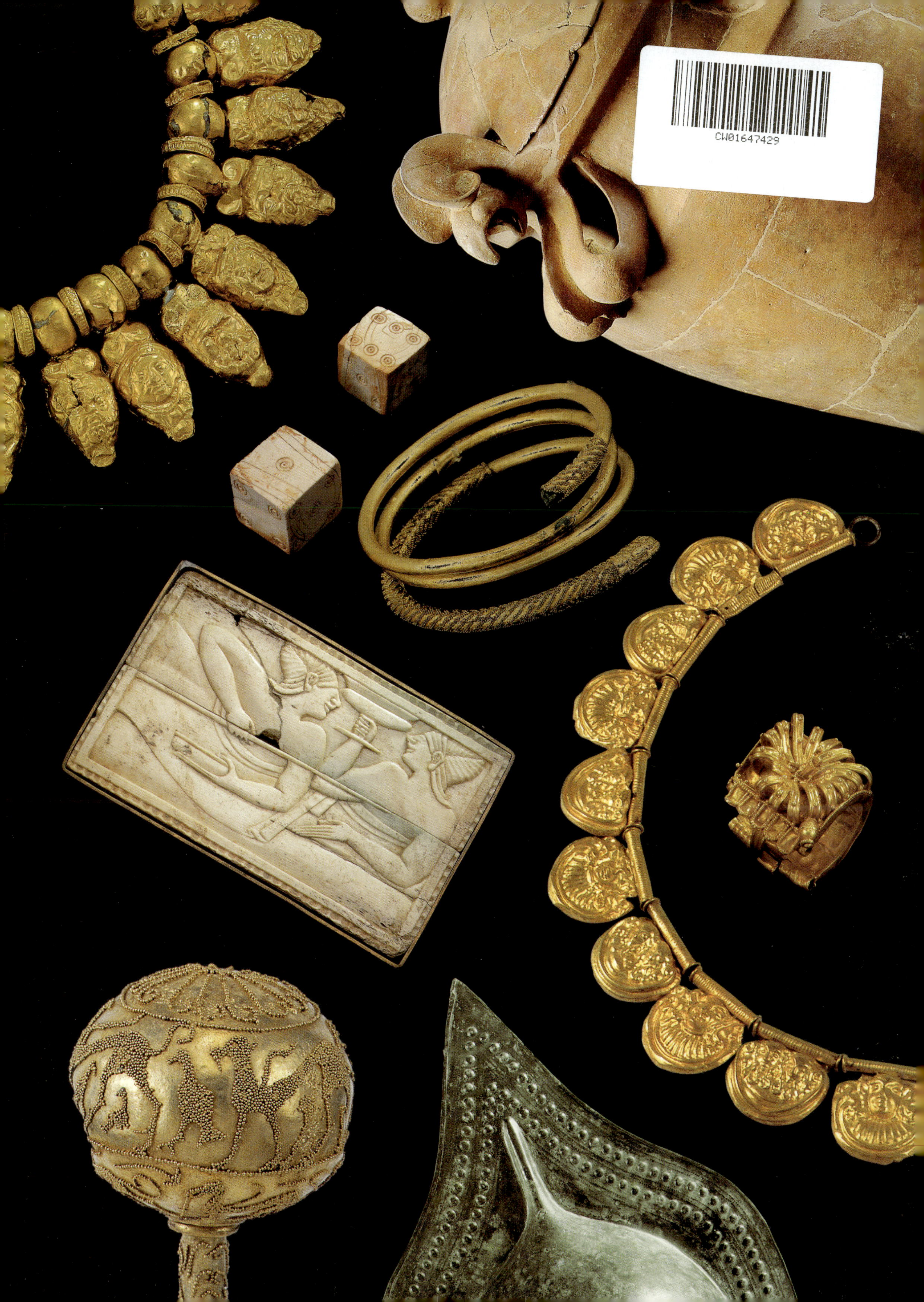

TREASURES FROM TUSCANY

THE ETRUSCAN LEGACY

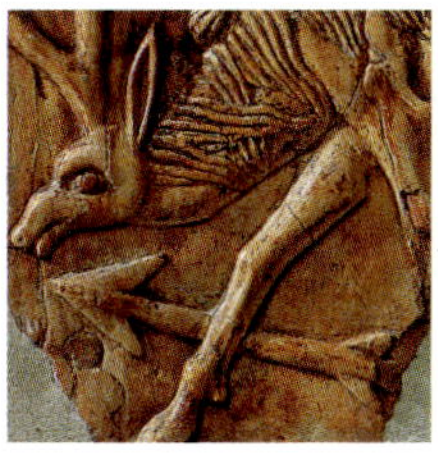
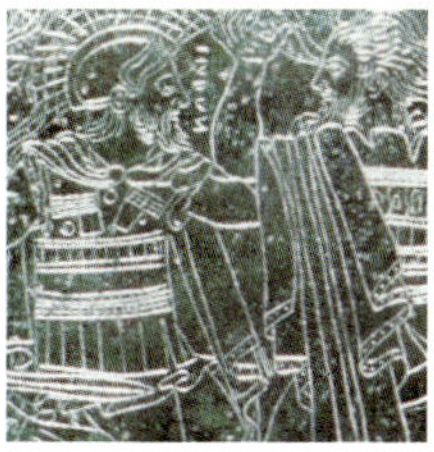
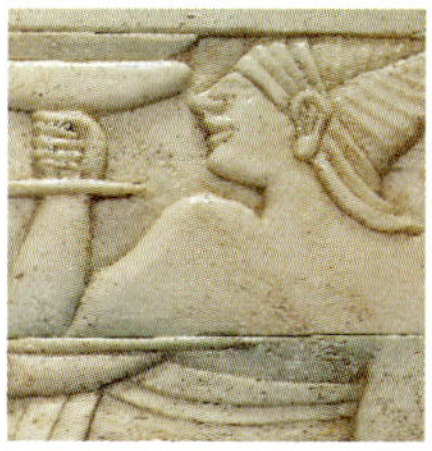

NMS National Museums of Scotland

Published by
NMSE Publishing
a division of NMS Enterprises Limited
National Museums of Scotland
Chambers Street
Edinburgh EH1 1JF

British Library Cataloguing in Publication Data
A catalogue record for this book
is available from the British Library

ISBN 1 901663 90 6

Cover, map and timeline design by Mark Blackadder
Internal design by NMS Enterprises Limited – Publishing

Printed and bound in the United Kingdom by Cambridge Printing

Treasures from Tuscany – The Etruscan Legacy
at the National Museums of Scotland
from 16 July to 31 October 2004

was organized and presented by the
Superintendence for Archaeological Heritage of Tuscany,
Tuscany Region and Centro Promozioni e Servizi, Arezzo, Italy

In collaboration with the Italian Cultural Institute, Edinburgh
and supported by Fondazione Monte dei Paschi di Siena

Also under the patronage of
The Italian Ministry for Cultural Assets
The Italian Ministry for Foreign Affairs

CONTENTS

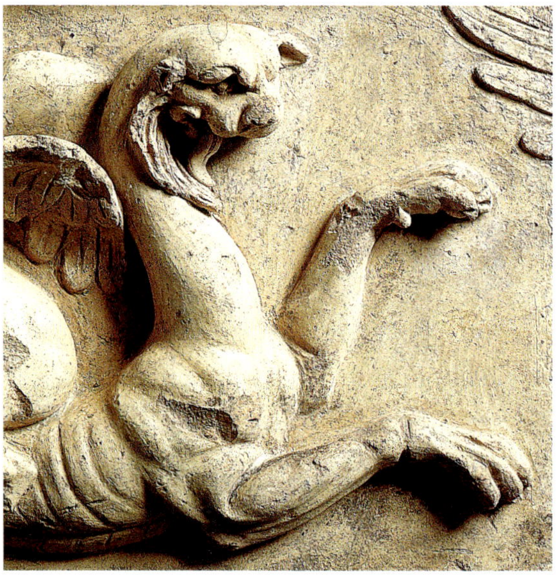

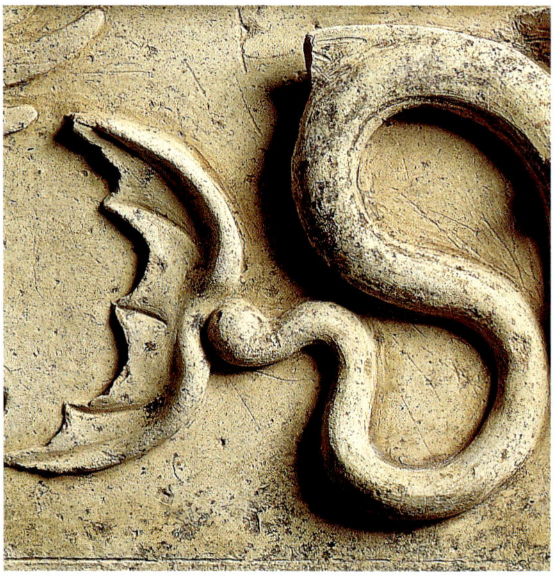

FOREWORD

ENNIO TROILI
Director
Italian Cultural Institute, Edinburgh

The opening of the exhibition *Treasures from Tuscany – The Etruscan Legacy* at the Royal Museum is an event of particular importance: it is in fact the first specifically Italian presentation housed by the Museum and the first large archaeological exhibition on the Etruscans.

Treasures from Tuscany is also the central event in the various activities marking the 40th anniversary of the Edinburgh-Florence twinning link, which will carry on until the end of September.

Alongside the archaeological exhibition there is a small, but extremely interesting, presentation of contemporary Italian design, '20 oggetti a reazione poetica', organized by two young architects, Matteo Ragni and Giulio Iacchetti.

The two exhibitions, though different in subject and intention, demonstrate the principles that have inspired the recent policies of the Italian Cultural Institute: that is to show the importance and wealth of our cultural patrimony and also to underline the continuity of our cultural tradition and the vitality of contemporary Italian culture in its different aspects.

Old and new, therefore, but bound together in a relationship which has remained uninterrupted for centuries, and in fact has been continually enriched by new and diverse sources of inspiration combining and assimilating influences from other cultures too.

With this in mind the Institute has also promoted the Italian Film Festival, now in its 11th edition, as well as retrospectives of the great Italian film directors, Pasolini, Olmi, Zurlini and Fellini (to mention only those undertaken this year). It has also promoted the publication of novels by contemporary writers, Ammaniti and Baricco; an exhibition of Italian fashion from 1950 to 1980; and events dedicated to the leading Italian cities – Siena, Florence, Venice, and shortly Palermo. With their long and complex historical and literary evolution, and their Old Masters, these cities have long been studied: in October 2004 an international conference is being held at the National Gallery of Scotland on the occasion of the exhibition *The Age of Titian – Venetian Renaissance Art from Scottish Collections.*

The wide range of events organized to accompany the exhibition of *Treasures from Tuscany* is part of this overall plan, and in the coming months will bring Italy into the forefront of the Scottish cultural scene, and will strengthen our collaboration with local institutions, which has proved so successful.

My warm thanks to the National Museums of Scotland for accepting my proposals and for timing them to coincide with the Edinburgh International Festival, and also my thanks to the Centro Promozioni e Servizi, Arezzo, and the Soprintendenza Archaeologica of Tuscany, with whom I have had very cordial and valuable relations for many years.

Previous page:
above: detail of plaque (no. 271e)
below: detail of tripod cup (no. 271f)

FOREWORD

GIANCARLO ARAGONA
Italian Ambassador
to the United Kingdom

It gives me great pleasure to welcome the exhibition *Treasures from Tuscany – The Etruscan Legacy* to the Royal Museum, Edinburgh.

This is the first event on the Etruscans ever held in Scotland and I would like to underline not only the beauty of the works of art – from jewels to bronze, from ceramics to ivory – but also their importance for the understanding of such an extraordinary civilization, the first to flourish on Italian soil, at the very origins of the history of Rome and, hence, of Western civilization.

Treasures from Tuscany also marks a significant moment in Scottish-Italian relations as it was initiated under the 'co-operation agreement' signed in 2002 between Scotland and Tuscany and coincides with the celebrations for the 40th anniversary of the Edinburgh-Florence twinning.

This long series of events will trace an ideal itinerary from the Etruscan world to our times, showing how skills and creativity have flourished in Tuscany side by side for centuries.

Treasures from Tuscany is a remarkable achievement, an example of co-operation between public and private institutions from both countries, and provides an excellent opportunity for creating even closer cultural links, paving the way for an increasingly vibrant collaboration between Italy and Scotland.

Finally, I would like to take this opportunity to thank all those who contributed to making this wonderful exhibition possible.

FOREWORD

CLAUDIO MARTINI
Chairman of the Tuscany Regional Assembly

The Etrurian civilization marked the development of central Italy and all the other Mediterranean cultures throughout the millennium. This led from the primitive cultures of the Bronze Age to the great Roman civilization. Etruscans influenced and moulded the character of the Roman society, whose complexity and cultural wealth took root in the Etrurian era.

Etruscan archaeological finds testify to the constant changes, development and progress undergone by this civilization, thanks to the economic and cultural relationships they established with nearly all the other Mediterranean peoples. Etruscans succeeded in building bridges between the east and west, north and south of the ancient world, and they mediated among all these different cultures. These peoples found the Etruscan environment the perfect place to meet each other.

The objects displayed in this exhibition provide an exhaustive outline of all the arts that flourished in Etruria. This was thanks to the talent and technical skill of its artists and craftsmen, who shaped new styles and summed up in amazing allegories the wealth of the Etruscan civilization. In any of these finds you can see the mark of individual inventiveness and the strength of the cultural syncretism that livened up the Etrurian world, a theme that is still important and topical.

Tuscany is regarded as the cradle of the Etruscan civilization. It is an honour, and extremely satisfying, to see the great interest still aroused by Etruscans all over the world. *Treasures from Tuscany – The Etruscan Legacy* deserves particular attention and approval, as it brings together an exhaustive selection of amazing Etrurian works of art with a selection of items belonging to the everyday life of the Etruscan citizens. This will enhance the familiarity of visitors with the habits, behaviours and features of this society.

The United Kingdom has always shown much interest in the Etrurian civilization. Etruscan collections are on display both in the British Museum in London and in the National Museums of Scotland in Edinburgh. *Treasures from Tuscany* gives all of us a further occasion to demonstrate the great passion and respect for ancient civilizations which is nourished by British institutions and the British people with a support evolved from in-depth knowledge and scientific authority.

The Etruscans, the bridge-builders between different European civilizations and the East, brought the shores of the Mediterranean Sea closer together. As such they exemplify the establishment of international cultural and economic relationships in a friendly and successful way. As the Etruscan legacy demonstrates, such relationships are bound to strengthen partnerships and make them richer.

Once again, I would like to thank the National Museums of Scotland for giving us the opportunity to encourage and enrich discussion and knowledge of the Etruscans.

FOREWORD

GORDON RINTOUL
Director
National Museums of Scotland

An important aspect of the work of the National Museums of Scotland is to enable visitors to see and to learn about cultures from around the world. We welcome the opportunity to show *Treasures from Tuscany – The Etruscan Legacy* at a time when links between this country and Tuscany are becoming ever stronger. This was recognized and encouraged by an agreement signed in 2002 between our First Minister, the Right Honourable Jack McConnell MSP, and President Claudio Martini, Chairman of the Tuscany Regional Assembly. The agreement is for the promotion of economic development in areas such as research, technological development and innovation, as well as cultural tourism.

Tuscany, as is well known, is a region rich in cultural treasures, ranging from prehistory to the present day. The objects carefully selected for our exhibition give a fascinating insight into the world of the Etruscans. Archaeologists used to talk about the mystery of this ancient European civilization, contrasting our ignorance of Etruscan culture with our abundance of knowledge of classical Greece and Rome. New discoveries and advances in scholarship have dramatically altered this picture. I fully expect that the exhibition will help demonstrate that the greatest mystery of all is how the treasures and achievements of the Etruscan people have remained so little known for such a long time.

Treasures there certainly are in our exhibition – not just gold and jewellery, but also beautifully crafted pieces of metalwork, stone and ceramics. Perhaps one of the exhibition's greatest strengths is the numerous portraits of the people themselves: images on their funerary equipment and objects of everyday use. This is not a display where people's lives are reconstructed from dry fragments. We are able to see the people for ourselves.

Treasures from Tuscany is about the Etruscan legacy. More and more we are all conscious of our European heritage, of which the Etruscans are a truly significant part. It is right that our exhibition should also encourage us to dwell on this. What contributions did the Etruscans make to the development of European civilization? How is this influence still with us today? We aim to provide some of the answers; you, the visitors, may detect many more.

A project like this depends on the co-operation of many people. It is a particular pleasure to record my thanks and those of my staff to Dr Ennio Troili, Director of the Italian Cultural Institute, Edinburgh, to the Soprintendenza Archaeologica of Tuscany and the Centro Promozioni e Servizi, Arezzo. Without their generosity, skill and hard work, the exhibition would not have been possible.

CONTRIBUTORS

Co-organized by
National Museums of Scotland
Superintendence for Archaeological Heritage of Tuscany, Italy
Tuscany Region
Centro Promozioni e Servizi, Arezzo, Italy

In collaboration with
The Italian Cultural Institute, Edinburgh
And supported by
Fondazione Monte dei Paschi di Siena

Also under the patronage of
The Italian Ministry for Cultural Assets
The Italian Ministry for Foreign Affairs

Lenders to the exhibition
Superintendence for Archaeological Heritage of Tuscany, Italy
National Archaeological Museum of Florence
National Archaeological Museum of Siena
National Archaeological Museum of Arezzo
Archaeological Museum of Chianciano Terme
Guarnacci Museum of Volterra
City Council of Colle Val d'Elsa

Scientific project
Guiseppina Carlotta Cianferoni

Exhibition management

Superintendence for Archaeological Heritage of Tuscany, Italy
Angelo Bottini, Superintendent
Giuseppina Carlotta Cianferoni

Ministry of Culture for Tuscany Region
Mariella Zoppi, Minister of Culture for Tuscany Region
Claudio Rosati
Maurizio Martinelli

Centro Promozioni e Servizi, Arezzo, Italy
Alberto Ricci
Daniel Virtuoso
Gloria Bastieri
Paola Cavigli
Laura Rossi

The Italian Cultural Institute, Edinburgh
Ennio Troili

Restorer
Ulisse Lazzeri

CATALOGUE TEXT

AM Adriano Maggiani
AME Anna Maria Esposito
AMi Alessandra Minetti
AP Alessandra Parrini
AR Anna Rastrelli
ARo Antonella Romualdi
BA Benedetta Adembri
DZ Donatella Zinelli
EG Elizabeth Goring
EM Elisabetta Mangani
FN Francesco Nicosia
GB Gilda Bartoloni
GC Gabriele Cateni
GCC Giuseppina Carlotta Cianferoni
GP Gabriella Poggesi
IO Ilaria Ottanelli
LP Lucia Pagnini
LP Laura Paoli
LV Laura Venuti
MCB Maria Chiara Bettini
MCy Mario Cygielman
MI Mario Iozzo
PG Pamela Gambogi
RW Rose Watban
SB Stefano Bruni
SR Silva Rosi

Text edited by
Elizabeth Goring

The National Museums of Scotland would like to thank the following individuals for their advice and assistance:

Carlotta Cianferoni
Richard De Puma
Linda Lewin
Elizabeth Moignard
David Ridgway
Francesca Serra Ridgway
Laura Rossi
Judith Swaddling
Ennio Troili
Daniel Virtuoso
Dyfri Williams

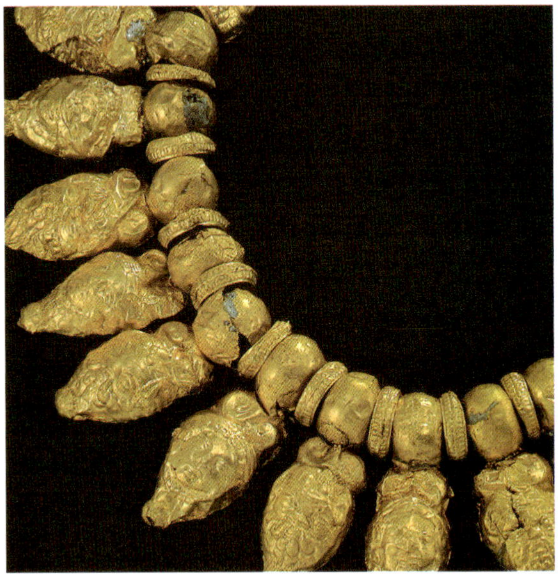

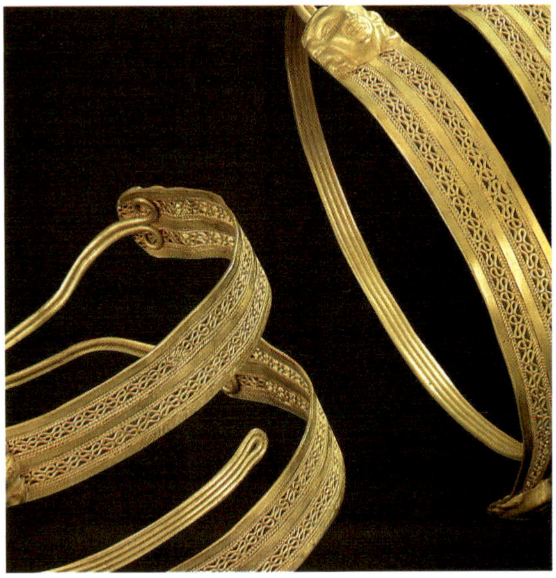

INTRODUCTION

The Etruscans were a highly sophisticated ancient people who lived in central Italy, in an area which lies largely between modern-day Florence and Rome. Their lands, bordered by the Tyrrhenian Sea to the west and the rivers Arno and Tiber to the north and south, included parts of modern Umbria, Tuscany and northern Lazio, all the way to Rome. They also expanded their commercial and political activities into Campania in the south and the Po valley in the north, leaving traces of their culture in those areas too.

The Greeks called the Etruscans the *Tyrrhenoi* or *Tyrsenoi*; the Romans called them *Etrusci* or *Tusci*; and the Etruscans apparently referred to themselves as *Rasenna*. Although they are widely perceived as an intriguing and fascinating people, it is no longer appropriate to refer to them (as they still so often are) as 'the mysterious Etruscans'. In fact, more is probably known about this culture than about any other pre-Roman culture of Italy.

The origins of the Etruscans have been much debated. Herodotus, the 5th century BC Greek historian, related that the Etruscans came from Lydia in Asia Minor. Driven from their homeland by famine, their leader Tyrrhenos, son of Atys, king of Lydia, brought them to Italy where they occupied the city that later became Caere (Cerveteri). Other classical authors thought they were originally Pelasgians. In the late 18th century AD, it was believed that the Etruscans were in the vanguard of migrants from Central Europe who had come to Italy through the transalpine regions to the north.

Today it is recognized that the origins of a people may be considerably more complex than these theories suggest, involving a mixture of ethnic and cultural processes. The roots of the Etruscan civilization may lie in the Late Bronze Age cultures of the local area, in the late 2nd millennium BC. The people who became known as the Etruscans first become visible in the archaeological record in the early Iron Age. The settlements of the Villanovan civilization (named after a site near Bologna) may provide the earliest evidence for the beginnings of Etruscan culture from about the 10th century BC. Although it is possible to refer to 'Etruscan culture', in fact the various Etruscan cities were independent city-states. Etruscan civilization continued to develop for many centuries until, in 27 BC, Etruria became the seventh region of Roman Italy and the Etruscans were finally integrated into the Roman world.

The Etruscan language is popularly perceived as a mystery. In fact Etruscan writing can be read, even though the meaning may not always be understood. The oldest Etruscan inscriptions date from about 700 BC. The language was written down in the alphabet brought to Italy by the first Greeks to settle there, adapted for the local needs. It was generally written from right to left. In the earliest texts there was no separation between words, although later the division between phrases was distinguished by dots. The pronounciation of the Etruscan language is uncertain. It was unlike the other languages spoken in Italy at that time, including Greek; and, unlike Greek, it has not been spoken in the last two thousand years. There are relatively few written texts (some 13,000) and many of them are short and formulaic. Most surviving texts relate to burials and give the name and family connections of the dead person.

Our understanding of the history of the Etruscans has been greatly enhanced by recent discoveries and research. The limited textual and literary evidence is balanced by a wealth of archaeological evidence, which allows us to follow the progress of this remarkable civilization from its earliest definable beginnings in the 9th century BC to its eventual demise in the 1st century BC. *GC/EG*

Previous page:
above: detail of necklace (no. 200)
below: detail of pair of bracelets (no. 62)

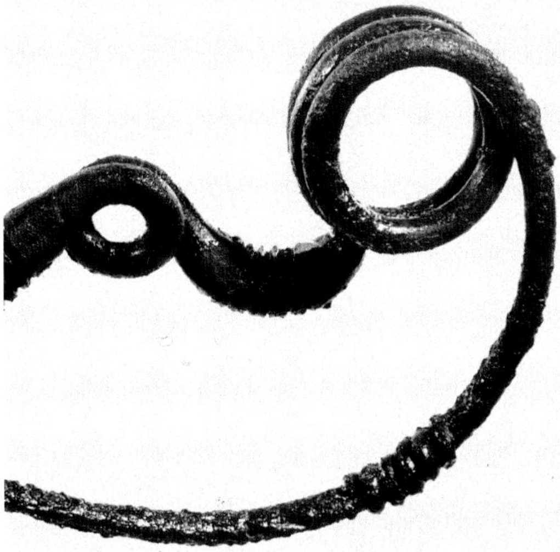

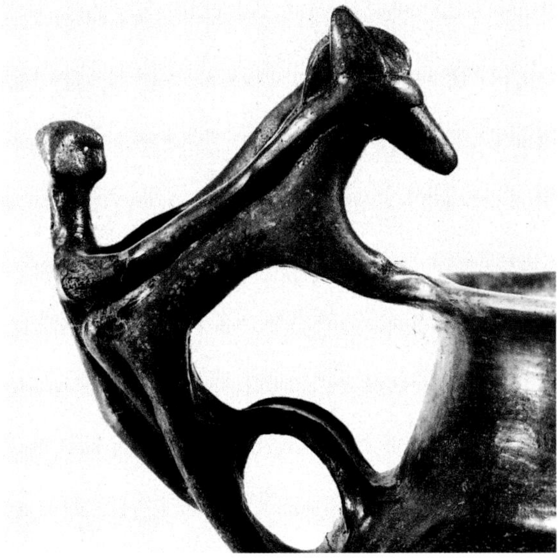

THE RISE OF THE ETRUSCANS

About 900-725 BC

The Early Iron Age civilization of the area that became Etruria is known as 'Villanovan', after a site near Bologna where the first finds that define it were discovered in the 1850s. Most Villanovan archaeological material comes from tombs. There is plenty of evidence for the cemeteries of these proto-Etruscans, which were located outside the settlements. Much less is known about their villages. There are several reasons for this. In the past, antiquarians and archaeologists tended to concentrate on unearthing tombs and sanctuaries, seeking objects which, at the time, were perceived to have greater historical and aesthetic value. They were less interested in settlement sites, which generally produced finds that were considered more mundane. Today the nature of archaeological investigation has changed significantly, and it is recognized that such objects can provide invaluable and evocative evidence for people's daily lives. The locations of the settlements have also played a part. Many Etruscan sites have been occupied continuously from antiquity into later periods, and sometimes to the present day. As a result many of the ephemeral traces of Etruscan habitation have been lost.

Villanovan villages were built on sites that could be easily defended, such as elevated plateaux between two rivers or on hills, and were surrounded by land suitable for farming, grazing and hunting. They were inhabited by small groups of a few hundred people who lived in circular or rectangular huts. Archaeological evidence suggests that these existed side by side, although the rectangular huts may be slightly later. The huts were apparently placed randomly and had some space between them, perhaps for cultivating crops or keeping animals. The larger huts could probably house up to ten people. The structures were made of perishable materials – posts, branches, wattle and daub. Their thatched roofs were supported on wooden frames with projecting eaves. Only traces of the huts now survive, marked by shallow foundation trenches, post holes and layers of habitation debris. Hut urns, used for burying the cremated remains of the dead from the 10th to the 8th centuries BC, provide the main evidence for the superstructures of these early dwellings.

During this period the dead were normally cremated and their burnt remains placed in urns. These were usually vessels made of a thick pottery called impasto, made from unpurified clay, which was worked by hand, burnished and fired at a low temperature. The urns were mainly biconical in shape and had lids shaped like cups or sometimes helmets. Occasionally, however, the burial urns were in the form of the huts of the living. These may have symbolized the houses of the dead or perhaps had implications of status. Grave goods placed with the cremated remains were buried with the ash urns in simple pits cut into the rock or earth. These indicate the sex or social role of the individual. Women's burials were accompanied by jewellery and implements used for spinning thread and weaving wool, such as spindle whorls, distaffs, spindles, spools and loom weights. Men were buried with razors and a particular type of fibula (garment fastener). During the 9th century BC the objects deposited in tombs were noticeably uniform, suggesting communities of people of relatively equal status. However, during the 8th century, especially in the later decades, the first signs of social differentiation are distinguishable. The objects buried in the graves were increasingly varied in both type and quality. There were more, and better, helmets, armour and weapons, and the first imports began to appear, from South Italy, Greece, Sardinia, Phoenicia and Central Europe.

The Villanovan civilization in the Etruria area was greatly influenced by the arrival of Greek colonists in Campania in South Italy. Euboean Greeks founded a trading settlement at Pithekoussai on Ischia around 775 BC, and a little later another at Cumae on the mainland. The presence of the Greeks led both to the import of large numbers of goods from the Greek world and to the arrival of more Greek traders and craftsmen who quickly established themselves on Italian soil. They were particularly attracted by the economic potential of the mining areas of the Tyrrhenian coast, especially the Campigliese and the Catena Metallifera near Populonia and Vetulonia, the island of Elba and the Tolfa mountains near Tarquinia and Cerveteri. The settlers integrated with the local inhabitants and played a significant role in the development of trade, agriculture and crafts. Impasto ware was replaced by pottery made of refined clay;

vessels were shaped on the potter's wheel, new decorative designs and types of vessel were introduced, and higher firing techniques in closed kilns were developed. The local bronze workshops, already very skilled, adopted new ideas and applied them to their own products. There were significant advances in agriculture too, including the introduction of drainage methods, better agricultural tools and new crops. Grapes and olives, ideally suited to Etruria's soil, were cultivated intensively for the first time from the 7th century BC, to produce wine and oil. The private ownership of land, the division of fields, and the growth of boundaries became evident.

All these changes transformed Villanovan society. The succeeding period was to be one of rapidly developing urbanization. Over time, the great Etruscan cities emerged. A more complex social structure evolved, with rich and important aristocratic families demonstrating their wealth and power through their lavish lifestyles and their prestigious and imposing funerary monuments.

GB/EG

Previous page:
above: detail of fibula (no. 3)
below: detail of tripod cup (no. 31)

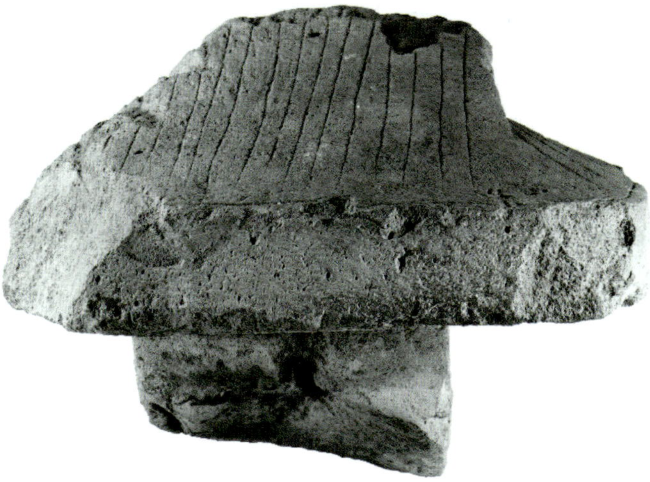

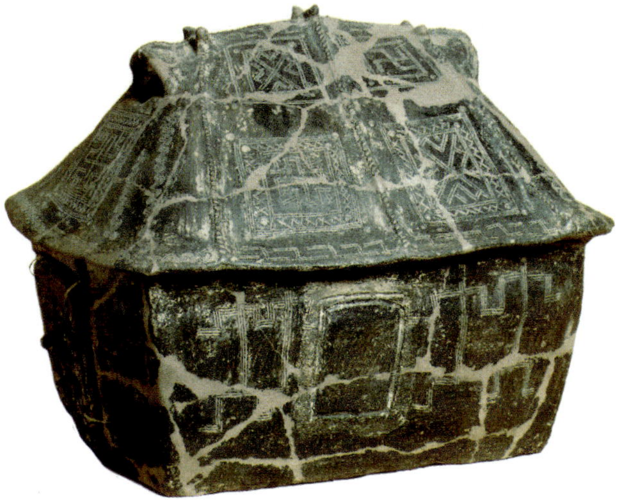

1 ## Cippus (grave marker)

Stone

Poggio Selciatello necropolis, Tarquinia

8th century BC

Height 62.0 cm

Grave markers were not common in the Villanovan period and this one in the shape of a hut roof is particularly unusual. However, hut-shaped ash urns were often used in the Iron Age cemeteries of Lazio and Etruria, especially in the early part of the period, where they have been found alongside the more common biconical urns. The Poggio Selciatello necropolis is one of the oldest cemeteries of Tarquinia. The urns from this cemetery are usually round or oval and represent the domestic huts used by the living. They had thatched roofs constructed of beams, with simple chimney holes set over a central hearth. The walls were of wattle and daub, made of reeds and branches covered with clay, with door and window openings. The hut models provide evidence for animals' and birds' heads or horns on the tops of the roofs, which may have had an apotropaic purpose, designed to turn away bad fortune. *AME*

National Museum of Archaeology, Florence, inv. 93833

2 ## Hut-shaped ash urn

Impasto

Tomb 45, Poggio Selciatello necropolis, Tarquinia

First half of the 9th century BC

Height 30.0 cm

This hut urn is different from most of the others from the same cemetery because of its relatively small size, its rectangular shape, the limited amount of applied ornament and its very rich surface decoration. A window is represented in the middle of one long wall. A pair of figures holding hands, shown to either side, may be taking part in a round dance. The ridge roof has three pairs of ridge logs that cross at the top, and its surface is covered with panels of elaborate incised decorative motifs. Only seven examples of this type of urn have been found in the five great necropolises excavated in Tarquinia. The fibula (number 3) is from the same tomb. *AME*

National Museum of Archaeology, Florence, inv. 21081

Civiltà 1985, 50, nos. 2.4.1, 2.4.2; Etruscos 1999, 210, no. 6; Haynes 2000, 7, fig. 5

3 Fibula

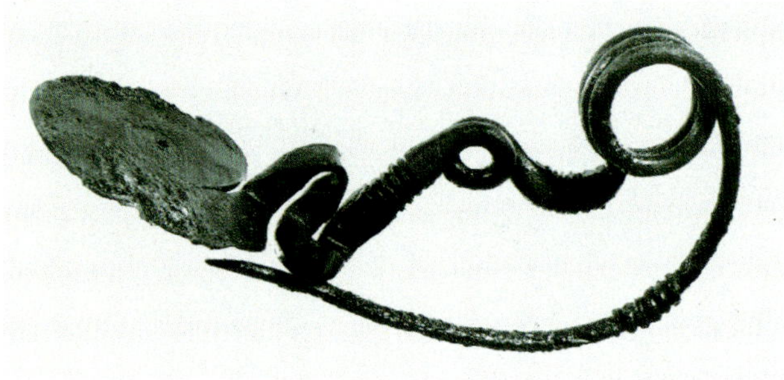

Bronze
Tomb 45, Poggio Selciatello necropolis, Tarquinia
First half of the 9th century BC
Length 10.5 cm

This fibula, with its decorated arch and end plate, belongs to a common type of the early part of the Iron Age, found both on the Tyrrhenian coast and in the Po valley. It supports the dating of the hut urn (number 2) to the earliest phase of Tarquinia's Villanovan period. *AME*

National Museum of Archaeology, Florence, inv. 21082

4 Biconical ash urn with lid bowl

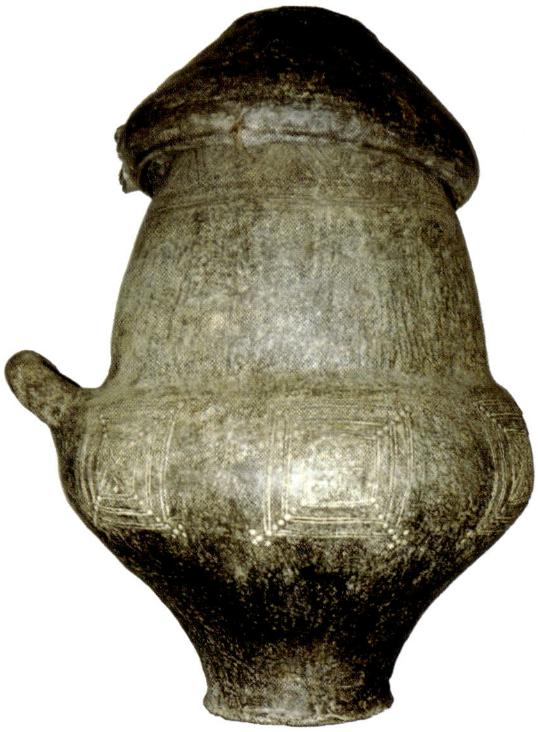

Impasto
Tomb 59, Poggio Selciatello necropolis, Tarquinia
First half of the 9th century BC
Height 40.0 cm

In the first part of the Villanovan period, the dead were normally cremated. Pottery ash urns, usually covered by a ceramic single-handled bowl or sometimes a helmet-shaped lid, were placed in simple pit tombs cut into the soil or rock, together with their associated grave goods. Urns with helmet-shaped lids indicate male graves, while those with lids in the shape of a cup or bowl are more common in women's graves. If the urn originally had two handles, one was often deliberately broken off to make it suitable for funerary use and the fragments placed inside the vessel. Male burials were accompanied by objects such as weapons, bronze fibulae with serpentine bows and razors, whereas female burials had simpler fibulae with arch-bows, jewellery, and equipment for spinning and weaving wool. During the 8th century BC the quality and quantity of the grave goods increasingly indicated the dead person's wealth and social status.

This urn was part of a burial group that also included numbers 5-9. It is a typical example of a woman's grave assemblage of the late Villanovan period in Tarquinia. The content of the group indicates the sex of the dead person. Before firing, the clay surface of the urn was incised with geometric motifs and patterns using a comb-like tool.

AME/GCC/EG

National Museum of Archaeology, Florence, inv. 83533A-B
Torelli 2000, 538, cat. no. 10

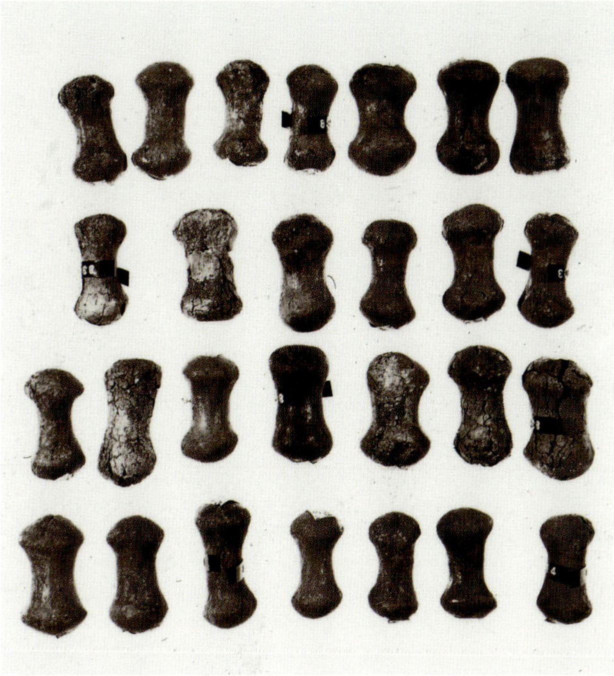

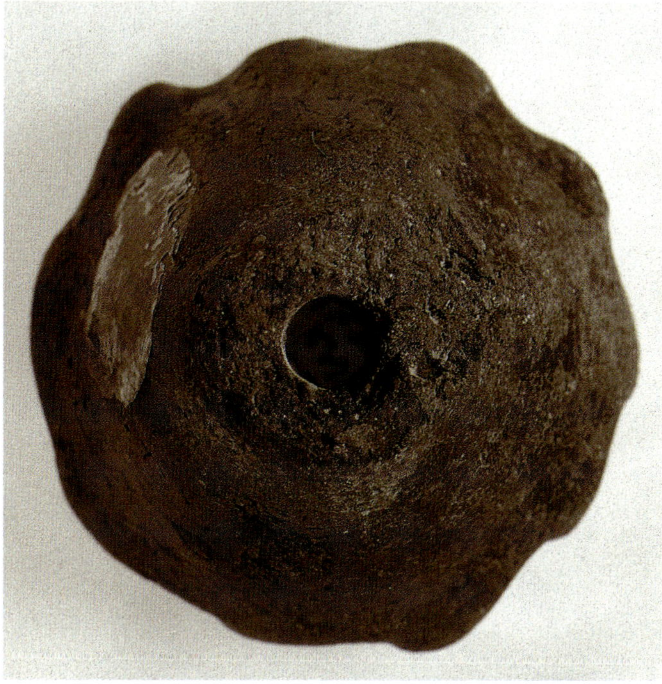

5 Twenty-seven bobbins

Impasto
Tomb 59, Poggio Selciatello necropolis, Tarquinia
First half of the 9th century BC
Length 4.2 to 5.2 cm

Female graves usually contained implements for working wool – spinning, weaving and sewing. These included spindle whorls, spindles, distaffs, loomweights and spools like these, used for thread. Twenty-nine spools were found in this tomb altogether, of which six were included in the exhibition. *EG*

National Museum of Archaeology, Florence, inv. 83533c3-29

6 Spindle whorl

Impasto
Tomb 59, Poggio Selciatello necropolis, Tarquinia
First half of the 9th century BC
Diameter 3.7 cm

National Museum of Archaeology, Florence, inv. 83533c30

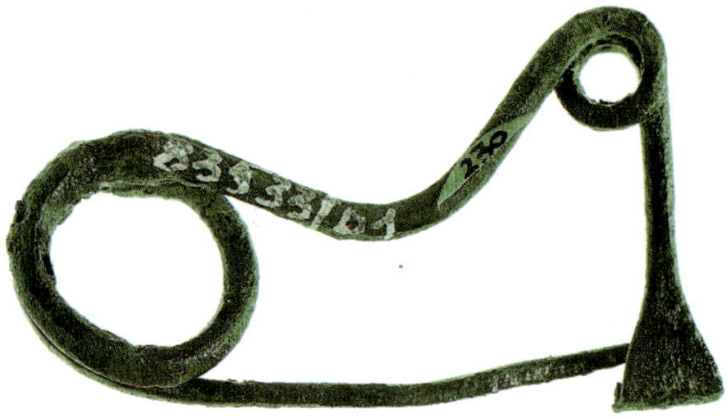

7 Fibula

Bronze
Tomb 59, Poggio Selciatello necropolis, Tarquinia
First half of the 9th century BC
Length 3.8 cm

This fibula has parallels from Sicily. *AME*

National Museum of Archaeology, Florence, inv. 83533d1

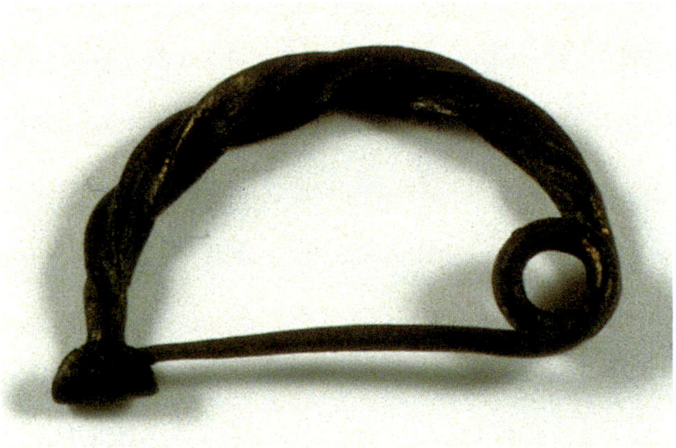

8 Fibula

Bronze
Tomb 59, Poggio Selciatello necropolis, Tarquinia
First half of the 9th century BC
Length 3.3 cm

The metal arch of this fibula has been twisted on itself to provide the decoration. *EG*

National Museum of Archaeology, Florence, inv. 83533d2

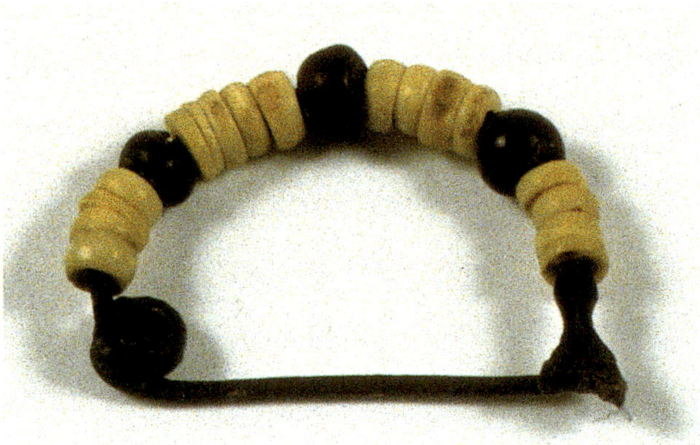

9 Fibula

Bronze and glass
Tomb 59, Poggio Selciatello necropolis, Tarquinia
First half of the 9th century BC
Length 3.5 cm

The arrangement of the beads on this fibula has been reconstructed. *AME*

National Museum of Archaeology, Florence, inv. 83533d3

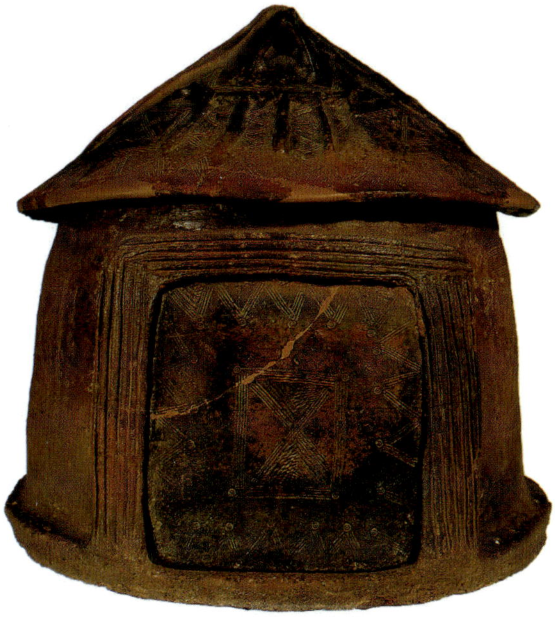

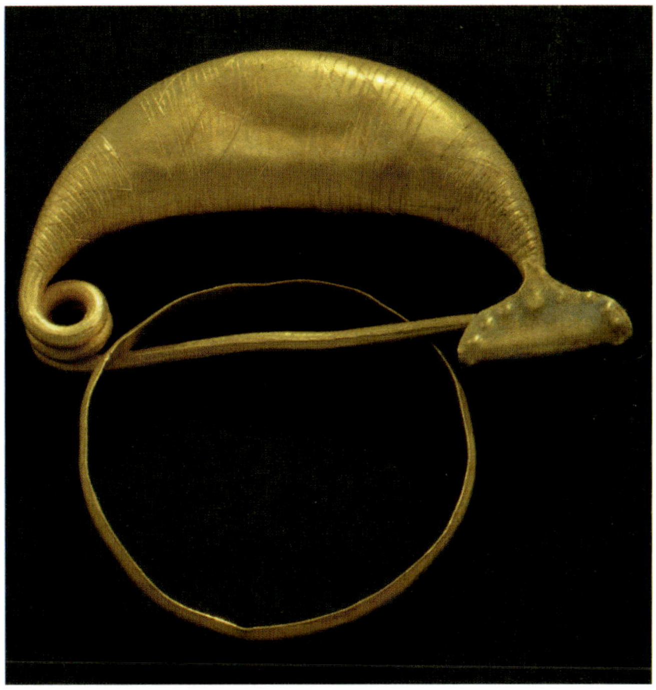

10 Hut-shaped ash urn with lid

Impasto
Poggio della Birbe necropolis, Vetulonia
Second half of the 9th century BC
Height 39.7 cm

Hut urns like this one, with its oval ground plan, offer useful clues to understanding the appearance of Etruscan houses. The geometric patterns on some of the urns suggest the real houses may have had painted decoration on their walls. Although hut urns have been found in several cemeteries in southern Etruria and in Lazio, in northern Etruria they are only known from Vetulonia.

MCy/EG

National Museum of Archaeology, Florence, inv. 6609

11 Fibula

Gold
Tomb 27, Selciatello Sopra necropolis, Tarquinia
Beginning of the 8th century BC
Length 3.4 cm

Bronze examples of this type of fibula were common in the early part of the Iron Age. This example, made from sheet gold, was found in a grave group that also included two gold hair spirals and silver and glass beads, suggesting the dead person was of high social status. The catchplate of the fibula has been decorated in repoussé, a technique where the gold is worked from the back, and the bow with chasing, which is worked from the front. *AME/EG*

National Museum of Archaeology, Florence, inv. 83565
Cristofani and Martelli 1983, 27, no. 2; Gioielli 1988, 137, no. 33

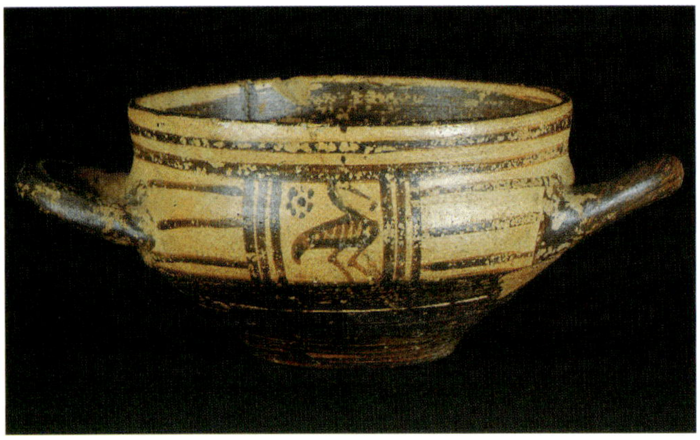

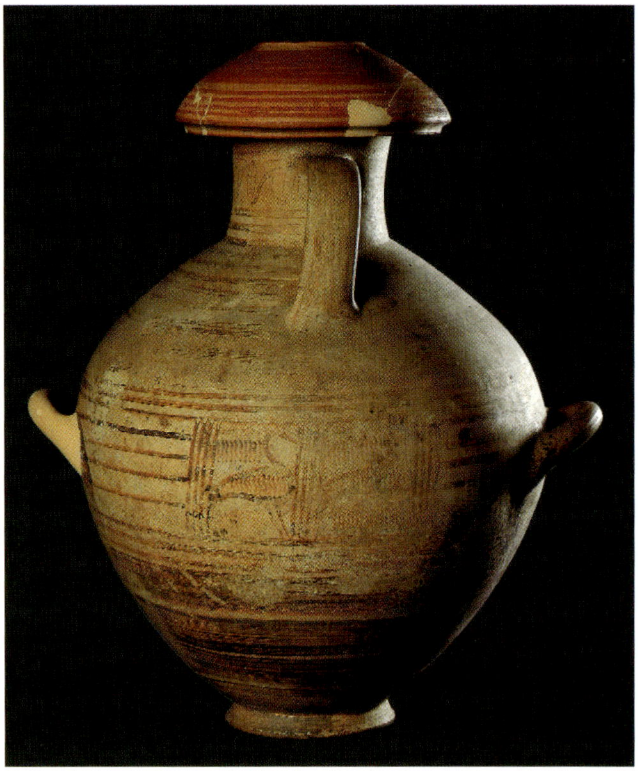

12 Euboean skyphos (drinking cup)

Painted ceramic
Tomb 174, Selciatello Sopra necropolis, Tarquinia
Second quarter of the 8th century BC
Height 7.0 cm

This cup has been recently identified as an Italian imitation of a type made on the island of Euboea, off the coast of Attica and Boeotia in Greece. The panel containing the bird closely resembles panels on vessels from the temple of Apollo at Eretria on Euboea, as well as Euboean-style examples from the Greek island of Naxos dating from around the middle of the 8th century BC.

During the 8th century, Euboeans had established colonies in Italy, at Pithekoussai (Ischia) and on the mainland at Cumae, and Euboea was extremely active in maritime trade. A few cups of this type have been found at several ceramic production centres on the Tyrrhenian coast (Veii, Narce, Cumae and Pithekoussai). It is not clear if they were imported or local imitations. This cup is important because it is one of the earliest examples of contact and interchange between Greece and the Tyrrhenian area after the founding at Pithekoussai of the first Greek colony in the Western Mediterranean.

SB/EG

National Museum of Archaeology, Florence, inv. 21332

13 Etrusco-geometric hydria (water vessel) and lid

Painted ceramic
Tomb 160, Selciatello Sopra necropolis, Tarquinia
First half of the 8th century BC
Height of hydria 40.6 cm; height of lid 6.0 cm

This was part of a burial group which differs from the normal Tarquinian burials of the period. The usual biconical ash urn was replaced by this water vessel with two horizontal handles and one vertical handle, and geometric-style decoration. It was covered with a bowl lid, like the usual types of ash urn. One of its horizontal handles was deliberately broken off, reflecting the custom of breaking one of the two handles of the standard type of burial urn. The hydria was made locally between 770 and 750 BC, imitating ceramics from Euboea in Greece. Its local manufacture is indicated by its decoration, which includes birds set inside rectangular panels. This is a decorative scheme generally used on cups (see number 12). The vessel provides evidence for the close commercial relationship between Etruria and Greece at this time, probably through the Euboean colony of Pithekoussai. The urn was accompanied by a bronze belt and three bronze fibulae, which together suggest a woman's burial of relatively high status. *MI*

National Museum of Archaeology, Florence, inv. 83669a-b
Civiltà 1985, 60-1, nos. 2, 4, 12

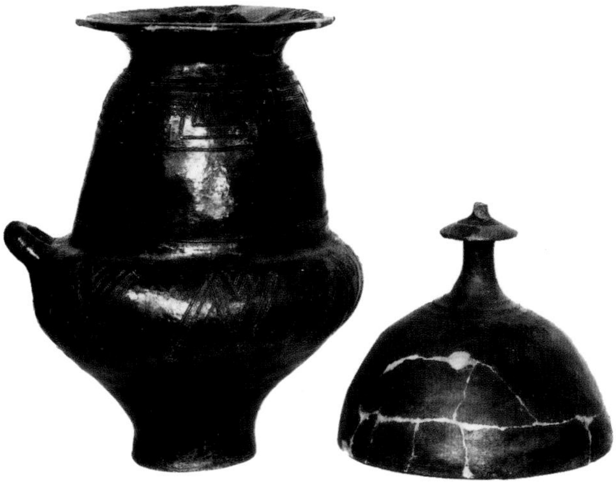

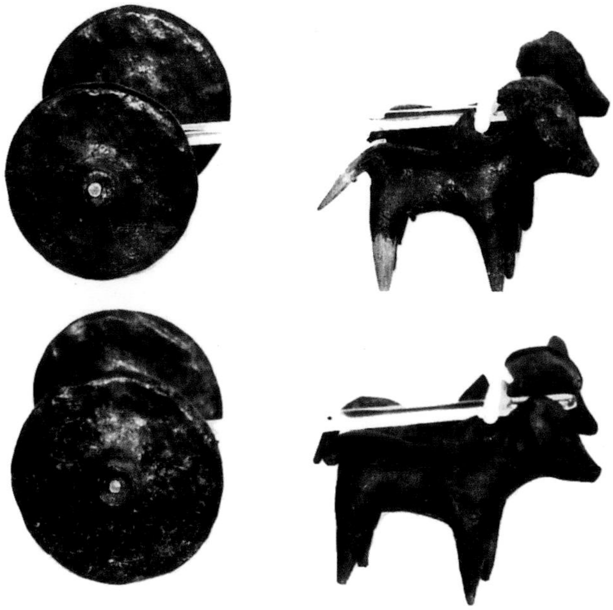

14 Ash urn with helmet-shaped lid

Impasto
Tomb 44, Selciatello Sopra necropolis, Tarquinia
First half of the 8th century BC
Height of urn 39.0 cm; height of lid 20.5 cm

The lid of this urn, which is a ceramic model of a bronze helmet, is an indication of a man's burial. The tomb containing this urn cannot be precisely dated, but the grave gifts were representative of those found in Tarquinian cemeteries in the first half of the 8th century BC. The urn was decorated with linear motifs incised with a double-pronged tool. Number 15 is from the same tomb. *MI*

National Museum of Archaeology, Florence, inv. 83577a-b
Civiltà 1985, 55, no. 56

15 Two model chariots

Impasto
Tomb 44, Selciatello Sopra necropolis, Tarquinia
First half of the 8th century BC
Height 6.7 cm

This type of chariot with its solid wheels originated in the Near East but spread widely throughout Europe. Two-wheeled chariots are less common than four-wheeled examples. Horse-drawn vehicles would have been associated with wealth and prestige. *MI/EG*

National Museum of Archaeology, Florence, inv. 83577c-d

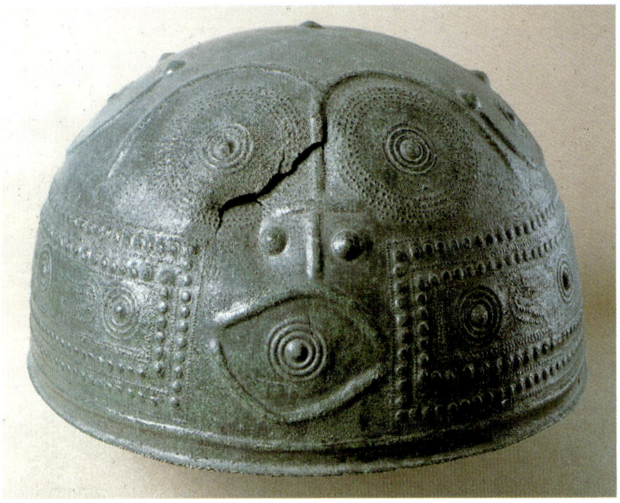

16 **Helmet**

Bronze

Tomb II (Tomb of the Priest), Poggio dell'Impiccato, Tarquinia

First half of the 8th century BC

Height 14.5 cm; diameter 29.0 cm

This helmet was found in the richly-furnished pit tomb of a warrior. Its decoration, which was applied in the repoussé technique, combines a stylized human face with motifs derived from central Europe. The face may have an apotropaic (protective) function. *SB*

National Museum of Archaeology, Florence, inv. 83380a

Civiltà 1985, 59, 60, nos. 2, 4, 11

17 **Ash urn with helmet used as lid**

Impasto (urn) and bronze (helmet)

Tomb I, Poggio dell'Impiccato, Tarquinia

The tomb group (numbers 17-26) dates from the late 9th to the early 8th centuries BC

Height of urn 39.0 cm; height of helmet 35.7 cm

This urn, with a helmet forming its lid, was found together with numbers 18-26 in a rectangular sarcophagus of volcanic stone (tufa). The ash urn contained the cremated remains of the dead man. The objects were found carefully arranged, as they had been left at the time of the burial. Necklaces had been hung from the neck of the urn, weapons were put beside it, and vases were placed at its foot. The tomb, which dates from the late 9th to the early 8th centuries BC, was one of the richest in the necropolis. The funerary equipment illustrates close links with South Italy and the so-called 'Urn Field' culture of Central Europe, as well as the high social rank of the dead man. The presence of weapons indicates that he was a warrior. The very fine helmet is the type on which the lid of number 27, the ash urn, was based. *AME*

National Museum of Archaeology, Florence, inv. 83379t-83379

Haynes 2000, 13, fig. 10; Torelli 2000, 559, cat. no. 56

18 **Ash urn**

Impasto

Tomb I, Poggio dell'Impiccato, Tarquinia

Height 17.5 cm

National Museum of Archaeology, Florence, inv. 83379s

19 **Six footed dishes**

Impasto

Tomb I, Poggio dell'Impiccato, Tarquinia

Height 7.0 cm to 4.3 cm

National Museum of Archaeology, Florence, inv. 83379 DI, DII, DIII, DIV, DV, DVI

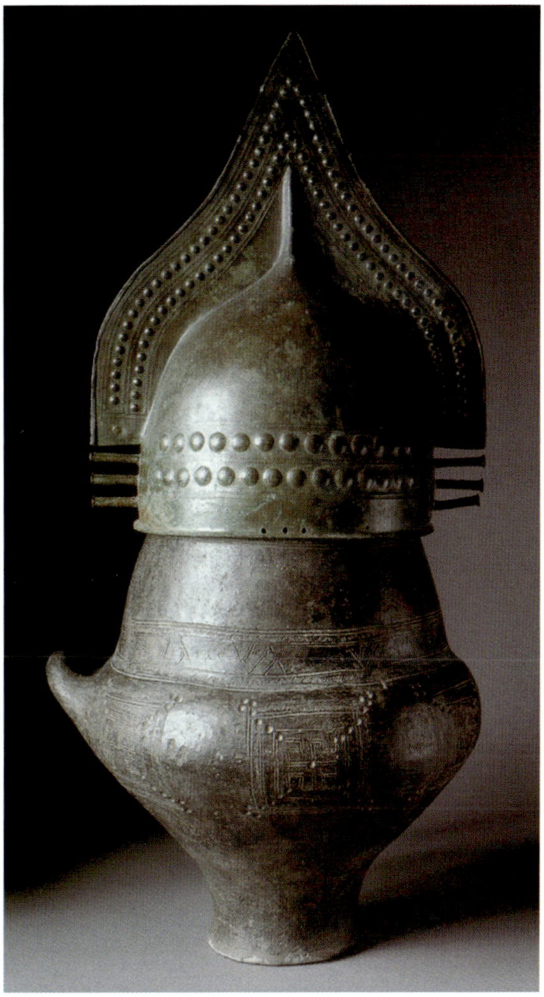

17

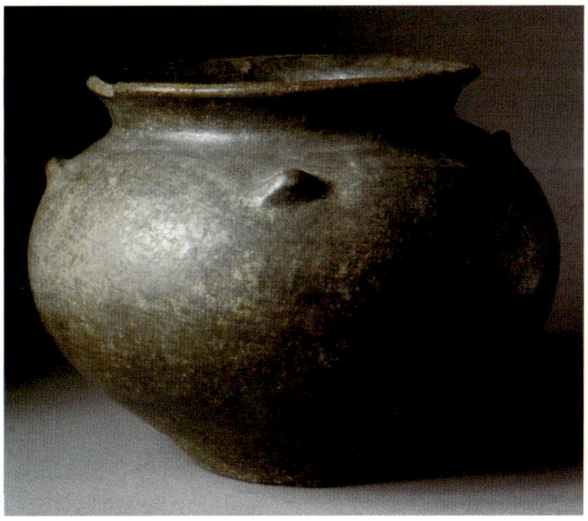

18

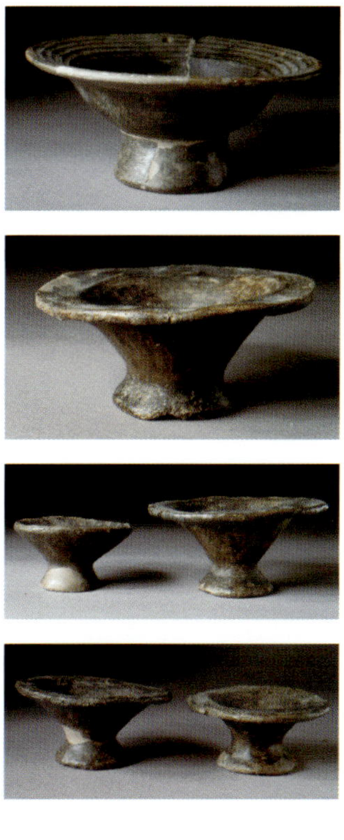

19

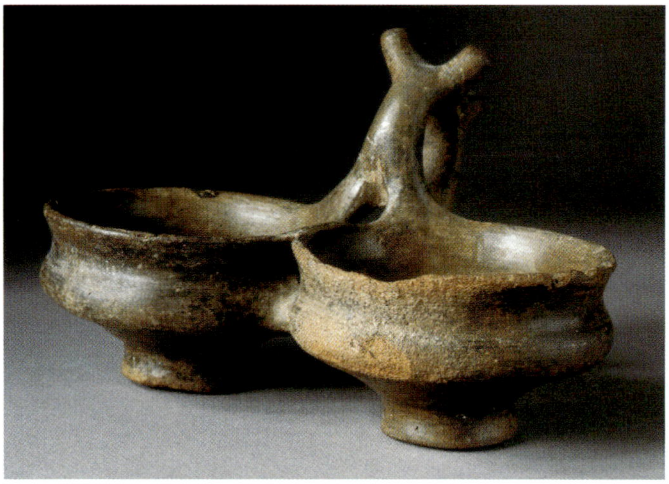

20

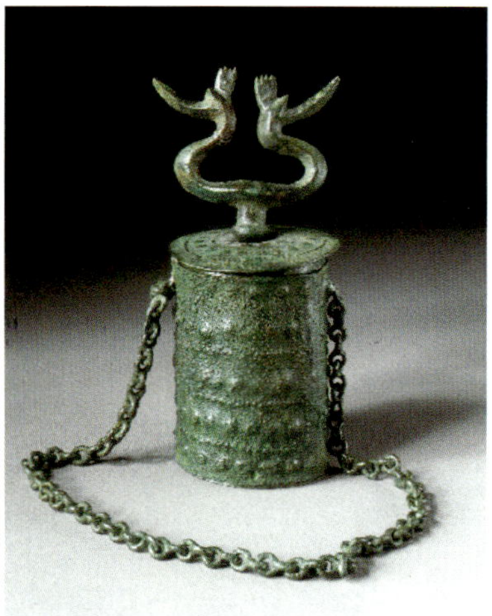

21

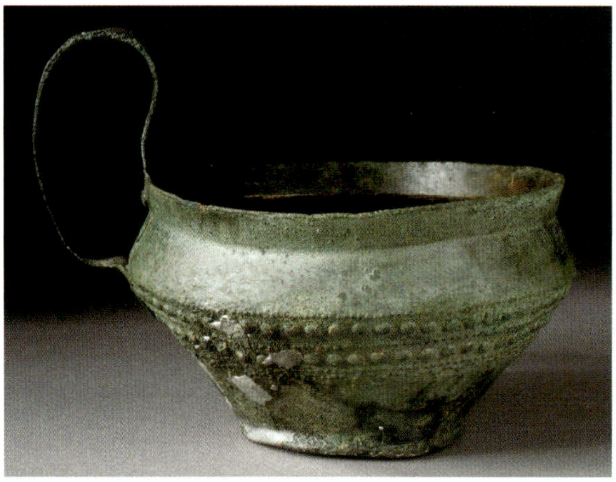

22

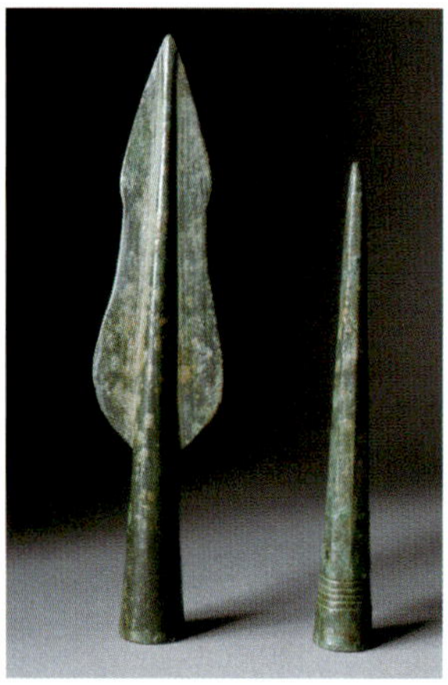

23

20 Double cup with an animal-shaped handle

Impasto
Tomb I, Poggio dell'Impiccato, Tarquinia
Height 10.0 cm

National Museum of Archaeology, Florence, inv. 83379f

21 Pyxis (lidded box)

Bronze
Tomb I, Poggio dell'Impiccato, Tarquinia
Height 10.0 cm

National Museum of Archaeology, Florence, inv. 83379e

22 One-handled cup

Bronze
Tomb I, Poggio dell'Impiccato, Tarquinia
Height 10.6 cm

National Museum of Archaeology, Florence, inv. 83379b

23 Spear head and butt

Tomb I, Poggio dell'Impiccato, Tarquinia
Length of spear head 20.5 cm; length of butt 16.5 cm

The pointed butt was attached to the shaft of the spear, at the opposite end to the spearhead. It is decorated with five concentric incised grooves.

National Museum of Archaeology, Florence, inv. 83379 GI, 83379 GII
Torelli 2000, 560, cat. no. 58

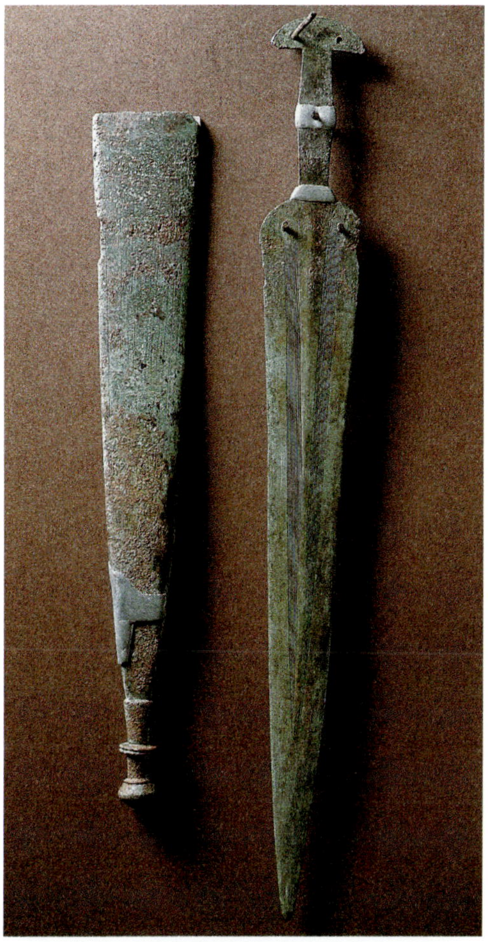

24 **Sword and sheath**

Bronze
Tomb I, Poggio dell'Impiccato, Tarquinia
Length of sword 43.0 cm; length of sheath 33.2 cm

Swords of this type (called the Pontecagnano type by archaeologists) have only been found in central Campania and a few sites on the Etruscan Tyrrhenian coast, illustrating the close links between Etruria and South Italy at this period. *GCC*

National Museum of Archaeology, Florence, inv. 83379P
Torelli 2000, 560, cat. no. 57

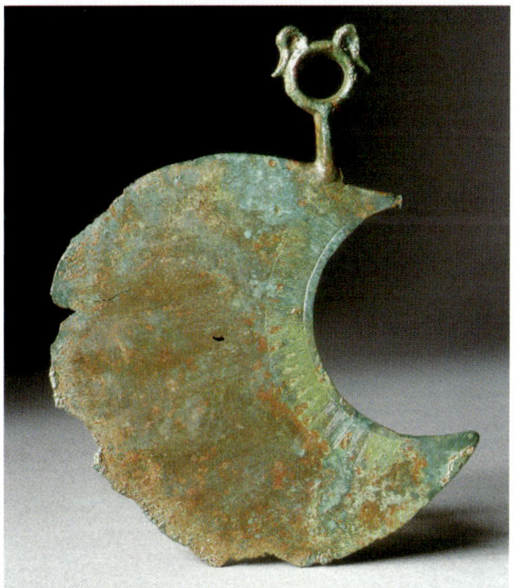

25 **Crescent-shaped razor**

Bronze
Tomb I, Poggio dell'Impiccato, Tarquinia
Length: 11.7 cm

Found with men's burials, examples of this type of razor are known both from early Etruria and Lazio. The decorative elements on the suspension loops usually took the form of stylized birds or birds' heads. *EG*

National Museum of Archaeology, Florence, inv. 83379V

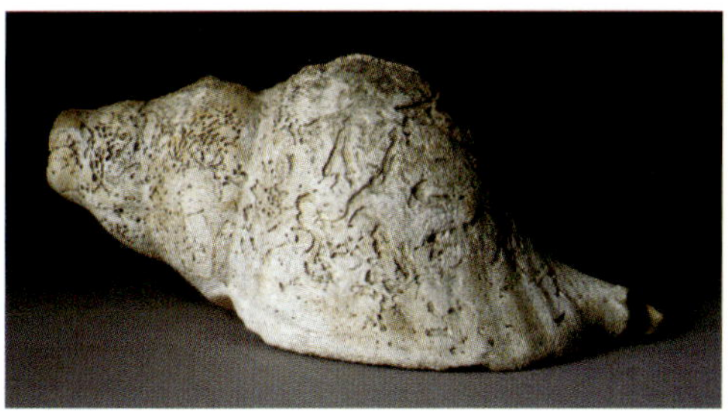

26 **Triton shell**

Charonia nodifera
Tomb I, Poggio dell'Impiccato, Tarquinia
Length 17.5 cm

This large shell had one end deliberately broken off, so that it could be blown like a trumpet. The use of charonia shells in this way is well-documented around the Mediterranean from the Neolithic period onwards. *AME/EG*

National Museum of Archaeology, Florence, inv. 83379C
For a discussion of the use of charonia shells in prehistoric Cyprus and elsewhere, see Ridout Sharpe 1991, 75-8 and references

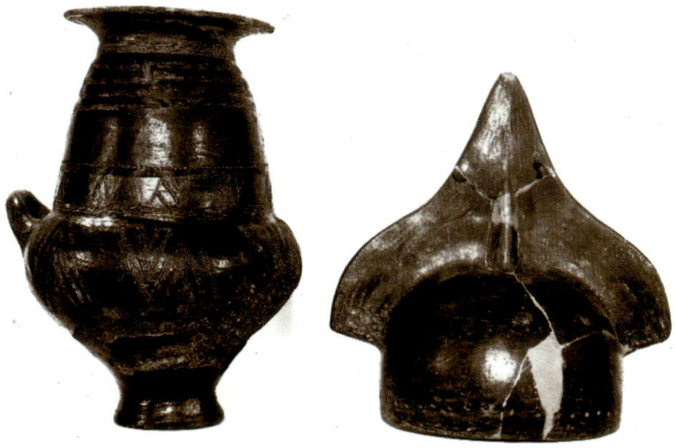

27

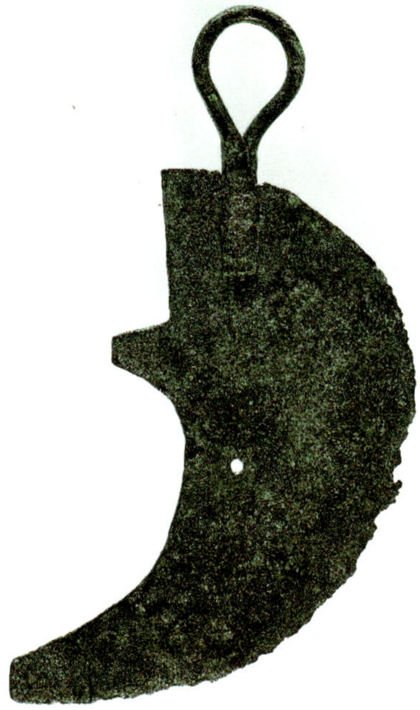

28

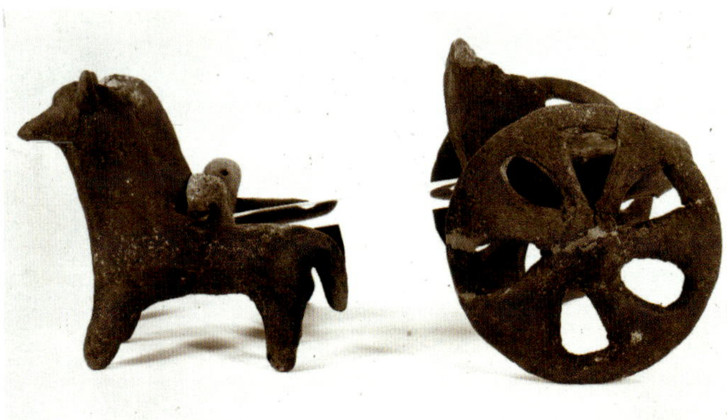

29

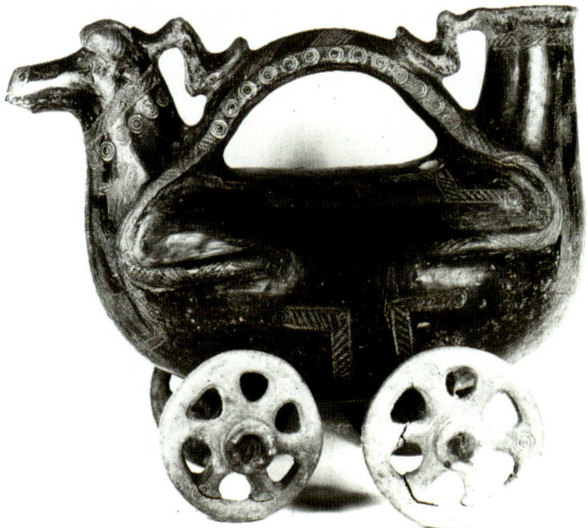

30

27 ## Ash urn with helmet-shaped lid

Impasto
Tomb 85, Poggio Selciatello Sopra necropolis, Tarquinia
First half of the 8th century BC
Height of urn 41.0 cm; height of lid 36.5 cm

The lid of this urn imitates a bronze crested helmet like number 17. The helmet-shaped lid and the associated grave goods (which included a bronze helmet and the razor, number 28) indicate the tomb was that of a warrior.

AME

National Museum of Archaeology, Florence, inv. 21000-21001

28 ## Crescent-shaped razor

Bronze
Tomb 85, Poggio Selciatello Sopra necropolis, Tarquinia
First half of the 8th century BC
Length 11.5 cm

National Museum of Archaeology, Florence, inv. 21003

29 ## Model two-horse chariot

Impasto
Bisenzio
Third quarter of the 8th century BC
Height 11.0 cm

Fast chariots of this type were usually used in battle. Models of this type were symbols of prestige. *GCC*

National Museum of Archaeology, Florence, inv. 71206

30 ## Wheeled askos (spouted jug)

Impasto
Tomb 4, Palazzetta necropolis, Bisenzio
Third quarter of the 8th century BC
Height 10.0 cm; length 21.0 cm

This unique and elaborate wheeled vessel in the form of a bird was found in the tomb of a person of high status. It may have contained precious oils or perfumes. Its surface was polished and impressed with cords and stamps to create geometric motifs. Two ducks were modelled in relief on the handle. *GCC*

National Museum of Archaeology, Florence, inv. 73463

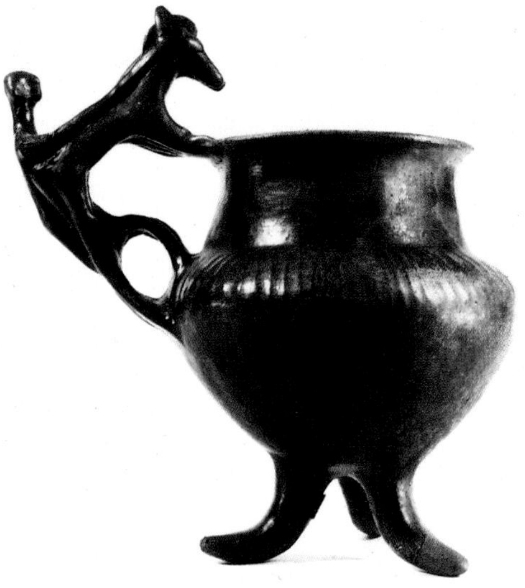

31

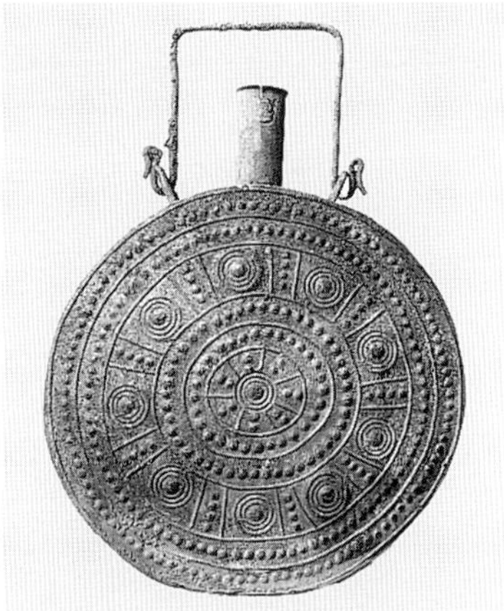

32

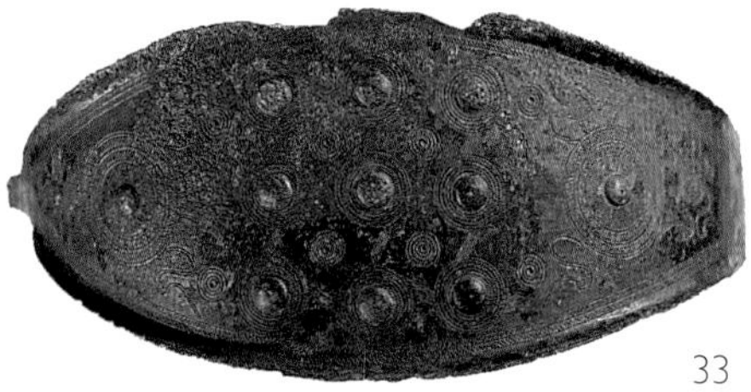

33

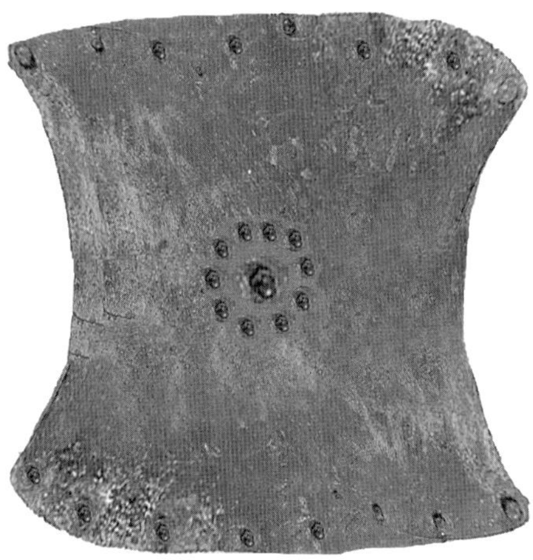

34

31 Tripod cup

Impasto
Tomb 3, Palazzetta necropolis, Bisenzio
Third quarter of the 8th century BC
Height 18.0 cm

Tripod (three-footed) cups are known from the end of the Bronze Age. They have often been found in Lazio and southern Etruria, especially in Bisenzio and Vulci and the surrounding areas. Examples with figurative handles, especially those in the form of charioteers, are characteristic of Bisenzio. This handle, in the form of a man holding the reins of two horses, may represent a 'Lord of the Animals'. *GCC/EG*

National Museum of Archaeology, Florence, inv. 75412

32 'Pilgrim' flask

Bronze
Tomb 1, Bucacce necropolis, Bisenzio
End of the 8th century BC
Height 14.0 cm

Vessels like this, with its swing handle, have flat sides so they can be worn comfortably against the body. They are found in the tombs of warriors of high status. Most examples are from the Tarquinia area, one of the main centres for the production of sheet bronze vessels with repoussé decoration. *GCC/EG*

National Museum of Archaeology, Florence, inv. 85532
Camporeale 1969, 17

33 Belt

Bronze
Tomb 1, Poggio delle Granate, Populonia
8th century BC
Length 40.0 cm; height 10.5 cm

This kind of belt was worn by women. It was decorated with bosses within incised concentric circles, perhaps representing the sun, as well as stylized birds. Similar examples have been found in Veii and Tarquinia. *GCC*

National Museum of Archaeology, Florence, inv. 113855
Minto 1921, 199, no. 3; L'Etruria mineraria 1985, 51, no. 48

34 Breastplate

Bronze
Certaldo (Florence)
Last quarter of the 8th century BC
Height 27.0 cm; width 28.0 cm

Breastplates were probably fastened over a fabric or leather tunic and protected the upper chest. They have mainly been found in southern Etruria and northern Lazio, but also occur at Volterra and in the Siena area. *GCC*

Museum of Archaeology, Siena, inv. 37427

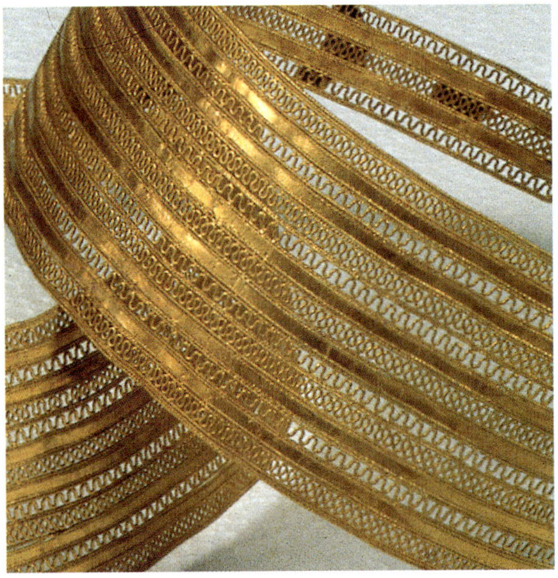

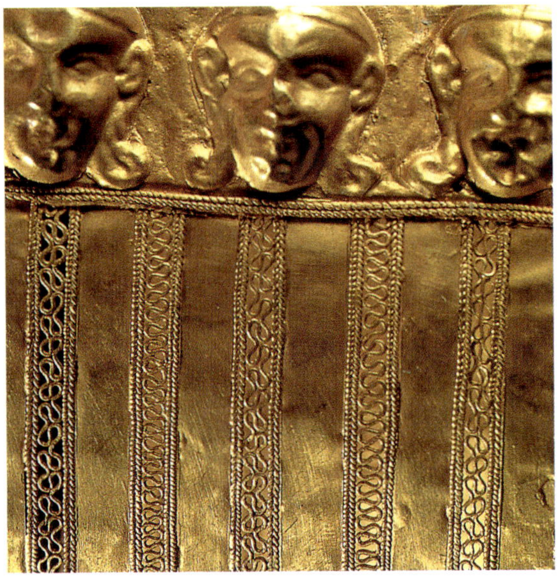

WEALTH AND POWER

About 725-580 BC

The last quarter of the 8th century to the first quarter of the 6th century BC is known to archaeologists as the 'Orientalizing period', reflecting the enormous influence exerted on the local culture by products and craftsmen from the Near East. It is one of the high points of Etruscan civilization. During the 7th century BC, Etruria's ships dominated the seas. It was now a powerful force in the Mediterranean, playing a major role in the political and economic relationships between the peoples of the Near East, Greece and Italy.

This period is marked by an abundance of luxury items such as gold jewellery, richly decorated silver and bronze vessels, ivories and fine ceramics. Huge quantities of high-quality imports reached Etruria from all over the Near East, Greece, Sardinia and central and eastern Europe, brought by Greek and Phoenician traders. Skilled craftsmen came too, bringing new ideas and techniques to the ceramics, bronze and goldworking industries. Products made in the Near East and Eastern and mainland Greece were often used as models to be adapted and re-worked to suit Etruscan taste. Expensive raw materials, such as ivory or amber, were imported to be worked locally. Perishable items like wine and olive oil were highly valued commodities. Imported from Greece and Phoenicia during the first part of the 7th century BC, by the second half of the century they were also being produced in Etruria as a result of the new, intensive cultivation of grapes and olives.

The arrival of Greek colonists in Italy eventually led to significant changes in Etruscan architecture and building techniques. Larger rectangular houses with rooms were introduced. The simple foundation trenches of the Villanovan period were replaced by stone foundations, and sun-dried bricks, stone blocks, wickerwork or wooden frameworks around a rubble core, took the place of wattle and daub. From the second half of the 7th century BC, roofs were covered with terracotta tiles. The more important private houses and the public buildings had roofs adorned with painted architectural terracottas including acroteria (the sculpted finials of pediments), antefixes and water-spouts and, later, friezes, large sculptural figures and other revetments. Most importantly, the 7th century saw the emergence of the city and town, together with urban planning, drainage and street systems, as well as the related development of organized social, administrative and political functions and structures.

Close links with the cultures of Greece and the Near East led to more than the adoption of artistic motifs and new skills. With the rise of the aristocratic class, the Etruscans incorporated many important elements of the sophisticated lifestyles of those cultures within their own society, including literacy, banqueting and a heroic funerary tradition.

At this time literacy was largely confined to the aristocracy. Writing was a new skill, a symbol of prestige, and it was used to express the individual ownership of possessions and tombs. The Etruscans used the Greek alphabet adapted for their own very different language. An aristocratic tomb of about 670 BC, in the rich Circolo degli Avori (Circle of the Ivories) at Marsiliana d'Albegna, contained an ivory writing tablet, once gilded and spread with wax which could be written on. A model alphabet, for copying, was incised on the frame. The tablet was equipped with styluses for writing on the wax and blades for erasing.

The arrival of a wide range of banqueting vessels marked significant changes in the lifestyle of the Etruscan aristocracy, as wine-drinking and feasting became important elements of noble society. The custom of drinking wine while reclining on couches was derived from the royal courts of Assyria, and reached the Etruscans via the Greeks. The society described in the Homeric epics had the rituals of the dining table at its core and the banquet was a central means of consolidating social relationships. Etruscan banquets involved the consumption of meat and drink, accompanied by speeches, music and ritual. Banquets, accompanied by sports and games, were also an important part of the funeral ceremony and the tableware from the feast was buried with the dead. The symposium was a less formal type of entertainment centred around the drinking of wine. An important occasion for socialising and cementing relationships, it was considered an essential aspect of the aristocratic lifestyle. The survival of numerous jars, bowls, drinking cups, wine jugs and containers for mixing wine and water (the customary way of drinking wine) from the end of 8th century onwards demonstrates how widespread the practice of wine-drinking had become.

Differences in tomb types and grave goods offer a clear indication that by this time Etruscan society was formed of distinct classes, based on family groups and relationships. The lords headed the hierarchical structure, their power and wealth based on the ownership of land and its resources, both agricultural and mineral. They also controlled roads, essential for trade and commercial exchange.

Most of the information about the Etruscan lords of the Orientalizing period comes from tombs. At this time the aristocracy used elaborate chamber tombs covered by mounds, or tumuli, reaching heights of up to ten metres, a mark of their status. Located in prominent positions, these mounds drew attention to the prestige and wealth of the family who commissioned them. Such large tombs could accommodate numerous burials from the same family, underlining the importance of family ties. In southern Etruria, with its softer local volcanic stone (tufa), the tombs were cut into the rock. In northern Etruria, aristocratic burials were at first placed in trench tombs dug into the ground and lined with stone. Groups of trenches were enclosed within large circles of worked stone slabs (known as circoli), up to 30 metres in diameter. Later the aristocracy built tomb chambers covered by false vaults and topped with monumental mounds. The tomb chambers were approached by a wide entranceway (known as the dromos). The chambers inside are architectural masterpieces, superbly built in a wide variety of styles. Resembling domestic houses, the tomb chambers were in effect the houses of the dead, and the cemetery, or necropolis, the 'city of the dead'.

The tomb contents provide much information about the status and lifestyle of their occupants. Wealthy tombs of this period were furnished with luxury items of ivory, bone, amber, gold, silver and glass. Fine ceramics and bronzes, such as the banqueting services, reflect functional needs, iron and bronze weapons suggest the heroic ideal, and insignia such as the fasces (double axes with rods – see number 72) and bronze fans (number 109) speak of secular power and ritual. Male burials were accompanied by richly-decorated weapons and armour, crested helmets, large circular shields, short swords and heavy spears. By the second half of the 7th century the Etruscans had adopted the type of arms and armour used by Greek hoplites (heavily armed infantry soldiers). The hoplites marched to the sound of horns, like number 74 from the Tomb of the Chariots in Populonia. The prince buried in this tomb was probably a military leader.

Etruscan aristocratic women apparently enjoyed a high level of social equality with men. They owned, and were buried with, the types of banqueting vessels in which wine and water were mixed. By the Archaic period, they certainly participated in banquets, drinking wine alongside the men. Women's tombs could include pairs of horse bits and by the end of the 8th century even two-horse chariots. These could have been used during the funeral ceremony, and would have indicated exceptionally high status. Women were also equipped with rich clothing and jewellery. Some of the jewellery found in the tombs may be objects of exchange from other areas; aristocratic marriages were probably used to seal alliances between noble families and communities.

The remarkable gold jewellery of the Orientalizing period perhaps provides the finest testimony to the wealth of the aristocracy. These jewels are masterpieces of the goldsmith's art, demonstrating the exceptionally high level of skill and sophistication attained by the craftsmen of Etruria. Their confident use of certain techniques of surface decoration – chasing, embossing, granulation and filigree – has rarely been surpassed.

GCC/EG

Previous page:
above: detail of a pair of bracelets (no. 44)
below: detail of a bracelet (no. 45)

35 Handle

Bronze
Vetulonia
End of the 8th to the beginning of the 7th century BC
Height 18.5 cm

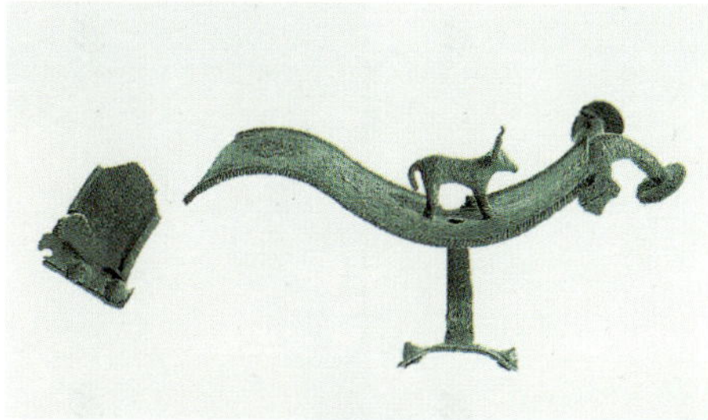

This bronze handle is decorated with the cast figure of a bull and a stylized bull's head. It was once attached to a sheet bronze jar, probably a local Vetulonian interpretation of a central European form. Most of the handles of this kind have been found in Vetulonia. *GCC*

Museum of Archaeology, Siena, inv. 37670
Camporeale 1969, 30

36 Axe head

Bronze
Vetulonia
End of the 8th to the beginning of the 7th century BC
Length 25.0 cm

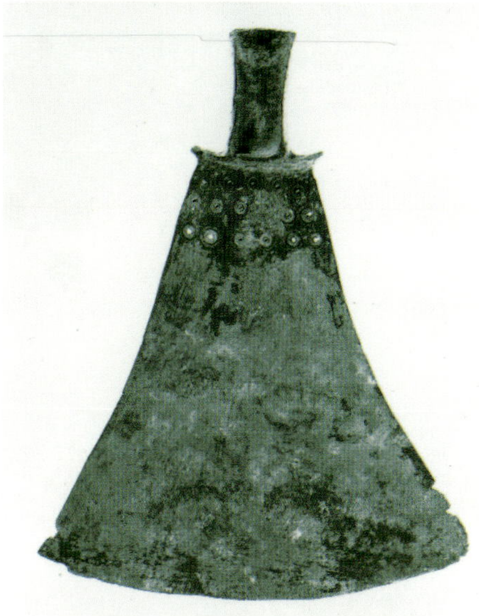

Axes were prestige items, and this example was probably buried with a high-ranking warrior. The blade is decorated with concentric circles. It would once have been mounted on a wooden handle. *GCC/EG*

Museum of Archaeology, Siena, inv. 37663

37 Axe with handle

Bronze (axe head) and iron with ivory and amber inlays (handle)
From a tomb near Chiusi, Siena
End of the 8th century BC
Length 64.0 cm

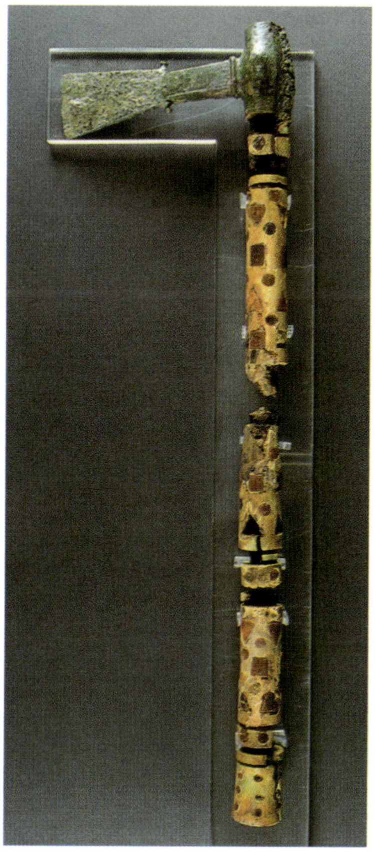

This type of bronze axe was common throughout the 8th century and examples are also known from the 7th century. The axe head was made using the 'lost wax' technique of casting. The well-preserved handle has a square-sectioned iron core faced with ivory, with amber inlays. These were set in tinned mounts, probably to reflect light through the amber. This technique was apparently characteristic of the Chiusi area and Paolone areas. Axes were symbols of authority. The purpose of this axe was probably purely ceremonial, intended to emphasize the high social status of its owner. *MCB*

National Museum of Archaeology, Florence, inv. 70787

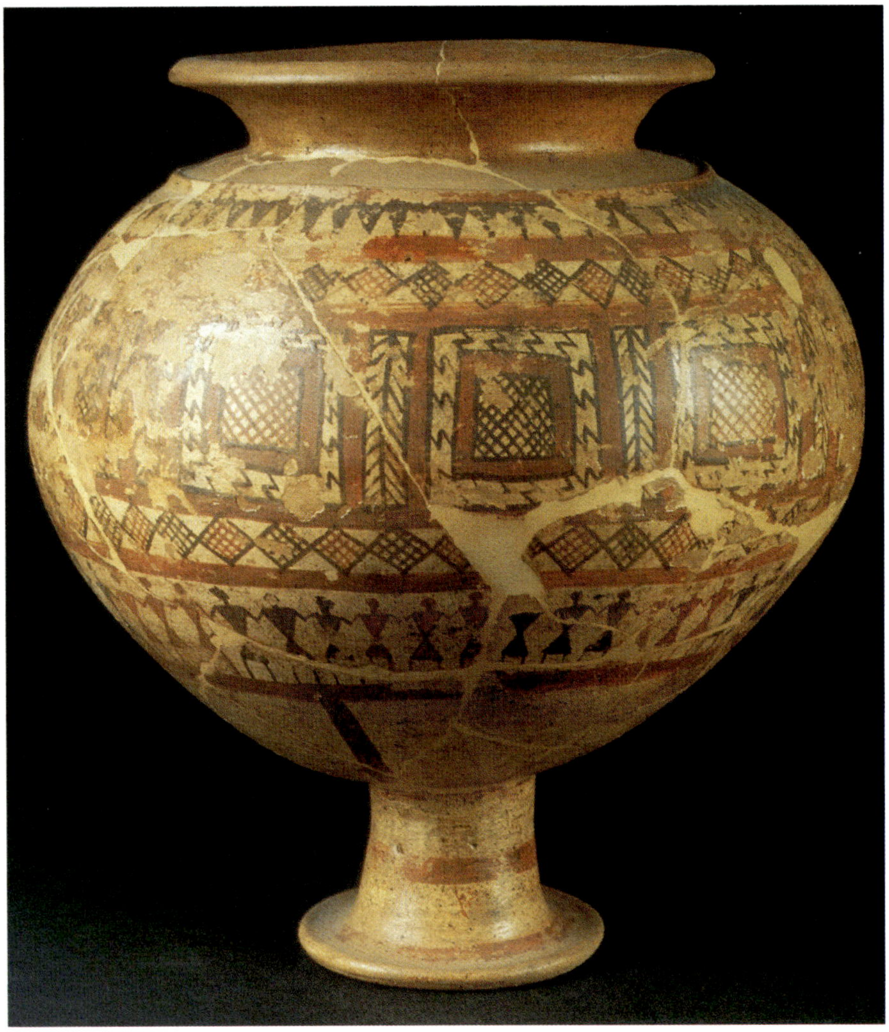

38 **Olla and stand**

Painted ceramic
Tomb 3, Bucacce necropolis, Bisenzio
About 700 BC
Height 35.5 cm; diameter 32.5 cm

This type of globular vase on a high foot, known as an 'olla', dates from the third quarter of the 8th century to the first quarter of the 7th century BC. The presence of many examples in Bisenzio suggests that there was a workshop making them locally. They have also been found at Tarquinia, Vetralla, in the Falisco marsh region around Civita Castellana and at Vulci.

This vase, which was reconstructed from fragments, is one of the finest examples known. It is made from purified impasto painted with red and black decoration on a creamy ground. The decoration is arranged in horizontal bands around the body, and includes rows of inverted triangles, hatched lozenges and squares, zigzags and a herringbone pattern. Like other examples, it has a band of decorated panels (metopes) around its belly. The geometric decoration is typical of Villanovan ornament. However, the lowest band depicts a row of 48 human figures in silhouette, apparently holding hands in a round dance, perhaps as part of a ceremony. The row of dancing figures was a new subject in Etruscan art of the period. Groups of three black figures alternate with groups of three red figures; the colour difference may be intended to differentiate men and women. If so, then this may be an early pictorial representation of the equality of men and women in Etruscan social and cultural life.

The vase was found in the tomb of a woman of very high status. She was buried with one of the richest assemblages so far known from this period. The contents of her tomb included gold, silver and amber jewellery, faience amulets and steatite scarabs imported from the East, impasto vessels and other fine ceramics, bronzes, a spool used in woolworking, horse bits, and bronze and iron shears.

MCB/EG

National Museum of Archaeology, Florence, inv. 85629

Haynes 2000, 24-5, figs. 25a-b; Torelli 2000, cat. no. 164

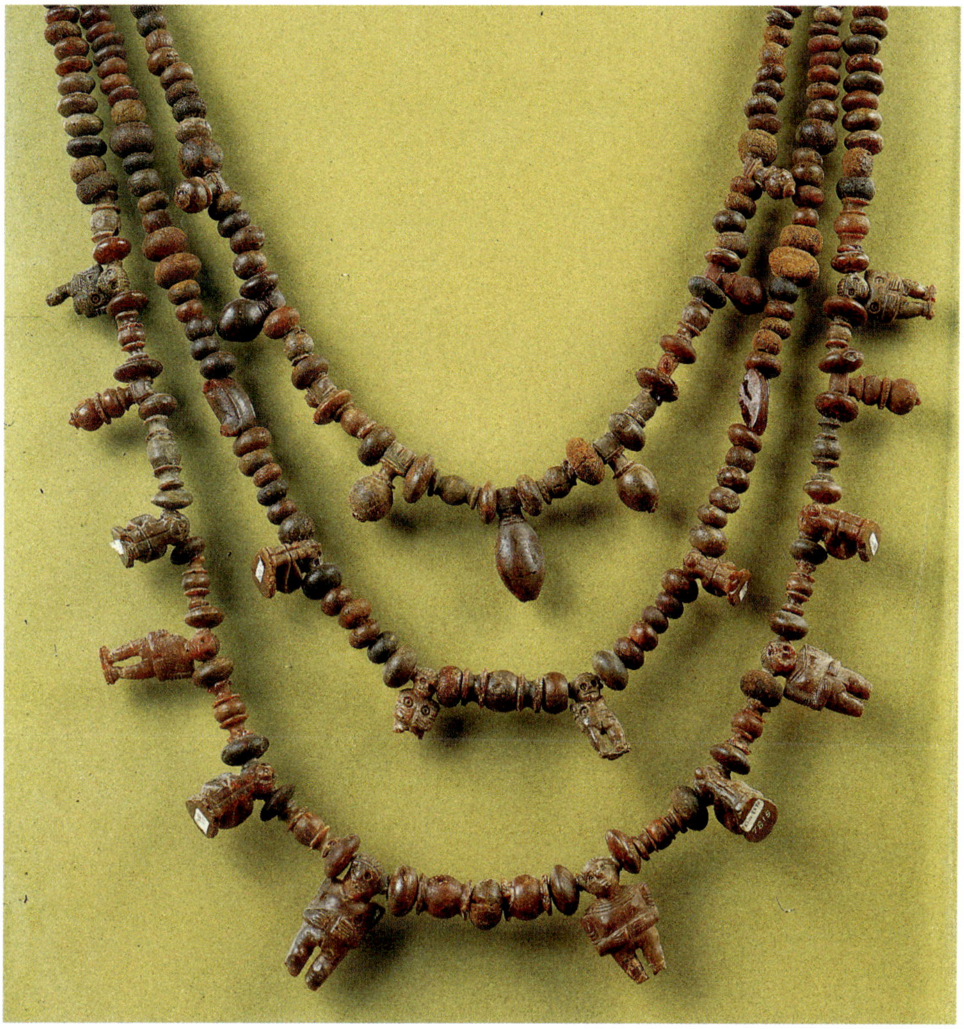

39 **Necklace**

Amber

Circolo dei Monili (Circle of the Jewellery), Poggio alla Guardia necropolis, Vetulonia

End of the 8th century BC

In the early Orientalizing period aristocratic inhumations and cremations at Vetulonia were placed in trench tombs dug in the ground and lined with stone. Groups of these trench tombs were enclosed within large circles of stone slabs. This necklace came from such a Circle.

The elements of this necklace have been re-strung in modern times and the arrangement is conjectural. The surviving elements consist of 111 beads of different shapes and sizes and 25 pendants. Several of the pendants are in the form of naked females standing with their hands resting on their bellies; others are in the form of seated monkeys with their elbows on their knees and their paws cupped under their chins. The rest are elaborate elongated drop shapes of various types. The pendant types are typical of Etruscan jewellery from the end of the Villanovan period and the early Orientalizing period. The monkey motif is particularly characteristic, and can be paralleled on various objects from Vetulonia and Marsiliana. The amber itself, however, had to be imported from the Baltic, although it was carved locally.

The material may have had some special significance. Apart from being prized for its glorious colour, it will have been recognized that amber, when rubbed, becomes charged with static electricity and will therefore attract light material to it. The Greek word for amber, 'elektron', provides the origin of the word 'electricity'.

The necklace was a luxury item which formed part of a rich assemblage. It must have belonged to a person of high status, and it provides an indication of the growing affluence of the aristocracy in Etruscan society. *LP/EG*

National Museum of Archaeology, Florence, inv. 7815

Camporeale 1969, 28; Haynes 2000, p. 100

40 Cup in the form of a boot

Impasto

La Sagrona tomb 3, Poggio alla Guardia necropolis, Vetulonia

End of the 8th to the beginning of the 7th century BC

Height 13.0 cm

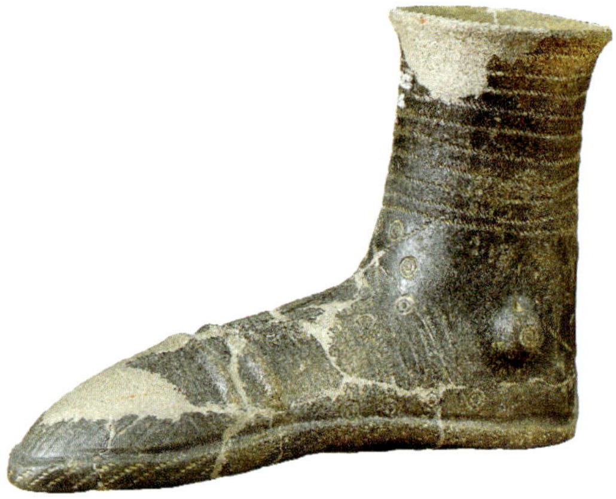

This cup is in the form of a right boot with a pointed toe. It is elaborately decorated with corded patterns and impressed circles, suggesting how the boot was laced, and the ankle is also indicated. The origins of this type of vessel can be found both in Italy and beyond; the oldest examples come from the Mycenaean world and the Bronze and Iron age cultures of central Europe. Similar examples to this one, of comparable date, are known from Vetulonia, Este, Bologna and Novilara. This example was found in the same tomb as a razor, and thus probably belonged to a man.

LP/EG

National Museum of Archaeology, Florence, inv. 8208

Falchi 1891, 185; Camporeale in L'Etruria mineraria 1985, 381; Magnificenza 1998, 39, no. 2

41 Three fibulae

Bronze

Unknown provenance

End of the 8th century BC

Lengths 18.8, 14.0 and 15.0 cm

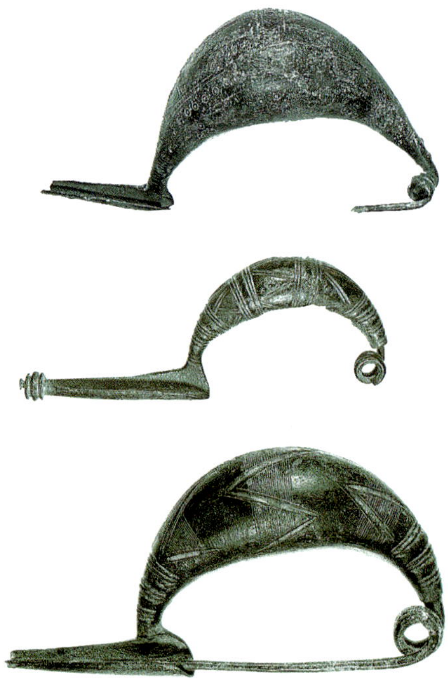

Fibulae were essential for fastening clothing, and were worn by both men and women. Leech- or boat-shaped fibulae like these, with their thick arched bows, were almost always worn by women. Many bronze and precious metal examples survive from the Orientalizing period in Etruria. They are found in pairs or groups of four. They were cast using the 'lost-wax' technique, and some have plain bows, while others are embellished with geometric motifs like these. Over time, the type developed progressively longer feet.

GCC/EG

Museum of Archaeology, Siena, inv. 37603, 37576, 37590

42 **Bracelet**

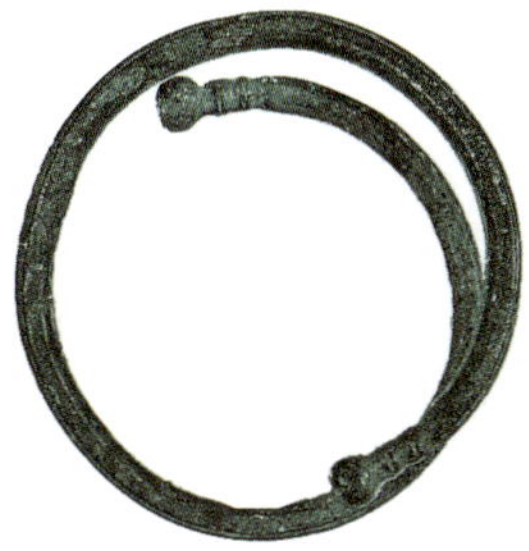

Bronze
Unknown provenance
Beginning of the 7th century BC
Diameter 10.0 cm

This was a popular type of bracelet during the Orientalizing period. It is solid cast and has decorated overlapping terminals. *GCC/EG*

Museum of Archaeology, Siena, inv. 37521

43 **Dinos (large bowl) on holmos (stand)**

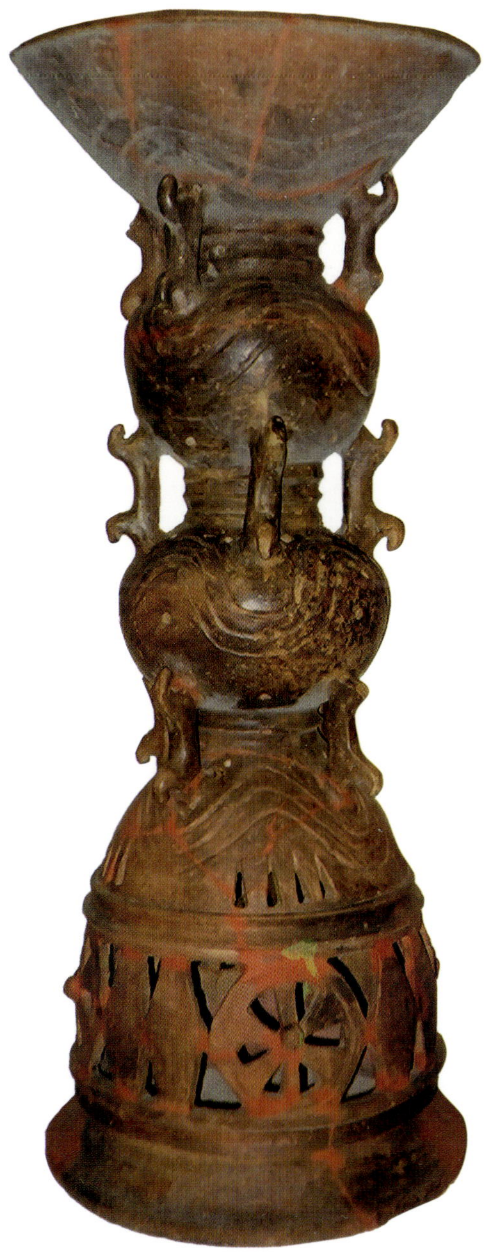

Impasto
Falerii
Beginning of the 7th century BC
Height of vessel 33.0 cm; height of stand 78.0 cm

Vessels and stands like these were used for banquets. The bowl was used for mixing wine and water. These are prestige items which marked the deceased as a person of aristocratic status. Banquets were an integral part of the aristocratic lifestyle. Stands like this one come from western central Italy, from Falerii in the south east of Etruria, or from Lazio, and are based on metal prototypes from Greece and the Near East. *GCC/EG*

National Museum of Archaeology, Florence, inv. 75493
Paribeni in MonAnt 1906, vol. 16; Magnificenza 1998, 45, no. 14

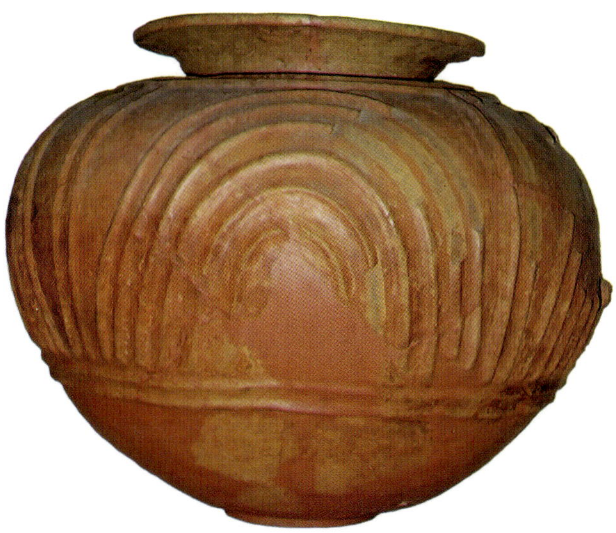

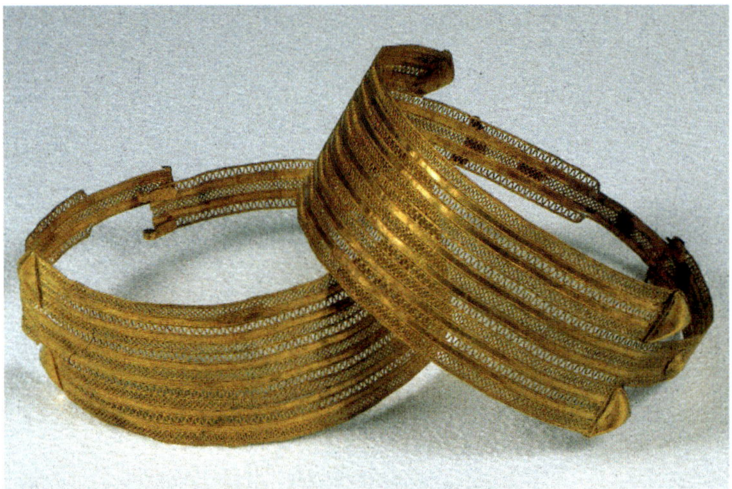

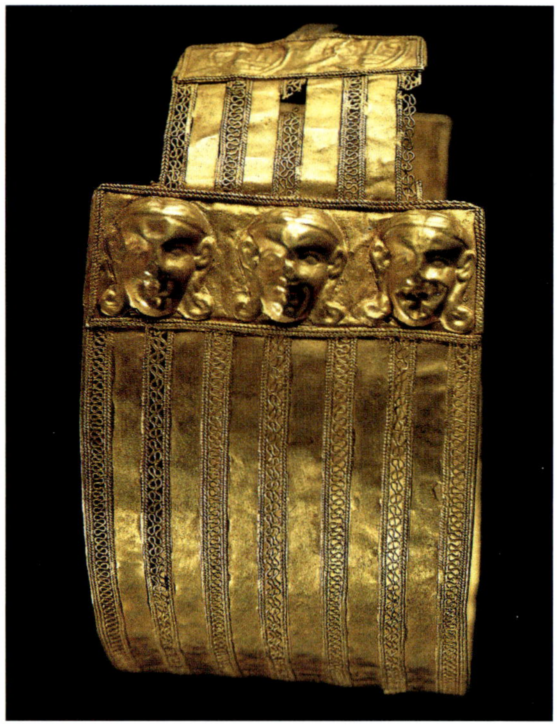

44 **Pair of bracelets**

Gold

Vetulonia

First quarter of the 7th century BC

Diameter 9.5 cm

This type of bracelet (known as an armilla) was made from alternating strips of gold sheet and open filigree work. This was a popular style, probably made in southern Etruria. Examples have been found in Vetulonia, Populonia, Tarquinia and Cerveteri. *GCC*

National Museum of Archaeology, Florence, inv. 73848, 73849

45 **Bracelet**

Gold

Tumulo delle Migliarine, Vetulonia

Second quarter of the 7th century BC

Diameter 7.0 cm

This is one of a pair of bracelets. It was formed from six plain strips of sheet gold alternating with seven bands of open wire work (filigree). The arrangement of the fine wires shows subtle variations. Gold strips set across either end of the bands are decorated with female heads, their hair arranged in Hathor locks, a style derived from Egypt and the Near East. The narrower ends of the bracelets were formed from four plain and five filigree bands. Gold strips set across their ends are decorated with Orientalizing (Syro-Phoenician) palmettes. The edges of all the strips are ornamented with wires arranged in a herringbone pattern. This jewel, with its characteristic Orientalizing decorative motifs, is a typical example of Vetulonian goldwork.

MCy/EG

National Museum of Archaeology, Florence, inv. 75511

Cristofani and Martelli 1983, 38 and note 31

46 Two fibulae

Bronze, blue and yellow glass
Tomb 2, Banditella necropolis, Marsiliana d'Albegna
First quarter of the 7th century BC
Length 4.7 cm

The bows of these two fragmentary leech-shaped fibulae consist of a square-sectioned bronze rod encased in blue glass. The glass was decorated with longitudinal chevrons which were originally filled with yellow glass, of which small traces remain. Glass fibulae are particularly rare.

GCC

National Museum of Archaeology, Florence, inv. 11125, 11126
Minto 1921, 38, pl. 11; Sundwall 1943, 194, no. 9

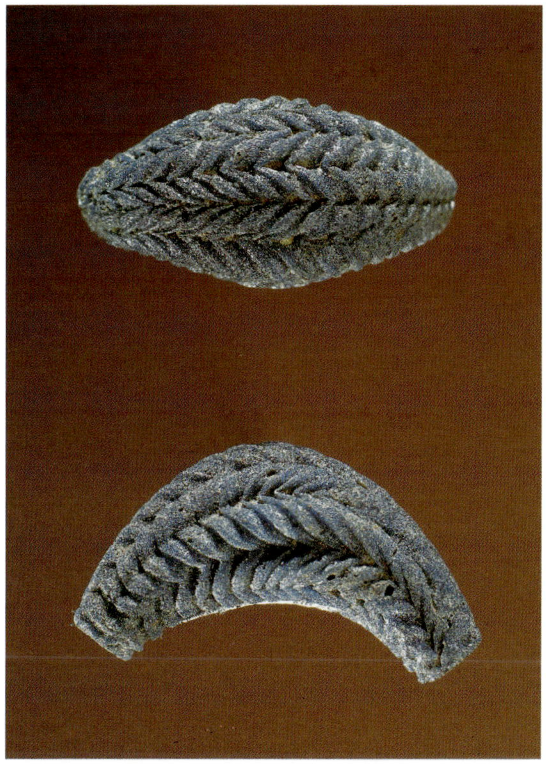

47 Two fibulae

Bronze, bone and amber
Tomb 2, Banditella necropolis, Marsiliana d'Albegna
First quarter of the 7th century BC
Length 5.6 cm

The bows of these fragmentary leech-shaped fibulae were originally ornamented with five bone and two amber segments which decrease in diameter towards the ends. The large bone elements in the middle were set with a square amber plaque surrounded by a series of concavities, each of which once held amber inlays. Fibulae of this type have been found widely in Etruria on sites of the early Orientalizing period.

National Museum of Archaeology, Florence, inv. 11121, 33789
Minto 1921, 38; Sundwall 1943, 190

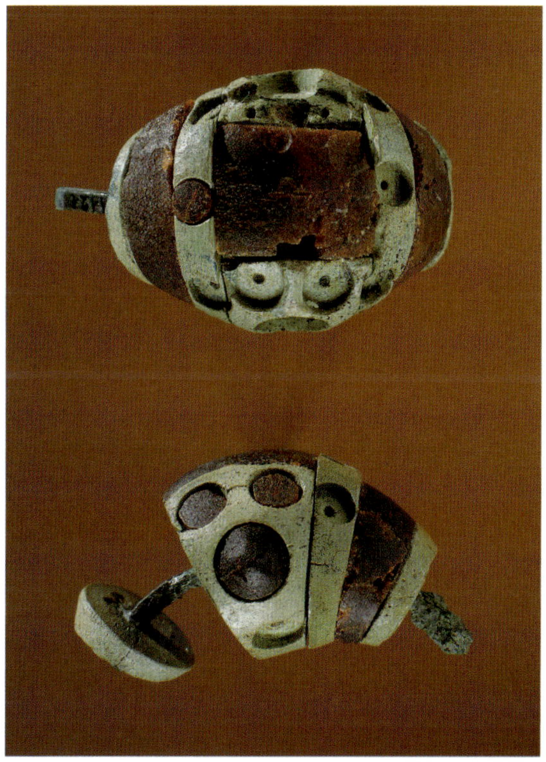

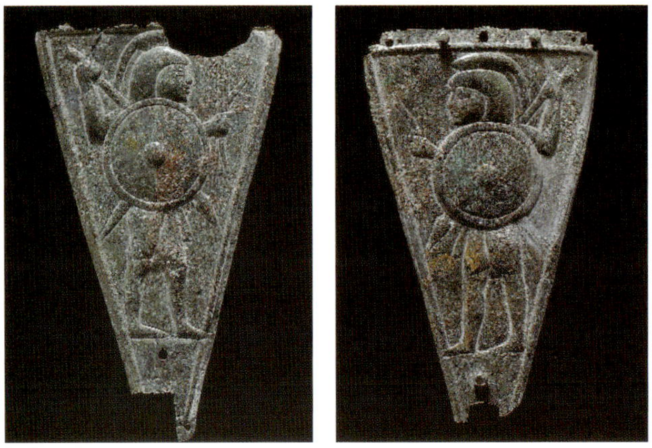

48

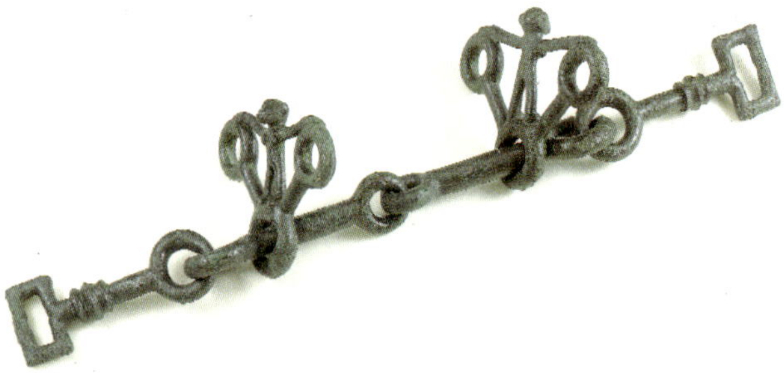

49

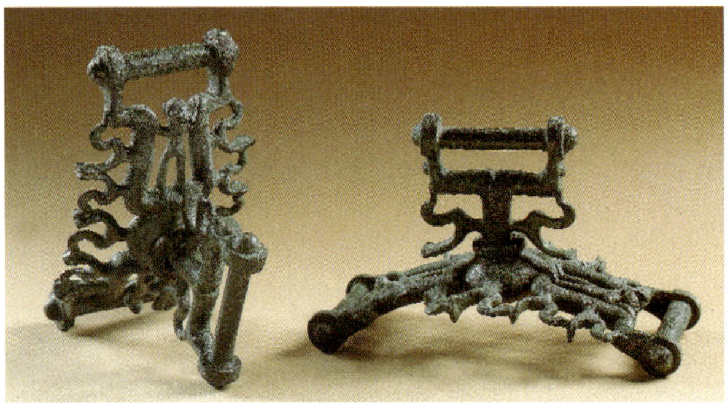

50

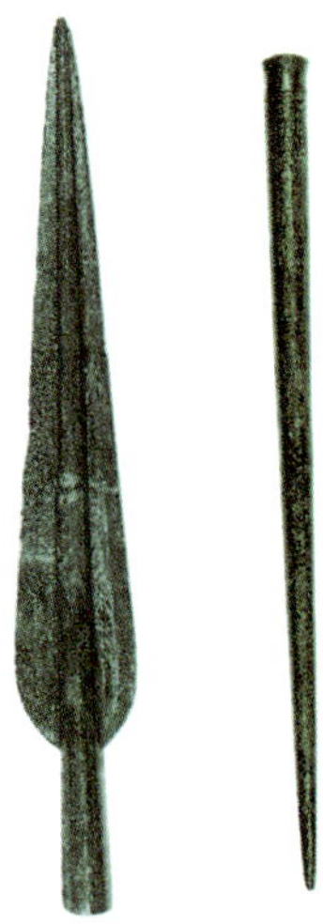

51

48 Harness trappings

Bronze
Banditella necropolis, Marsiliana d'Albegna
Second quarter of the 7th century BC
Heights 20.8 cm, 21.1 cm

These unique sheet bronze plaques are from the bridle of a pair of horses. Etruscan bridle plaques are usually round. Holes along the ends of these examples suggest that they were originally backed with leather. Each plaque is decorated with an armed warrior wearing a crested helmet and holding a bow and arrows and a spear. Their upper bodies are protected by round shields, apparently slung over one arm. The pointed end of a sword is visible below the lower edge of the shields. The decoration was applied in repoussé, the detail sharpened with chasing applied from the front. *GCC*

National Museum of Archaeology, Florence, inv. 33918, 33919
Camporeale in St Etr 1967, vol. 35, 31 and pl. 12; Magnificenza 1998, 51, no. 29

49 Pair of horse bits

Bronze
Banditella necropolis, Marsiliana d'Albegna
Second quarter of the 7th century BC
Lengths 33.5 cm, 35.4 cm

Horse bits are sometimes found in rich tombs of the late Villanovan and early Orientalizing period. They occur in groups of two or four, and were used in life as part of the harness for chariots drawn by two or four horses. These examples have cheekpieces decorated with stylized human figures, which are characteristic of the harness mountings from Vetulonia. *GCC/EG*

National Museum of Archaeology, Florence, inv. 33916, 33917
Minto 1921, 169, pl. 32; Magnificenza 1998, 52, no. 30

50 Harness trappings

Bronze
Banditella necropolis, Marsiliana d'Albegna
Second quarter of the 7th century BC
Length 15.3 cm

The function of these horse trappings is uncertain, but it has been suggested that they were used around the horse's body as part of the saddle, linked by straps to the rest of the harness. They are elaborately decorated with human figures and stylized ducks. *GCC*

National Museum of Archaeology, Florence, inv. 33914, 33915
Minto 1921, 171, 269, pl. 34; Magnificenza 1998, 53, no. 31

51 Spear head and butt

Bronze
Tomb 14, Banditella necropolis, Marsiliana d'Albegna
Middle of the 7th century BC
Length of spear head 38.0 cm; length of butt 40.0 cm

Spears made of bronze are rare in the Marsiliana necropolis: 35 of the 39 spears from the site were made of iron. Almost a quarter of the tombs in this necropolis contained weapons, but there was very little armour – three shields and no helmets.

National Museum of Archaeology, Florence, inv. 11273, 11274
Minto 1921, 525, fig. 27, no. 6

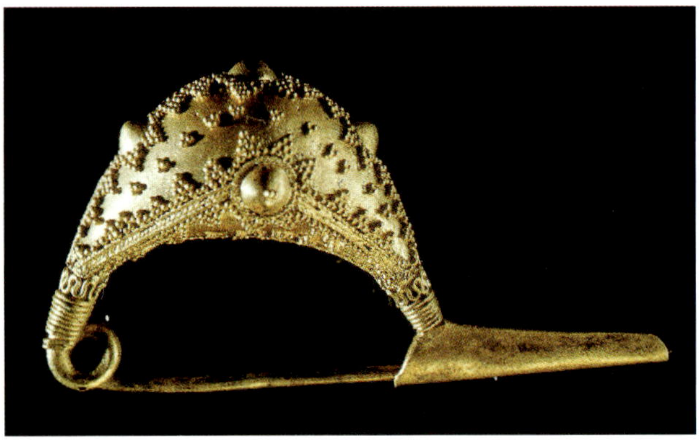

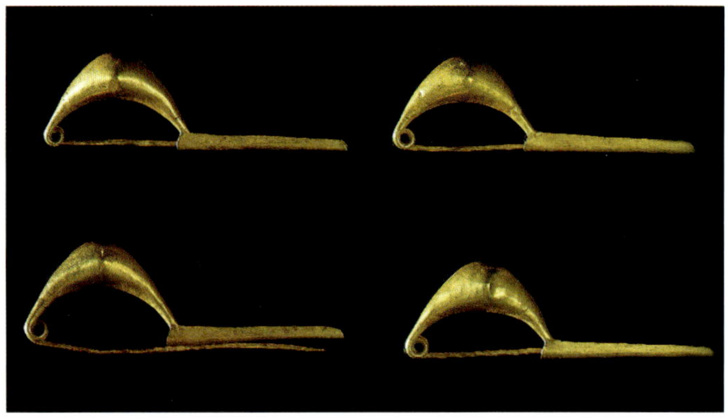

52 Fibula

Gold
Circolo degli Acquastrini, Vetulonia
Second quarter of the 7th century BC
Length 3.4 cm

This leech-shaped fibula belongs to a group which was probably made locally in Vetulonia. It is embellished with decoration of fine granules (granulation) and wires (filigree). *MCy*

National Museum of Archaeology, Florence, inv. 73597
Etrusker 1987, 186, nos. 36-48; Magnificenza 1998, 53-4, nos. 32-9

53 Four fibulae

Gold
Circolo degli Acquastrini, Vetulonia
Second quarter of the 7th century BC
Lengths 4.2 to 4.4 cm

Many examples of these simple leech-shaped fibulae have been found in Vetulonia. *MCy*

National Museum of Archaeology, Florence, inv. 73592-73595

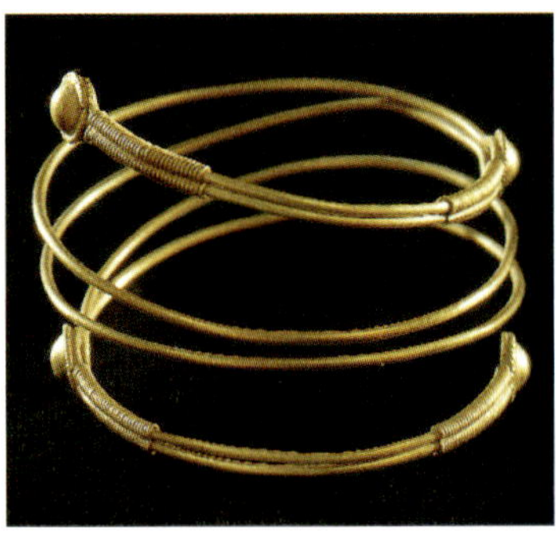

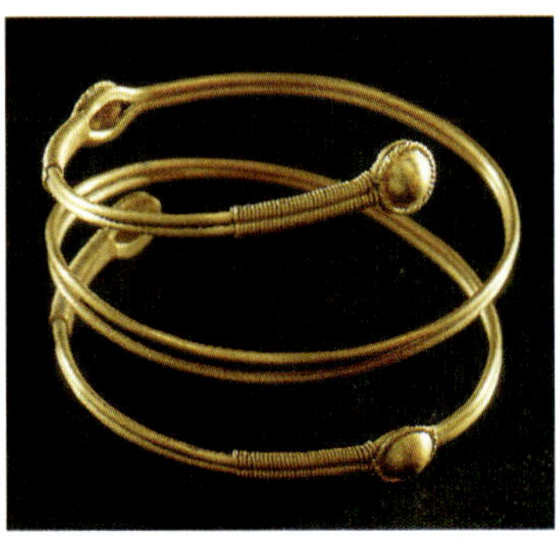

54 Hair spirals

Gold
Circolo degli Acquastrini, Vetulonia
Second quarter of the 7th century BC
Diameter 3.5 cm

These gold spirals decorated with filigree were probably used as hair ornaments. Gold and silver hair spirals were very popular in northern Etruria during the Orientalizing period. *MCy*

National Museum of Archaeology, Florence, inv. 73599, 73600
Etrusker 1987, 188, nos. 45-6; Magnificenza 1998, 55, no. 40

55 **Three fibulae**

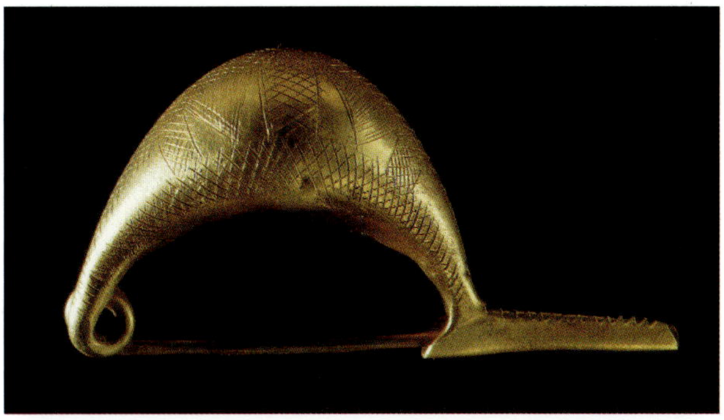

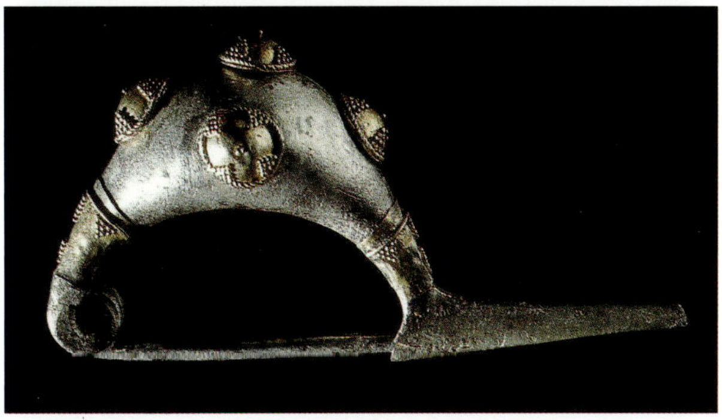

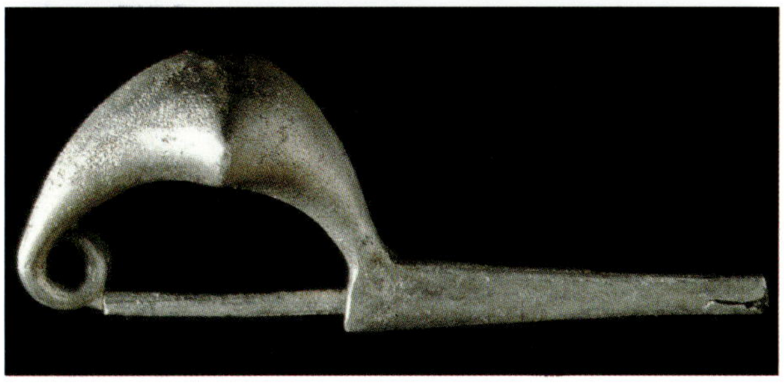

Gold; silver and electrum; silver
Circolo degli Acquastrini, Vetulonia
Second quarter of the 7th century BC
Lengths 3.8 cm, 4.5 cm, 3.2 cm

The chased linear decoration on the gold fibula is unusual at this date. The silver and electrum example decorated with granulated bosses belongs to a group probably made in Vetulonia in the first half of the 7th century. (Electrum is gold which contains a high proportion of silver.) The simple fibula made from silver sheet has many parallels in Vetulonia (see the gold fibulae, number 53). *MCy*

National Museum of Archaeology, Florence, inv. 73596bis, 73603, 73605
Sundwall 1943, 198

56 **Axe head/adze**

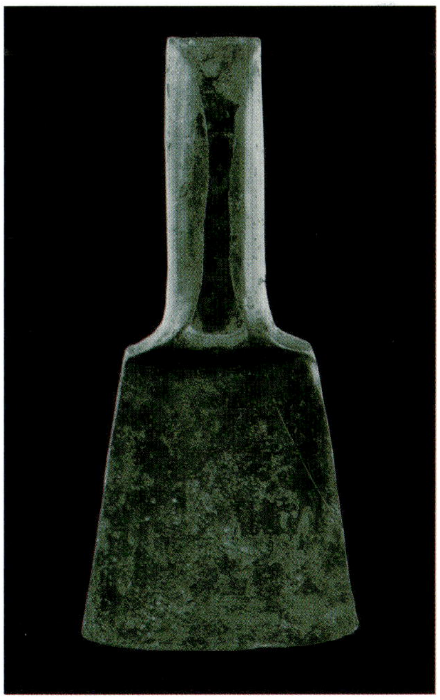

Bronze
Circolo degli Acquastrini, Vetulonia
Second quarter of the 7th century BC
Length 5.6 cm

Similar examples are known from Vetulonia, Veii and Volterra. *MCy*

National Museum of Archaeology, Florence, inv. 7367
Etrusker 1987, 205, no. 107; Magnificenza 1998, 56, no. 42

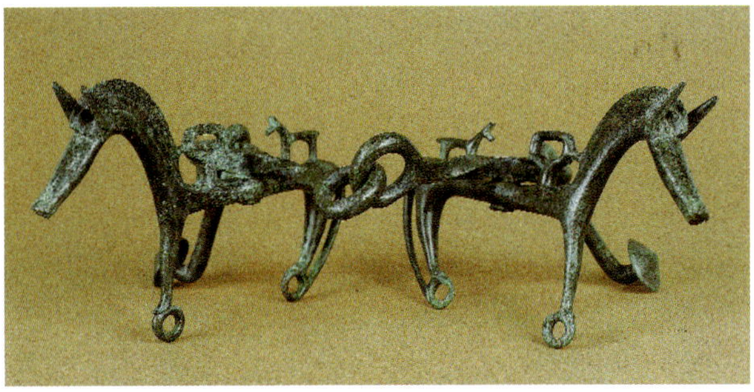

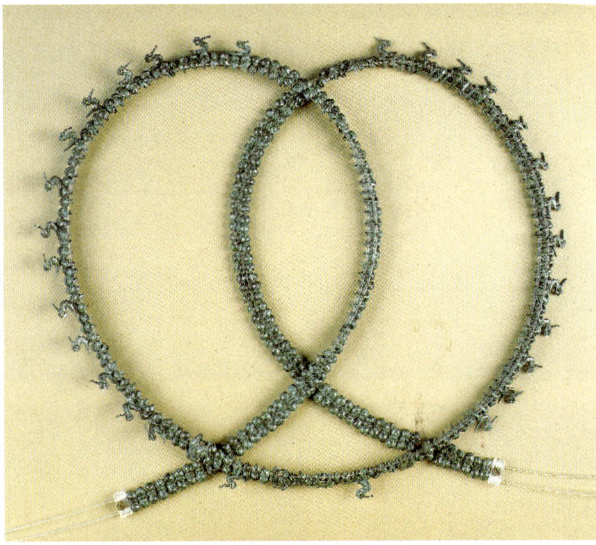

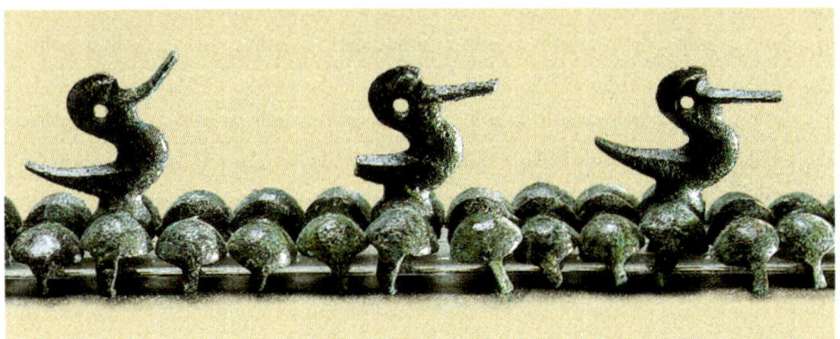

57 Pair of horse bits

Bronze
Circolo degli Acquastrini, Vetulonia
Second quarter of the 7th century BC
Length 17.8 cm

This type of bit with cheekpieces in the form of horses was very popular in Etruria and in the area north of the Appennines, and many examples have been found in Vetulonia. Horses were often represented on bronzes from Vetulonia. *MCy*

National Museum of Archaeology, Florence, inv. 7380, 7381
Magnificenza 1998, 56, no. 43

58 Horse harness (and detail)

Bronze
Circolo degli Acquastrini, Vetulonia
Second quarter of the 7th century BC
Length 185.0 cm

This harness consists of more than 250 separate bronze elements, 30 of them decorated with small cast bronze ducks. This type of harness has been found over a wide geographical area from southern Russia to Baden-Württemberg in south-west Germany, although only a few examples are known from Italy. The presence of this harness in a tomb in Vetulonia provides evidence of the city's links with central Europe, probably via Bologna. *MCy*

National Museum of Archaeology, Florence, inv. 7346
Etrusker 1987, 191, no. 79; Magnificenza 1998, 56, no. 44

59 **Tripod**

Bronze
Circolo degli Acquastrini, Vetulonia
Second quarter of the 7th century BC
Height 19.8 cm

This is believed to be one of the oldest examples of this characteristic product of the bronze workshops of Vetulonia. Similar tripods were exported further north to the Padania area, the valley of the river Po.

National Museum of Archaeology, Florence, inv. 7325

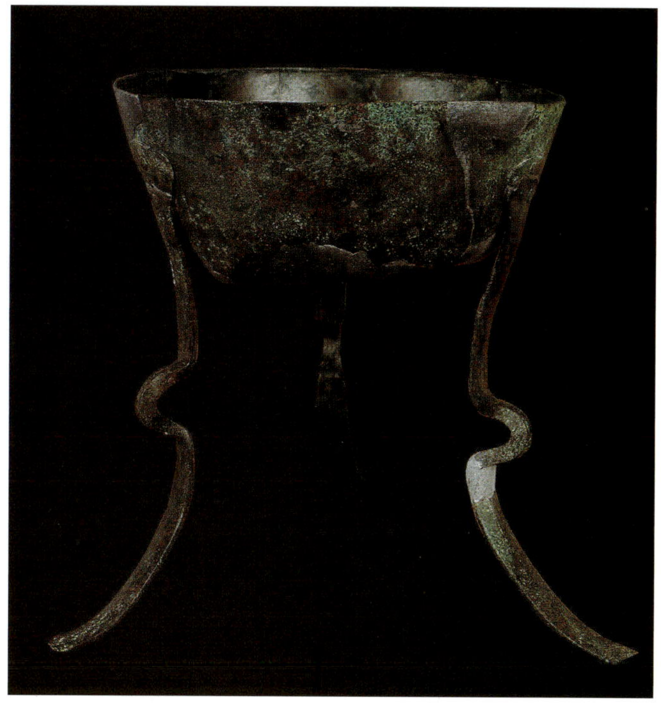

60 **Fibula**

Silver and gold
Tomb 10, Banditella necropolis, Marsiliana d'Albegna
Second quarter of the 7th century BC
Length 7.5 cm

This fine so-called 'dragon' fibula is very similar to two others from Marsiliana, from the Circolo di Perazetta, as well as two more from Vetulonia and Volterra. This distinctive group will have been made in a northern Etruscan workshop. Dragon fibulae were probably worn by men. *GCC/EG*

National Museum of Archaeology, Florence, inv. 11248
Minto 1921, 47, 194, pl. 12, 10; Magnificenza 1998, 48, no. 21; see also Cristofani and Martelli 1983, 268, no. 54; Minto 1921, 162, pl. 13, 3 and 7

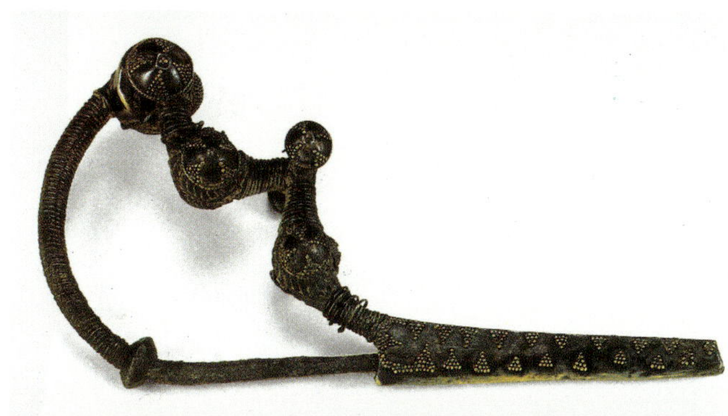

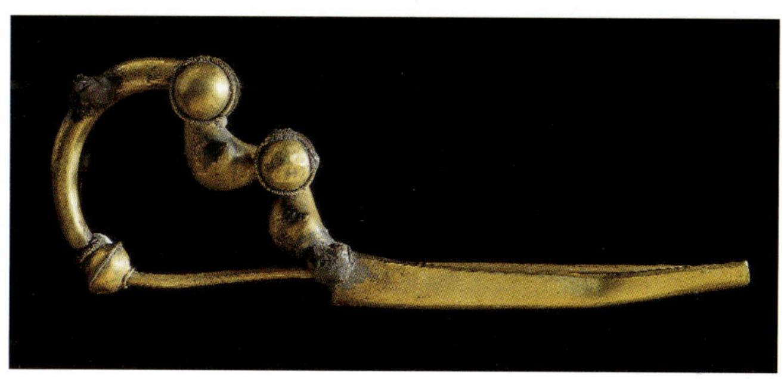

61 **Fibula**

Silver and gold
Circolo di Perazetta, Banditella necropolis, Marsiliana d'Albegna
Second quarter of the 7th century BC
Length 11.3 cm

This is another, simpler example of the dragon fibula type, of which there were numerous varieties. *GCC*

National Museum of Archaeology, Florence, inv. 117918

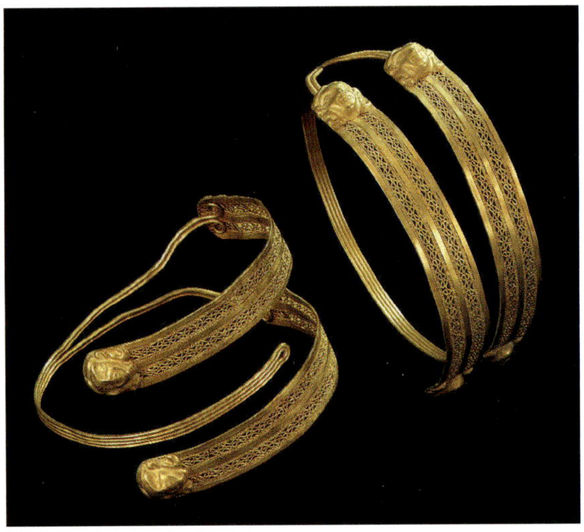

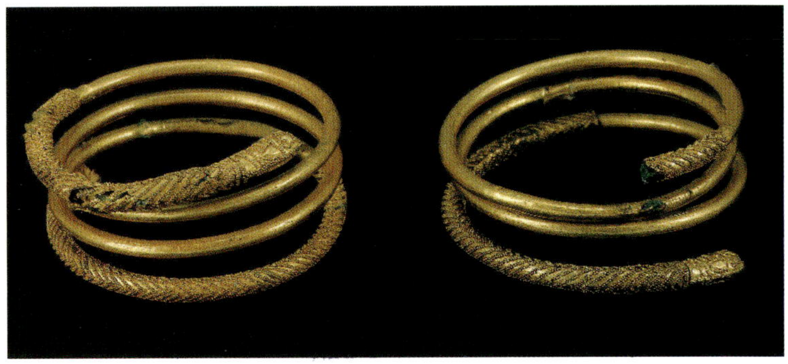

62 Pair of bracelets

Gold
Le Pellicce necropolis, Vetulonia
Middle of the 7th century BC
Diameter 7.0 cm

These bracelets, a necklace and several other items of gold and silver jewellery were found with a woman's cremation burial. They are decorated with filigree wire-work and female heads of sheet gold. Although the filigree technique was first developed in southern Etruria, workshops in northern coastal Etruria, especially in Populonia and Vetulonia, produced many fine examples of filigree jewellery, developing distinctive new forms.

GCC

National Museum of Archaeology, Florence, inv. 81244, 81245
Mágico 1996, 117, no. 31

63 Hair spirals

Gold sheet over a bronze core
Tarquinia
Middle of the 7th century BC
Diameter 3.5 cm

Simple versions of hair ornaments like these are known from the Villanovan period, usually made of bronze. They became very common in the Orientalizing period, when they were made in more elaborate forms and often of precious metals. Examples like these, with fine granulated decoration and terminals in the shape of snakes' or lions' heads, were popular in southern Etruria.

AME

National Museum of Archaeology, Florence, inv. 124966a-b
Gioielli 1988, 139, no. 45; Magnificenza 1998, 61, no. 56

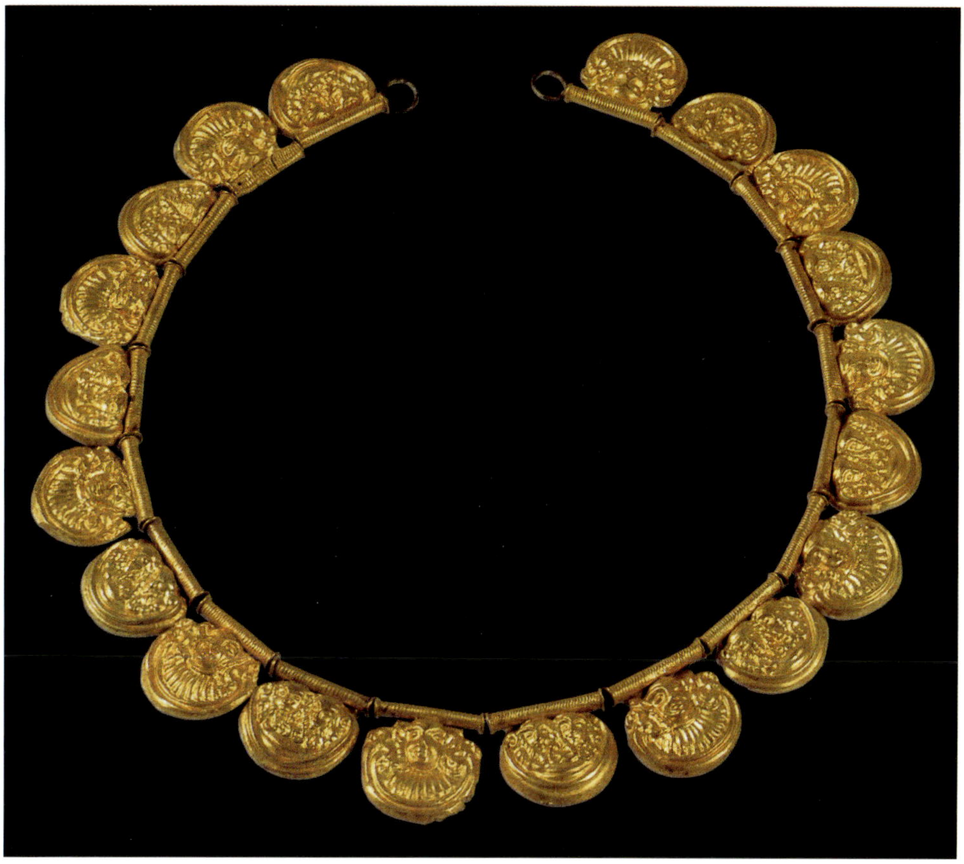

64 **Necklace**

Gold
The Pietrera tumulus, Vetulonia
Third quarter of the 7th century BC
Diameter of pendants approx. 2.0 cm

The Pietrera tomb was a monumental tumulus (mound) containing vaulted burial chambers. This necklace from the tomb is composed of 20 gold sheet pendants of two different types. They are decorated with the heads of females with their hair dressed in 'Hathor locks' (based on the style worn by the Egyptian goddess Hathor) and stylized lotus ornaments. Both are Orientalizing motifs. Other similar necklaces are known from Vetulonia. *MCy*

National Museum of Archaeology, Florence, inv. 74833a
cf. Cristofani and Martelli 1983, 280; Mágico 1996, 113, no. 21

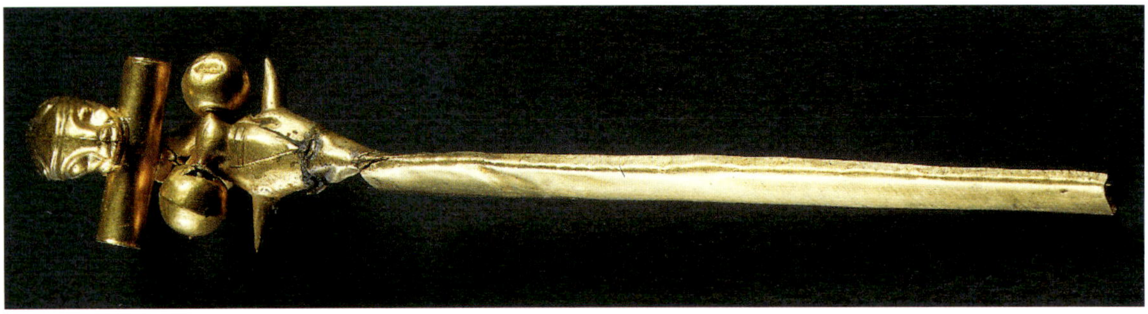

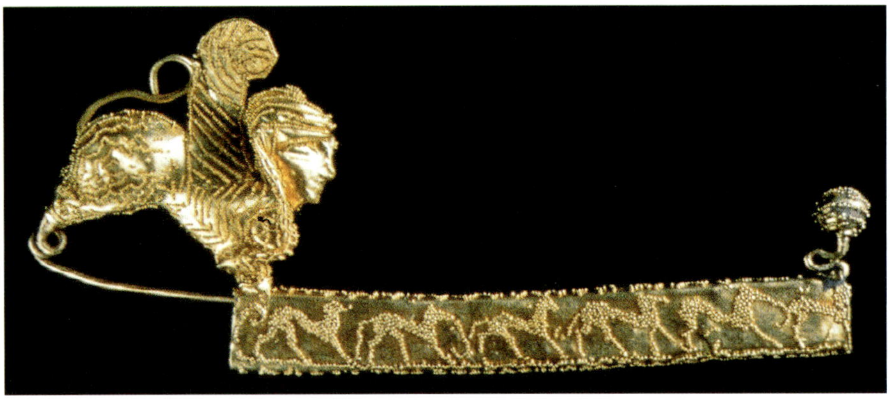

65 **Fibula**

Gold
Tomba del Littore (Tomb of the Lictor), Vetulonia
Third quarter of the 7th century BC
Length 11.7 cm

This important dragon fibula was found in the Tomb of the Lictor, together with numbers 66-71. This rich tomb, excavated in 1897, contained a miniature iron fasces, a bundle of rods around a double axe (see number 72). The fasces was a traditional symbol of power which in Republican Rome was carried by the lictors, the public attendants of the consuls, the two principal magistrates of the state. The fibula has a bull's head and a unique lion's head at one end. It was probably made in Vetulonia. *MCy/EG*

National Museum of Archaeology, Florence, inv. 77263
Cristofani and Martelli 1983, 270, 271, no. 61; Mágico 1996, 114, no. 25

66 **Fibula**

Gold sheet, silver core
Tomba del Littore (Tomb of the Lictor), Vetulonia
Third quarter of the 7th century BC
Length 8.5 cm

This elaborate fibula, with its bow in the form of a sphinx, has been skilfully decorated in the technique known as 'a pulviscolo', or powder granulation. The technique, which uses minute gold granules to create pattern and texture, is characteristic of Vetulonia. There is granulation on the sphinx, the ball-shaped terminal and the foot, where it has been used to create a row of six quadrupeds. The maker of this jewel has produced an eclectic mix of ideas drawn from various sources. The fabricated body of the sphinx, made in two halves, is typical of objects from southern Etruria; the powder granulation is typical of Vetulonia; and the sphinx is an Orientalizing motif. *MCy*

National Museum of Archaeology, Florence, inv. 77262
Cristofani and Martelli 1983, 272, no. 66; Cento Preziosi 1984, no. 20; Civiltà 1985, 104, no. 3, 15, 37

67 **Two fibulae**

Gold sheet, silver core
Tomba del Littore (Tomb of the Lictor), Vetulonia
Third quarter of the 7th century BC
Length 20.8 cm

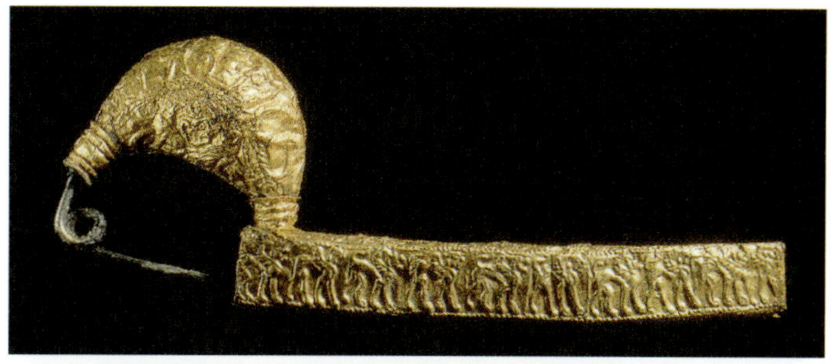

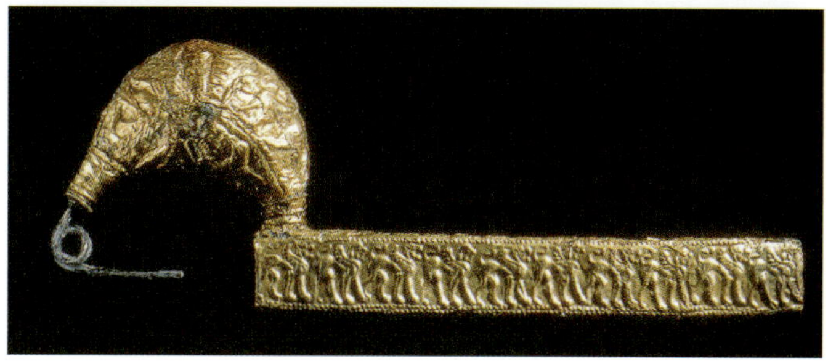

These are two identical examples of three very closely-related leech-shaped fibulae from the same tomb. The third (National Museum of Archaeology, Florence, inv. 77259, not included in the exhibition) has some minor differences, but all three must have been made in a single workshop using the same matrices. On each the sheet gold bow is decorated with sphinxes, griffins and palmettes. The feet are decorated differently on each of their faces, with rows of sphinxes, lions, griffins and Phoenician palmette motifs. Fibulae like these, which were popular in Vetulonia, are considered to be local versions of the more elaborate and sophisticated examples found in tombs like the Regolini-Galassi tomb in Cerveteri. *MCy*

National Museum of Archaeology, Florence, inv. 77257, 77258
Cristofani and Martelli 1983, 271, nos. 62-4; Mágico 1996, 115, no. 26

68 **Fibula (front and back views)**

Gold
Tomba del Littore (Tomb of the Lictor), Vetulonia
Third quarter of the 7th century BC
Length 15.6 cm

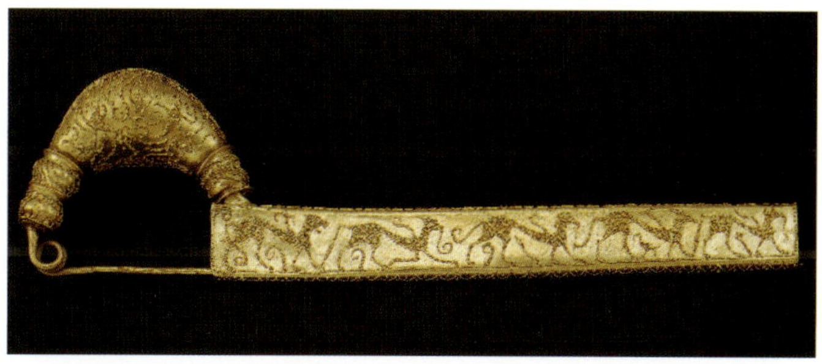

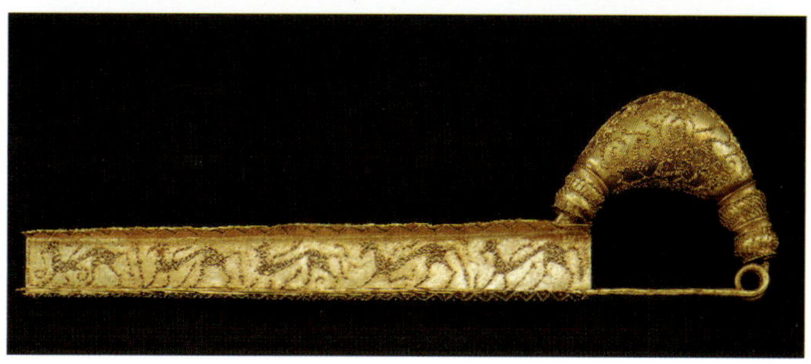

This is another fine leech-shaped fibula decorated with motifs in the 'a pulviscolo' (powder granulation) technique typical of the goldsmiths of Vetulonia. There are animal and plant motifs on the bow, together with a type of meander pattern along the upper face. The foot is decorated with rows of fantastic creatures, amongst them, on one side nearest the bow (front face), one of the earliest Etruscan representations of the monster called the chimaera. On the same side a tiny bird has been used as a filling ornament. *MCy*

National Museum of Archaeology, Florence, inv. 77261
Cristofani and Martelli 1983, 272, no. 65; Etrusker 1987, 188, no. 21; Mágico 1996, 114, no. 23

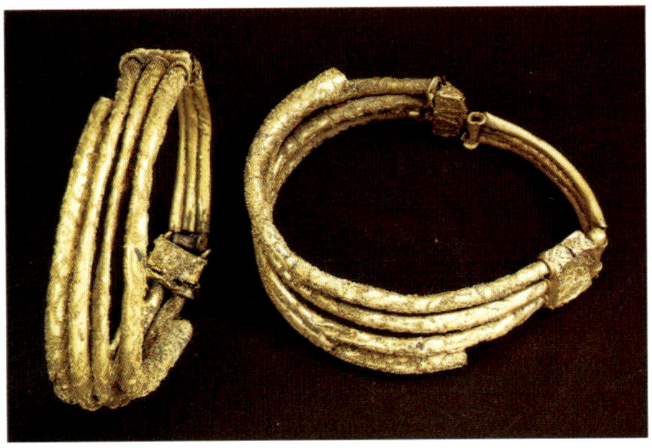

69

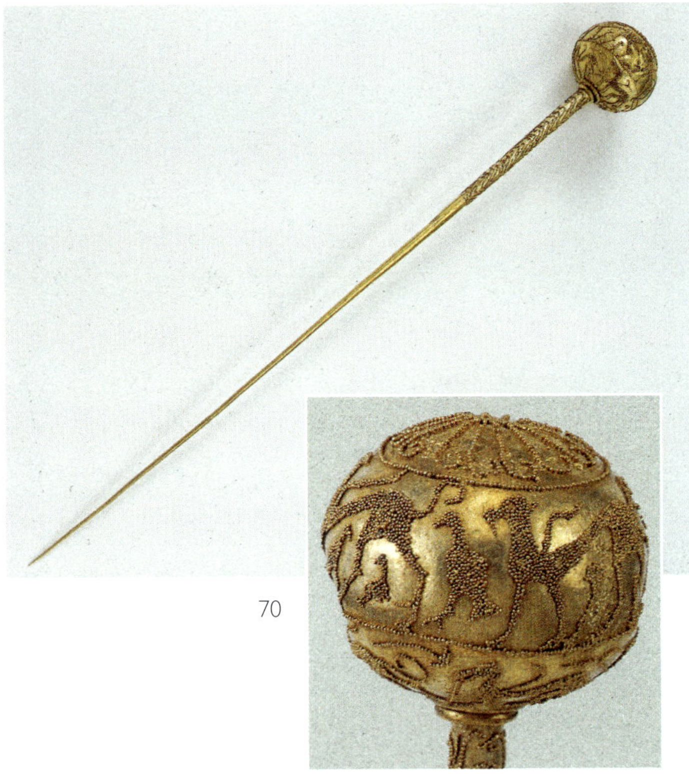

70

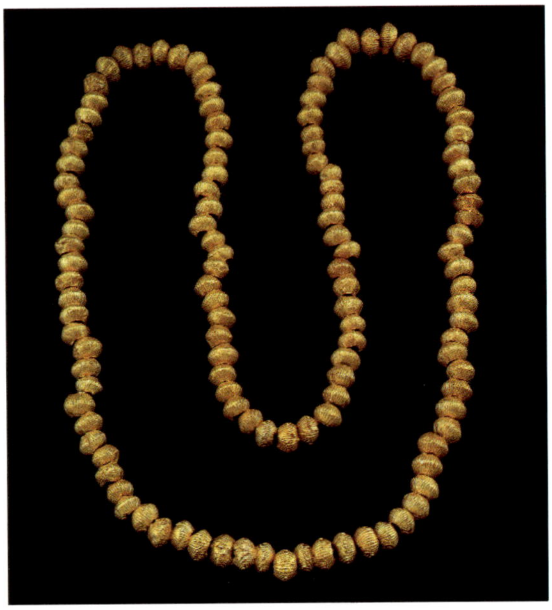

71

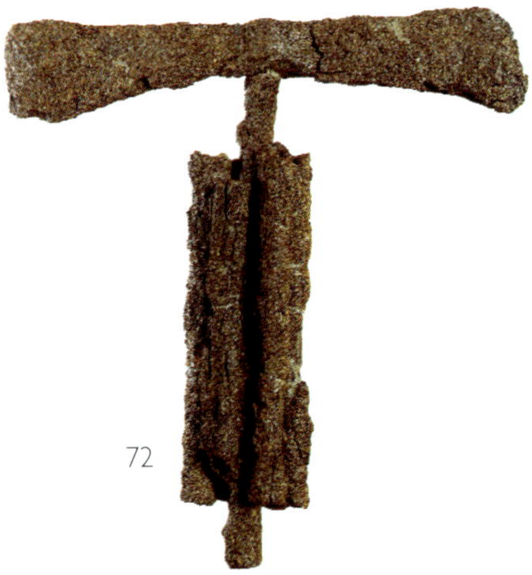

72

69 Pair of bracelets

Gold
Tomba del Littore (Tomb of the Lictor), Vetulonia
Third quarter of the 7th century BC
Diameter 6.5 cm

These unusual gold sheet bracelets are skilfully decorated with 'a pulviscolo' granulation (powder granulation). The curved surfaces of the main tubular elements are richly covered with lions, sphinxes, plants and geometric motifs in the style of the Vetulonian goldsmiths. The bracelets were fastened with a carefully-designed hinge and pin mechanism. *MCy*

National Museum of Archaeology, Florence, inv. 77266, 77267
Cristofani and Martelli 1983, 272, no. 67; Etrusker 1987, 188, nos. 22-3

70 Pin (and detail)

Gold
Tomba del Littore (Tomb of the Lictor), Vetulonia
Third quarter of the 7th century BC
Length 20.7 cm; diameter of pin head 2.2 cm

The upper part of the shaft of this very long, slender pin is decorated with curvilinear geometric motifs in powder granulation. The spherical head is decorated with curvilinear motifs, fantastic creatures, birds and plants in the same skilfully-executed technique. This remarkable pin from Vetulonia has been compared to one from Chiusi, unfortunately now lost. *MCy*

National Museum of Archaeology, Florence, inv. 77260
Cristofani and Martelli 1983, 270, no. 58; Mágico 1996, 114, no. 24

71 Necklace

Gold
Tomba del Littore (Tomb of the Lictor), Vetulonia
Third quarter of the 7th century BC
Average diameter of beads 0.7 cm

These 125 biconical 'melon' beads, made from gold sheet decorated with longitudinal striations, have been re-assembled to form this necklace. Similar beads are known from Vetulonia and Marsiliana d'Albegna.

National Museum of Archaeology, Florence, inv. 77265
Cristofani and Martelli 1983, 271, no. 60

72 Fasces (double axe with rods)

Iron
Vetulonia
Second half of the 7th century BC
Height 25.0 cm

This object consists of a double-headed axe with a hollow handle, projecting from a bundle of cylindrical rods. This group of objects became the Roman fasces, carried by the lictors, public attendants of the principal Roman magistrates, as symbols of their judicial powers. The Roman writer Silius Italicus recorded that the origins of the Roman fasces lay in Vetulonia. This object would have been associated with a person of high political and military status. *GCC*

National Museum of Archaeology, Florence, inv. 8608

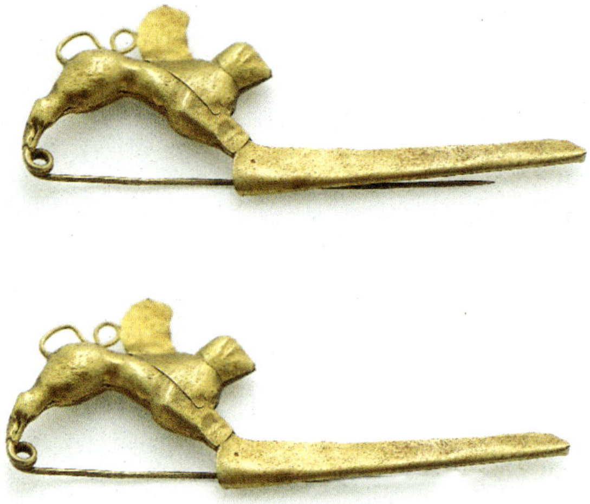

73

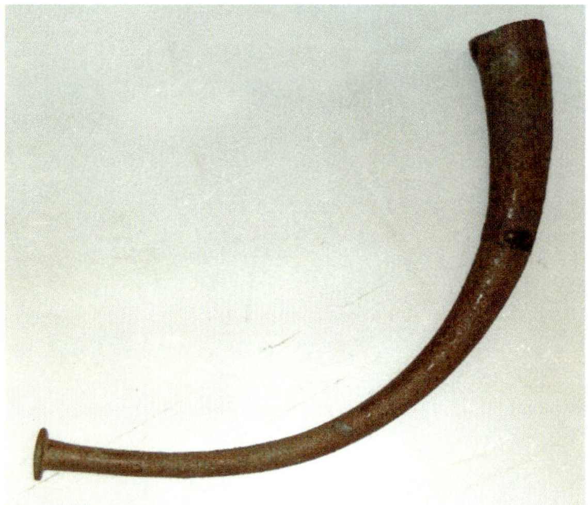

74

75

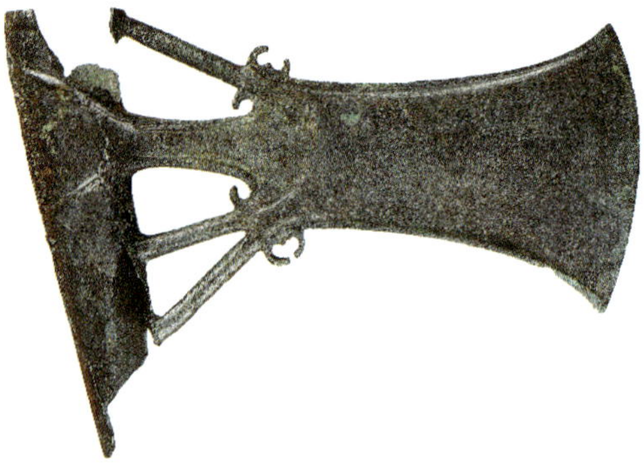

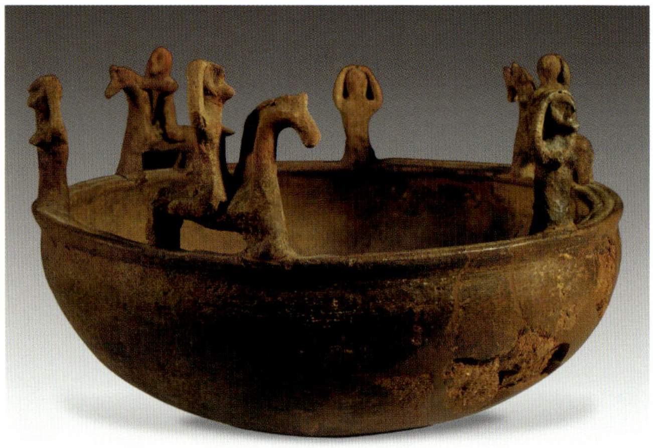

76

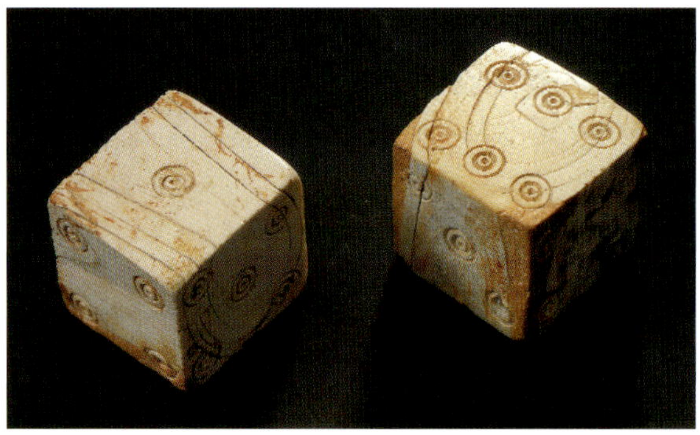

77

73 Two fibulae

Gold
Unknown provenance
Second quarter of the 7th century BC
Length 5.3 cm

The bows of these sheet gold fibulae are in the form of sphinxes. Fibulae with animals on the arch are typical of southern Etruria, which has produced many examples in the form of lions and horses. Another, more elaborate, sphinx-shaped fibula was found in the Tomba del Littore at Vetulonia (number 66). *GCC*

National Museum of Archaeology, Florence, inv. 75513, 75514

74 Cornu (war trumpet)

Bronze
Tomba dei Carri, San Cerbone necropolis, Populonia
Second half of the 7th century BC
Length 40.0 cm

The belief that the war trumpet originated in Etruria has been supported by the discovery of this early example from the necropolis of San Cerbone. Representations of similar horns from the 6th century regularly show them in association with hoplites (well-armed foot soldiers). The shape and size of these trumpets changed in the 5th century, eventually developing into the standard form of the Roman cornu. *GCC*

National Museum of Archaeology, Florence, inv. 152342

75 Axe head

Bronze
Trestina
7th century BC
Length 30.0 cm

This large cast bronze axe head is from a rich deposit of votive objects, but similar axes have sometimes been found in the tombs of high-status warriors of the Orientalizing period. By this date iron was being used for practical purposes, such as for weapons, but bronze axes like this one were highly valued as symbols of authority. *GCC*

National Museum of Archaeology, Florence, inv. 84507

76 Lebes (bowl)

Impasto
Valle Rodeta, Pitigliano
Second half of the 7th century BC
Height 14.0 cm; diameter 38.5 cm

This remarkable bowl was found in a chamber tomb in 1939. Its rim is ornamented with six small figurines drawn from the local stylistic traditions of the late Villanovan period. Three horsemen alternate with three mourning women, subjects illustrating the aristocratic rank of the dead person, as well as aspects of funerary ritual. *AP*

National Museum of Archaeology, Florence, inv. 89852
Torelli 2000, 597, cat. no. 173

77 Pair of dice

Ivory
Unknown provenance
Third quarter of the 7th century BC
Height 2.0 cm

As on modern dice, the circles with dots represent the numbers one to six. *AR*

National Museum of Archaeology, Florence, inv. 01565a-b

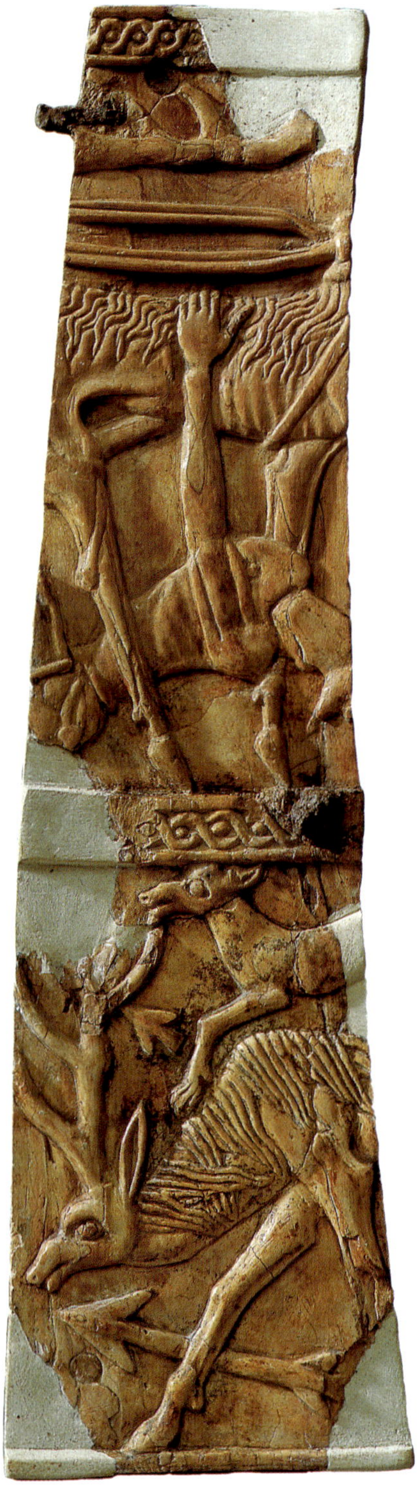

(a)

78 Mounting plaques

Ivory

The tholos tomb, Montefortini tumulus, Comeana (Florence)

Second half of the 7th century BC

The tholos (beehive-shaped) tomb within the tumulus of Montefortini consisted of a huge chamber more than seven metres in diameter. Although ivories have frequently been found in wealthy burials of the Orientalizing period, an exceptionally large number of high quality ivories was recovered from the entrance to this tomb. They illustrate the wide range of techniques employed by the very skilled ivory-workers who made them, including high and low relief, engraving and fretwork.

Some of these techniques indicate the ready access the craftsmen must have had to ivory. Relief carving and in particular fretwork, or openwork, are 'wasteful' of what was a very precious material, and it is likely that even the smallest fragments of waste material would have been re-used. Ivories like these from the Montefortini tumulus are representative of the burgeoning demand from the aristocratic class for luxury items in the Orientalizing period: other exotic materials included glass, faience and ostrich shell. The long-established trade in luxury raw materials around the Mediterranean has been highlighted by the discovery of the Late Bronze Age (14th century BC) Ulu Burun shipwreck off the south coast of Turkey. The ship had been carrying unworked elephant and hippopotamus ivory, ostrich eggs and ingots of blue glass, as well as finished products such as precious metal vessels and weapons.

More ivory objects have been found in northern Etruria than anywhere else in Etruria, or indeed in Italy. Ivory-carving was a long-established art in the Near East and finished objects were imported to Italy from there. However, immigrant ivory-workers from the East were also working in Etruria to meet the specific demands of the local market and, like foreign craftsmen working in other materials, they will have passed on their skills to the Etruscans. Examination of large groups of material, such as the Montefortini ivories, may eventually enable the identification of the work of individual carvers.

Flat or curved plaques like these were used as mounts for objects made from other materials, such as chests and boxes, or furniture such as chairs and beds, and were fixed in place using bone or ivory pins. It has been suggested these plaques came from a chest, an important chair, or even (though less likely) a chariot (see Torelli 2000, 577-8).

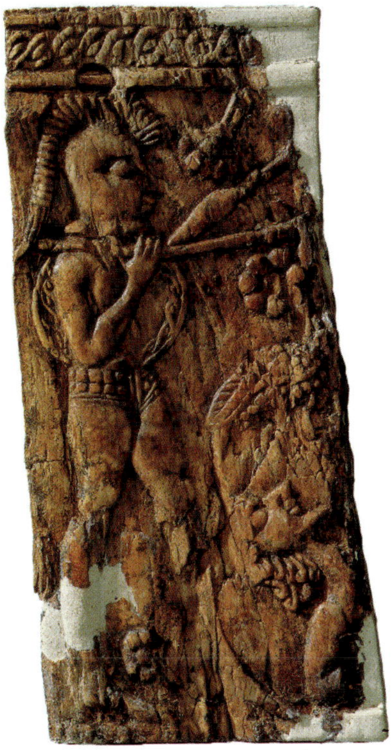

(b)

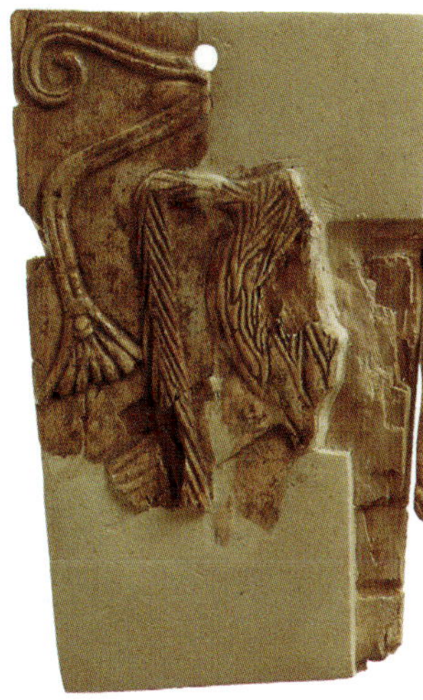

(c)

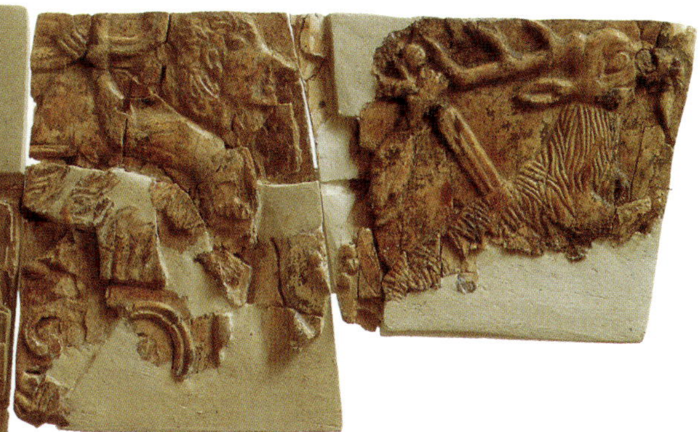

(a) Height 20.2 cm

The upper part of this plaque shows part of a scene which includes a large quadruped with long antlers, apparently a stag. The shaft of a chariot is just visible between the animal's legs. A man is shown clinging to the underside of the animal's belly, his head hanging down. Although this recalls the story of Odysseus escaping with his companions from the cave of the Cyclops Polyphemus by hiding amongst his sheep and goats, the animal's antlers and the presence of what seems to be a chariot make such an identification unlikely. The scene may show a stag and another animal drawing a chariot, a motif known from an engraved gem from Campania dated to the 7th-6th centuries. The lower part of the plaque shows another stag with a dog above it. Arrows are visible in the back-ground. *MCB/FN*

National Museum of Archaeology, Florence, inv. 194659
Torelli 2000, 577

(b) Height 10.5 cm

This plaque shows a hoplite (a heavily armed infantry soldier) walking to the right. He is wearing a high-crested Corinthian helmet and carries a round shield and a spear. A spear thrown by an unseen enemy is shown piercing him from above. At his feet lies a fallen man. The scene may show a fight between heroes. The presence of horizontal pins at the left edge indicate it is incomplete. *MCB/FN*

National Museum of Archaeology, Florence, inv. 194655

(c) Length 17.2 cm

This plaque shows a centaur brandishing a sword, hunting a deer. *MCB/FN*

National Museum of Archaeology, Florence, inv. 240155

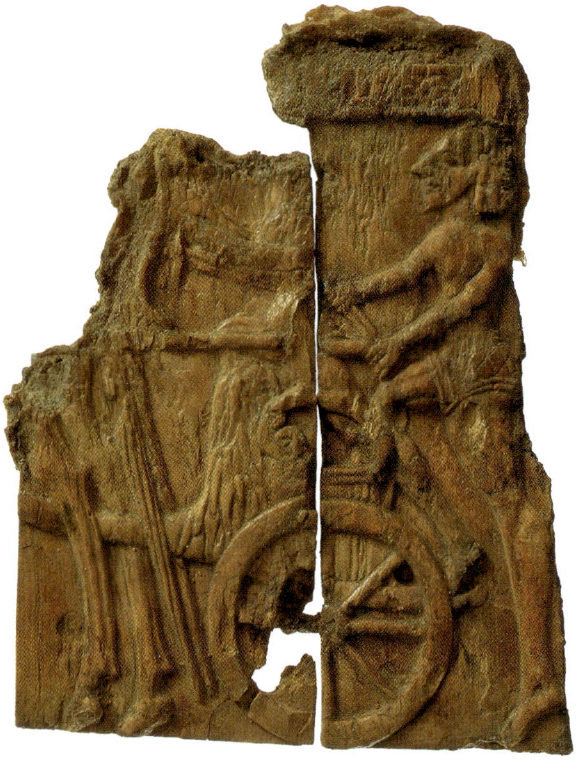

(d)

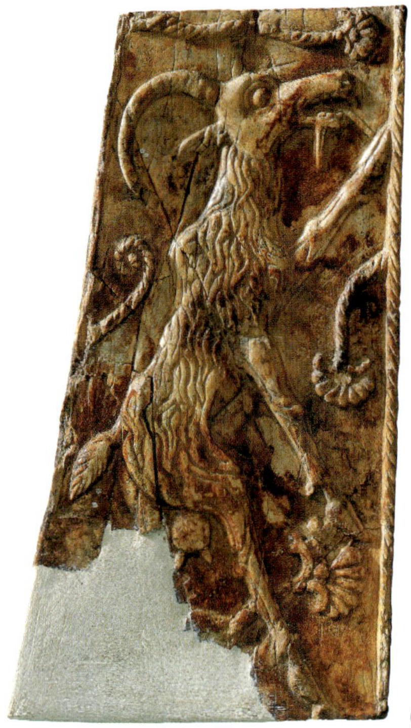

(e)

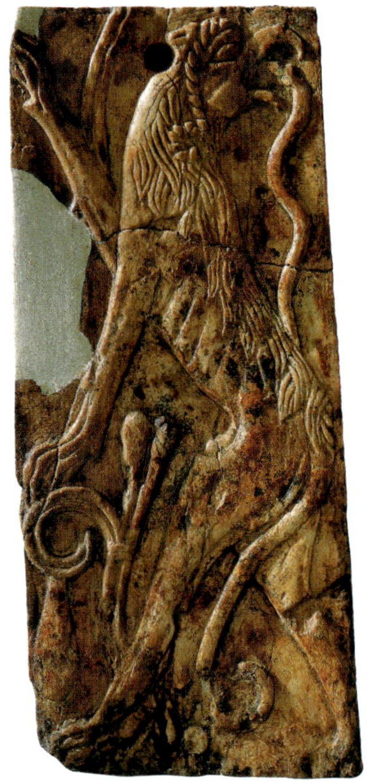

(f)

(d) Height 10.8 cm

This plaque shows two heroes, apparently Herakles and Iolaus, in a chariot. Iolaus was Herakles' nephew and charioteer, and took part in the battle with the Hydra of Lerna. The heads of the two figures are shown level, an artistic device to indicate that they are of equal status. Herakles is identified by his lionskin and Iolaus by his bow. In this scene only part of the biga (a two-horse chariot) is visible. A heavy lionskin is draped over it. One figure is mounting the chariot, holding a long rod in one hand. The other figure is badly damaged, but can be seen standing on the chariot holding a bow. *MCB*

National Museum of Archaeology, Florence, inv. 224109

(e) Height 10.2 cm

This plaque shows a goat rampant (standing on its hind legs: a heraldic pose). It is surrounded by floral ornament. In the centre there is a hole and an ivory pin for fixing the plaque to its background. This plaque may have been mounted symmetrically confronting number 78(f) on the same object. Despite differences in detail, it is possible they were made by the same craftsman. *MCB*

National Museum of Archaeology, Florence, inv. 194658

See Torelli 2000, p. 578, where the goat is identified as possibly Amalthea.

(f) Height 10.5 cm

This plaque shows a griffin rampant. Its head is turned back, and one front foreleg is supported on a floral ornament, in a common heraldic pose. A snake is gripped in its jaws. Two holes for mounting pins are visible. *MCB*

National Museum of Archaeology, Florence, inv. 194657

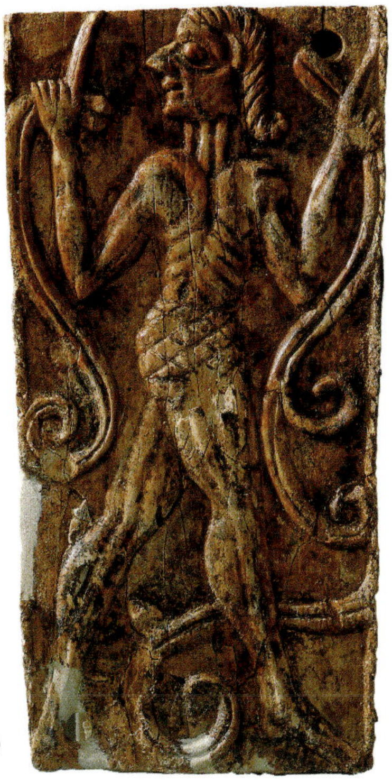

(g)

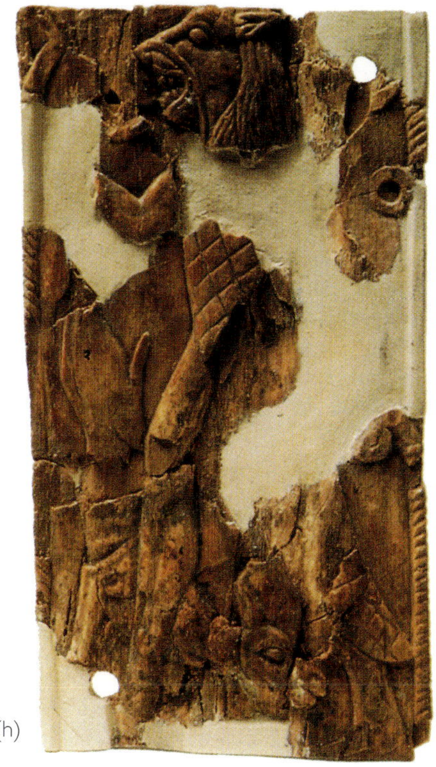

(h)

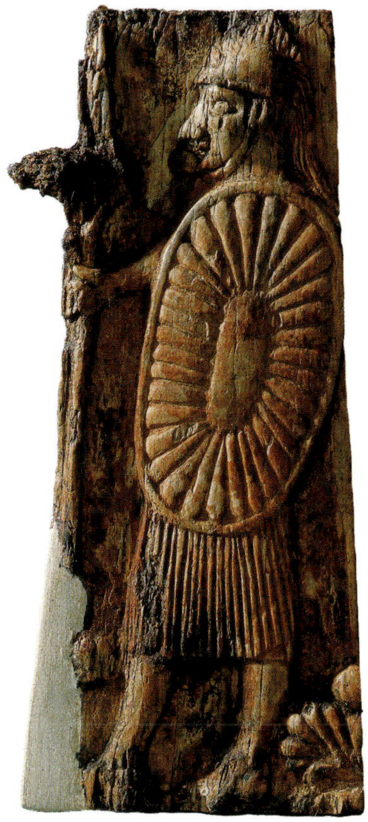

(i)

(g) Height 10.5 cm

This plaque shows a male figure, perhaps Aristaeus, son of Apollo and Cyrene, father of Actaeon. He is shown walking to the right, his head turned back, wearing a short garment of typical Etruscan late Orientalizing style. He grasps long spiralling plant ornaments in his upraised hands. His face and muscled body are carefully detailed. This plaque may be associated with number 78(h), which has similarly located mounting pins and also shows a male figure. *MCB/FN*

National Museum of Archaeology, Florence, inv. 194660

(h) Height 10.8 cm

This plaque shows another male figure, possibly Herakles. The figure appears to have a lion's head. He is shown wearing a long garment and walking to the left. In his right hand he grasps a fawn, its tail and head raised, apparently still alive. The plaque was mounted with three pins. *MCB/FN*

National Museum of Archaeology, Florence, inv. 240154

(i) Height 9.2 cm

This plaque shows a heavily-armed warrior walking to the left. He wears a helmet with a long flowing crest and a pleated garment, and carries a spear in his right hand. The carver has paid great attention to the detailing of the man's shield and tunic. The surface of the shield has been carefully textured using a special carving technique. The pleated tunic, large oval shield and helmet are unusual features. The tunic has some parallels with garments shown on Phoenician and Cypriot vessels, but may be related to those worn by figures on objects such as the ivories from the Bernadini tomb in Cerveteri (Caere), inspired by Egyptian art. The shield has parallels from the north and east of Italy, especially Romagna and Piceno, but these are generally later in date. The helmet and spear recall those represented on the Benvenuti situla from Este. The chinstrap is an unusual feature in Etruscan armour. It has been suggested that the style of the helmet either reflects an older cultural tradition in Etruria or was based on an entirely foreign type. *MCB/FN*

National Museum of Archaeology, Florence, inv. 194656

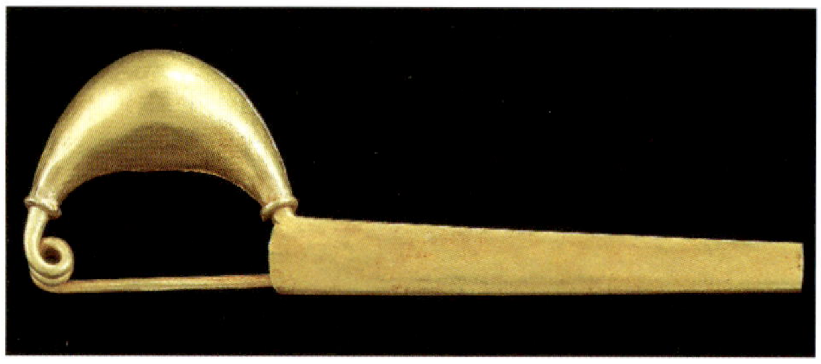
79

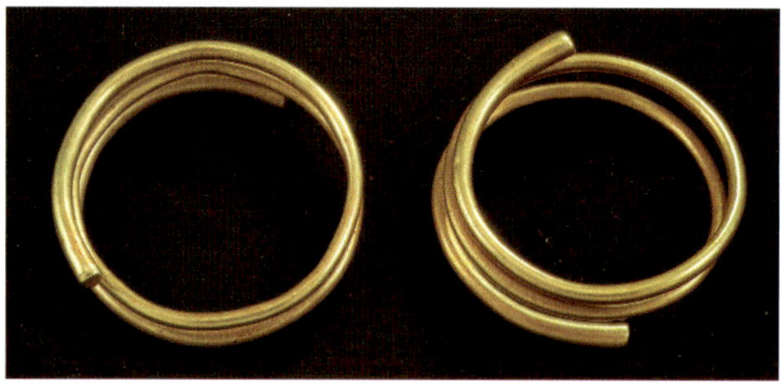
80

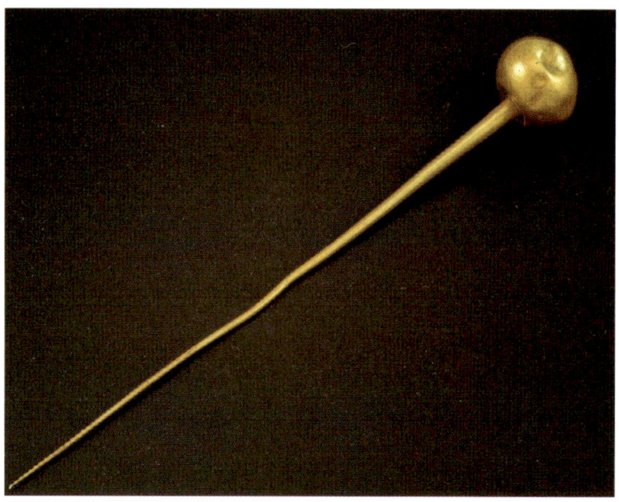
81

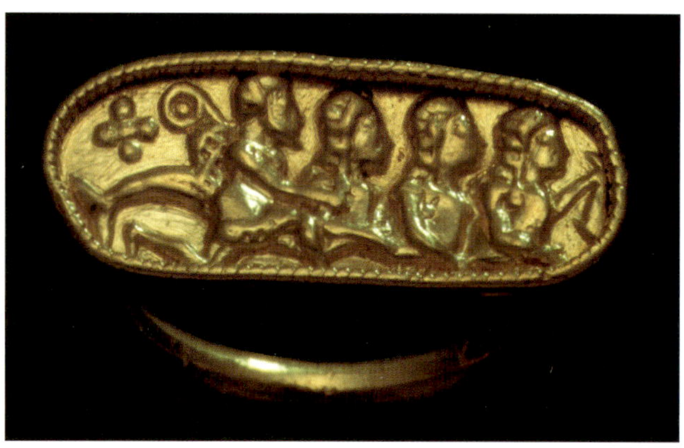
82

Objects from the Tomba dei Flabelli (Tomb of the Fans), Porcareccia necropolis, Populonia (numbers 79-130)

The Tomb of the Fans was a richly-equipped monumental chamber tomb used over a number of generations. This remarkable intact tomb, found by Antonio Minto in 1927, was part of a necropolis which had been buried under the debris of a deep slag mound resulting from the ancient smelting of iron ore. It consisted of a chamber with a false vault. Two plain upright limestone stelae stood to either side of the entrance to the passage (or dromos) leading to the chamber, a mark of the importance of the occupants. The chamber contained three funerary beds, one to either side and a third at the end. The end wall was divided by an upright stone slab. Examination of the bones showed that the remains of four individuals were placed in the tomb, at different times during the last quarter of the 7th century BC and the second quarter of the 6th. A rich assemblage of jewellery and other objects indicated that a woman's burial had been deposited on the left-hand funerary bed. This extensive group included a gold ring (number 82), a pin (number 81), hair spirals (number 80), earrings (numbers 114-15), some fragmentary alabaster perfume bottles (number 117), and many other precious and prestigious objects.

See Minto 1932

79 Fibula

Gold
Middle of the 7th century BC
Length 8.0 cm

Gold fibulae seem to be typical of several communities in northern Etruria. A gold leech-shaped fibula of the same type was found in the Tomba dei Carri (Tomb of the Chariots) in Populonia, and similar examples are known from Vetulonia and Volterra.

National Museum of Archaeology, Florence, inv. 89268

80 Hair spirals

Gold
Middle of the 7th century BC
Diameter 3.6 cm

Hair spirals like these, made in gold or silver, were common in northern Etruria at this time. *GCC*

National Museum of Archaeology, Florence, inv. 89266, 89267

81 Hair pin

Gold
Third quarter of the 7th century BC
Length 16.0 cm

Precious metal pins like this are unusual. They began to appear from the middle of the Orientalizing period, gradually increasing in popularity. The later examples are generally much shorter. This example has no close parallels, but it can be compared with the longer granulated pin from the Tomba del Littore in Vetulonia (number 70). *SB*

National Museum of Archaeology, Florence, inv. 89261

82 Finger ring

Gold
Second quarter of the 6th century BC
Length 2.7 cm

The oblong bezel of this ring has a mythological scene apparently representing Herakles subduing Nereus, a sea god. The ring was probably made in one of the skilled workshops in Vulci, in southern Etruria, and is one of the earliest examples of a type which was very popular in the 6th century BC. *SB*

National Museum of Archaeology, Florence, inv. 89260
Cristofani and Martelli 1983, 298-9, no. 182

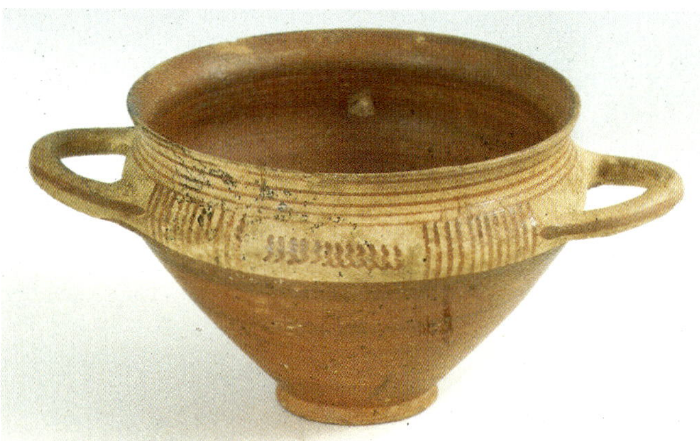

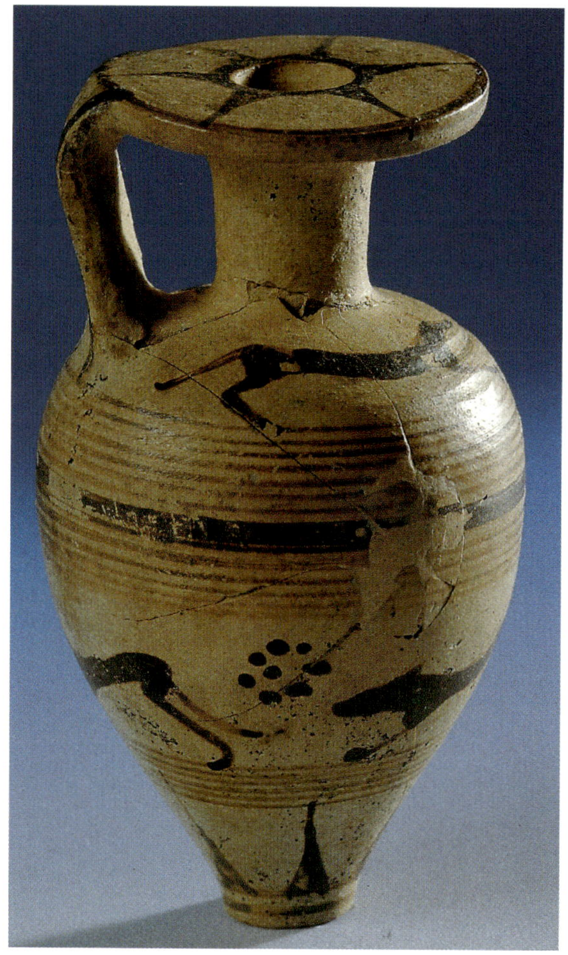

83 **Protocorinthian skyphos (drinking cup)**

Painted ceramic

End of the first quarter of the 7th century BC

Height 6.1 cm

This small cup of the middle Protocorinthian period was imported from Greece. *ARo*

National Museum of Archaeology, Florence, inv. 89411

Minto 1932, 356, pl. 14, no 15, fig. 24; Magnificenza 1998, 83, no. 100

84 **Protocorinthian aryballos (perfume bottle)**

Painted ceramic

About 630 BC

Height 7.0 cm

This small perfume bottle is one of a large group of Greek aryballoi decorated with running dogs. Numerous examples have been found in Populonia. *ARo*

National Museum of Archaeology, Florence, inv. 89407

Minto 1932, 310, pl. 14, no 14; Neeft 1983, 174, list 80, no. 1 (Durand Painter); Magnificenza 1998, 83, no. 102

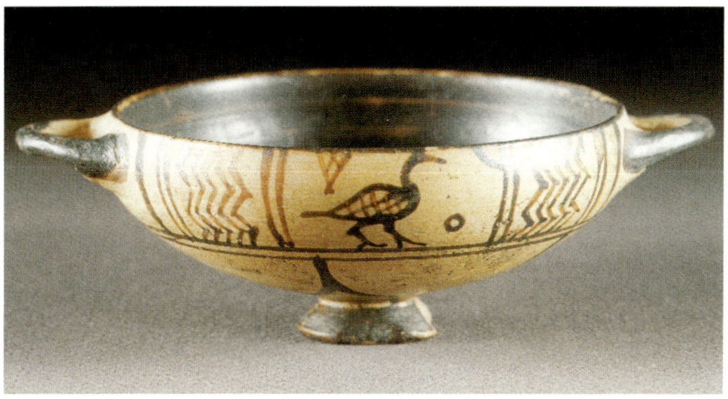

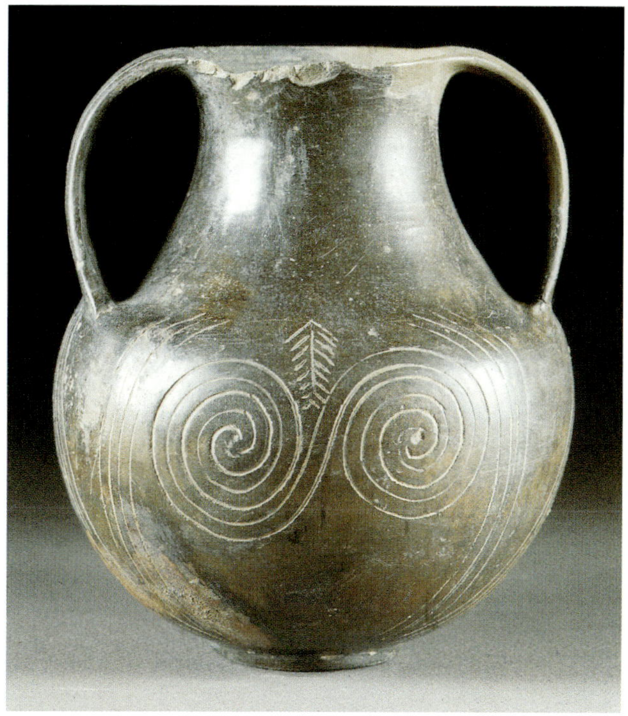

85 **Rhodian cup**

Painted ceramic
Middle of the 7th century BC
Height 3.7 cm

A similar cup decorated with birds has been found in Populonia, and other examples are known from Vetulonia and Poggio Pelliccia. They are amongst the oldest examples of East Greek ceramics known from northern coastal Etruria. *ARo*

National Museum of Archaeology, Florence, inv. 89410
Minto 1932, 355, pl. 14, no. 9, fig. 23; Magnificenza 1998, 82, no. 100

86 **Amphora (container for liquids)**

Impasto
Third quarter of the 7th century BC
Height 12.6 cm

Small amphorae like this one, with the same double spiral motif, are well-known in southern Etruria, from Cerveteri and Veii. The presence of the herringbone motif may suggest this example came from Cerveteri, where it was used extensively. It is certainly an import from southern Etruria, and is an indication of the active trade between Populonia in the north and the cities of the south in the middle and late Orientalizing period. *ARo*

National Museum of Archaeology, Florence, inv. 89390
Minto 1932, 308, pl. 14; Minto 1922, 152, pl. 38, 3; Etrusker 1987, 252, no. 54; Torelli 2000, 600, cat. no. 181

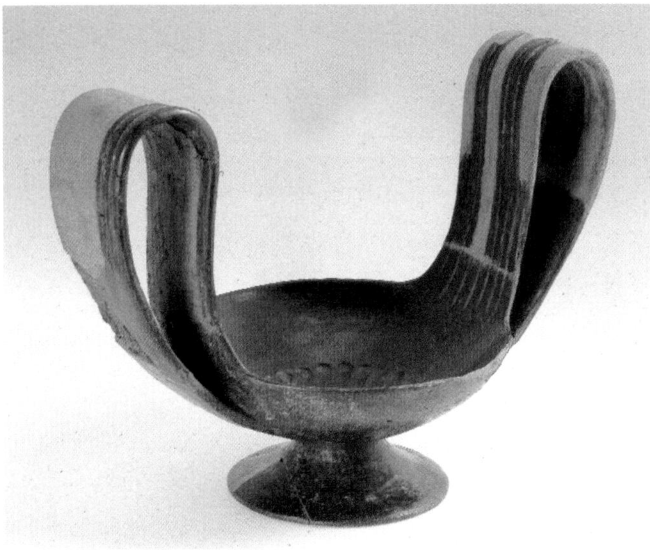

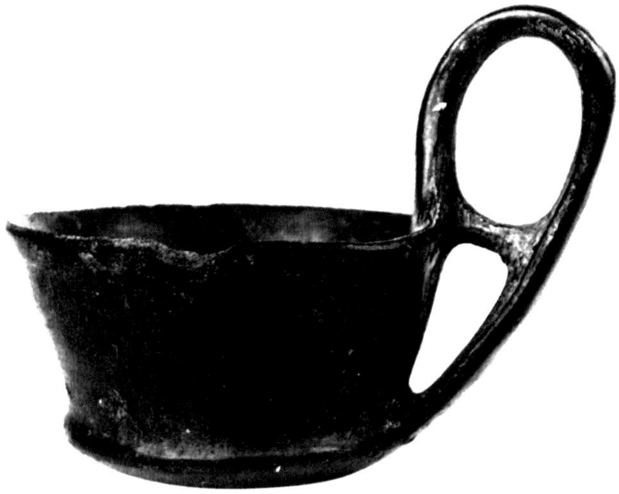

87 Kantharos (drinking cup)

Bucchero
Third quarter of the 7th century BC
Height 14.6 cm

Bucchero pottery, a ceramic with a shiny black surface and dark grey core, was first made by southern Etruscan potters, probably in Cerveteri, and there is good evidence for production centres in southern and inland Etruria. Later the manufacture of bucchero ware also spread north, but much less is currently known about the development of workshops in northern coastal Etruria.

SB/EG

National Museum of Archaeology, Florence, inv. 89395
Minto 1932, 309, pl. 14, no. 7; Magnificenza 1998, 84, no. 103

88 Kyathos

Bucchero
Middle to third quarter of the 7th century BC
Height 4.5 cm

The kyathos, with its single high handle, was used for ladling wine out of wine vessels. Many of the bucchero vessels from Populonia share the same shapes and decorative motifs as those produced in Cerveteri from the middle of the 7th century BC. However, there are some Populonian vessels with distinctive features which are more likely to have been made locally (see also number 90). Nevertheless, the ceramic output of the city seems to have been extremely limited in variety and quantity at this early period.

National Museum of Archaeology, Florence, inv. 89391

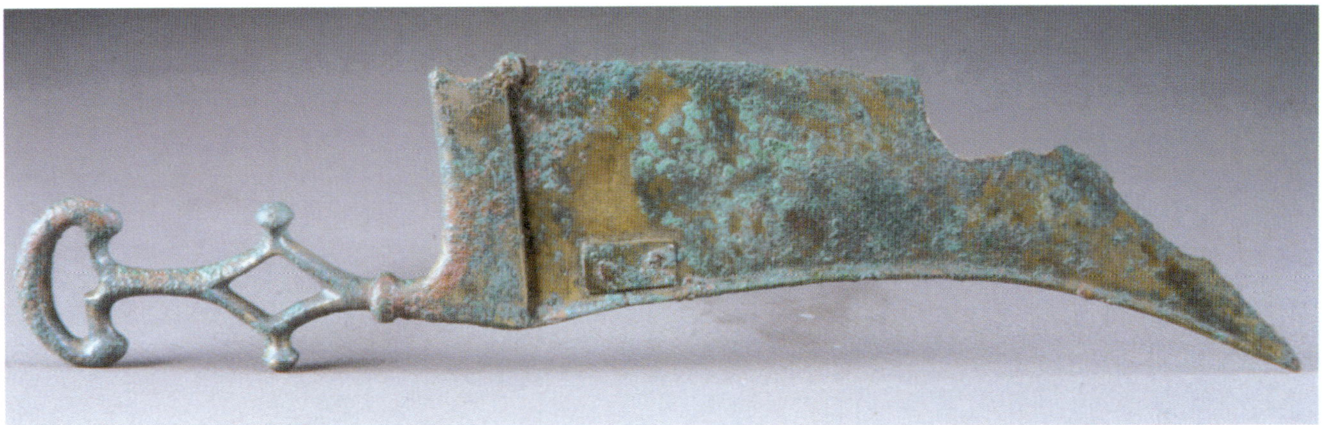

89 **Knife**

Bronze
First half of the 7th century BC
Length 21.4 cm

This knife, which probably had a ritual function, is typical of Bologna. Related examples were made in central northern Europe. This example, and a slightly different type from Vetulonia, seem to be the only ones known from Etruria. It provides important evidence for contact between Bologna and the mining area of northern Etruria, already well-established in the Villanovan period.

National Museum of Archaeology, Florence, inv. 89328

90 **Kyathos**

Bucchero
Middle of the 7th century BC
Height 5.4 cm

National Museum of Archaeology, Florence, inv. 89393

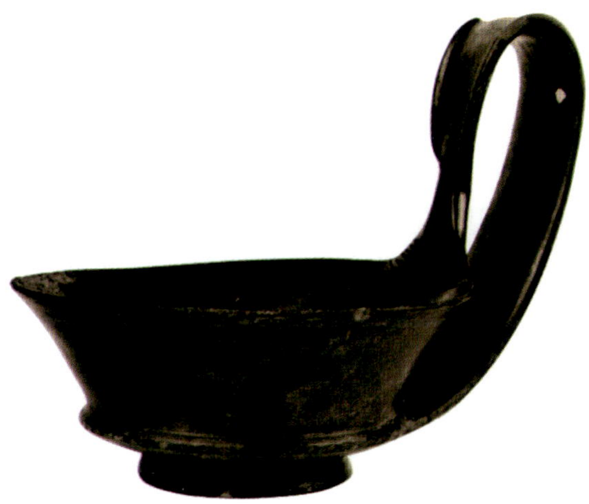

91 **Cup**

Impasto
Third quarter of the 7th century BC
Height 6.0 cm

This is a common Etruscan shape at this date.

National Museum of Archaeology, Florence, inv. 89389

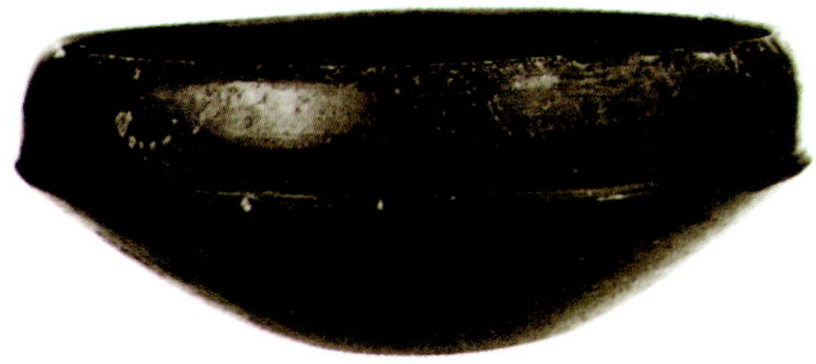

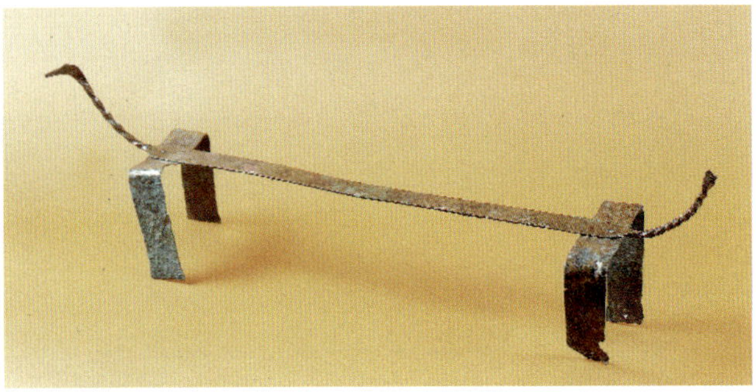

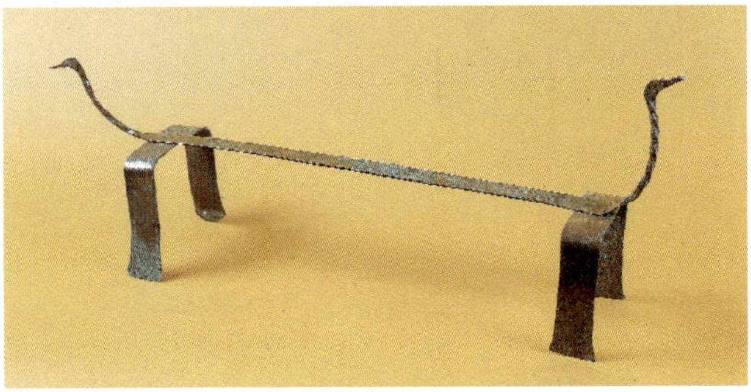

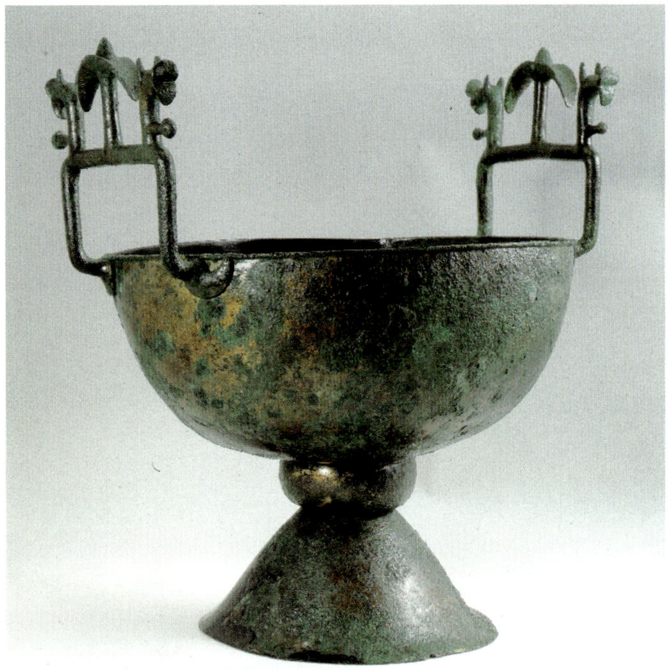

92 Pair of firedogs

Bronze
Third quarter of the 7th century BC
Length 52.0 cm; height 19.4 cm

In Greece, firedogs and spits were placed in the tombs of high-ranking warriors, a custom reflecting Homeric tradition that continued into the first half of the 8th century BC. Firedogs and spits were both found in the Tomb of the Fans. In daily life such objects, generally made of iron, were used for the preparation of roasted food, but their presence in high-status tombs like this one was probably connected to social rank and ritual. These bronze firedogs, with their decorative finials in the form of stylized birds, do not seem to have been functional. *ARo*

National Museum of Archaeology, Florence, inv. 89323, 89324

93 Lebes (cauldron)

Bronze
Middle of the 7th century BC
Height 32.6 cm; diameter 26.6 cm

This large water vessel of sheet bronze with cast bronze handles is the product of a Vetulonian workshop. It belongs to a well-known type of cauldron found in Populonia and at Fabbrecce in the upper Tiber valley. An example found in the sanctuary at Olympia in Greece indicates the value and prestige of this object. The technique of decoration recalls bronzes from Cyprus. *SB*

National Museum of Archaeology, Florence, inv. 89337
Minto 1932, 344, pl. 10, no. 7, fig. 16; Magnificenza 1998, 76, no. 90

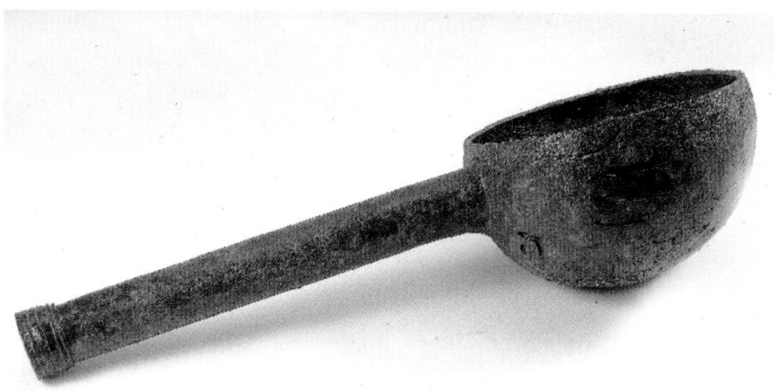

94 **Simpulum (ladle)**

Bronze
Second quarter of the 7th century BC
Length 28.8 cm

Like number 93, this ladle was made in Vetulonia. Part of a drinking service, it is strikingly decorated with human hands at the junction between the bowl and the handle. Similar examples are also known from Vetulonia, Bisenzio, Lazio and the Po valley. *ARo*

National Museum of Archaeology, Florence, inv. 89333
Minto 1932, 302, pl. 11, no. 29; Magnificenza 1998, 75, no. 89

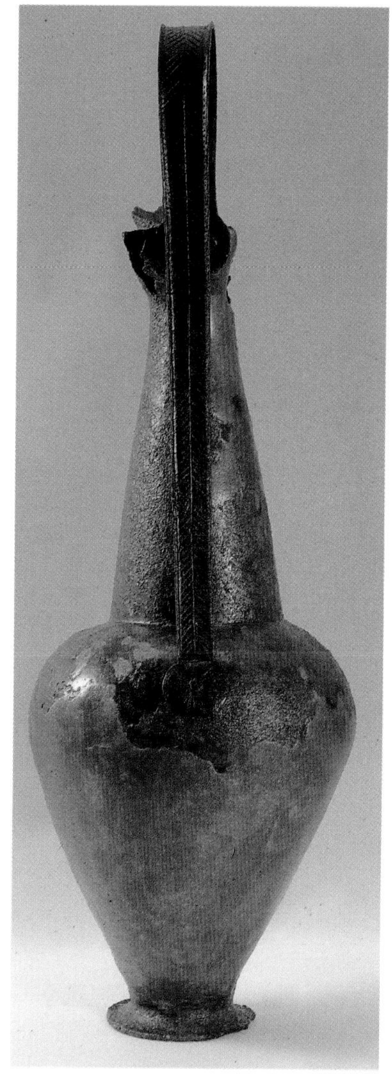

95 **Oinochoe (wine jug)**

Bronze
Third quarter of the 7th century BC
Height 40.3 cm

This large jug, with its finely-decorated cast bronze handle, is one of a group thought to be of local Etruscan manufacture, although it has no exact parallel. They apparently imitate originals from Cyprus, examples of which have been found in aristocratic tombs at Pontecagnano (Salerno). *ARo*

National Museum of Archaeology, Florence, inv. 89361
Culican in Syria 45, 1968, 281, no. 2; Magnificenza 1998, 77, no. 91

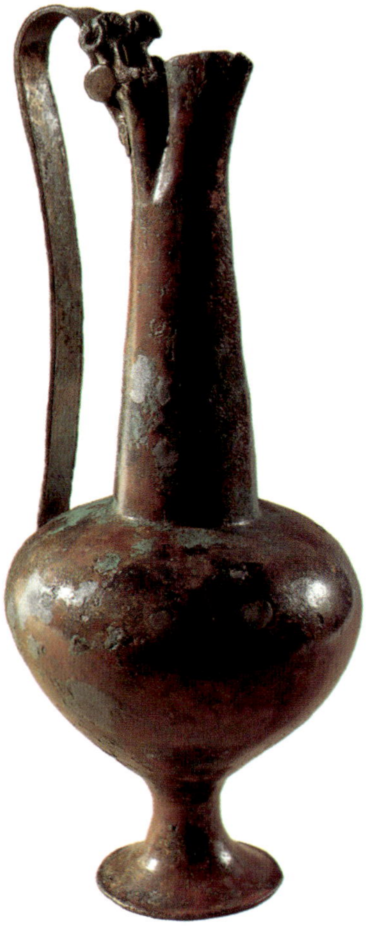

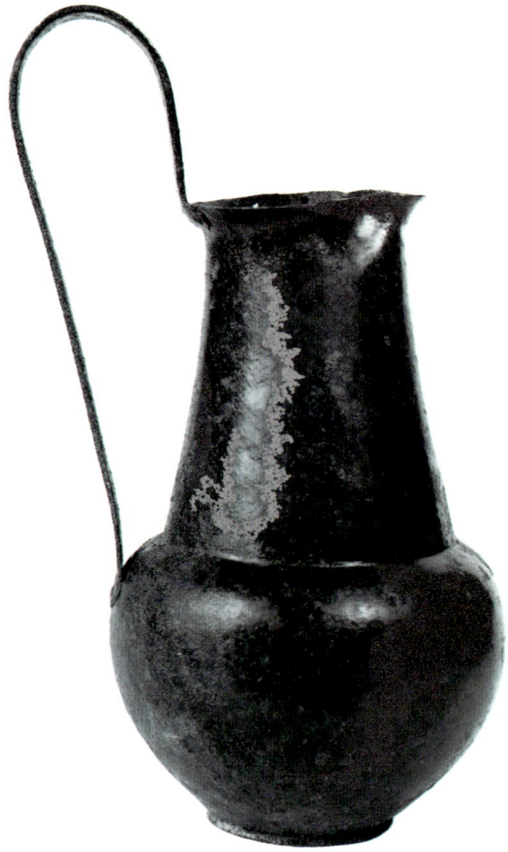

96 **Oinochoe (wine jug)**

Bronze
Third quarter of the 7th century BC
Height 32.1 cm

This vessel is thought to be of Etruscan manufacture, although it recalls Phoenician originals.

National Museum of Archaeology, Florence, inv. 89362

97 **Round-mouthed pitcher**

Bronze
Second half of the 7th century BC
Height 28.7 cm

National Museum of Archaeology, Florence, inv. 89359

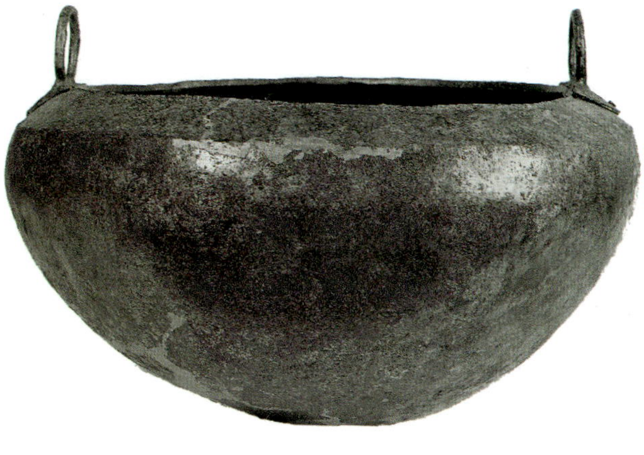

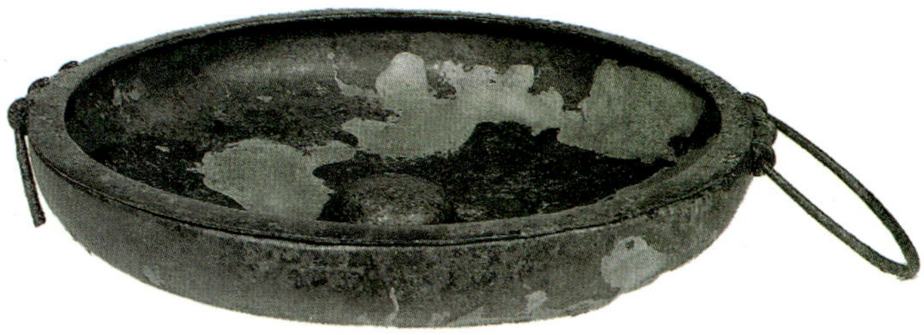

98 **Lebes (cauldron)**

Bronze
7th century BC
Height 26.0 cm; diameter 38.4 cm

This large vessel was raised from a single thin sheet of bronze. Cauldrons like these were standard items of funerary equipment in Etruscan tombs from the 7th century.

National Museum of Archaeology, Florence, inv. 89338

99 **Phiale mesomphalos (dish with a domed centre)**

Bronze
Third quarter of the 7th century BC
Diameter 36.4 cm

This large flat dish with moveable handles was made locally. The form is based on a type from Cyprus.

National Museum of Archaeology, Florence, inv. 89349

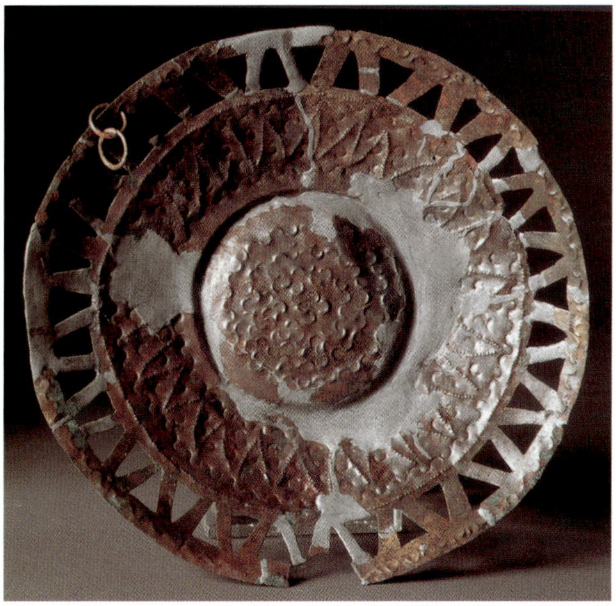

100 **Tray**

Bronze
Second half of the 7th century BC
Diameter 28.0 cm

There is no parallel known for this unusual object, and its function is not clear. It was probably part of the dining equipment used for banquets. The tray has openwork sides, and rings for hanging it up when it was not in use.

National Museum of Archaeology, Florence, inv. 89336

101 **Grater**

Bronze and wood
7th century BC
Height 9.3 cm; width 6.0 cm

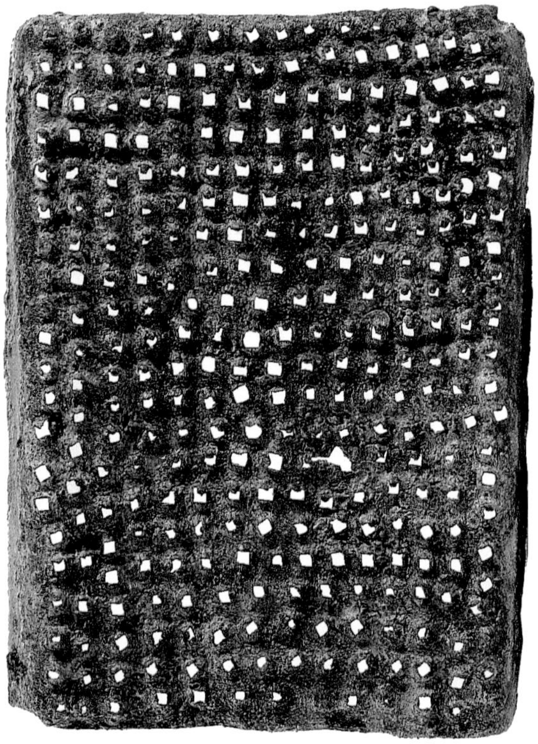

Made from a perforated rectangular sheet of bronze, this grater was equipped with a wooden handle carved in the shape of a crouching fawn which is now in a very poor state of preservation. Graters have been found in burial assemblages from the 9th century BC in Greece. Examples were discovered in the tombs of three warriors buried in the Toumba cemetery at Lefkandi in Euboea. They have also been found Italy, in the 7th century BC aristocratic tombs of Campania and Lazio, as well as in rich tombs in Populonia and Vetulonia in the mining area of northern Etruria. According to Homer's *Iliad* (XI, 628-43), graters were used to prepare a special drink called 'kykeion' which was made from wine, barley and goat's cheese ('In this cup, their comely attendant mixed the pottage with Pramnian wine, and after making it ready by grating into it some goat's milk cheese with a bronze grater and sprinkling white barley on top, she invited them to drink', Rieu 1966, 214). This drink was believed to have healing properties and could cure wounds. The Etruscan princes may have learnt the use of this 'heroic' drink from the Euboeans who came to northern Etruria in search of metal ore. Bronze graters were also offered at sanctuaries, and examples have been found at the Heraion on Samos. *ARo/EG*

National Museum of Archaeology, Florence, inv. 89330
Minto 1932, 341-2, pls. 10, 2, 6, 8; Ridgway 1997, 16, 3, 334-5; Torelli 2000, 611, cat. no. 225

102 **Oinochoe (jug)**

Bronze
First half of the 6th century BC
Height 25.0 cm

This fine jug was a luxury item used during banquets. It is one of a large group of bronze jugs known as 'Rhodian' oinochoe, found particularly widely in Etruria, Umbria, Piceno, Campania, Apulia, Sicily, the Rhône area, southern Spain and central Europe. However, most of them come from the rich aristocratic tombs of Etruria. Some of these jugs were imported to Italy from East Greece (perhaps Rhodes); others seem to have been copied by Etruscan bronze-workers although it is not certain exactly where. Populonia enjoyed close trade contacts with East Greece. The shape of these jugs provided inspiration for Etruscan bucchero ware as well as Etrusco-Corinthian pottery.

National Museum of Archaeology, Florence, inv. 89366
Shefton 1979, 79, pls. 6, 1-2; Torelli 2000, 611, cat. no. 226

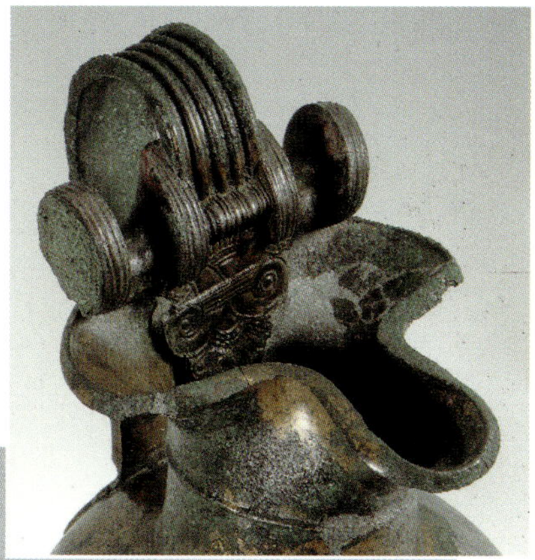

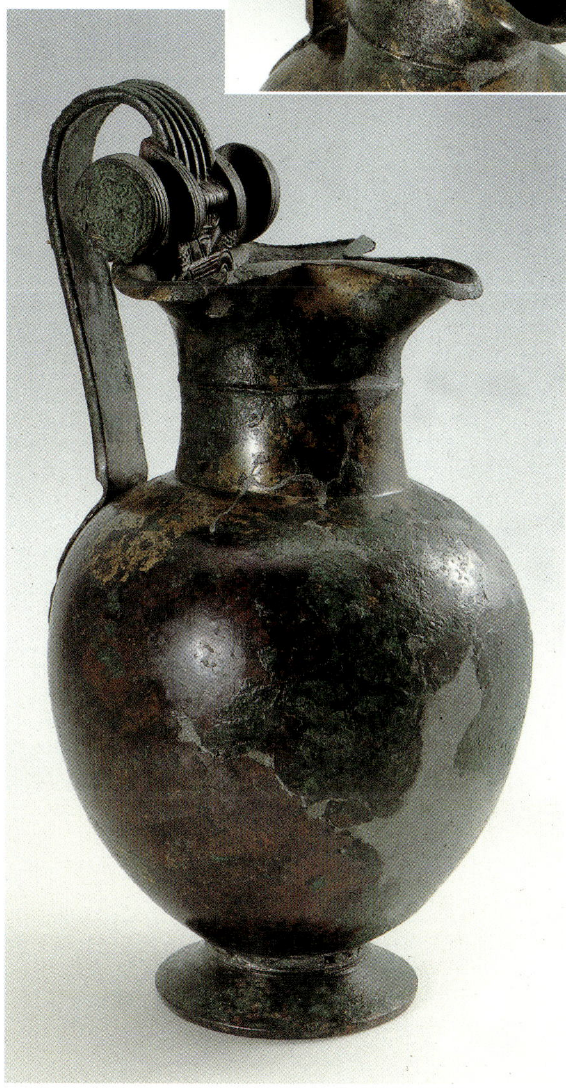

103 ## Situla (pail)

Bronze
First to second quarter of the 7th century BC
Height 30.8 cm

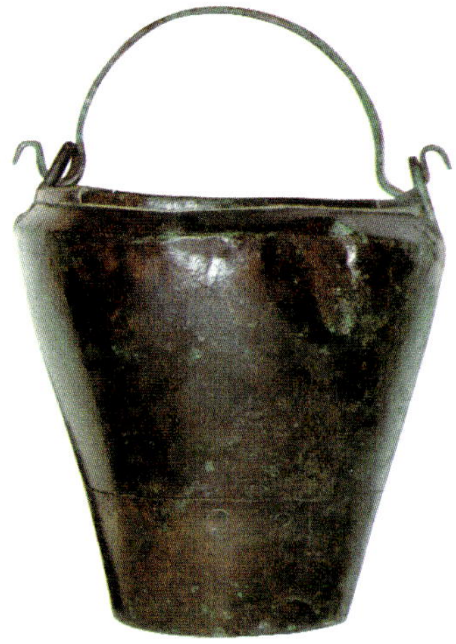

Examples of this type of bronze pail have also been found in Vetulonia, which was probably the production centre. It is derived from a northern European type.

National Museum of Archaeology, Florence, inv. 89354

104 ## Situla (pail)

Bronze
Second quarter of the 7th century BC
Height 20.0 cm

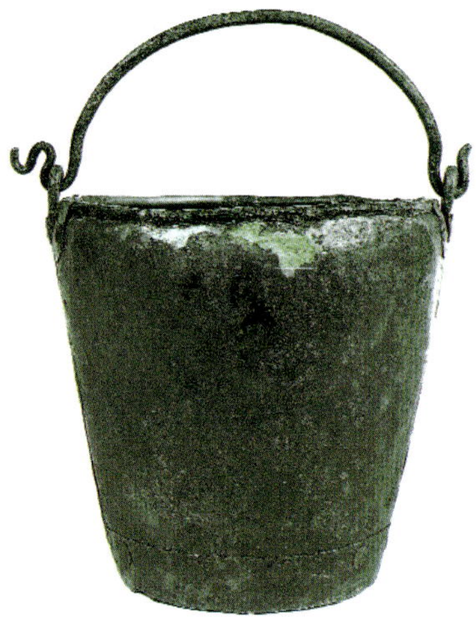

National Museum of Archaeology, Florence, inv. 89355

105 ## Basin

Bronze
End of the 8th century to the middle of the 6th century BC
Height 4.5 cm

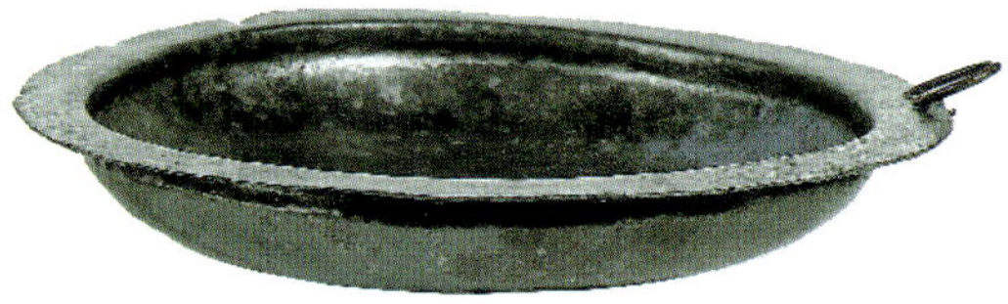

This undecorated basin was probably part of the drinking service used for banquets, although its function is not known. Basins like these were commonly used over a long period in Etruria.

National Museum of Archaeology, Florence, inv. 89346

106 **Olpe (jug)**

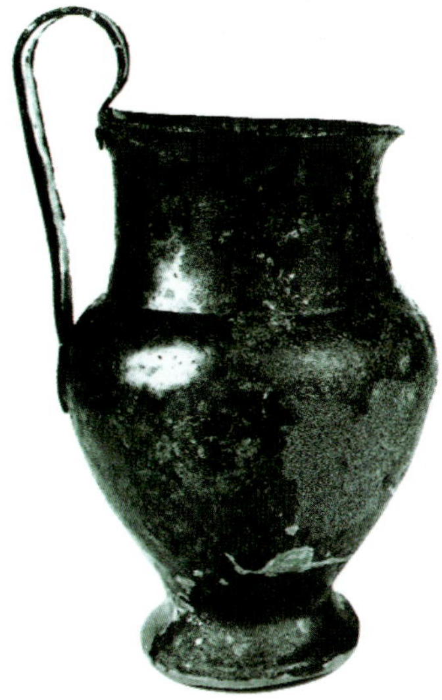

Bronze
First half of the 6th century BC
Height 15.8 cm

This jug is one of a common group found very widely over central Italy (at Vulci, Trevignano, Orvieto, Populonia, Chiusi, Fiesole and Narce). The type is based on an East Greek form. It has been suggested these olpai were produced in workshops in Orvieto. *SB*

National Museum of Archaeology, Florence, inv. 89360

107 **Situla (pail)**

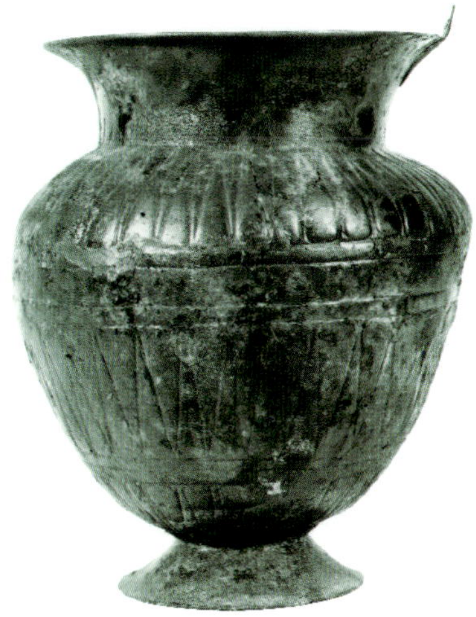

Bronze
Second quarter of the 6th century BC
Height 18.3 cm

National Museum of Archaeology, Florence, inv. 89358

108 **Infundibulum (strainer-funnel)**

Bronze
Second quarter of the 6th century BC
Length 33.6 cm

The Etruscans used strainers to remove the lees from wine before serving. These strainer-funnels were once thought to have been made in Populonia or Vulci, but it is now believed they were produced in Orvieto. This handled example, with its removable sieve and its hook for hanging, is one of the oldest known. The strainer and other products of Orvieto in this tomb provide evidence for the close relationship between Populonia and inland Etruria. *SB*

National Museum of Archaeology, Florence, inv. 89332

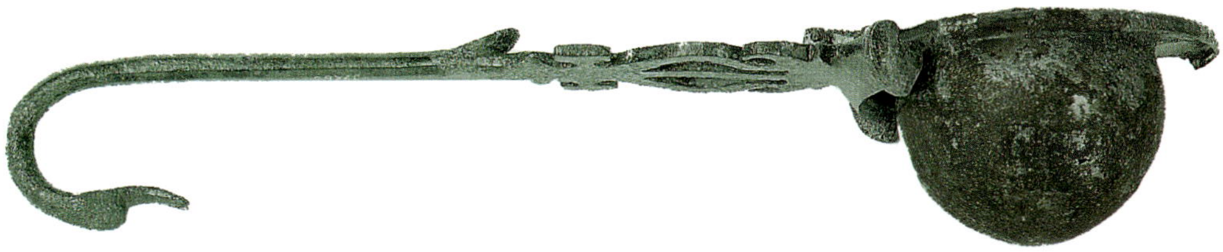

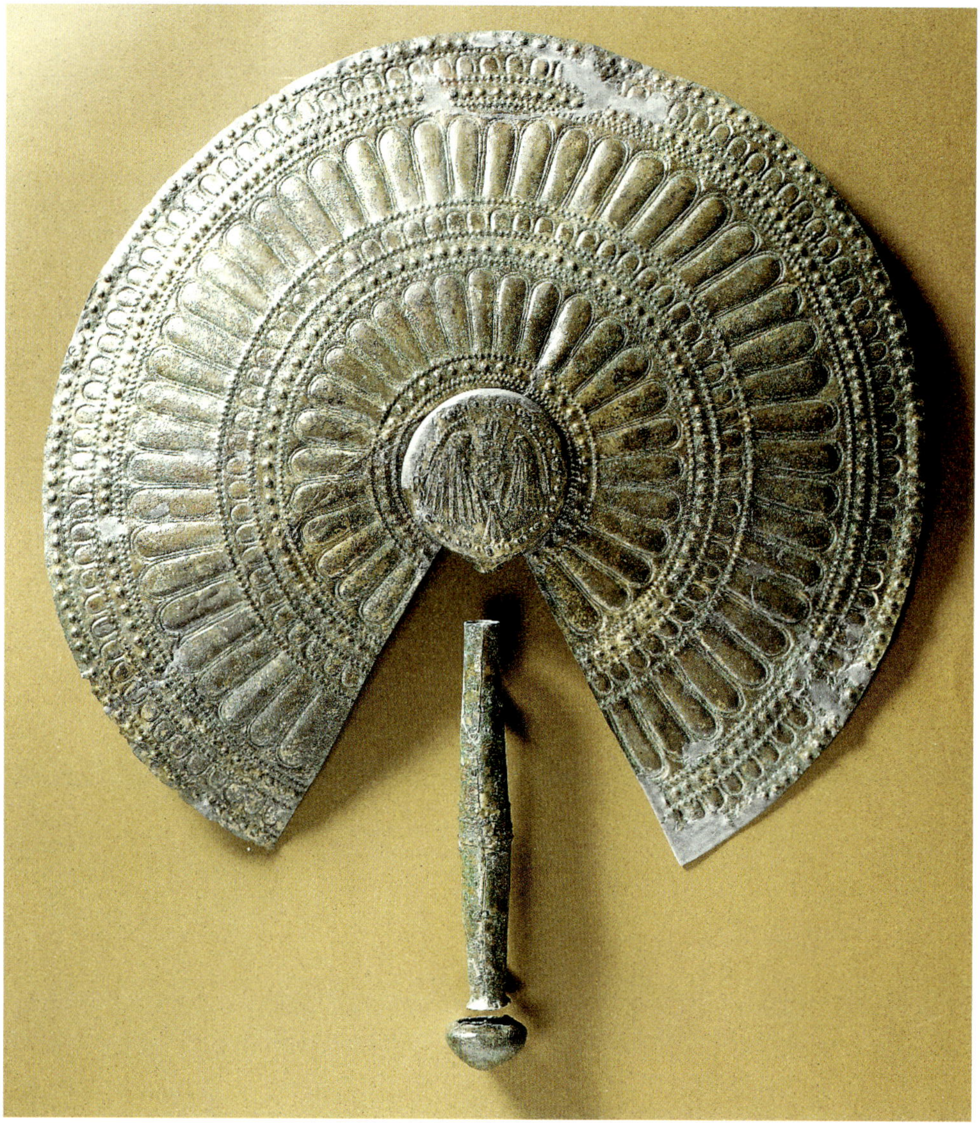

109 Flabellum (fan)

Bronze
Third quarter of the 7th century BC
Height 21.0 cm; diameter 50.0 cm

Fans were formal insignia used in processions, an idea derived from the Near East. In Etruria they were important status symbols belonging to people of very high rank. Evidence suggests they were associated with both men and women during the Orientalizing period. At Murlo, representations of fans on funerary stelae are related to women, and examples were included in the burial assemblage of a recently-discovered princely tomb at Veii. There were three sheet bronze fans in the Tomb of the Fans at Populonia. Other fans, of bronze, wood and even straw, have been found in rich tombs elsewhere in Etruria and Lazio.

This example is decorated in repoussé with alternating rows of bosses and tongue motifs. There is a plant motif resembling a lotus flower in the central disc. It is flanked by two women wearing long cloaks, who are facing each other. One woman appears to be offering a wreath or a dish, in the form of a dotted circle, to the other. The significance of this scene is not clear. The figurative style and the technique of the decoration suggest northern Etruscan influence.

Many traces of the original wooden core survive within the sheet bronze handle. The bronze was attached to the wood with tiny bronze nails. The round fan head would have been mounted on leather or fabric. *ARo*

National Museum of Archaeology, Florence, inv. 89325

Minto 1932, 332, nos. 10, 10a, pl. 7; Minto 1922, 149, nos. 54a-b, 3; Etrusker 1987, 234, no. 32; cf. Haynes 2000, 105, fig. 88

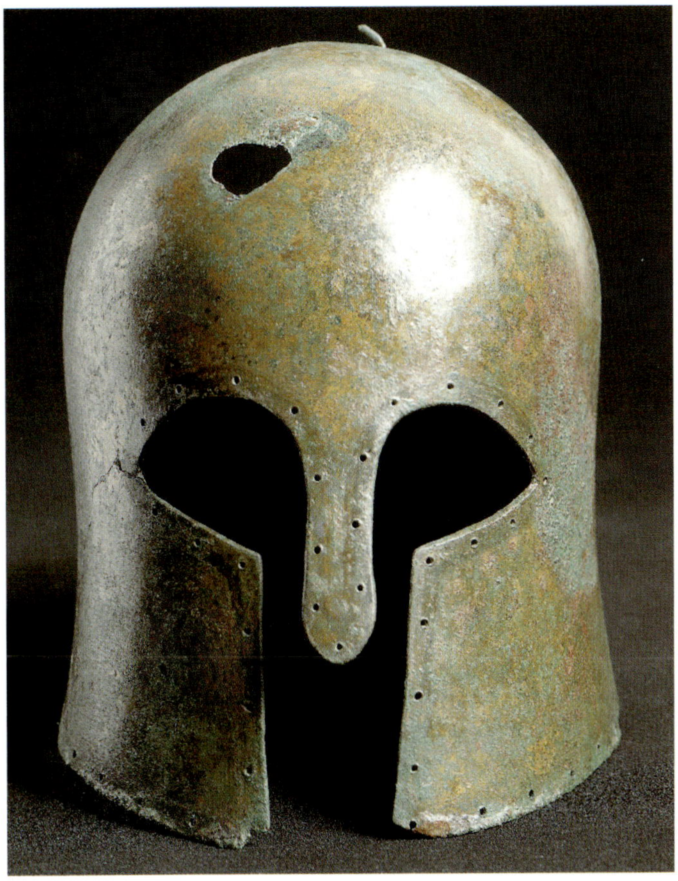

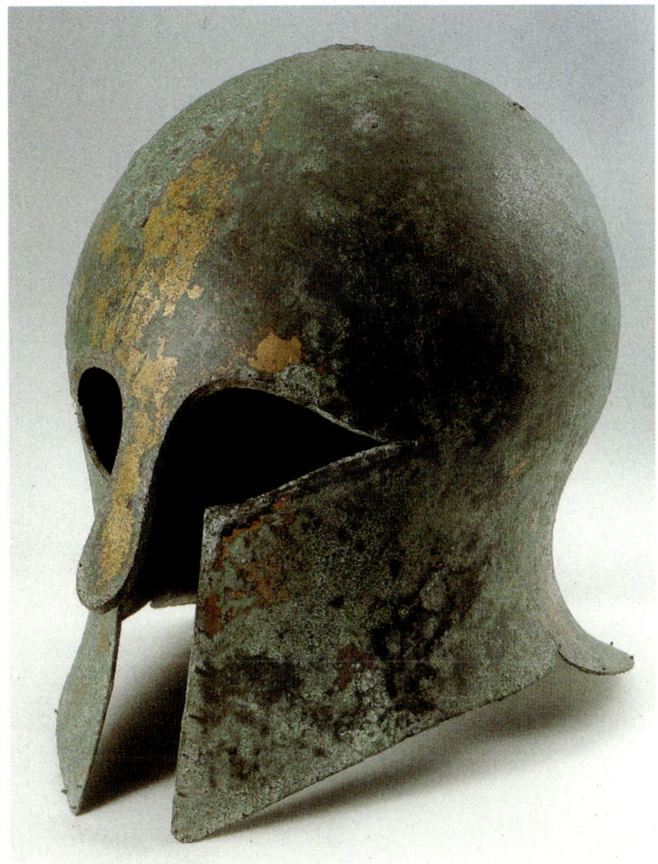

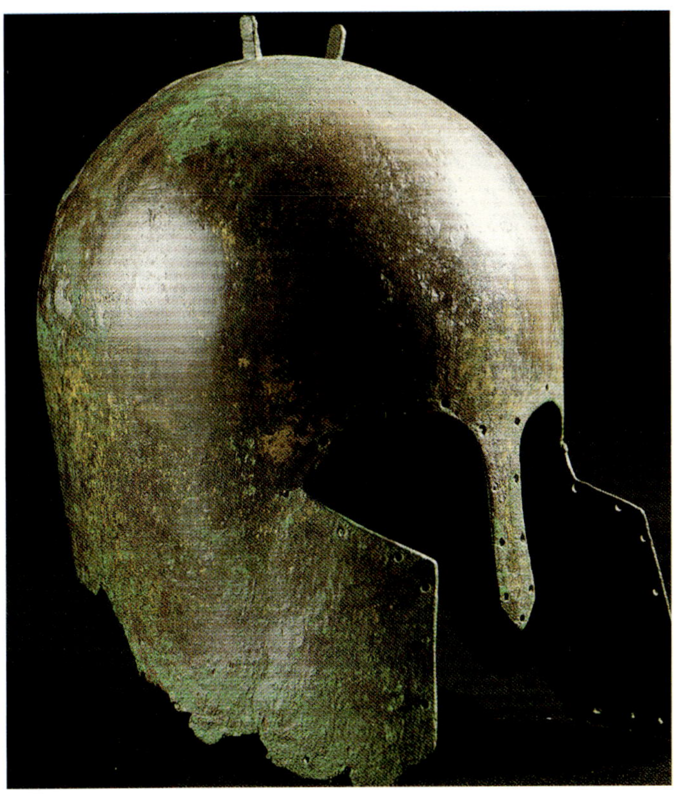

110

Three helmets

Bronze

Second half of the 7th century BC

Heights 25.0 cm, 23.0 cm, 23.0 cm

Heavy body armour was used in Etruria from the middle of the 7th century BC. These Corinthian helmets are amongst the oldest examples of Greek armour known from an Etruscan funerary context. One of these helmets is of particularly high quality, and was probably viewed as an especially prestigious import. It was associated with the finest of the pairs of greaves (leg armour) from the tomb, number 112. The Tomb of the Fans contained four helmets in total: the fourth (number 111) is of central European origin. These, together with the greaves, suggest four sets of armour. There were also the fragments of a bronze shield. The whole group reflects the power and prestige of the Populonian aristocracy. *ARo*

National Museum of Archaeology, Florence, inv. 89310, 89309, 89311

Minto 1932, 329, pl. 3; Magnificenza 1998, 78, no. 93

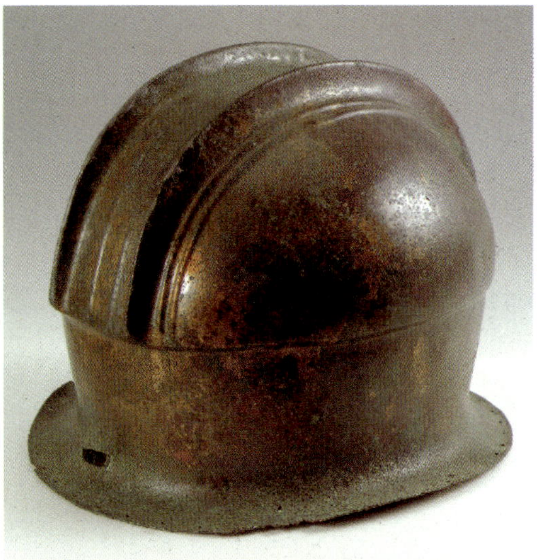

111 **Helmet**

Bronze
Middle of the 7th century BC
Height 26.0 cm

This remarkable double-crested helmet is of central European origin. Many examples are known from sites of the Hallstatt culture (the Iron Age culture of central-western Europe, named after a site in Austria), most of them from Slovenia. In Italy, examples have been found at Piceno, but this helmet from the Tomb of the Fans is the only one with an Etruscan provenance. It provides further evidence of the Populonian aristocracy's wide-ranging connections. *ARo*

National Museum of Archaeology, Florence, inv. 89312

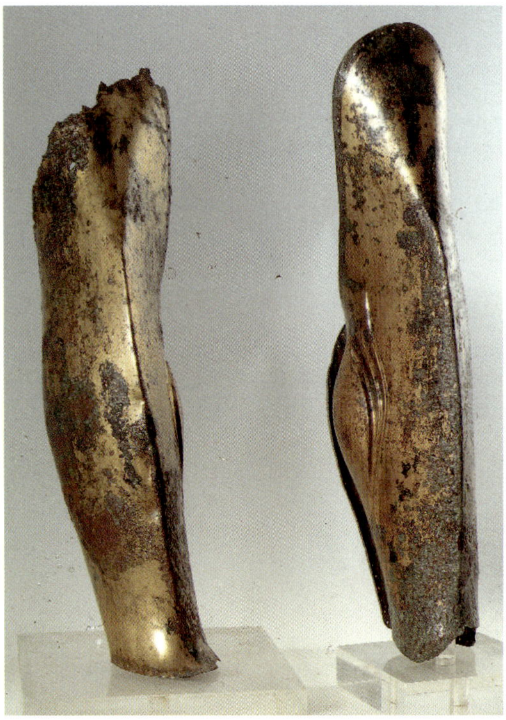

112 **Pair of greaves**

Bronze
Middle of the 7th century BC
Height 43.0 cm

The calf muscles are carefully indicated. Small holes along the edges of these high-quality greaves show they were probably once lined with leather or fabric. *ARo*

National Museum of Archaeology, Florence, inv. 89315, 89316
Minto 1932, 320, pls. 7, 8; Magnificenza 1998, 80, no. 96

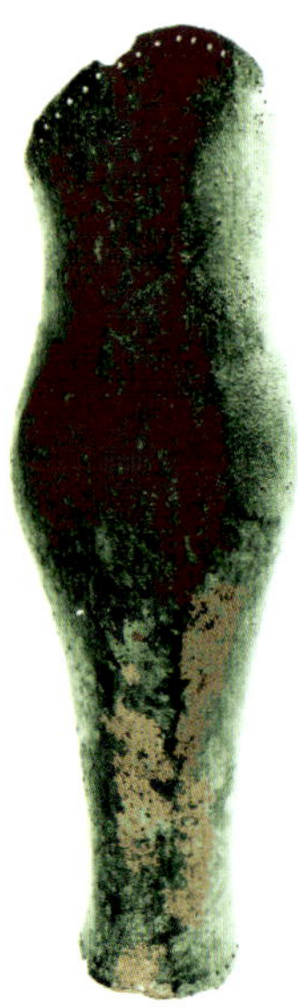

113 **Greave**

Bronze
Middle of the 7th century BC
Height 40.0 cm

Two single greaves were found in the tomb, of which one is shown. They were both for the left leg. Single greaves have been found in other funerary assemblages and presumably had a purely symbolic function. Alongside these and number 112, a further pair of greaves was found in the Tomb of the Fans, which, together with the four helmets, indicates four sets of armour. *GCC*

National Museum of Archaeology, Florence, inv. 89314

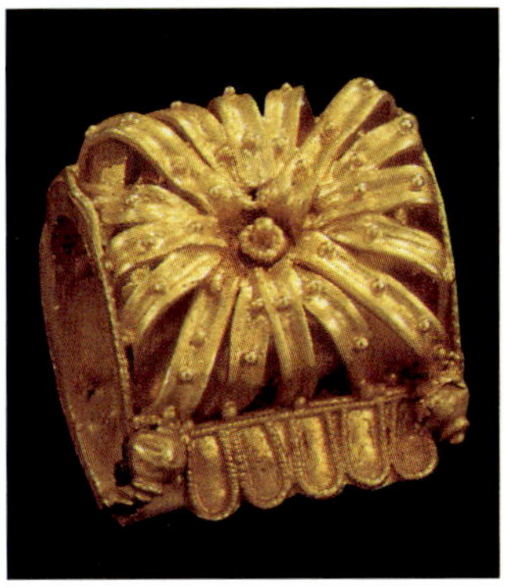

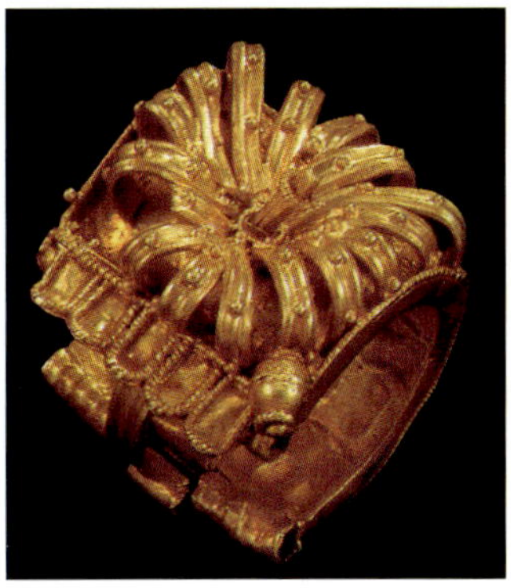

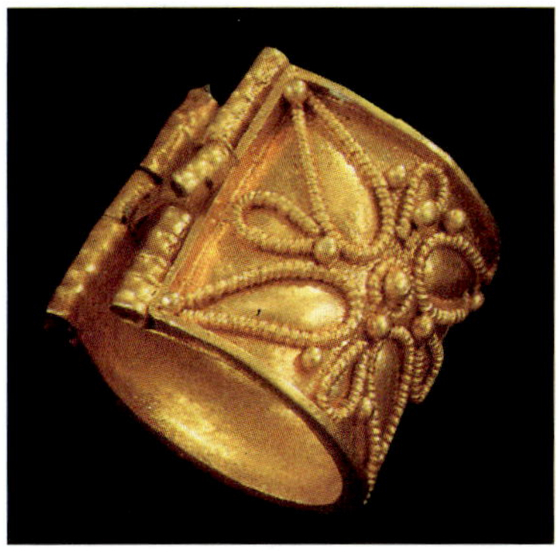

114 Pair of earrings

Gold
Second quarter of the 6th century BC
Height 1.9 cm; width 1.9 cm

These earrings were made by bending a rectangular sheet of gold into a cylinder, leaving the ends open. They originally hung from ear wires. Their decoration consists of sheet gold petals ornamented with tiny granules, and filigree wires. This type of earring, known as 'a bauletto', probably originated in the goldsmiths' workshops of Vulci. The type became extremely common all over Etruria in the Archaic period and was made in many different production centres. This pair was made in Vulci. They were associated with the woman buried on the left bed of the tomb chamber, and they and number 115 are regarded as being amongst the earliest known examples of this popular type. *SB*

National Museum of Archaeology, Florence, inv. 89262, 89263
Minto 1932, 295, pl. 2.7; Torelli 2000, 572, cat. nos. 91-2

115 Earring

Gold
Second quarter of the 6th century BC
Height 1.9 cm; width 1.9 cm

Of similar form to number 114, this single earring is decorated with oval filigree petals and granules in what became a very common decorative design. There is an exact parallel for this earring from the tumulus of Molinello di Asciano. *SB*

National Museum of Archaeology, Florence, inv. 89264
Minto 1932, 295, pl. 2.9; Torelli 2000, 572, cat. no. 93

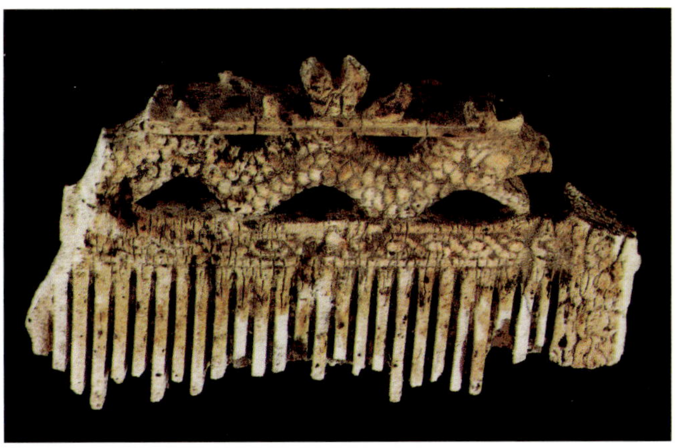

116 Comb

Ivory
End of the 7th century BC
Length 5.1 cm

This comb was associated with the woman buried on the left bed of the tomb chamber. It was an important prestige item, carved in Etruria from a precious imported material. The fragmentary top of the comb is carved with a snake in an openwork design. Its scaly body is carefully patterned and textured. Above the snake are traces of two animals, perhaps felines, to either side of a palmette and lotus. *ARo*

National Museum of Archaeology, Florence, inv. 89295

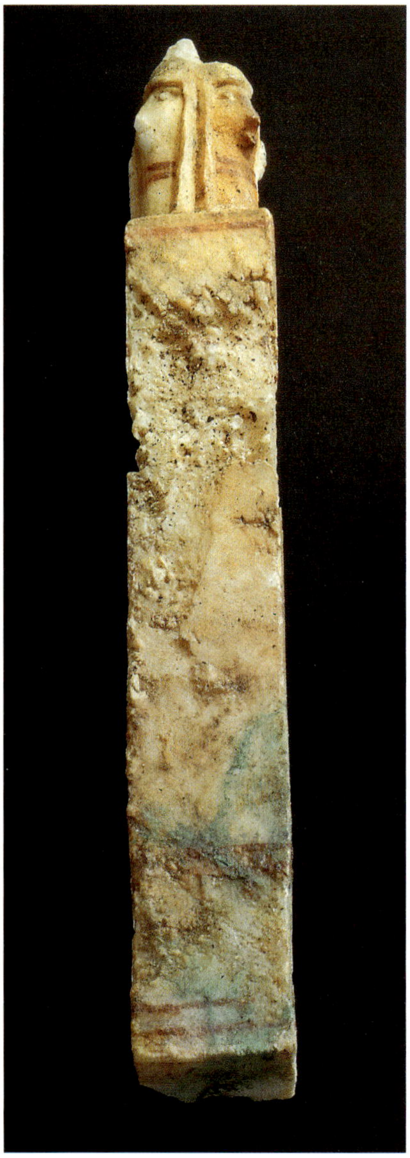

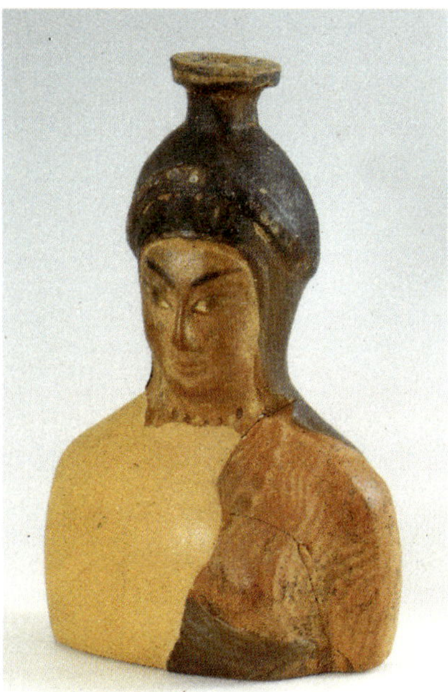

117 Alabastron (unguent bottle)

Painted alabaster

First half of the 6th century BC

Height 21.0 cm

This is one of several fragmentary alabaster unguent bottles associated with the woman's burial in the tomb. The other examples are cylindrical with tops in the form of a woman's head, and were luxury items probably imported from East Greece, perhaps Rhodes or Samos. This one, however, has a long square-sectioned body topped by four roughly-worked women's heads, with necklaces indicated by painted red lines. Its style and form are unlike the East Greek alabastra, and it is thought to have been made locally in a northern Etruscan workshop. Alabastra like these would have held perfumed oils and essences.

National Museum of Archaeology, Florence, inv. 89284

cf. Torelli 2000, 576, cat. no. 115; Haynes 2000, 104

118 Perfume flask

Painted ceramic

Second quarter of the 6th century BC

Height 11.7 cm

This perfume flask is in the form of a woman's head and upper body. She is dressed in a chiton (tunic) and himation (mantle), and wears a diadem and necklace. The vessel was made in Rhodes. Many East Greek perfume flasks are known from Populonia; most of them came from Rhodes, but some may have originated in Samos and Miletus. A few imported types more commonly found in South Italy and Sicily have also been discovered in Etruria. *ARo*

National Museum of Archaeology, Florence, inv. 89423

119 **Perfume flask**

Painted ceramic
Second quarter of the 6th century BC
Length 10.3 cm

This perfume flask is in the form of a reclining deer. The lid, in the shape of its head, was made separately and is missing. The flask is one of a group made in Etruria. It is not known exactly where they were produced, but they may have come from more than one centre. Similar flasks have also been made in bucchero ware.

National Museum of Archaeology, Florence, inv. 89427

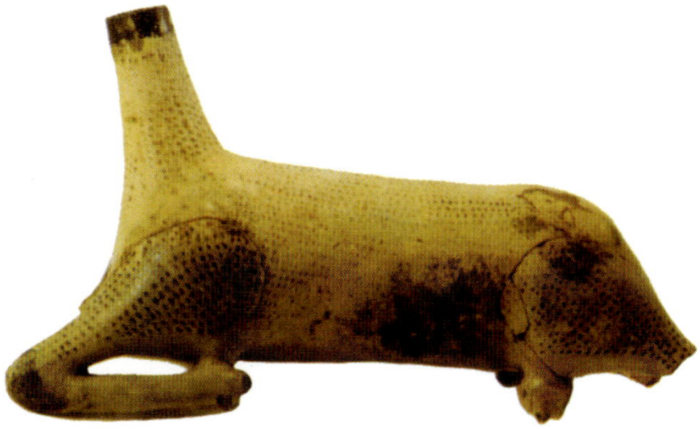

120 **Perfume flask**

Painted ceramic
First decades of the 6th century BC
Length 20.1 cm

This perfume flask is in the form of a running hare.

National Museum of Archaeology, Florence, inv. 89429

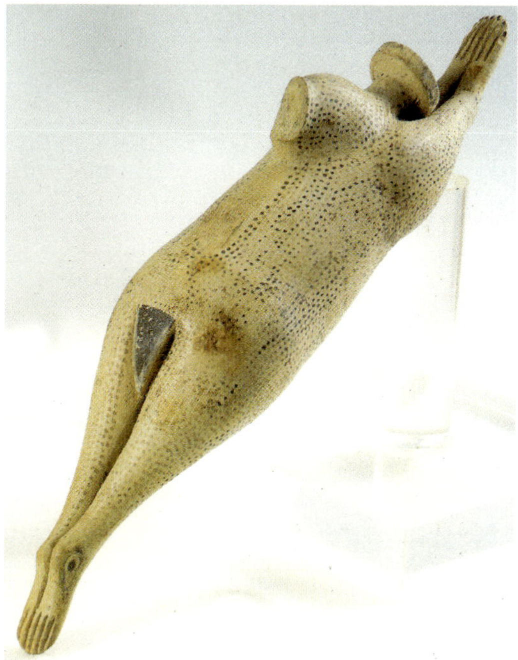

121 **Perfume flask**

Painted ceramic
Second quarter of the 6th century BC
Length 10.3 cm

This is one of three perfume flasks in the form of ducklings found in the tomb. It is an uncommon type in this part of northern Etruria; besides these three, two more are known from Vetulonia.

National Museum of Archaeology, Florence, inv. 89426

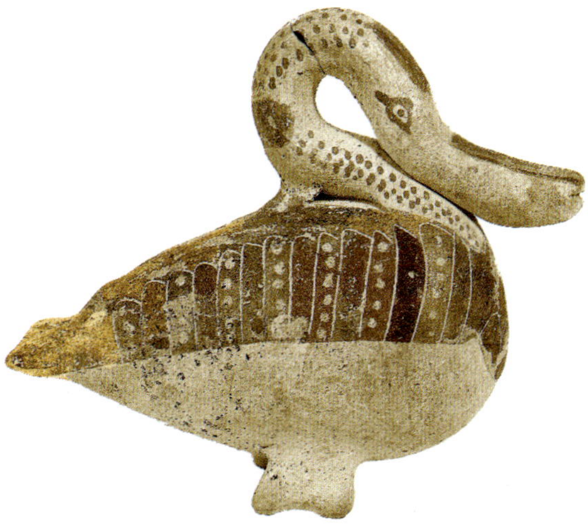

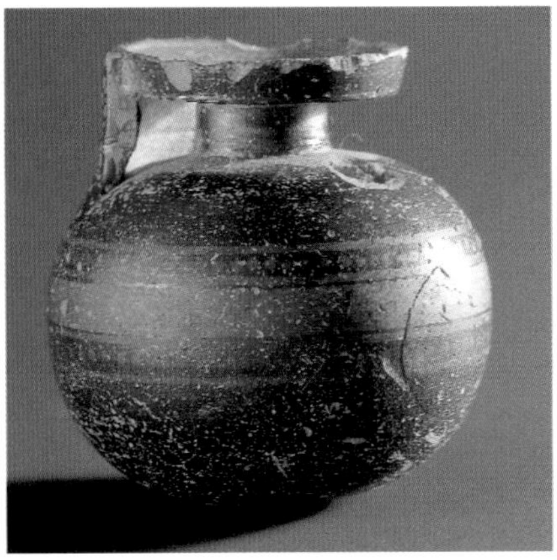

122

Laconian aryballos (perfume flask)

Painted ceramic

First decades of the 6th century BC

Height 6.1 cm

This small vessel and one other aryballos mark the arrival in Populonia of pottery from Greek Sparta in the second quarter of the 6th century BC. Spartan ceramics were probably brought to Etruria, together with pottery from other parts of Greece, by traders from Eastern Greece. The large number of East Greek objects in the cemeteries of Populonia provide good evidence for the presence of merchants from that area, probably from Samos. Populonia benefited from the only natural port on the Tyrrhenian coast. *GCC*

National Museum of Archaeology, Florence, inv. 89396

Torelli 2000, 579, cat. no. 125

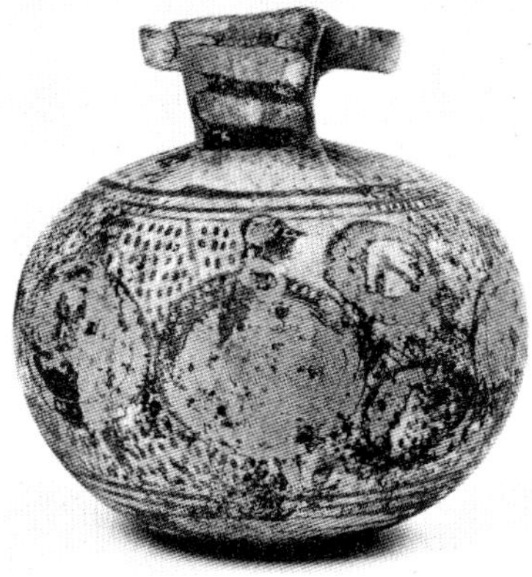

123

Corinthian aryballos (perfume flask)

Painted ceramic

First quarter of the 6th century BC

Height 7.3 cm

This small perfume flask, now rather worn, is decorated with a row of eight warriors. It is one of a group of similarly-decorated vessels made in Corinth. The details of the warriors' shields suggest this aryballos dates from the Middle Corinthian period.

ARo

National Museum of Archaeology, Florence, inv. 89412

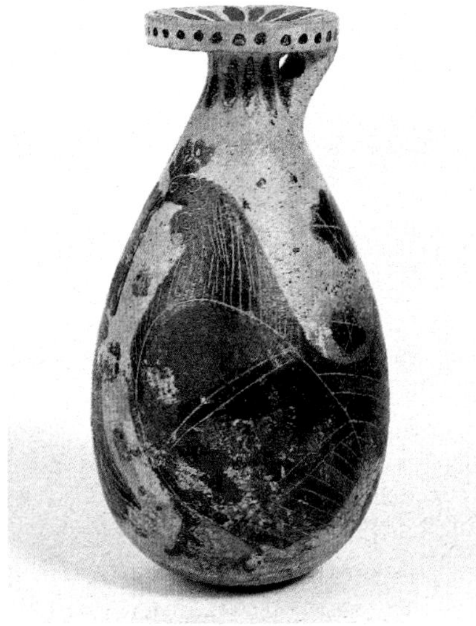

124

Corinthian alabastron (perfume flask)

Painted ceramic

First quarter of the 6th century BC

Height 11.7 cm

National Museum of Archaeology, Florence, inv. 89419

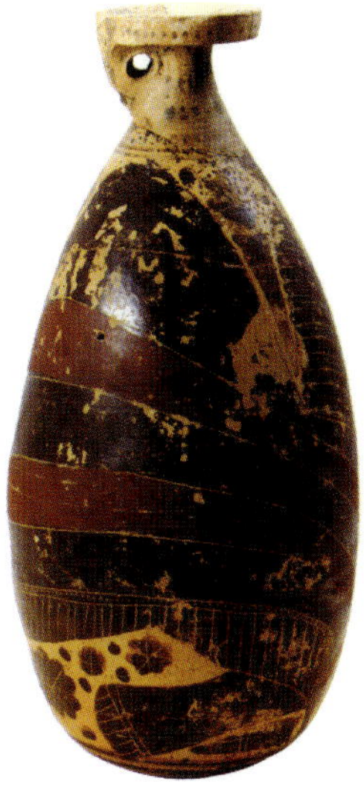

125

Corinthian alabastron (perfume flask)

Painted ceramic

End of the first quarter of the 6th century BC

Height 23.6 cm

This flask is decorated with a large figure of a siren, a mythical bird with a woman's head. It has been attributed to a Corinthian vase-painter of the Middle Corinthian period known as the Populonia Painter, named after this alabastron. Nine other vessels have been identified as being by his hand. The single large figure of a siren on the body of the alabastron is typical of his work. *ARo*

National Museum of Archaeology, Florence, inv. 89417

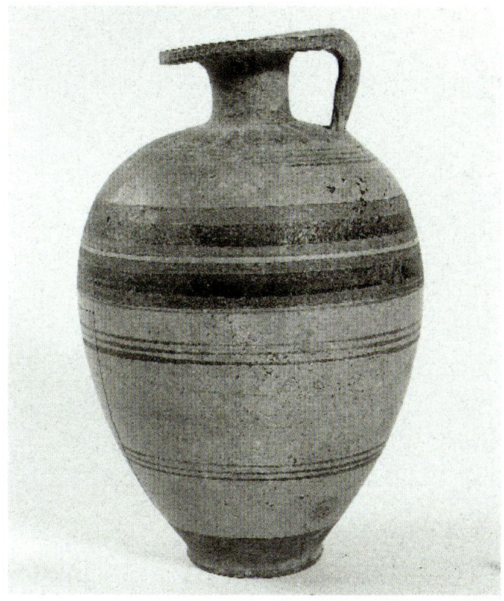

126

Etrusco-Corinthian aryballos (perfume flask)

Painted ceramic

End of the 7th to beginning of the 6th century BC

Height 11.7 cm

This Etruscan-made flask copies middle Early Corinthian pottery. This is a very common Etrusco-Corinthian type, found both in southern Etruria (at Cerveteri, Tarquinia and Vulci) and in the north (at Populonia and Chiusi).

National Museum of Archaeology, Florence, inv. 89398

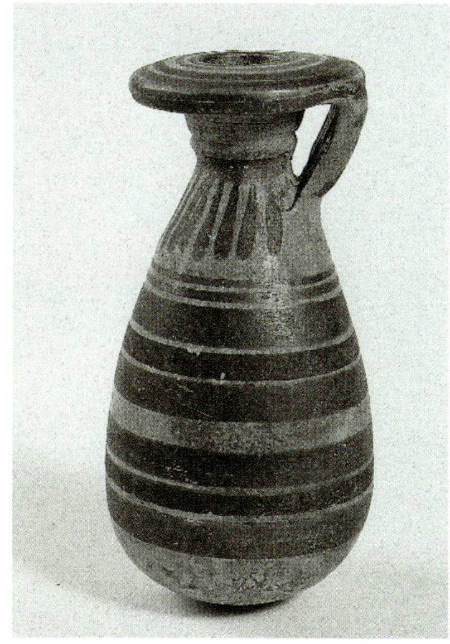

127

Etrusco-Corinthian miniature alabastron (perfume flask)

Painted ceramic

End of the 7th to the middle of the 6th century BC

Height 6.0cm

Perfume flasks with simple banded decoration are extremely common in Etruscan tombs. *GCC*

National Museum of Archaeology, Florence, inv. 89403

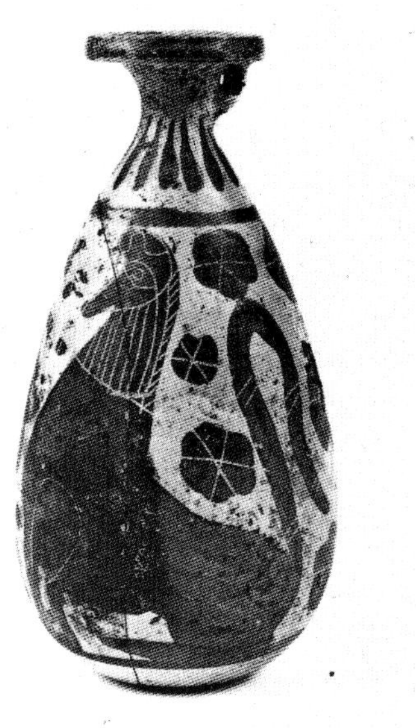

128

Etrusco-Corinthian alabastron (perfume flask)

Painted ceramic
First decades of the 6th century BC
Height 13.6 cm

This flask, now rather worn, is decorated with two confronted lions with a bird standing between them. It was made in Vulci, one of the principal centres for the production of Etrusco-Corinthian pottery, and has been attributed to the Bobuda Painter, one of that city's more prominent vase-painters of the period.

National Museum of Archaeology, Florence, inv. 89420

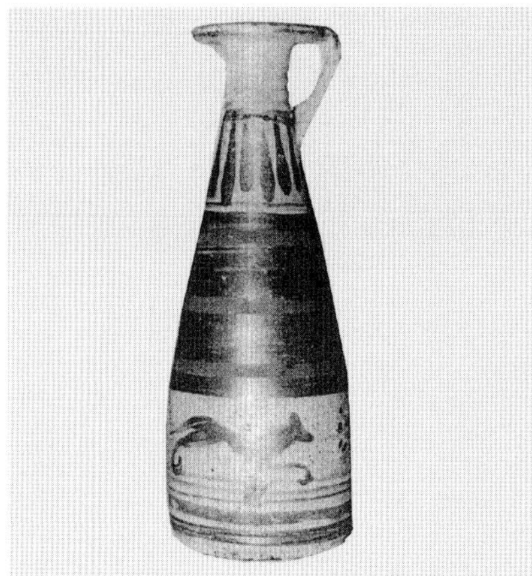

129

Etrusco-Corinthian alabastron (perfume flask)

Painted ceramic
Middle of the 7th century BC
Height 12.6 cm

This Etruscan-made flat-based alabastron was made under East Greek influence. *EM*

National Museum of Archaeology, Florence, inv. 89405

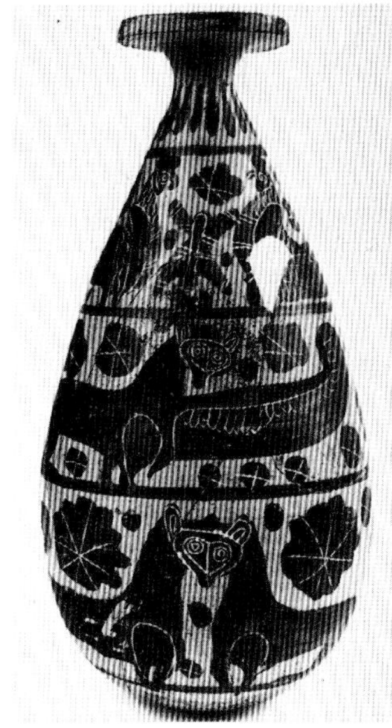

130

Etrusco-Corinthian alabastron (perfume flask)

Painted ceramic
First half of the 6th century BC
Height 22.0 cm

This alabastron, with its elaborate decoration of animal friezes, has been attributed to a workshop in Vulci. At that time Vulci was the leading city for the production of painted vases under the influence of Corinthianizing and East Greek vase-painters. It belongs to what is known as the 'Matsch' group.

National Museum of Archaeology, Florence, inv. 89416

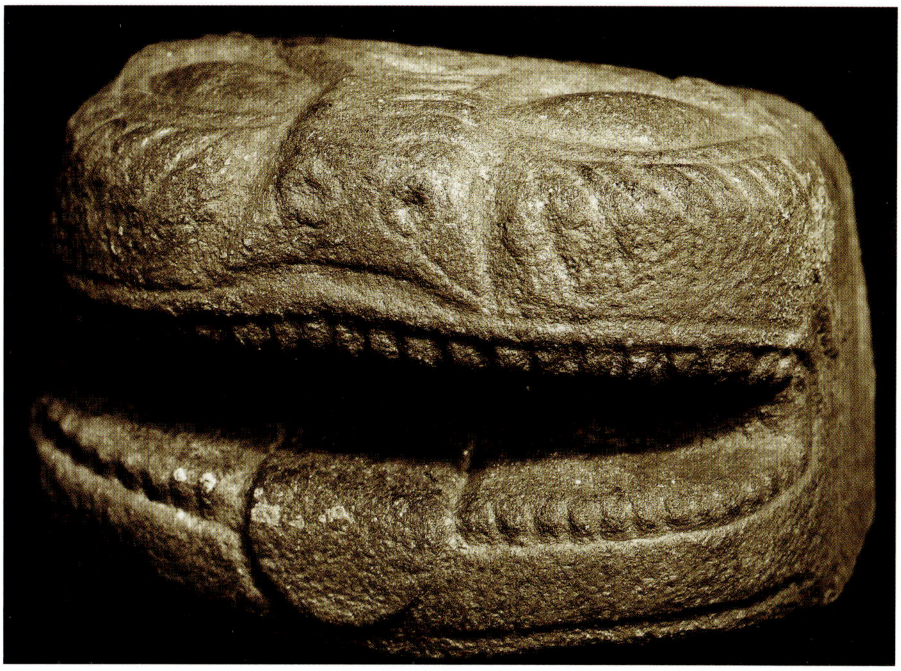

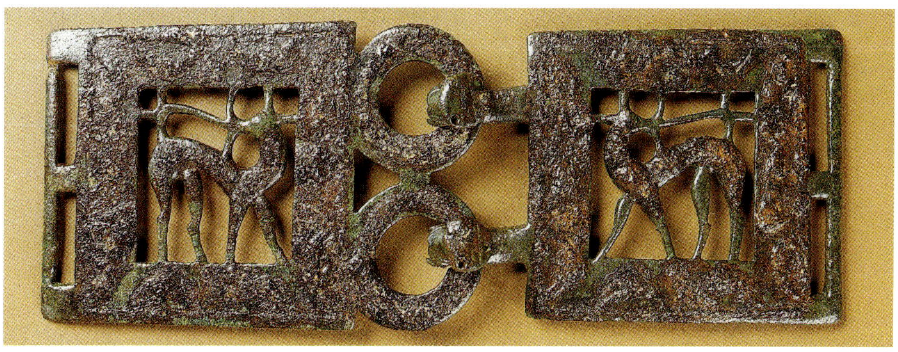

131 **Base**

Stone
Castellina in Chianti
Last decades of the 7th century BC
Height 30.0 cm

This stone base was set into the left side of the doorway of one of the four tombs within the Montecalvario tumulus. It was probably intended to ward off bad fortune. The cavity in its upper surface suggests it was originally intended to support a cippus (grave marker) or statue. This is a very unusual object although it has some parallels in the Near East. *GCC*

National Museum of Archaeology, Florence, inv. CMC100

132 **Belt buckle**

Bronze with iron inlay
Castelnuovo Berardenga
Third quarter of the 7th century BC
Widths of the two halves 12.5 cm, 11.5 cm; height 8.0 cm

This belt buckle is an example of a rare decorative technique: bronze inlaid with iron. It is one of a small number of similarly-decorated cast-bronze buckles found in the Siena area, at Murlo and Castellina in Chianti, but also at Cerveteri in southern Etruria and as far afield as the southern Tyrol and Lyons. The same technique was also used on a chariot from the Tomb of the Chariots at Populonia. The workshop producing this unusual metalwork was probably located in northern Etruria, most likely in Populonia. The technique was used in the Caucasus from the 8th century BC. *GCC/EG*

Museum of Archaeology, Siena, inv. CB1
von Hase 1971, 86, 1749

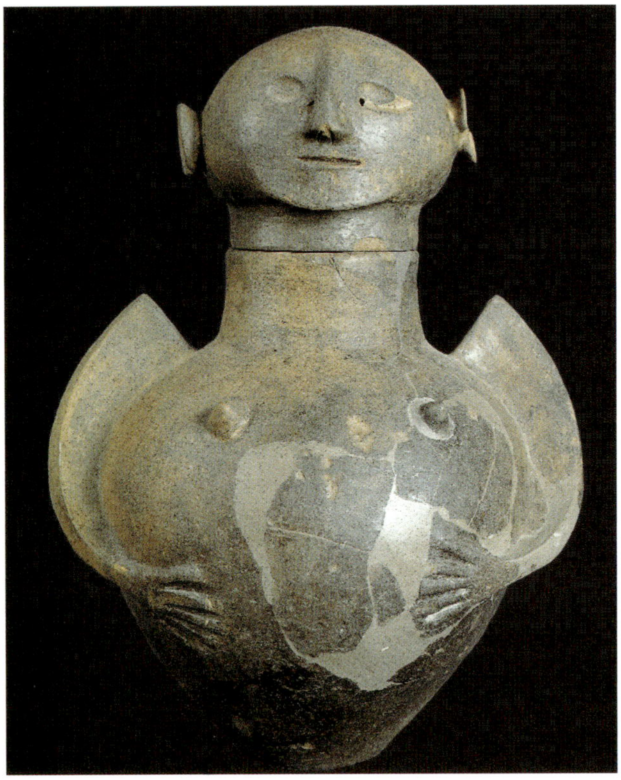

133 **Female 'canopic' ash urn**

Impasto
Castiglione del Lago
Second half of the 7th century BC
Height 50.0 cm

The people of the inland area around Chiusi, unlike those of coastal northern and southern Etruria, did not practise inhumation in the Orientalizing period, but continued to cremate their dead. The ash urns and grave goods were often placed within tombs consisting of terracotta storage jars buried in pits and covered with stone slabs. The lids of the ash urns gradually developed human features. They are called 'canopic' because they resemble the canopic jars of Egypt which were used to hold the organs of the mummified dead. In Etruria, the human form of the ash urns may have been intended to provide a 'body' for the cremated person. The urns were often placed on small stone, ceramic or bronze thrones within the tombs, presumably intended to reflect or enhance the status of the deceased person in the social hierarchy (see number 134). The presence of breasts indicates this urn belonged to a woman. *AR/EG*

National Museum of Archaeology, Florence, inv. 72782a-b
Magnificenza 1998, 71, no. 79; Haynes 2000, 106, fig. 89

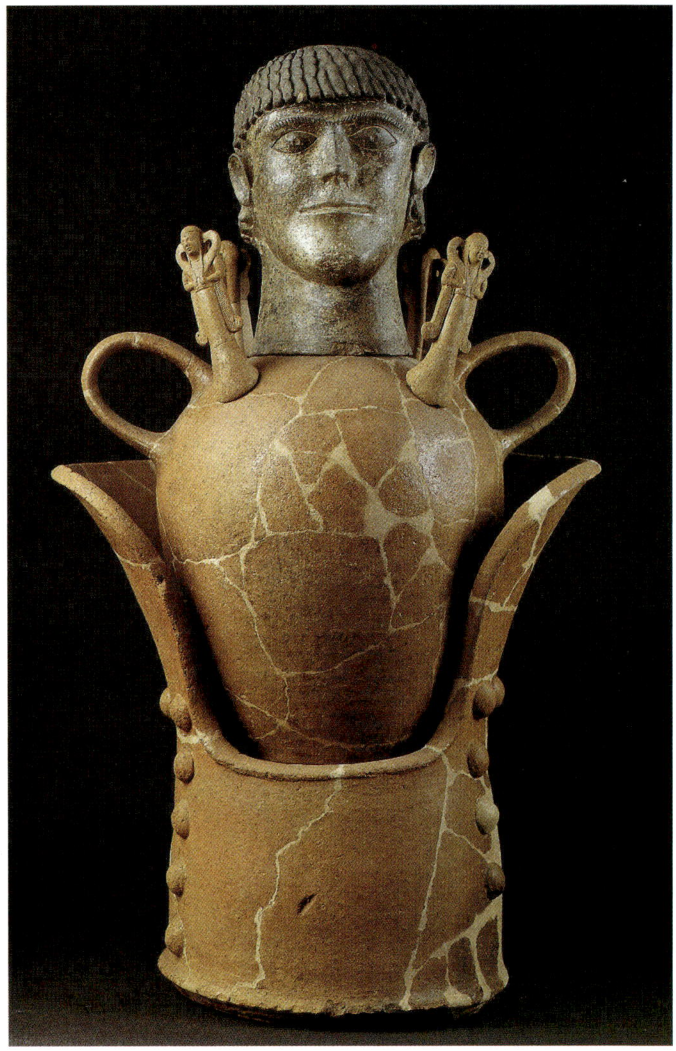

134 **'Canopic' ash urn on throne**

Impasto
Cetona (near Chiusi)
Second half of the 7th century BC
Height 85.0 cm

The face and hair of this ash urn have been finely detailed. The studded decoration on the throne recalls metalwork. *GCC*

National Museum of Archaeology, Florence, inv. 79199

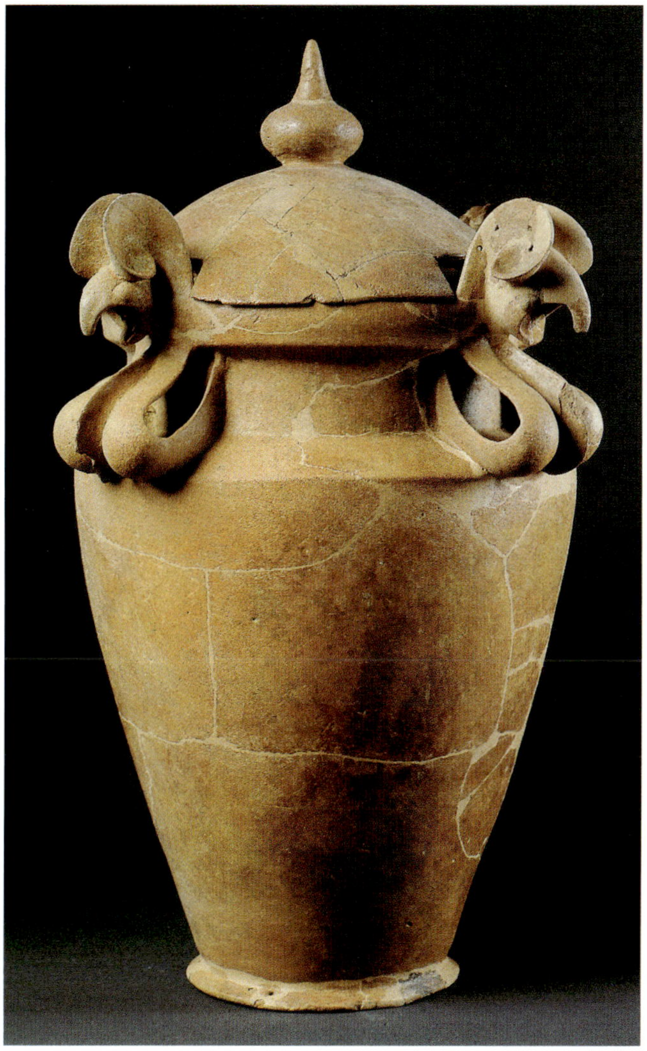

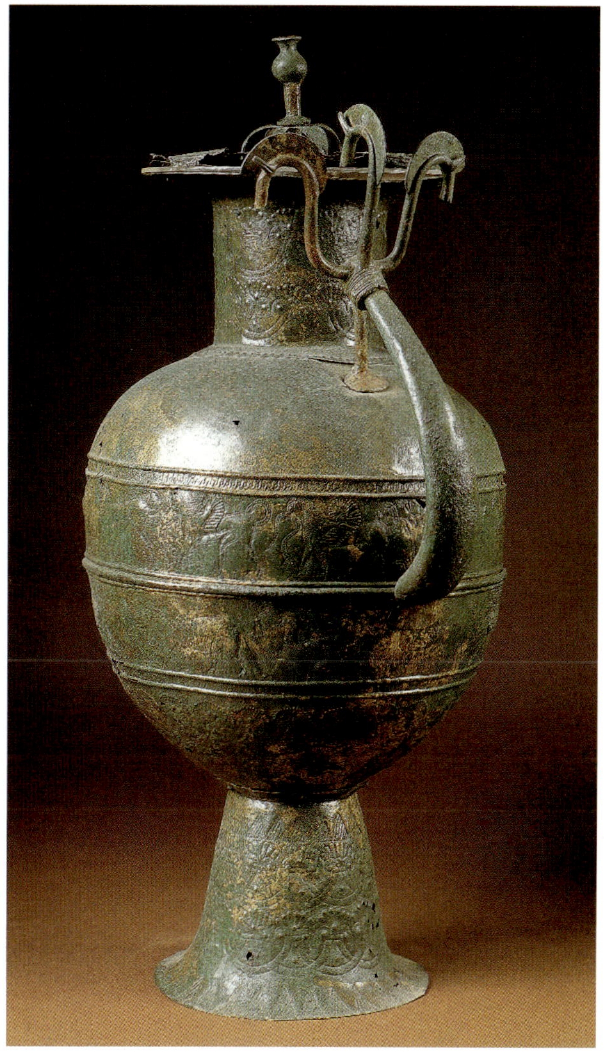

135 **Ash urn**

Impasto
Sarteano (near Chiusi)
Second half of the 7th century BC
Height 85.0 cm

The upper part of this urn is decorated with four griffin's heads. The griffin was a mythical creature often associated with funerary ritual. The urn was made in Chiusi. *GCC*

National Museum of Archaeology, Florence, inv. 73000

136 **Amphora**

Bronze
Cannicella necropolis, Orvieto
End of the 7th century BC
Height 69.0 cm

This bronze amphora, which was used as a cinerary urn, was probably made in Chiusi. Its body, neck and foot are decorated with Orientalizing imagery and there are cast stylized horse heads on the handle. *GCC/EG*

National Museum of Archaeology, Florence, inv. 73087
Magnificenza 1998, 62, no. 58

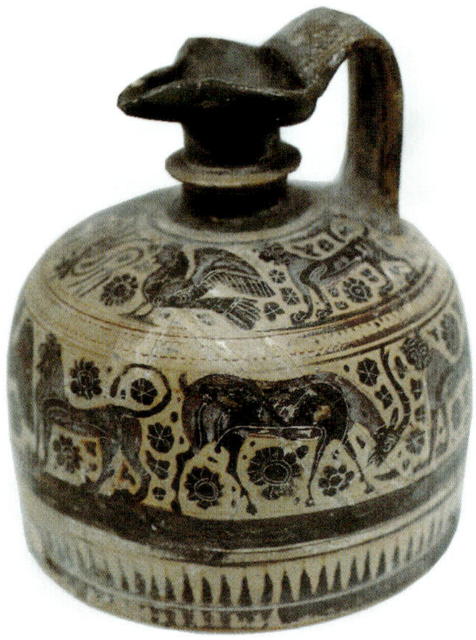

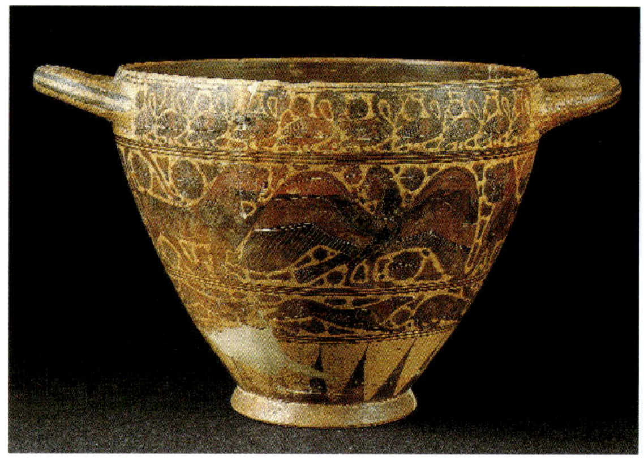

138 **Corinthian kotyle (cup)**

Painted ceramic
Tomb B, Vulci
Beginning of the 6th century BC
Height 19.5 cm

National Museum of Archaeology, Florence, inv. 76139
Magnificenza 1998, 87, no. 108

137 **Corinthian oinochoe (wine jug)**

Painted ceramic
Unknown provenance
First part of the 6th century BC
Height 37.5 cm

This jug, which was imported from Greece, has been attributed to the Middle Corinthian vase-painter known as the Dodwell Painter (about 600-575 BC), who concentrated on animal friezes. Corinthian ceramics were imported into Etruria from the beginning of the 7th century BC, increasing greatly in number by the middle of the century. Later, however, the expansion of local ceramics workshops under the influence of immigrant potters led to a decline in imports until the second quarter of the 6th century. *LV*

National Museum of Archaeology, Florence, inv. 3722
Payne 1931, 315, no. 1115

139 **Corinthian aryballos (perfume flask)**

Painted ceramic
Unknown provenance
First quarter of the 6th century BC
Height 6.5 cm

This type of Corinthian perfume flask is very common, and has been found widely from the last quarter of the 7th century to the end of the 6th. This Middle Corinthian example has a woman's head in profile painted on the handle. *GCC*

National Museum of Archaeology, Florence, inv. 3750

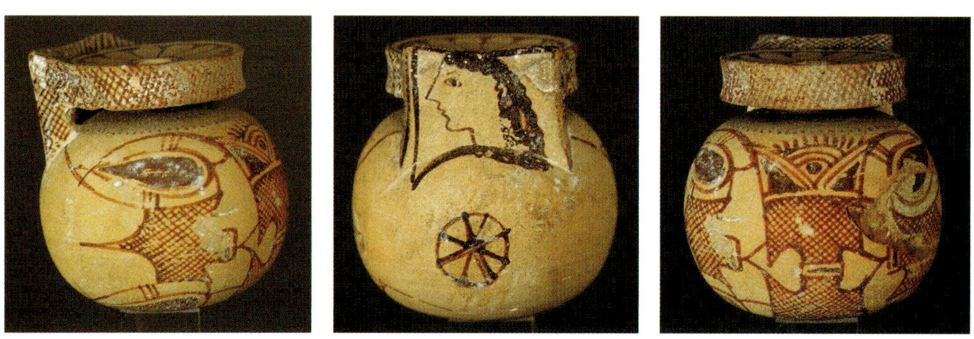

139

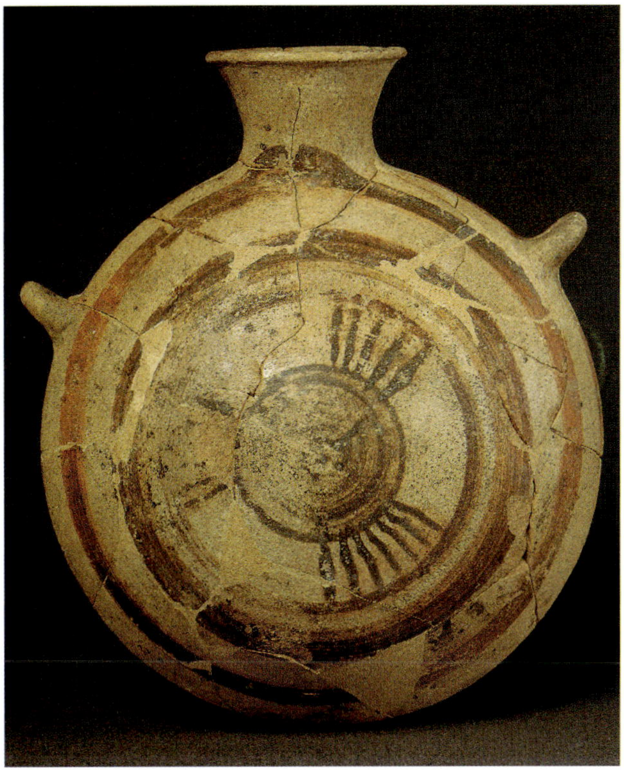

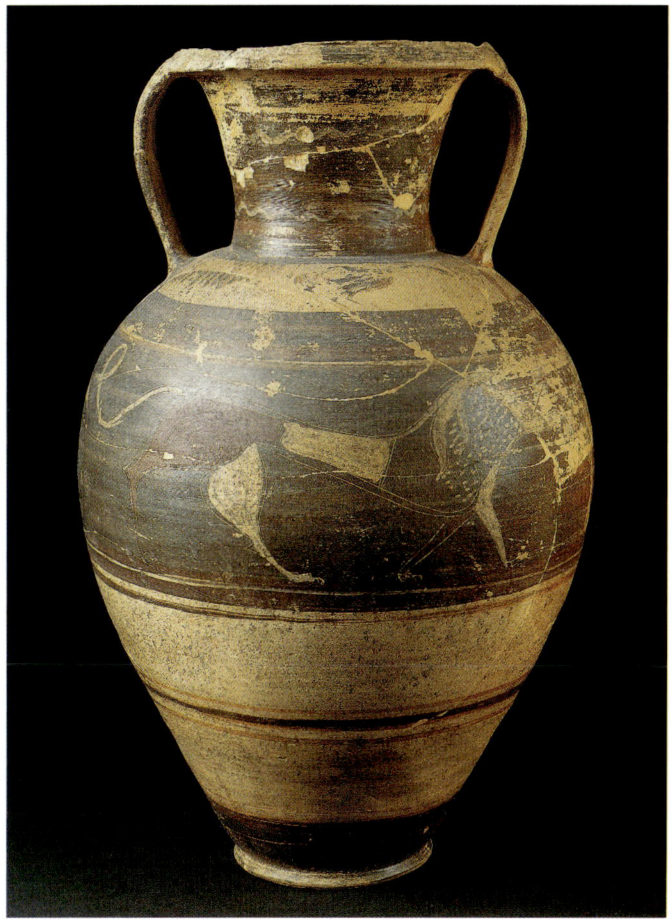

140 **Etrusco-Corinthian flask**

Painted ceramic
Chiusi
Last quarter of the 7th century BC
Height 24.5 cm

The form of this ceramic vessel is based on a type of blue faience flask made in Egypt and Rhodes. They were imported to Etruria, where the form was imitated in the local impasto and bucchero ceramic wares. *GCC*

Museum of Archaeology, Siena, inv. BC38
Magnificenza 1998, 45, no. 15

141 **Etrusco-Corinthian amphora**

Painted ceramic
Chamber tomb 2, Merellio, Bisenzio
End of the 7th to the beginning of the 6th century BC
Height 54.0 cm

The outlines of the deer, lion and eagle around the body of this wine vessel have been incised into the clay. The amphora belongs to a group of vases called the Monte Abbatone group. *GCC*

National Museum of Archaeology, Florence, inv. 73397
NSc 1886, 310, no. 3; Szilágyi 1967, 550, no. 9, pl. 102, 2; Magnificenza 1998, 87, no. 109

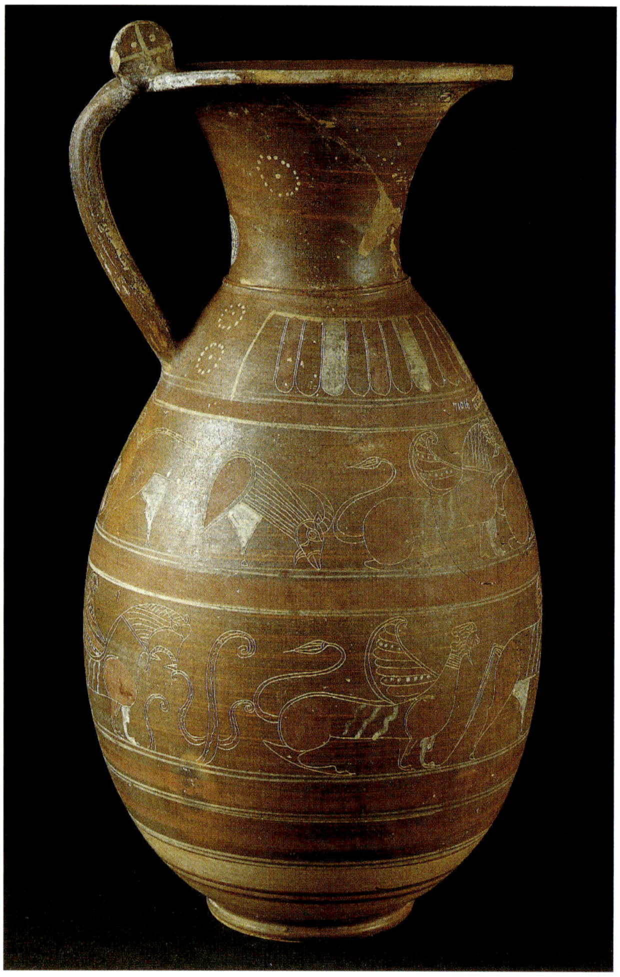

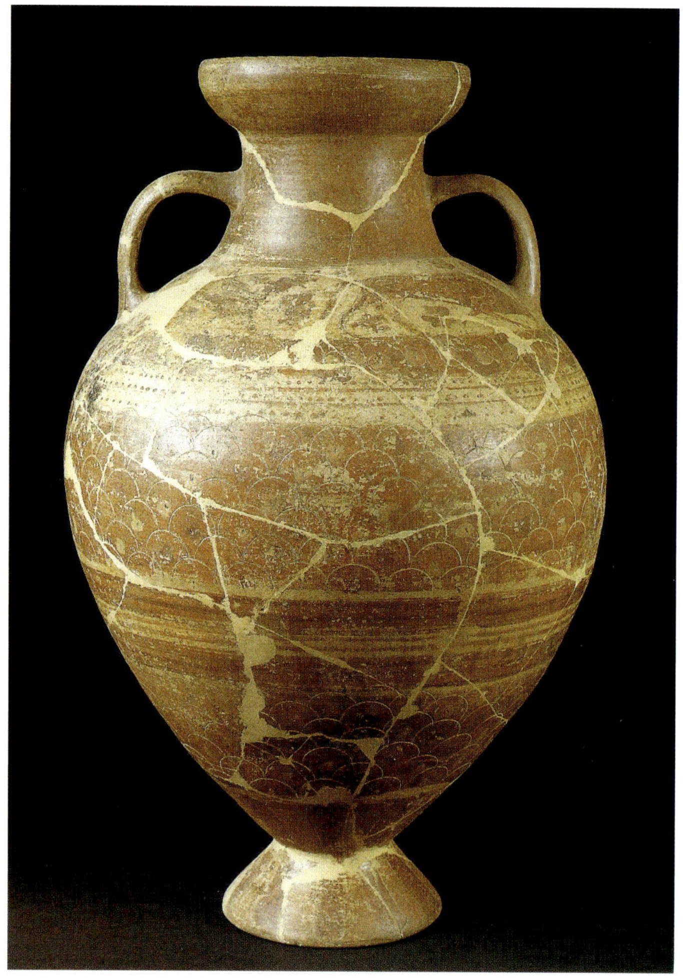

142 **Etrusco-Corinthian olpe**

Painted ceramic
Pescia Romana (near Montalto di Castro)
End of the 7th to the beginning of the 6th century BC
Height 40.5 cm

This jug decorated with friezes of animals has been attributed to an artist known as the Pescia Romana Painter, who worked in Vulci. *GCC*

National Museum of Archaeology, Florence, inv. 71016
Magnificenza 1998, 88, no. 111

143 **Etrusco-Corinthian amphora**

Painted ceramic
Cerveteri (Caere)
End of the 7th to the beginning of the 6th century BC
Height 63.8 cm

This wine vessel is one of a class of large vases typical of Cerveteri known to archaeologists as 'the Group of Large Scaled Amphorae'. They are decorated with broad bands of scale pattern and guilloches. Dots in the centre of each scale motif show they were incised using compasses. *GCC/EG*

National Museum of Archaeology, Florence, inv. 96498
Magnificenza 1998, 88, no. 112

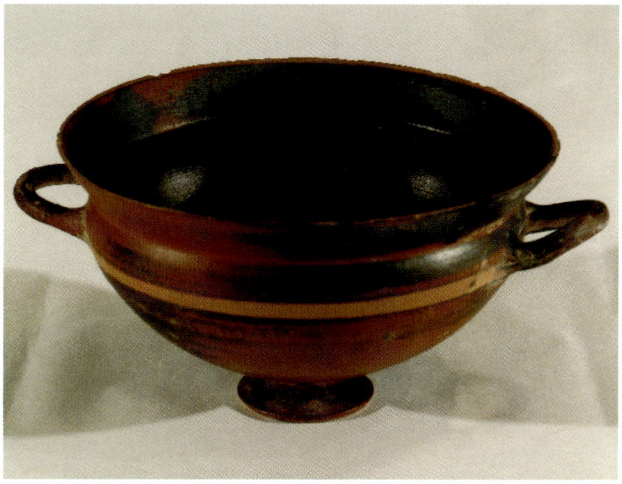

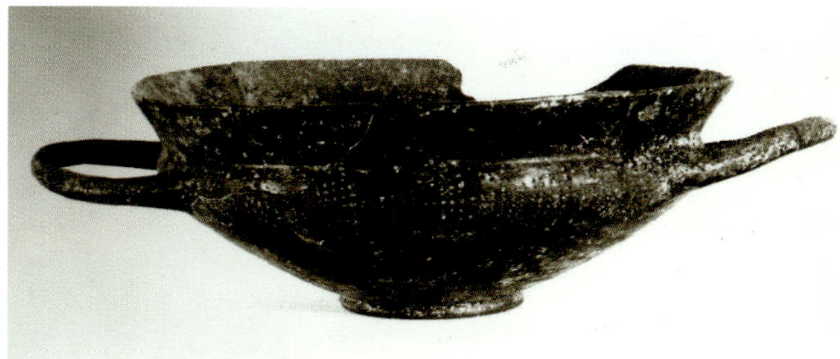

144 **Ionian cup**

Painted ceramic
Pescia Romana
Last quarter of the 7th century BC
Height 13.6 cm; diameter 13.0 cm

This cup is East Greek in origin. Most of the Ionian cups from Etruria have been found in the south, especially around Cerveteri and Vulci, like this one. *GCC*

National Museum of Archaeology, Florence, inv. 71030
Magnificenza 1998, 91, no. 119

145 **Ionian-style cup**

Bucchero
Tomb D or E, Monte Michele, Veii
Last decades of the 7th century BC
Height 4.9 cm; diameter 11.5 cm

This is a locally-made version of an Ionian cup in typical southern Etruscan bucchero ware. The dotted fan decoration is a very common motif which was used on many types of vessel. *GCC*

National Museum of Archaeology, Florence, inv. 94642
Magnificenza 1998, 92, no. 122

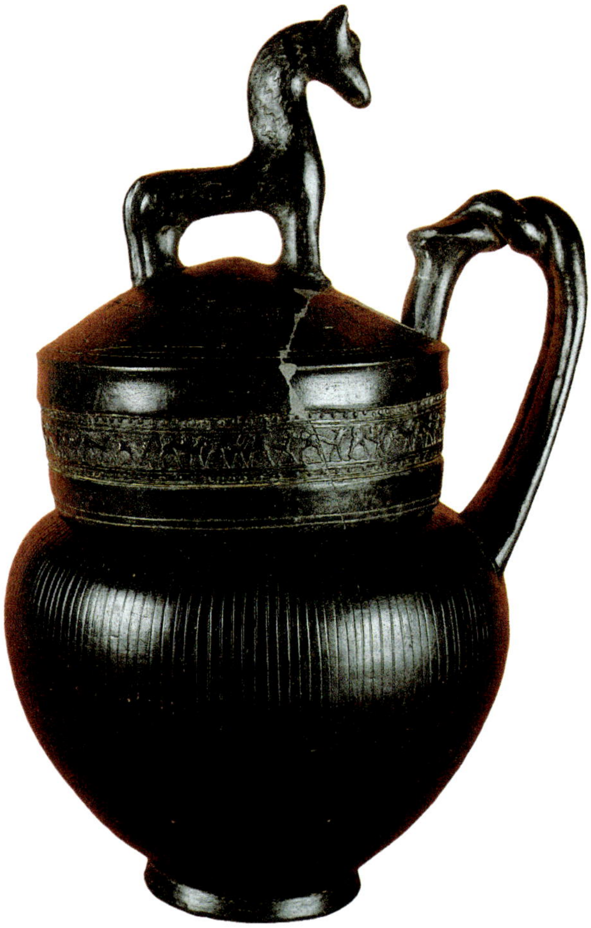

146 **Olpe (jug)**

Bucchero
Orvieto
Last decades of the 7th century BC
Height 25.0 cm

Etruscan bucchero pottery, with its shiny black surface and dark grey inner core, is easily recognizable. ('Bucchero' is not an ancient name; it is a corruption of the word 'bucaro', which refers to sweet-smelling black vases which were imported from South America by the Spanish and Portuguese.) The ware was extremely popular and was exported widely outside Italy. The earliest examples seem to be from Cerveteri, and date from the second quarter of the 7th century. The first vessels of bucchero ware (known as 'bucchero sottile') had thin walls and bright surfaces. Workshops were soon established in other Etruscan cities such as Veii, Vetulonia, Tarquinia and Vulci and, in due course, Chiusi and Orvieto. Later bucchero vases had much thicker walls ('bucchero pesante'). The shapes and decoration usually imitate metalwork, and the range of types is dominated by vessels for use in the serving of wine. Decorative techniques included incision, later replaced by quicker methods involving stamps or the rolling of engraved cylinders over the surface of the clay, as used here around the lid of this jug. Rows of animals facing in the same direction can be found on Etrusco-Corinthian olpai as well as on red impasto storage jars from Cerveteri. *BA/LV/EG*

National Museum of Archaeology, Florence, inv. 71212

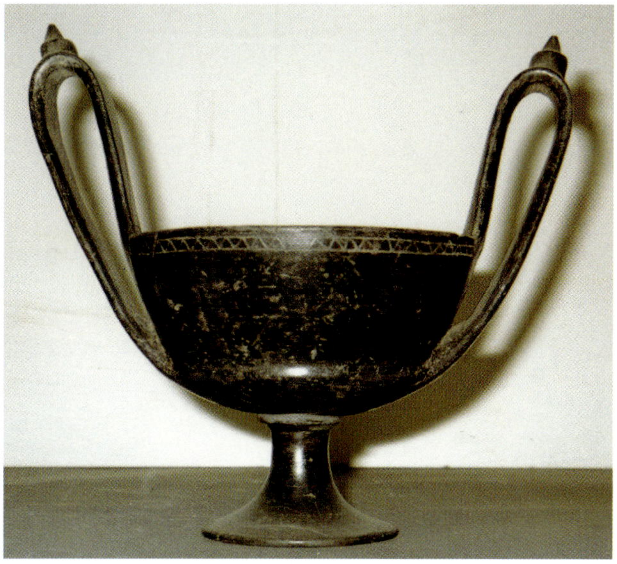

147 ## Kantharos (two-handled cup)

Bucchero
Cerveteri (Caere)
End of the 7th to first part of the 6th century BC
Height 17.0 cm

Bucchero pottery was being widely exported by this period through trade networks connecting France and Spain to Greece and Asia Minor. *GCC*

National Museum of Archaeology, Florence, inv. 96485

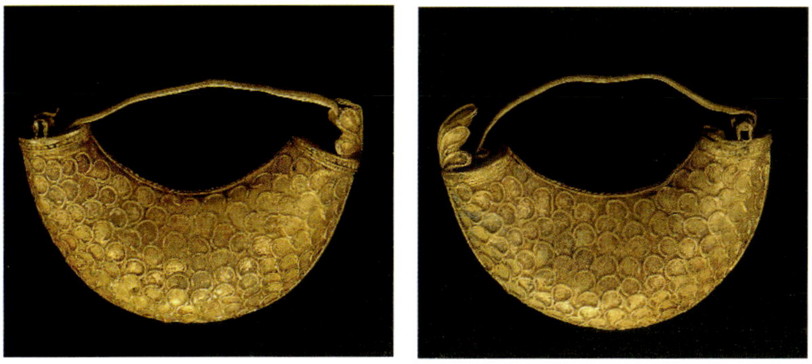

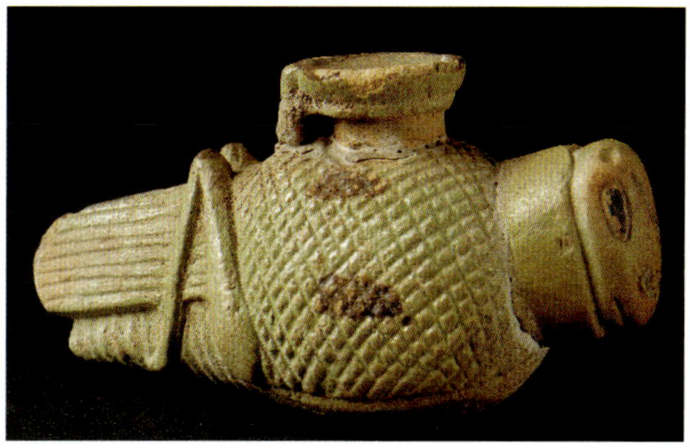

148 ## Pair of earrings

Gold
Chiusi
End of the 7th to the first quarter of the 6th century BC
Length 3.2 cm

The earliest 'leech-shaped' earrings appeared in Etruria in the second quarter of the 7th century. This pair is decorated with a scale pattern and simple palmettes in filigree (wirework). *SB/EG*

National Museum of Archaeology, Florence, inv. 74630
Gioielli 1988, 140, no. 52; Mágico 1996, 117, no. 32. For the shape, see Marshall 1911, pl. 16, no. 1308

149 ## Perfume flask

Faience
Pescia Romana
About 600 BC
Length 9.2 cm

This flask, in the form of a grasshopper, was probably made on Rhodes. Although imported East Greek perfume flasks are common in Etruria, where they must have been valued for both their precious contents and their form, this example is unusual. Egyptian faience is a kind of glazed quartz frit. *GCC/EG*

National Museum of Archaeology, Florence, inv. 71197
Martelli 1978, 167; Magnificenza 1998, 91, no. 120

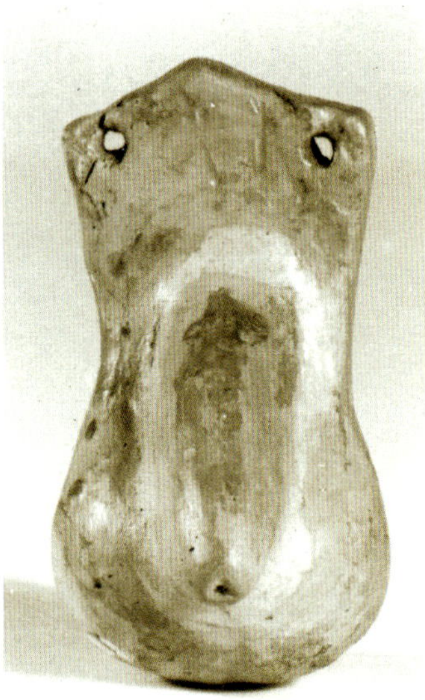
152

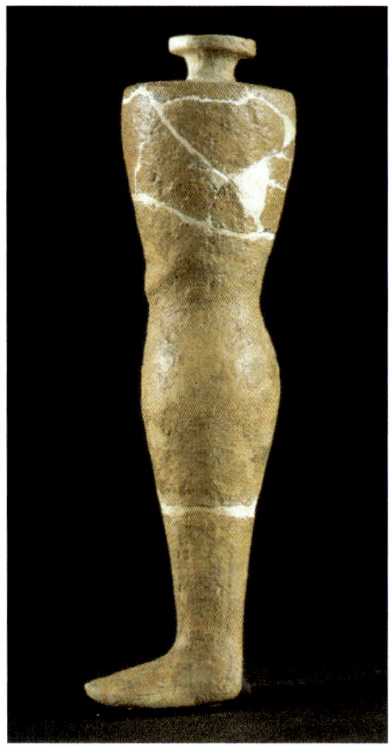
153

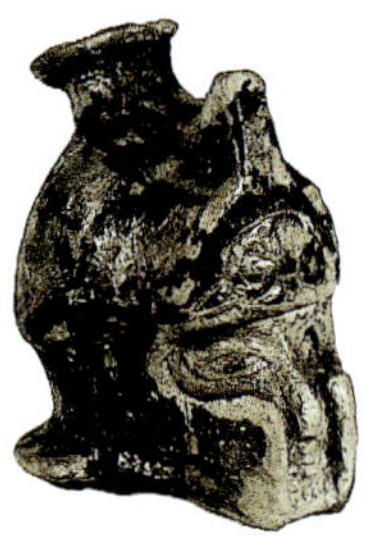
150

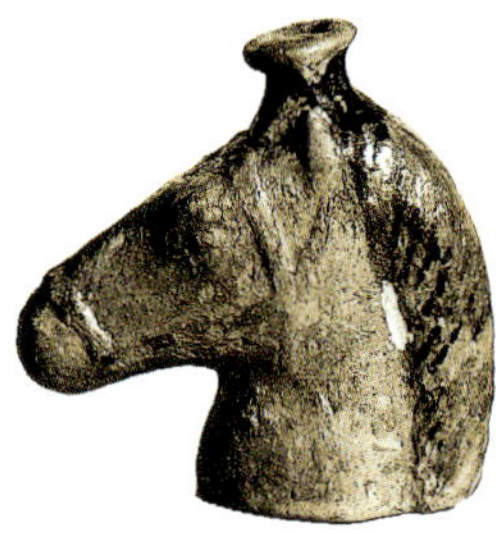
151

150 Warrior's head perfume flask

Painted ceramic
Figulo tomb, Le Migliarine, Vetulonia
Early 6th century BC
Height 6.3 cm

This and the following three perfume flasks all come from the same tomb. Excavated in 1983, in an area at the edge of the cemeteries of Vetulonia, the Figulo tomb was a simple earth-cut grave covered by a mound five metres high and ten metres in diameter. Cremated remains had been placed in a bronze ash urn and a basin. The presence of weapons indicates the burial of a man. The tomb, dated to the first half of the 6th century BC, contained extremely rich funerary offerings, many of which had been imported to Vetulonia from elsewhere in Etruria, from mainland Greece and East Greece. As well as Etrusco-Corinthian, Corinthian and East Greek ceramics, there were some iron objects, rather poorly preserved, and bronzes, both Etruscan-made and imported from East Greece. The tomb's contents reflect the very active trade networks operating at this time, which may have been direct with Vetulonia, in northern Etruria, or channelled through one of the cities of southern Etruria. Vetulonia's commercial activities were closely linked to its expanding mining industry and its trade in copper products. The city's wealth in the 7th century was founded on its control of the rich mining centres within its territory. The Figulo tomb is located on the route to the mining area of Il Massetano. *MCy*

National Museum of Archaeology, Florence, inv. 8362

151 Horse's head perfume flask

Painted ceramic
Figulo tomb, Le Migliarine, Vetulonia
Beginning of the 6th century BC
Height 9.3 cm

National Museum of Archaeology, Florence, inv. 8363

152 Perfume flask in the form of a phallus

Ceramic
Figulo tomb, Le Migliarine, Vetulonia
Beginning of the 6th century BC
Height 5.8 cm

National Museum of Archaeology, Florence, inv. 8367

153 Perfume flask in the form of a leg

Painted ceramic
Figulo tomb, Le Migliarine, Vetulonia
Beginning of the 6th century BC
Height 20.2 cm

The lacing on the front of the leg and foot and a rosette on the knee are indicated with incised lines, and traces of a dark slip survive. *MCy*

National Museum of Archaeology, Florence, inv. 8348

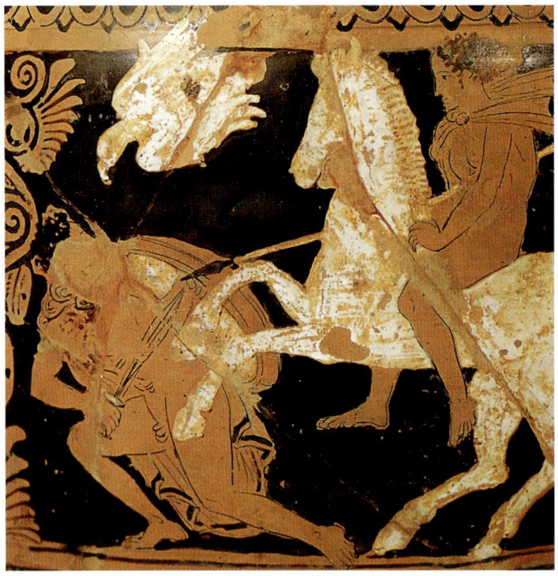

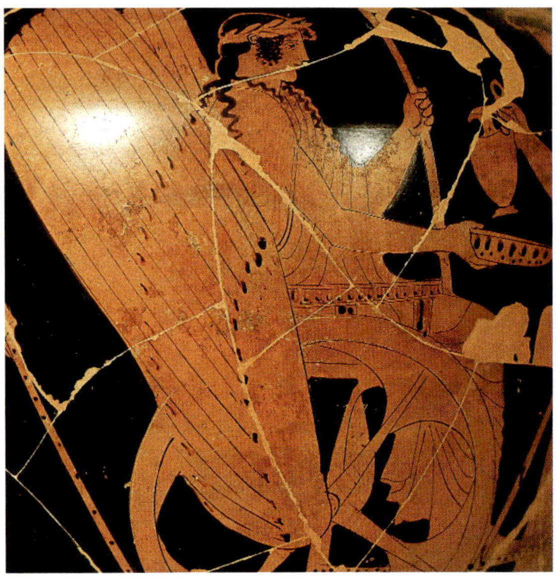

URBAN SOCIETY
About 580-325 BC

In this period Etruscan urban society prospered. The cities were independent of each other. They controlled their own territories, had their own administrative structures, and their distinct cultural identities were reflected in different customs and artistic styles. Their urban infrastructure was largely in place by the end of the 7th century BC. The largest towns and cities were surrounded by walls protecting their houses, public buildings and temples. As in Greece, one of the characteristic features of the city as a political entity was an acropolis (citadel), occupying a dominant strategic position, with access to water and easy to defend. The city leaders could call upon their local men to serve as soldiers.

In the previous period wealth had been concentrated in the hands of a limited group of aristocratic families. During what archaeologists call the Archaic period (580-480 BC) the power of the lords waned. The wider distribution of wealth led to the formation of a new middle class which increasingly dominated commerce and craftsmanship. People were linked by common interests rather than their obligations to noble families. Drawn from skilled artisans, craftsmen, merchants and traders, able to own property, the middle classes began to monopolize Etruria's economy and politics. The 6th century also marked the beginning of a system of pre-monetary currency based on weights, rather than the old system of exchange and barter. The evidence of social change is well documented in the cemeteries. The new middle classes built smaller, simpler and more standardized family tombs recalling domestic architecture, carefully arranged along planned streets.

Etruria's rich mineral resources were intensively exploited and efficient trading networks were in place. Throughout the 6th century Ionian merchants from eastern Greece (particularly Samos, Miletus and Phokaia) replaced the Phoenicians in dominating trade with Etruria. Through them, Etruria received a wide range of luxury goods including perishable products such as perfumes, textiles, wine and olive oil. Fine ceramics for the table were imported from Corinth, eastern Greece and Athens. As in the previous period, specialized foreign workshops were established in Etruria, exerting a strong influence on locally-made crafts, from ceramics to wall paintings and architectural terracottas. Greek art was a continuing source of inspiration for the Attic craftsmen who settled in Etruria.

Etruria's exports to Greece largely consisted of metals and food, rather than its own artistic products. However, they did export these to the coast of southern Gaul (France). Wine amphorae, bronze vessels, the highly valued black bucchero ware and painted Etrusco-Corinthian ceramics were all traded to that area. These goods also reached Corsica, Sardinia, Carthage on the North African coast, and the Greek colonies in Sicily.

Complex relationships existed between the various trading powers. There were constant struggles between the Etruscans, Carthaginians and Greeks for control over the trade routes in the Tyrrhenian Sea. The Etruscans strengthened their control by forming an alliance with Carthage around 540 BC. Etruscans, probably from Orvieto, Chiusi, Volterra and Fiesole, also spread north, establishing settlements in the Po valley and reinforcing their presence at important centres like Bologna. The Etruscan dynasty of the Tarquins ruled Rome for much of the 6th century BC, and the Roman kings Tarquinius Priscus, Tarquinius Superbus and Servius Tullius all had Etruscan origins. Literary tradition records that Rome was attacked by the Etruscans under the leadership of Porsenna, king of Chiusi at the end of the 6th century BC. The details of this confrontation are not clear, but it is probable that the Etruscans briefly occupied Rome. At the start of the 5th century the Etruscans were still expanding their sphere of influence, but their power had waned considerably. A century later, in 396 BC, Rome annexed Veii and began its advance into the territories of central Italy.

One cause of Etruscan decline in what is known as the Classical period (480-325 BC) was undoubtedly the loss of control of their important Tyrrhenian trade routes due to the rising power of Carthage and Syracuse. The key moment in this power struggle was the battle of Cumae (474 BC), when the Etruscan fleet faced the combined forces of the Cumaeans from Campania on the South Italian mainland and their Syracusan allies from Sicily.

The Etruscans lost the battle and with it their control over shipping routes in the south Tyrrhenian Sea. Greek trade, dominated by Athens, turned instead towards the Adriatic coast, especially the port of Spina at the mouth of the River Po.

By no means all the Etruscan city states were affected by defeat at Cumae. The most damaged were the coastal cities of southern Etruria, whose economies were dependent on maritime trade with Greece. Other cities continued to prosper, especially those inland, on the north Tyrrhenian coast and the Adriatic coast. Populonia, which had developed an important metalworking industry towards the end of the 6th century, retained important trade links with the Greeks, as did the mining regions on the island of Elba. It is indicative of the economic stability of Populonia that it was apparently the first Etruscan city to mint coins, probably during the second half of the 6th century.

The Etruscan class structure was profoundly affected by these economic upheavals. The middle classes, largely dependent upon commercial activities and trade, lost their dominant status by the 4th century, and power reverted to the aristocracy. Internal problems within some of the cities had to be resolved by calling on the assistance of others. Further difficulties were becoming apparent too. Around 430 BC the town of Capua in Campania, largely an Etruscan city in the previous century, had fallen to Samnites, an Italic people from the Apennines, probably mercenaries. In the north, the Po valley region was no longer able to resist the incursions of the Gauls who had already occupied large areas of Lombardy. In 390 BC the Gauls also threatened Rome. Significant changes were on the way, and Rome was to play the leading role. *GCC/EG*

Previous page:
above: detail of Faliscan red-figure stamnos (no. 219)
below: detail of Attic red-figure stamnos (no. 217)

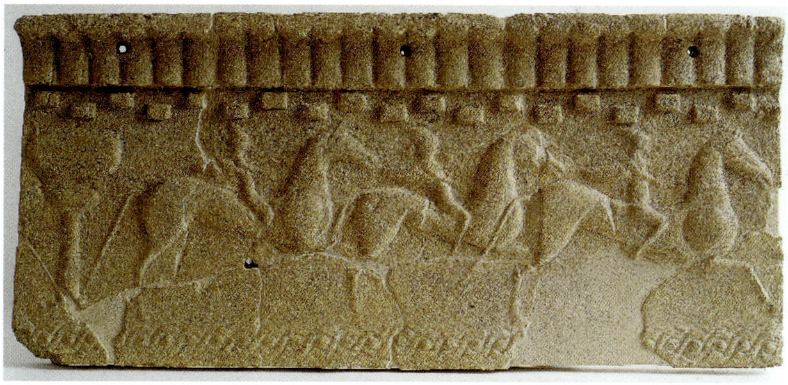

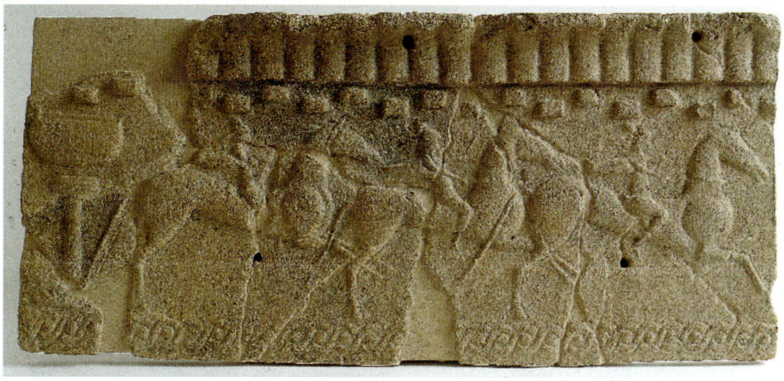

154 Two frieze plaques

Terracotta
From the Archaic building complex at Poggio Civitate (Murlo)
First quarter of the 6th century BC
Height 24.5 cm; length 54.8 cm

Poggio Civitate is located on a prominent hill near Murlo. It was the site of a large and impressive building complex of the Archaic period, apparently the princely residence of the local aristocratic dynasty. The roofs of the building complex were decorated with locally-made roof tiles and architectural terracottas, including these plaques. They were part of a long moulded frieze comprising four different figurative scenes which included a carriage procession and a banquet. While the plaques were influenced by a number of sources including Near Eastern and South Italian Greek friezes and Corinthian pottery, their subject matter also provides evocative evidence for some characteristic features of Etruscan aristocratic life at this period. These two plaques show a horse race with three riders. The prize is the large cauldron on a column which is shown to the left. It is possible the four themes were directly related to the building on which the frieze was placed. The local prince served as chief, judge and priest. This building may have served as a focus for these roles, so the decoration may have drawn upon the ceremonial activities of the people who occupied it. Later, architectural friezes like these at Poggio Civitate were more often used for the adornment of temples, as in Greece. *GCC/EG*

Museum of Archaeology, Siena, inv. 112627, 112628
Haynes 2000, 122, figs. 102 and 114-26; Borelli and Targio 2003, 36-7

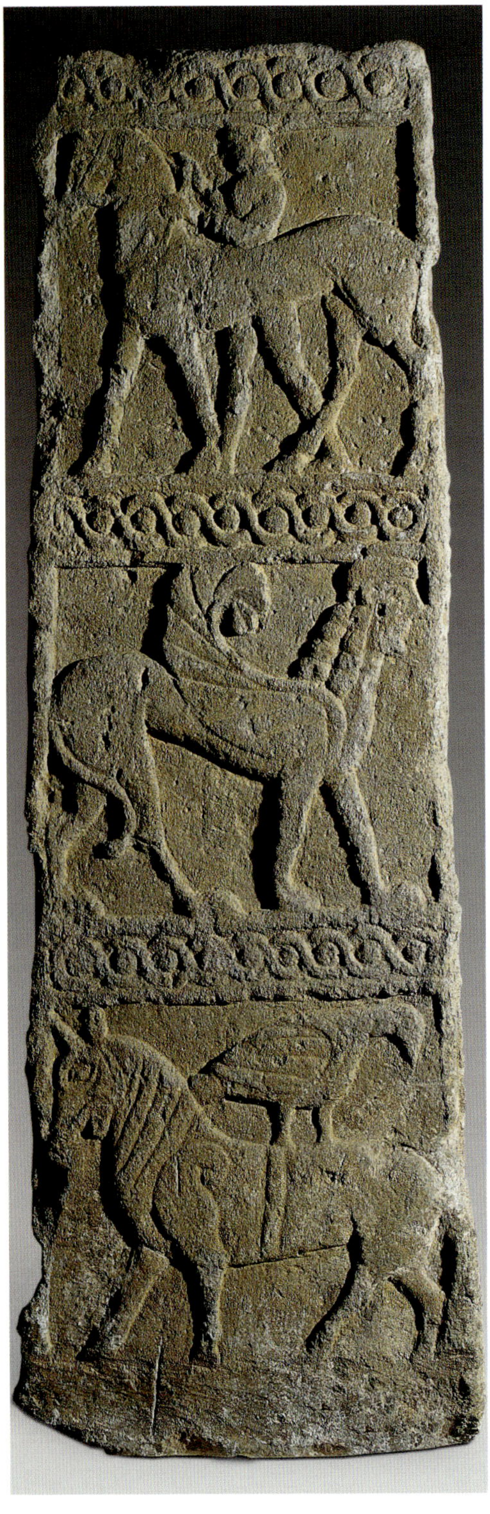

155 Cippus (grave marker)

Nenfro
Probably from Vulci (Campari collection)
Beginning of the 6th century BC
Height 150.0 cm

Nenfro is a friable grey volcanic stone (or tufa) local to Vulci. Vulci was an influential centre for the production of stone sculpture. This is the best-known carved stone monument from the beginning of the Archaic period in southern Etruria. Its style and decoration were strongly influenced by Corinthian and Ionian (East Greek) imagery. Only one face and parts of the two sides of the grave marker have survived. In the upper register a man is shown leading a horse by the reins. There is a sphinx in the middle register and a bull with a bird perched on its back in the lowest register. Similar animals and fantastic creatures probably decorated the missing parts of the sculpture. *SB/EG*

National Museum of Archaeology, Florence, inv. 75840
Magnificenza 1998, 345, no. 453

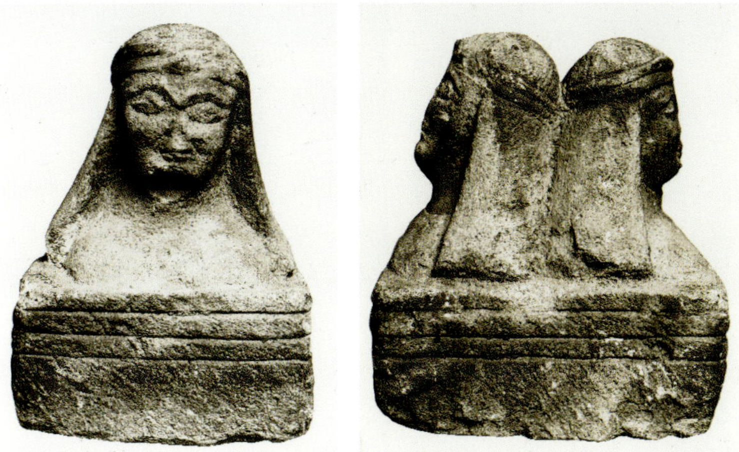

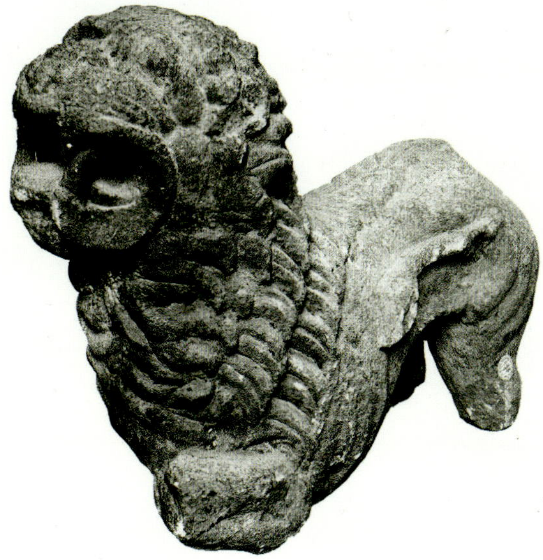

156 **Cippus (grave marker) [two views]**

Tufa
Orvieto
First half of the 6th century BC
Height 48.0 cm

Tufa is a porous and friable volcanic stone, a by-product of lava. In the Archaic period at Orvieto, burials were often placed in chamber tombs covered with small mounds topped by various types of cippi, or grave markers. Many Etruscan grave markers survive from the Archaic period, varying greatly in character from cemetery to cemetery and according to the gender, age and status of the dead person. The two female heads on this one may represent women mourners. *GCC/EG*

National Museum of Archaeology, Florence, inv. 73138

157 **Funerary sculpture**

Tufa
Montalto di Castro (near Vulci)
Middle of the 6th century BC
Height 50.0 cm

Pairs or groups of sculptures were placed in tombs from the end of the 7th century BC onwards. It is not certain exactly how they were positioned as so many of the tombs have been looted, but examples are known from Vulci, Tarquinia, Cerveteri and Veii. At Vulci, sculptures of mythological creatures, such as sphinxes, centaurs and winged lions, like this one, were placed at the entrances of tombs. These had symbolic meaning, often evoking the underworld, or were designed to offer protection. *SB*

National Museum of Archaeology, Florence, inv. 75963

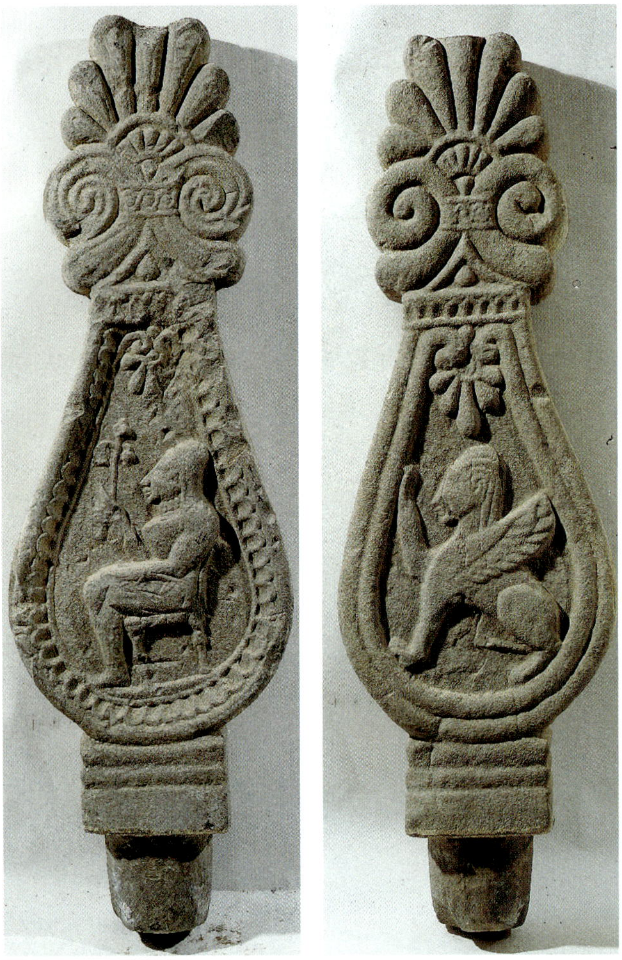

158 ## Funerary stela (grave marker) [two views]

Limestone
Londa, Florence
Second half of the 6th century BC
Height 104.0 cm

This is one of a number of limestone stelae and grave markers, carved in shallow relief, from the Fiesole area near Florence (see also number 159). They represent the products of a distinctive local school of sculpture. Oval examples like this one were associated with women's graves. On one side the dead person is shown as a veiled woman seated on a throne and holding a pomegranate branch. On the back there is a seated sphinx. The upper part of the stela is crowned with a palmette and volutes. *GCC/EG*

National Museum of Archaeology, Florence, inv. 5862
Haynes 2000, 251, fig. 208

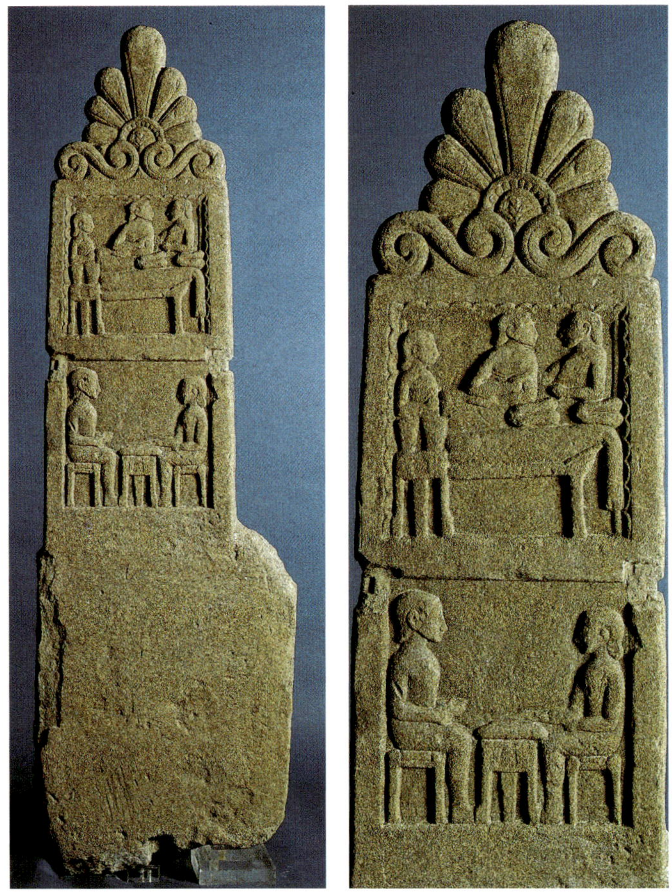

159 ## Funerary stela (grave marker) [view and detail]

Limestone
Antella, Florence
Second half of the 6th century BC
Height 159.0 cm

Another of the series of stone stelae from Fiesole, this belongs to the rectangular type carved in low relief with figurative scenes usually of banqueting or dancing. In the upper register a couple are shown reclining on a couch at a banquet. They are attended by a servant standing behind a small table bearing wine vessels. The lower register shows two people seated to either side of a low table. Like number 158, the stela is crowned by a palmette. *MI*

National Museum of Archaeology, Florence, inv. 75347
Etruscos 1999, 250, no. 309; Torelli 2000, 366

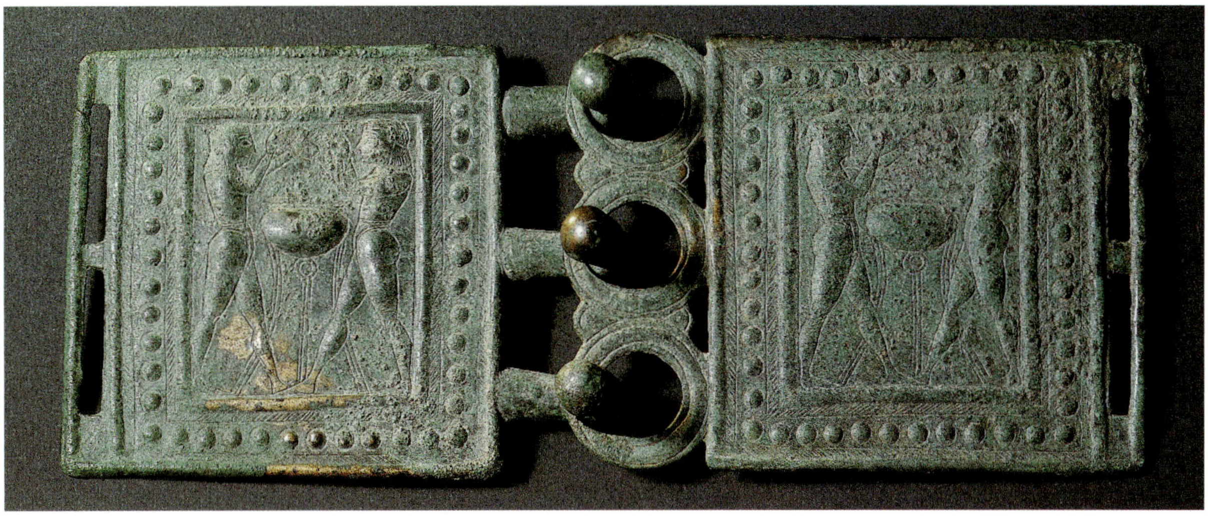

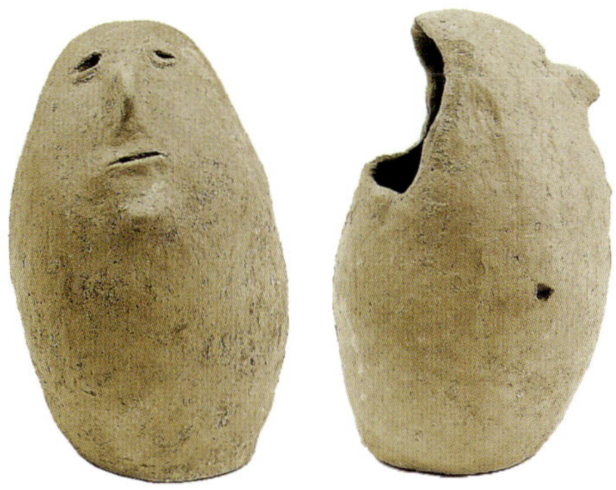

160 **'Canopic' ash urn**

Impasto
Sferracavalli necropolis, Sarteano (Siena)
First half of the 6th century BC
Height 28.5 cm

This locally-made urn was inspired by the 'canopic' ash urns of Chiusi, which also have faces representing the dead (see numbers 133, 134). However, unlike the Chiusi examples, which have separate lids in the form of human heads, this urn was made in one piece. It has an opening at the back.

GCC

Museum of Archaeology, Siena, inv. B878

161 **Belt buckle**

Bronze
Casole d'Elsa, Siena
First half of the 6th century BC
Length 20.3 cm

This buckle was found with another, identical example in the same tomb. Although they have no exact parallels, they are related to a small group of more complex silver-plated bronze buckles which were probably made in southern Etruria. This is possibly the earliest representation of a boxing match in the Etruscan world. Boxing was a favourite Etruscan sport, which formed part of the funerary games. Two boxers are shown confronting each other in front of the prize, a cauldron on a tripod. The scene is based on Greek prototypes.

GCC/EG

Museum of Archaeology, Siena, inv. MS31
von Hase 1971, 21, fig. 24; Mágico 1996, 121, no. 40

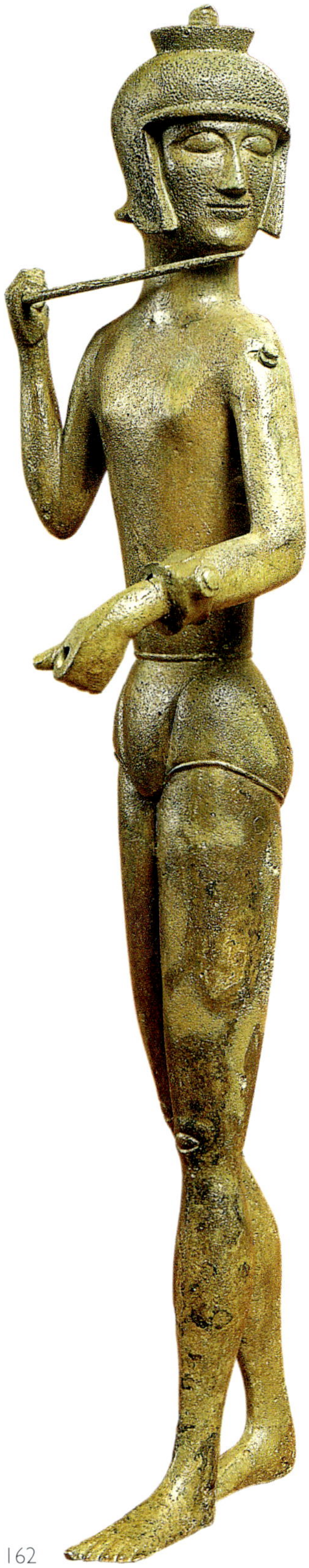

162

162 Statuette of a warrior (attachment or mounting)

Bronze
Brolio (Arezzo)
About 550 BC
Height 36.2 cm

This cast bronze figure, together with numbers 163-165, comes from Brolio in the Chiana valley, the site of one of the most important deposits of votive objects from Archaic Etruria. Excavated in 1863 it comprised a large body of bronze and ceramic material dating from the early 6th to the 5th centuries BC. The statuettes must have been dedicated in a sanctuary, probably established and controlled by a local aristocratic family. The remains of a fixing can be seen on the tops of the heads of all four figures indicating they were originally attachments or supports, presumably from a prestigious vessel such as a cauldron or an item of furniture like a throne. The warrior brandishes a spear with his right hand. A shield was once held on his left arm. He wears the loincloth known as a 'perizoma' and a sturdy helmet with long cheekpieces. The statuettes were probably the work of bronzesmiths from Chiusi. *ARo/EG*

National Museum of Archaeology, Florence, inv. 562
Torelli 2000, 621, cat. no. 272

163 Statuette of a warrior (attachment or mounting)

Bronze
Brolio (Arezzo)
About 550 BC
Height 35.7 cm

See number 162.

National Museum of Archaeology, Florence, inv. 563
Torelli 2000, 621, cat. no. 273

164 Statuette of a warrior (attachment or mounting)

Bronze
Brolio (Arezzo)
About 550 BC
Height 36.1 cm

See number 162.

National Museum of Archaeology, Florence, inv. 564
Torelli 2000, 621, cat. no. 274

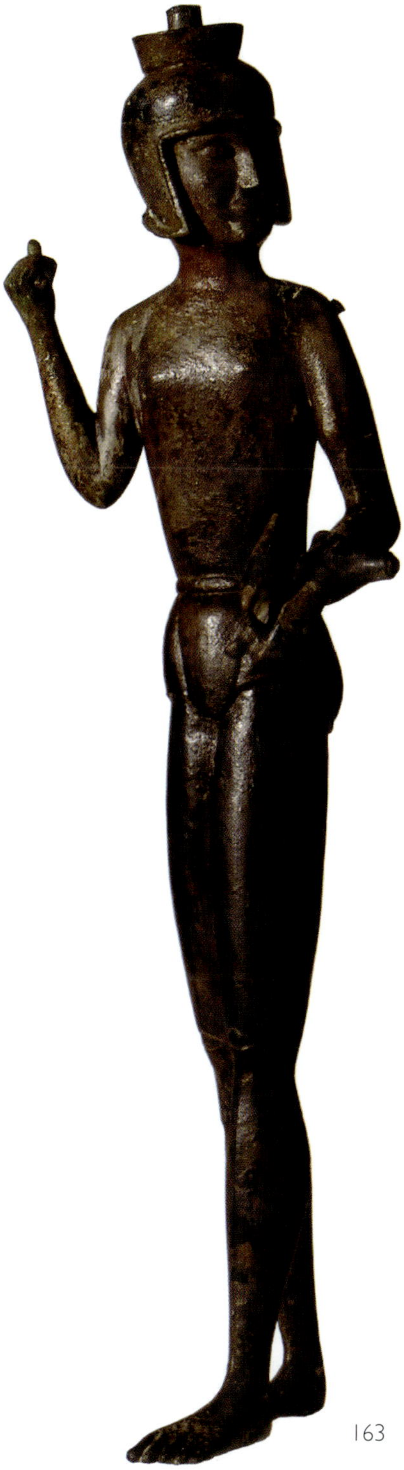
163

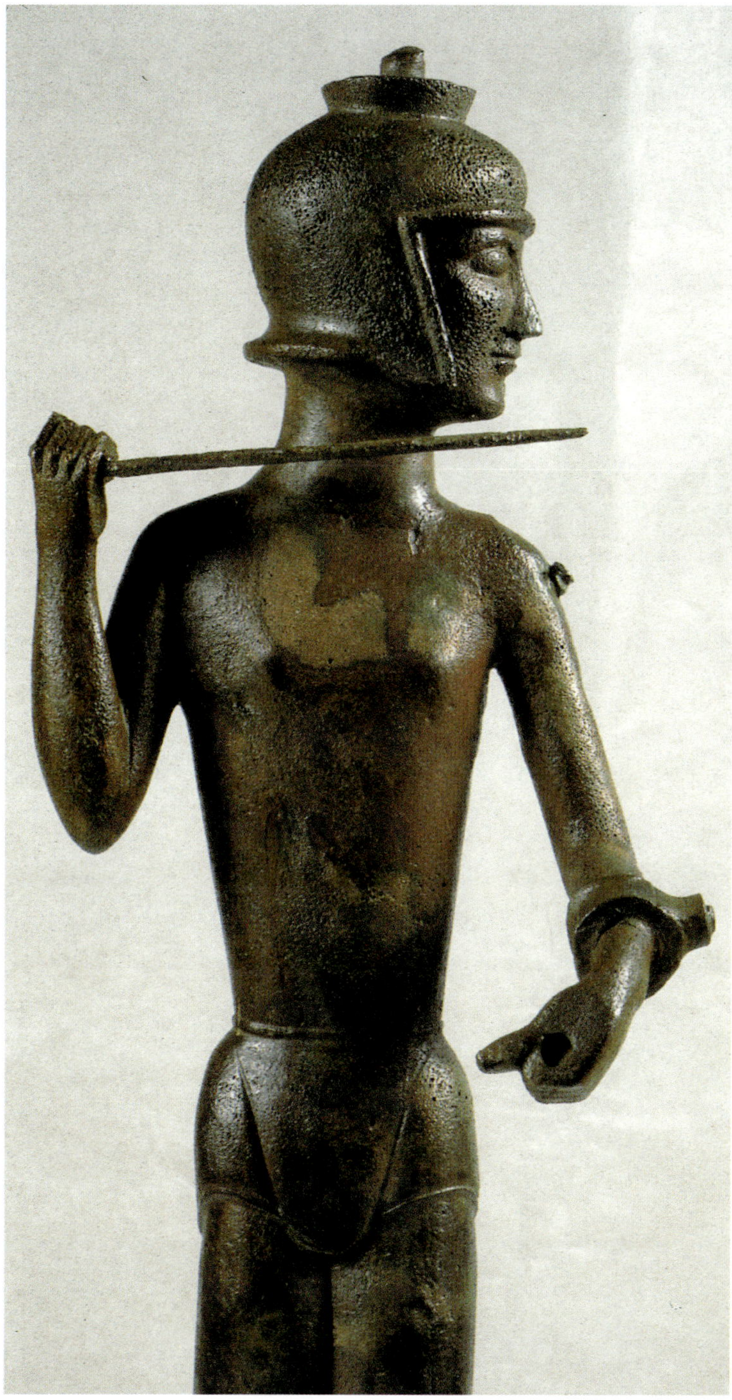
162 (detail)

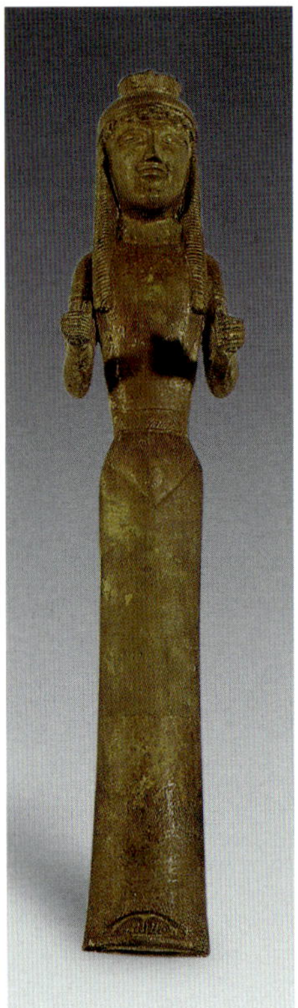

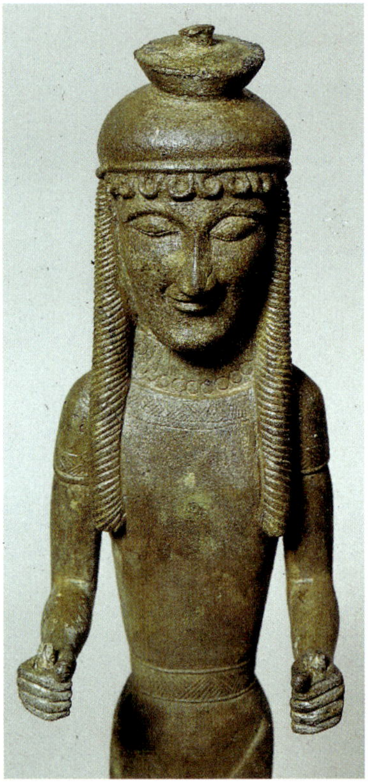

165 **Statuette of a woman (attachment or mounting)**

Bronze
Brolio (Arezzo)
About 550 BC
Height 36.1 cm

See number 162. This female figure is wearing a long belted dress and a necklace with circular pendants. *ARo*

National Museum of Archaeology, Florence, inv. 561
Torelli 2000, 622, cat. no. 275; Haynes 2000, 129, fig. 110

166 **Pair of earrings**

Gold
Chiusi
Second half of the 6th century BC
Height 1.7 cm

The 'a bauletto' earring was one of the most popular earring types of the Archaic period, found in many places in Etruria and South Italy. Three of the earliest examples of the type are numbers 114 and 115 from the Tomb of the Fans in Populonia. It has been suggested that the hollow inner part of the earrings held perfumed resins, the scent being released when the earrings were worn next to the warm skin. The skill and quality of the goldsmithing is remarkable. Etruscan jewellers had a highly sophisticated understanding of techniques such as filigree and granulation, creating an extensive repertoire of decoration. *SB/EG*

National Museum of Archaeology, Florence, inv. 77553
For some of the range of decoration, see Cristofani and Martelli 1983, nos. 142-7

167 **Earring**

Gold
Vetulonia
Second half of the 6th century BC
Height 1.4 cm

National Museum of Archaeology, Florence, inv. 132292

166

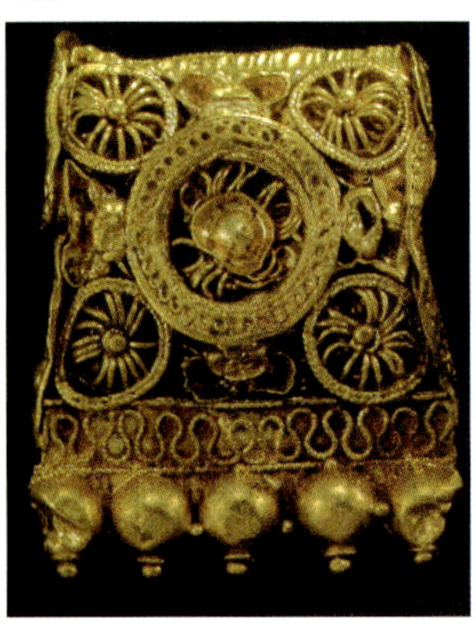

166

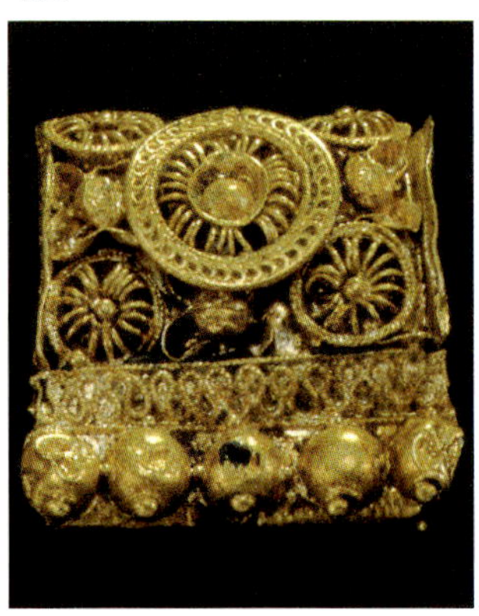

167

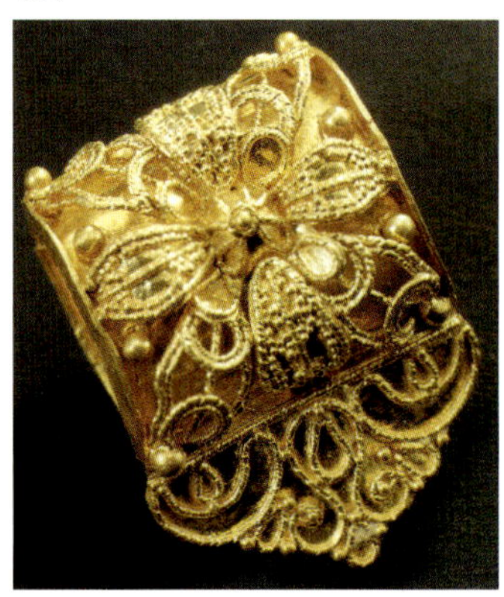

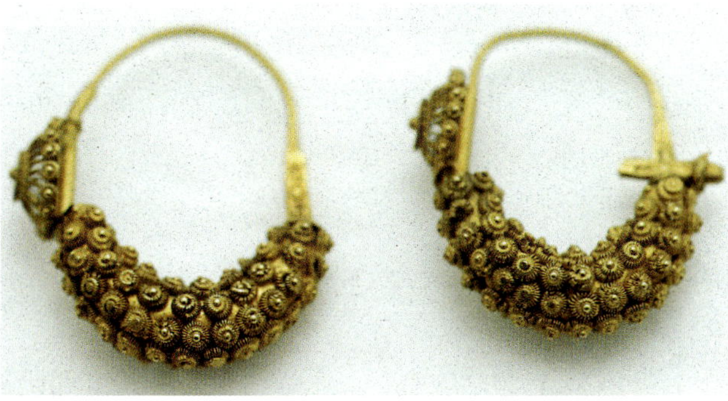

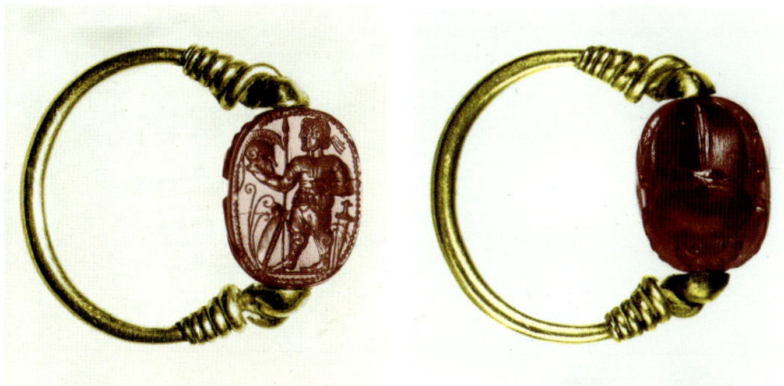

168 **Pair of earrings**

Gold
Unknown provenance
End of the 6th century BC
Length 3.5 cm

There were many different varieties of the so-called 'leech' earring. This pair has elaborate textured decoration created using fine gold filigree and granules.

GCC/EG

National Museum of Archaeology, Florence, inv. 77554

169 **Scarab ring (two views)**

Gold, carnelian
Unknown provenance
Last quarter of the 6th century BC
Length 1.3 cm

This gold swivel ring is mounted with a carved gemstone in the form of a scarab beetle. It is engraved on the underside with a representation of the Greek hero Achilles with the armour and weapons made for him by the god Hephaestus. The subject matter reflects the interest of the Etruscan aristocracy in identifying with the Greek heroes. The Etruscans became highly skilled in the art of gem-engraving, and this example is the work of a talented artist known as the Boston Master of Dionysus.

National Museum of Archaeology, Florence, inv. 15260
Civiltà 1985, 222, no. 8

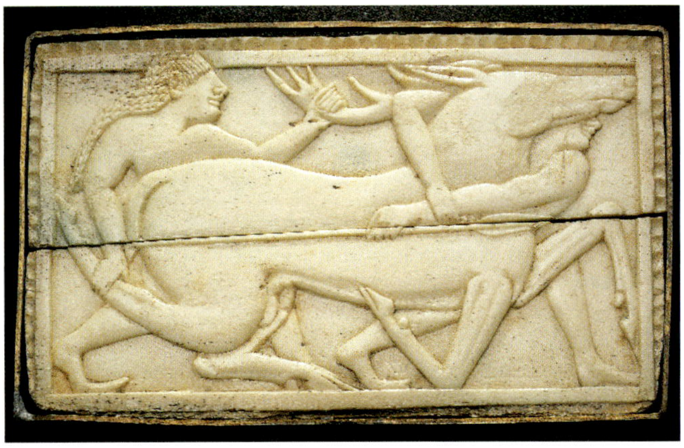

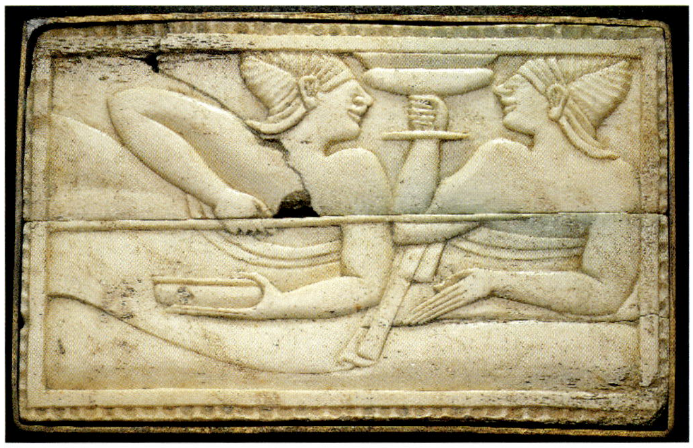

170 **Relief plaque**

Ivory
Pananatenaica tomb, Crocifisso del Tufo necropolis, Orvieto
Third quarter of the 6th century BC
Length 11.2 cm

Plaques of this kind, carved in low relief, were attached to the sides of the small wooden caskets used by wealthy Etruscan women to hold jewellery. Number 171 belonged to the same box. The lively and powerful scene of two hunters bringing down a stag was executed by a skilled Etruscan ivory-carver. *PG*

National Museum of Archaeology, Florence, inv. 01507
Gioielli 1988, 163, no. 49; Mágico 1996, 159, no. 125; Haynes 2000, 160, fig. 140

171 **Relief plaque**

Ivory
Pananatenaica tomb, Crocifisso del Tufo necropolis, Orvieto
Third quarter of the 6th century BC
Length 10.6 cm

Another mounting from the same casket as number 170, this plaque shows two men reclining on a banqueting couch, one holding a patera (dish), the other a drinking cup. *PG*

National Museum of Archaeology, Florence, inv. 01506
Gioielli 1988, 163, no. 50; Mágico 1996, 160, no. 126

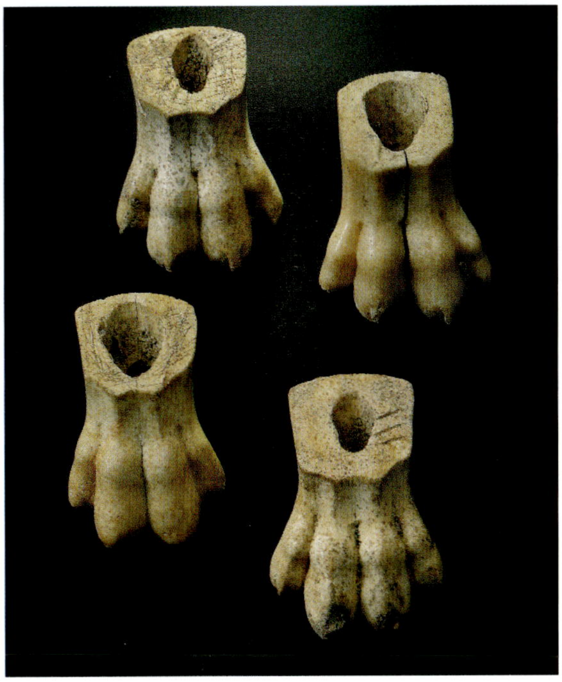

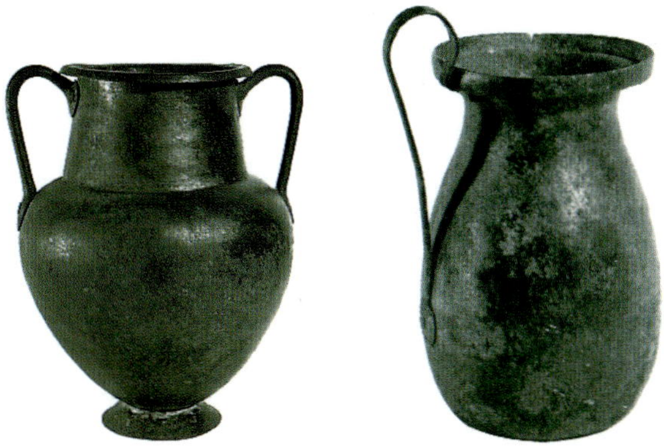

172 **Feet from a box**

Ivory
Pananatenaica tomb, Crocifisso del Tufo necropolis, Orvieto
Third quarter of the 6th century BC
Height 3.0 cm

This set of lions' feet may have come from the same casket as numbers 170 and 171. *PG*

National Museum of Archaeology, Florence, inv. 01492
Gioielli 1988, 163, no. 48; Mágico 1996, 159, no. 124

173 **Amphora (container for liquids)**

Bronze
Tomb of the Olives, Cerveteri (Caere)
Second quarter of the 6th century BC
Height 27.0 cm

This was originally one of a pair (the second now lost). It was made in Sparta in Greece. *GCC*

National Museum of Archaeology, Florence, inv. 75435
Cristofani 1979, 11, no. 19, figs. 10, 13

174 **Olpe (jug)**

Bronze
Tomb of the Olives, Cerveteri (Caere)
6th century BC
Height 17.0 cm

This jug has been compared to tapered olpai from Orvieto and more elongated olpai from Vulci, but this example is older and rather different in form. *GCC*

National Museum of Archaeology, Florence, inv. 75439
Cristofani 1979, 20, no. 23, figs. 16-18

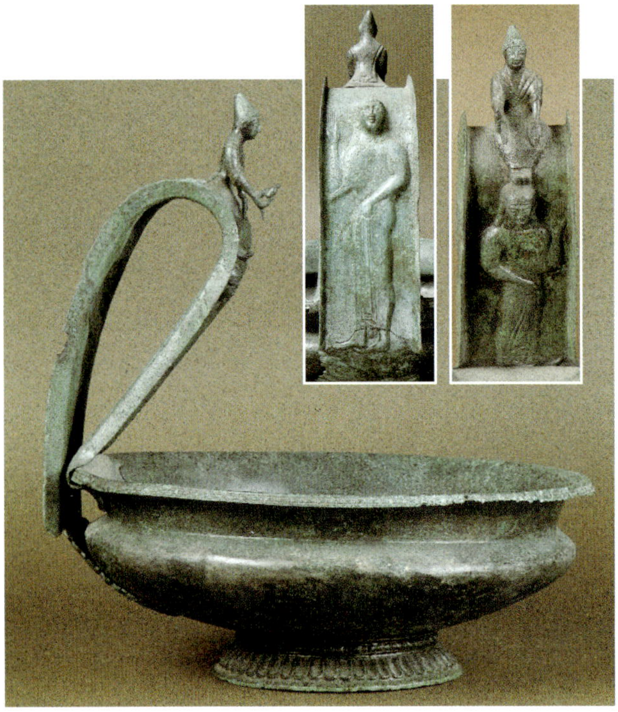

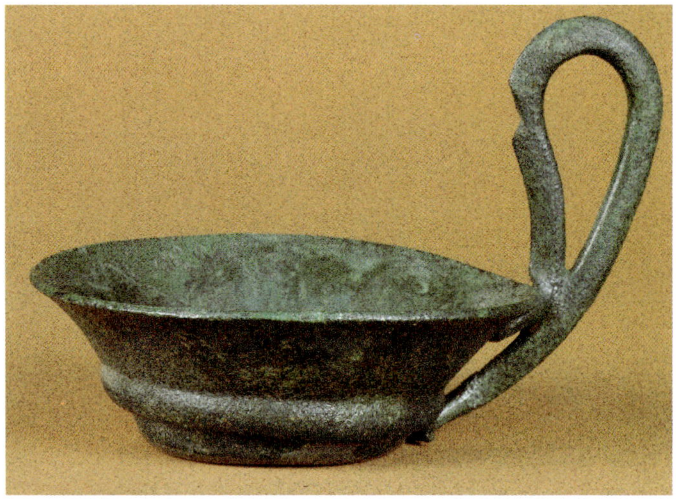

175 **Kyathos (ladle)**

Bronze
Bisenzio
Last decades of the 6th century BC
Height 21.0 cm

The handle of this unusually large and elaborate kyathos is decorated with two female figures in relief. A third cast bronze figure is shown seated on the top, holding an oblong object in her outstretched hand, her feet resting on the head of one of the relief figures. *GCC*

National Museum of Archaeology, Florence, inv. 74913

176 **Kyathos (ladle)**

Bronze
Bisenzio
Last decades of the 6th century BC
Height 8.5 cm

A simpler version of number 175, this type of vessel was frequently made of ceramic and used to ladle and serve wine during banquets. *GCC*

National Museum of Archaeology, Florence, inv. 74916

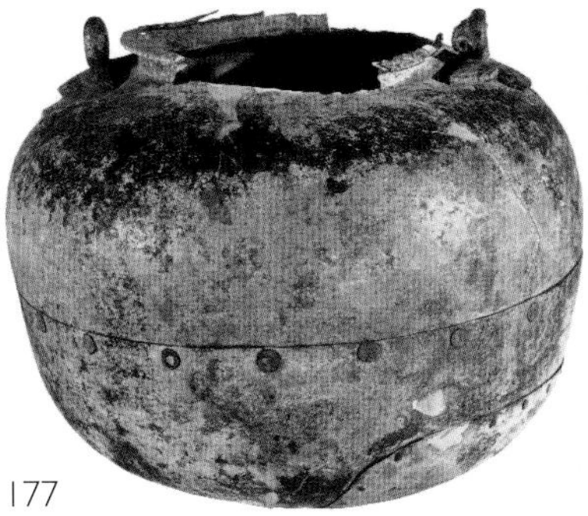
177

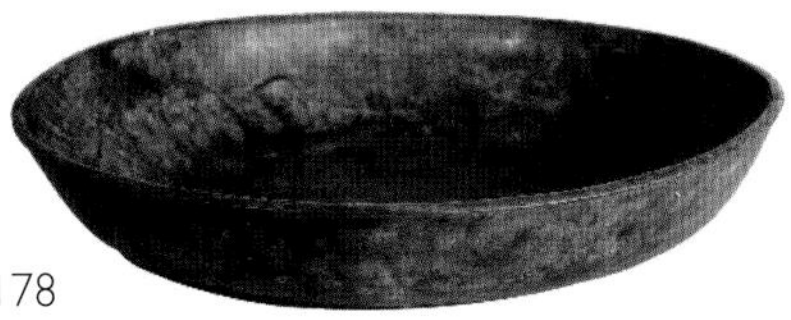
178

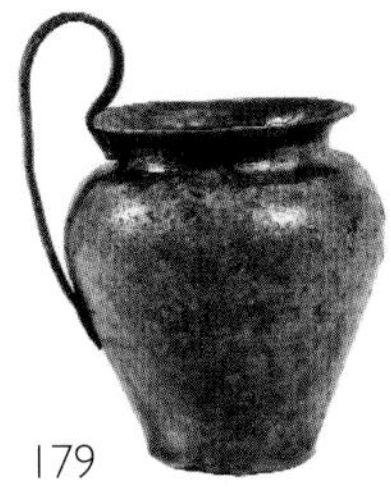
179

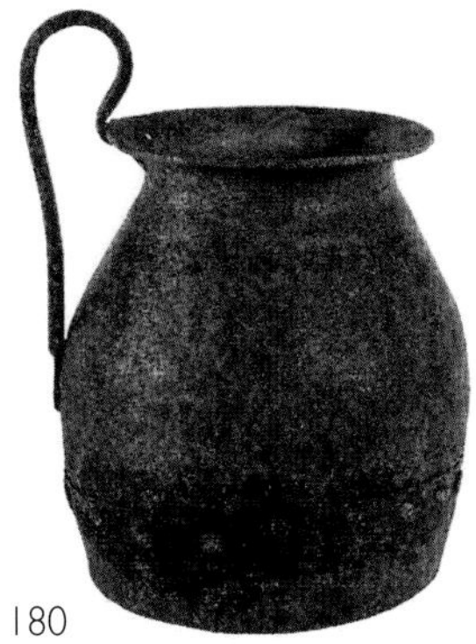
180

177 Cauldron

Bronze
Crocifisso del Tufa necropolis, Orvieto
Third quarter of the 6th century BC
Height 30.0 cm

This and numbers 178-180 come from the Crocifisso del Tufo necropolis at Orvieto which was established in the second half of the 6th century and continued in use throughout the 5th. The necropolis consisted of small rectangular built tombs of tufa set next to each other along narrow streets and covered with small mounds topped with cippi (grave markers). The name of the first owner of the tomb was usually inscribed over the doorway, and the dead were placed on stone benches inside.

Banqueting equipment, dedicated to the preparation and service of food and, especially, wine was commonly buried in Etruscan tombs. This cauldron with moveable handles, one of two from the same tomb, was probably used to cook meat. It was constructed of bronze sheets riveted together. Similar examples have been found in the important Monteleone tomb at Spoleto, but most have been found in Orvieto where they were probably made. Bronze vessels were often repaired, suggesting that they were both well-used in life and highly valued. There is an old repair on this example, and it was probably the oldest vessel in this group.

National Museum of Archaeology, Florence, inv. 75713

178 Basin

Bronze
Crocifisso del Tufo necropolis, Orvieto
End of the 6th to the first decades of the 5th centuries BC
Diameter 28.8 cm

National Museum of Archaeology, Florence, inv. 75721

179 Small jug

Bronze
Crocifisso del Tufo necropolis, Orvieto
End of the 6th to the first decades of the 5th centuries BC
Height 8.9 cm

National Museum of Archaeology, Florence, inv. 75716

180 Jug

Bronze
Crocifisso del Tufo necropolis, Orvieto
End of the 6th to the first decades of the 5th centuries BC
Height 23.5 cm

The bottom of this jug has been restored.

National Museum of Archaeology, Florence, inv. 75714

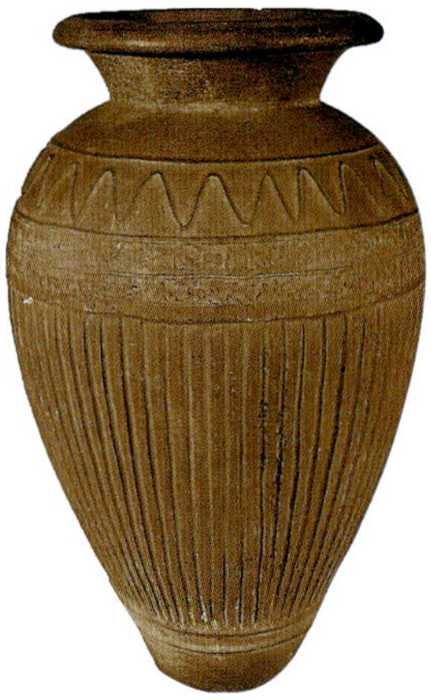

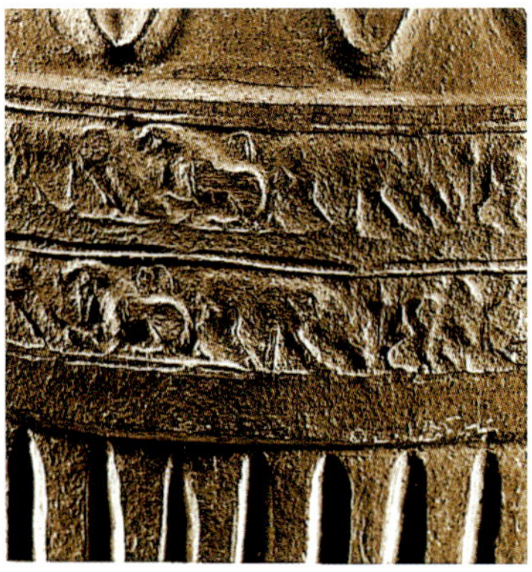

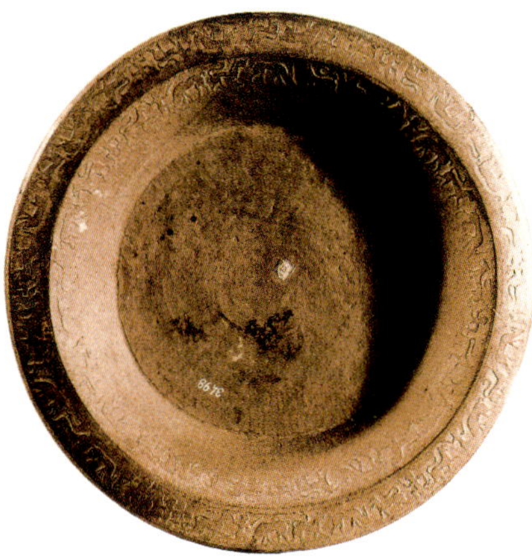

181 Pithos (storage vessel) [and detail]

Impasto
Cerveteri (Caere)
Second quarter of the 6th century BC
Height 79.5 cm

This type of storage jar belongs to a distinctive group of ceramics from Cerveteri, made for about a century from the last quarter of the 7th to just after the middle of the 6th century BC (see also number 182). The double frieze decoration around the upper part of the vessel was made by rolling a cylinder decorated with animals including griffins, lions, deer and boar. The pattern is repeated eight and a half times. The less formal arrangement of the animals (which in early examples all face in the same direction), together with the introduction of plant motifs, date the pithos to the latter part of the production period. *GCC*

National Museum of Archaeology, Florence, inv. 75403

182 Brazier

Impasto
Cerveteri (Caere)
Second quarter of the 6th century BC
Diameter 50.0 cm

Like number 181, this brazier was decorated with animal friezes produced with a cylinder. The pattern was repeated six times on the rim and four and a half times inside the upper edge. The motifs include boars, lions, panthers and goats as well as human figures. The latter feature helps to clarify the dating. Similar examples of the same motifs have been found on other braziers and pithoi. *GCC*

National Museum of Archaeology, Florence, inv. 3498
Camporeale 1984, 84-5, pl. 28e; Civiltà 1985, 142, no. 5

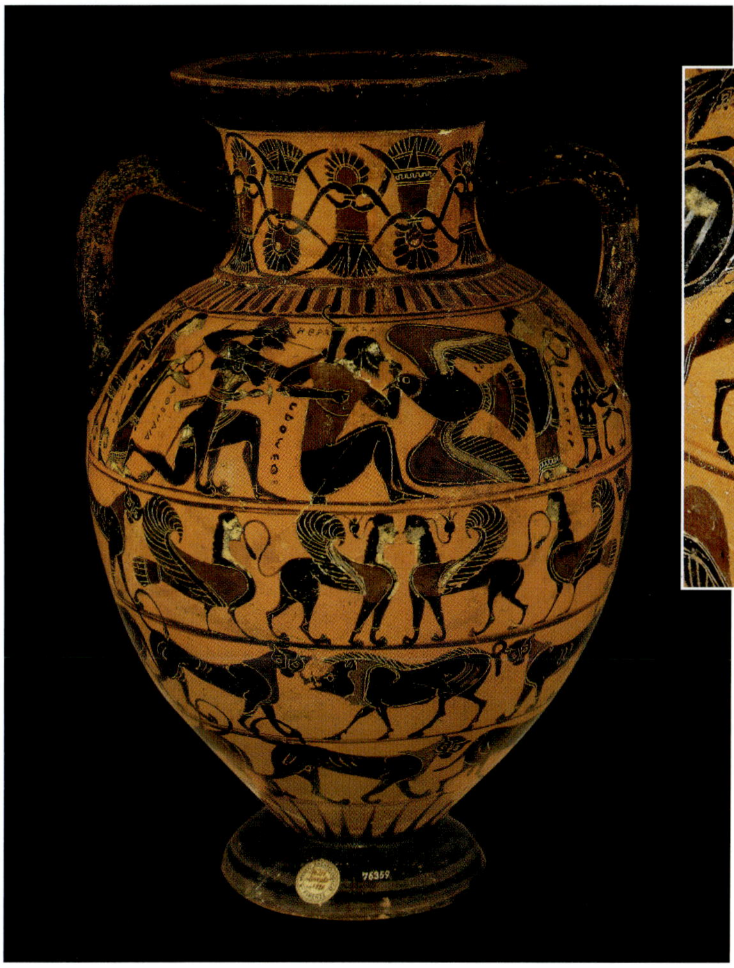

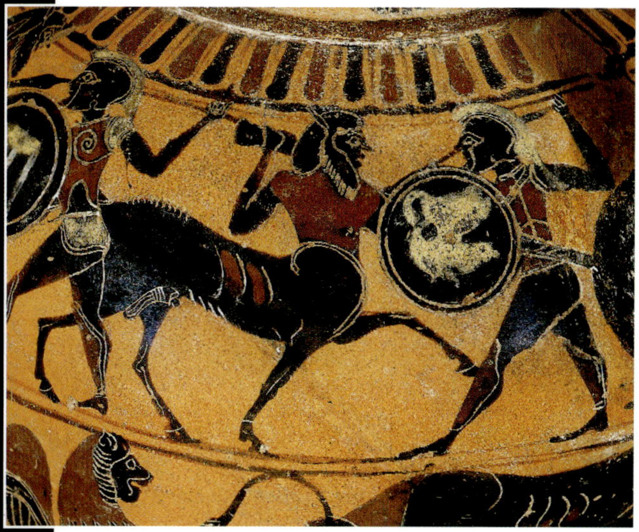

183 Tyrrhenian amphora (container for liquids)

Painted ceramic
Unknown provenance
About 560 BC
Height 40.0 cm

The so-called 'Tyrrhenian amphorae' were produced in Attica in Greece during the second quarter of the 6th century specifically for export to the Etruscan market. They arrived in Italy mainly through the ports of the Tyrrhenian coast, and have been found all over Etruria. Vases like these were very influential in transmitting Greek mythological subjects to Etruria. They had a significant influence on the development of the local ceramic industry and Etruscan potters soon imitated them. Imported Attic ceramics outnumbered those from other areas of Greece from 550 BC onwards. Despite a downturn in trade following the defeat of the Etruscan fleet by the Syracusans off Cumae in 474 BC, they continued to reach the main Etruscan cities until the 4th century. Tyrrhenian amphorae are decorated with several horizontal friezes over the neck and body in 'black-figure' style. (Black-figure is a vase-painting technique which produces figurative designs in black silhouette on a light-coloured ground; the black and red were not 'paints' but were produced by firing clay slip under specific firing conditions. Internal details were incised or applied using added colour, usually red or white.) Tyrrhenian amphorae usually depicted scenes from Greek mythology. This example shows the story of Herakles and Prometheus and a battle with the Centaurs, with rows of animals, mythical and real, below. *AR/EG*

National Museum of Archaeology, Florence, inv. 76359

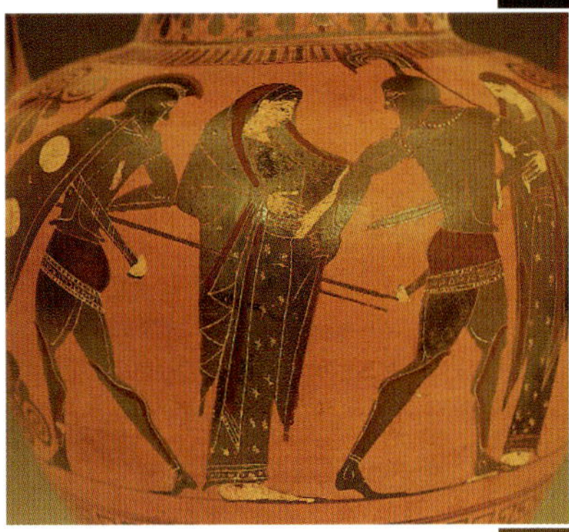

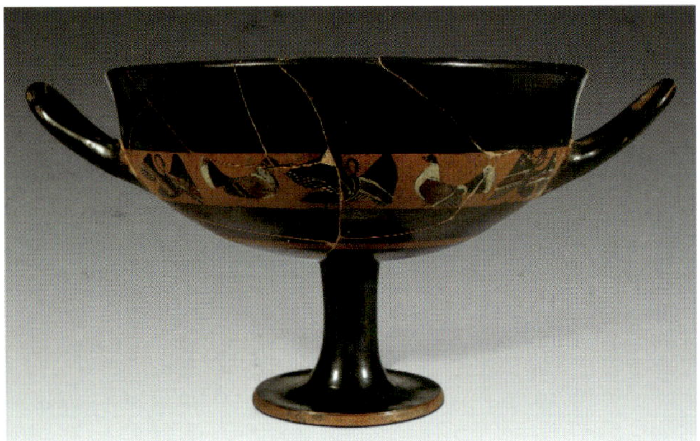

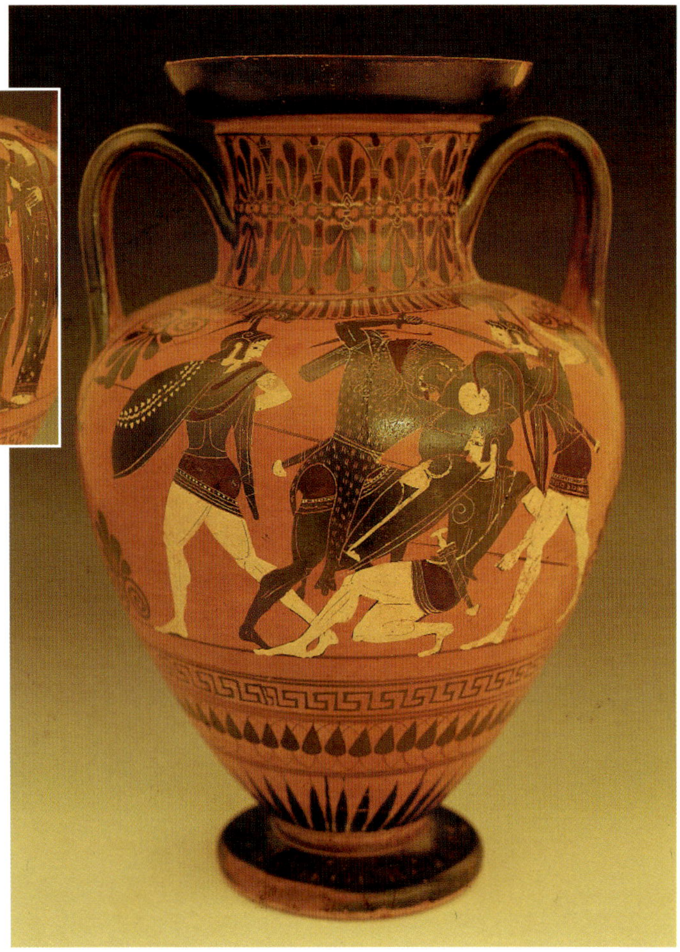

184 **Attic black-figure kylix (drinking cup)**

Painted ceramic
Tomb C, Vulci
Middle of the 6th century BC
Height 15.0 cm

This black-figure cup is another import from Attica. It is a so-called 'Little Master' cup, with decoration painted in a miniaturist style in a narrow frieze in the handle zone. *GCC*

National Museum of Archaeology, Florence, inv. 76160

185 **Attic black-figure amphora (container for liquids) [and detail]**

Painted ceramic
Tomb D, Vulci
About 530-510 BC
Height 40.0 cm

Another import from Attica, this black-figure amphora has a representation of Herakles fighting the Amazons on one side and Paris' abduction of Helen on the other. The vase was painted by the artist known as the Antimenes Painter. Herakles was one of his favourite subjects. *GCC/EG*

National Museum of Archaeology, Florence, inv. 76179
Beazley 1956, 269, no. 38

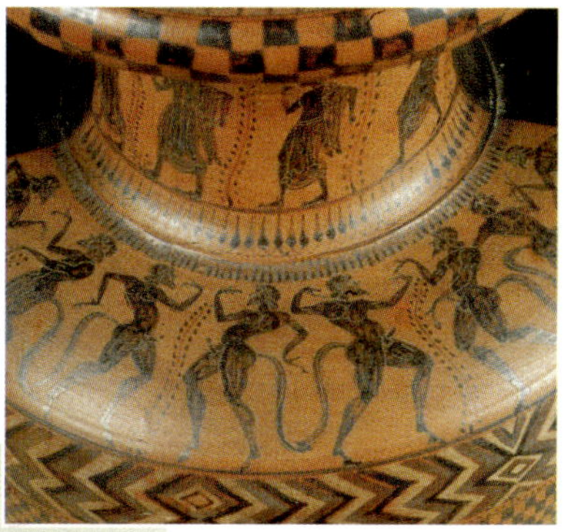

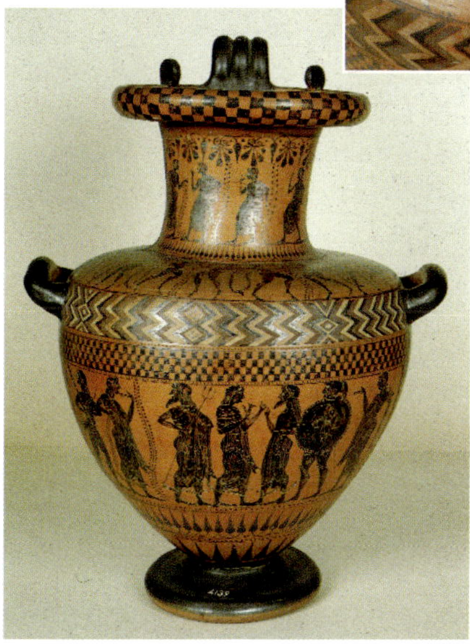

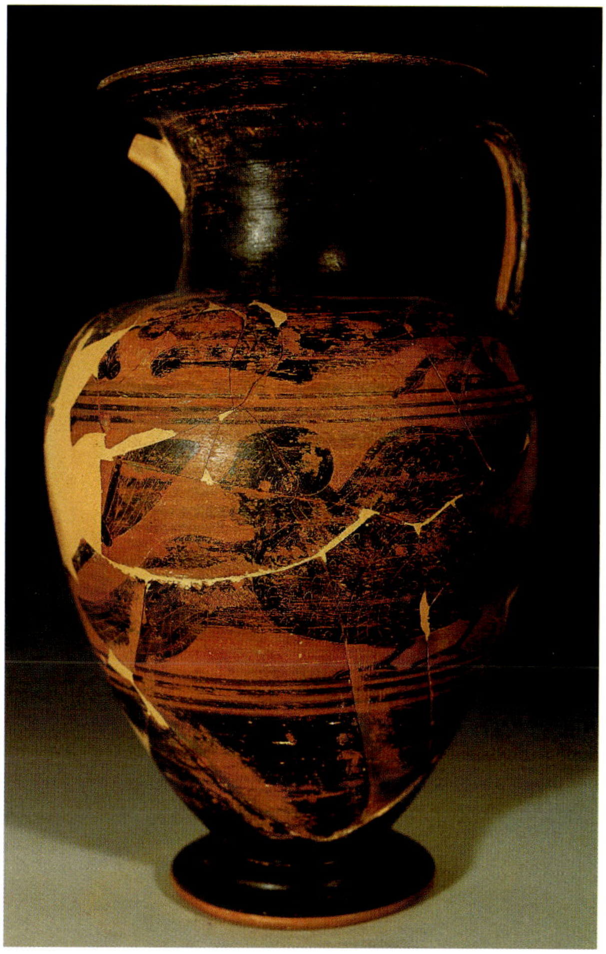

186 **Etruscan black-figure hydria (water vessel) [and detail]**

Painted ceramic
Pitigliano
510-500 BC
Height 46.0 cm

This vessel is attributed to an important Etruscan artist known as the Micali Painter, who worked in Vulci during the last two decades of the 6th and the start of the 5th century BC. He is known to have produced some two hundred vases. Originally influenced by Ionian (East Greek) vase-painting, this vessel shows the influence of Attic vases on his mature style. The decoration includes dancing satyrs on the shoulder, while the principal scene shows Herakles among the gods of Olympus. *GCC/EG*

National Museum of Archaeology, Florence, inv. 4139
Civiltà 1985, 169, no. 5

187 **Etruscan black-figure amphora (container for liquids)**

Painted ceramic
Unknown provenance
End of the 6th century BC
Height 39.5 cm

This vase belongs to a series known as the Orbetello group, and was painted by a follower of the Micali Painter (see number 186). The Micali Painter had many assistants in his very active workshop, and some seem to have set up their own workshops outside Vulci. The shoulder of this vase is decorated with lions, the body with three sirens. *EM/EG*

Museum of Archaeology, Siena, inv. 38477
Mangani 1991, 64, no. 42

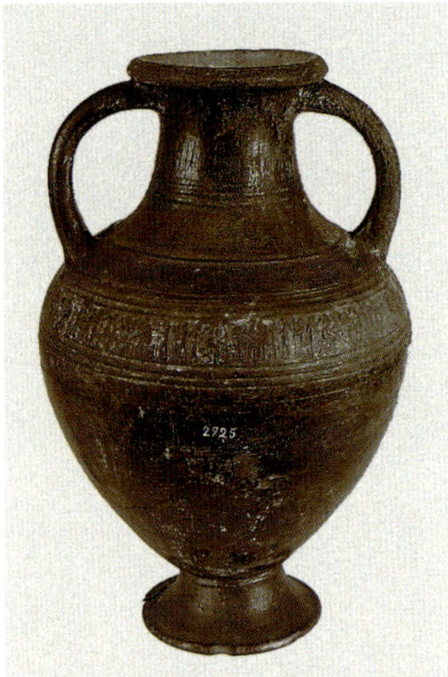

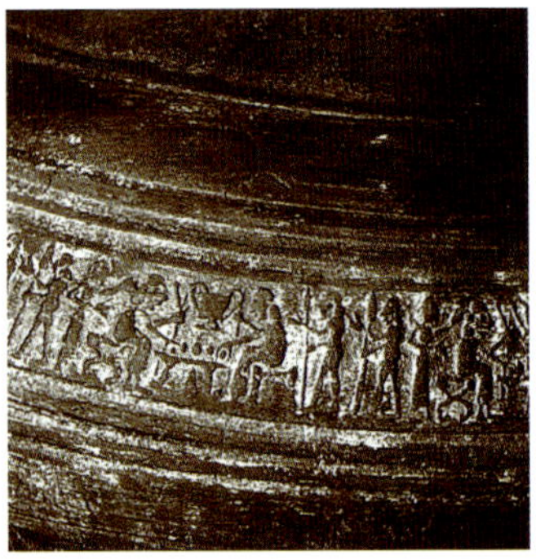

188 **Amphora (container for liquids) [and detail]**

Bucchero pesante
Chiusi region
Second half of the 6th century BC
Height 28.7 cm

The shoulder of this vase of bucchero pesante ('heavy bucchero', characterized by thick walls) was decorated by rolling an engraved cylinder over the surface of the clay. Chiusine bucchero vases decorated in this way have been found only in the Chiusi area, which suggests that they were made locally and specifically for a local market. Chiusi was an important production centre for bucchero ware throughout the 6th century BC. The decoration is of a scene, repeated eleven times, involving a female figure, two male figures seated to either side of a table playing with gaming pieces, and two warriors, which may recall scenes of Ajax and Achilles playing a board game in the presence of Athena. *LV/EG*

National Museum of Archaeology, Florence, inv. 2925
Civiltà 1985, 163, no. 2

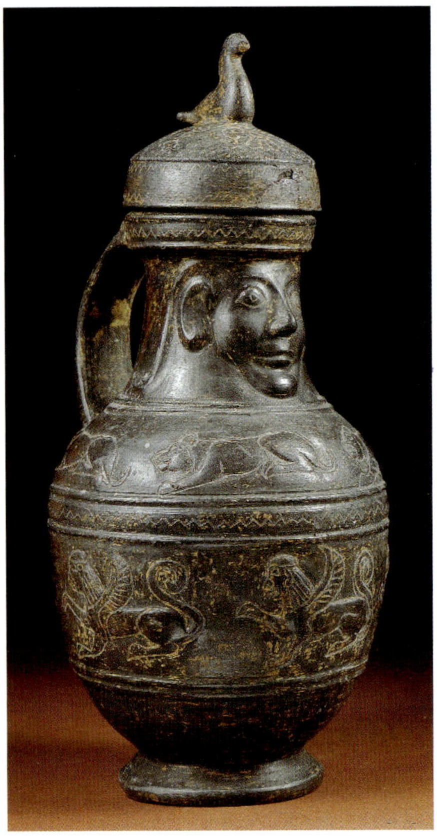

189 **Oinochoe (wine jug)**

Bucchero pesante
Chiusi
6th century BC
Height including lid 36.4 cm

Like numbers 190-194, this wine jug was made in Chiusi and formed part of a bucchero pesante table service (although the pieces are not from the same set). New shapes and forms were introduced in this ware, including foculi like number 192. The decoration was moulded or modelled in the round. The body of this jug is decorated with sphinxes, and there is a human head on the neck which recalls the 'canopic' jars of an earlier period at Chiusi (see numbers 133 and 134). On the lid there is a bird modelled in the round. *SR/EG*

National Museum of Archaeology, Florence, inv. 3179

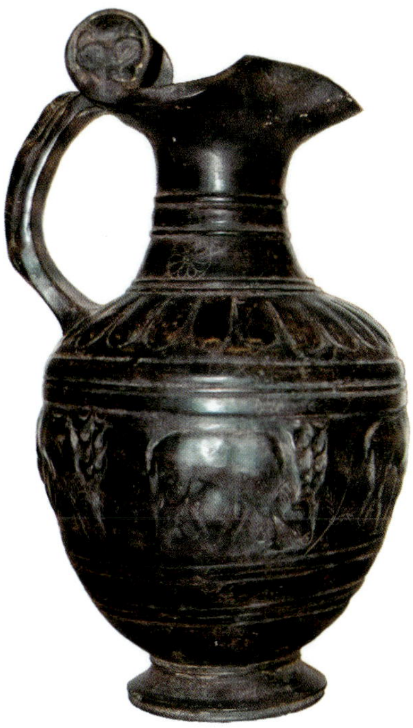

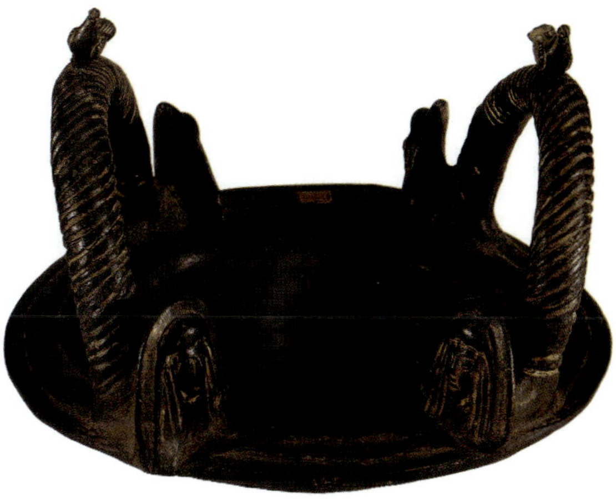

190 **Oinochoe**

Bucchero pesante
Chiusi
6th century BC
Height 35.7 cm

The handle of this jug is decorated with a female in relief, and there is an animal frieze around the body. *DZ*

Museum of Archaeology, Siena, inv. BC217

191 **Tray**

Bucchero pesante
Chiusi
Second half of the 6th century BC
Diameter 37.5 cm; height 20.5 cm

There is a moulded female head in front of the inner face of both ends of the large loop handles. *SR*

National Museum of Archaeology, Florence, inv. 3083

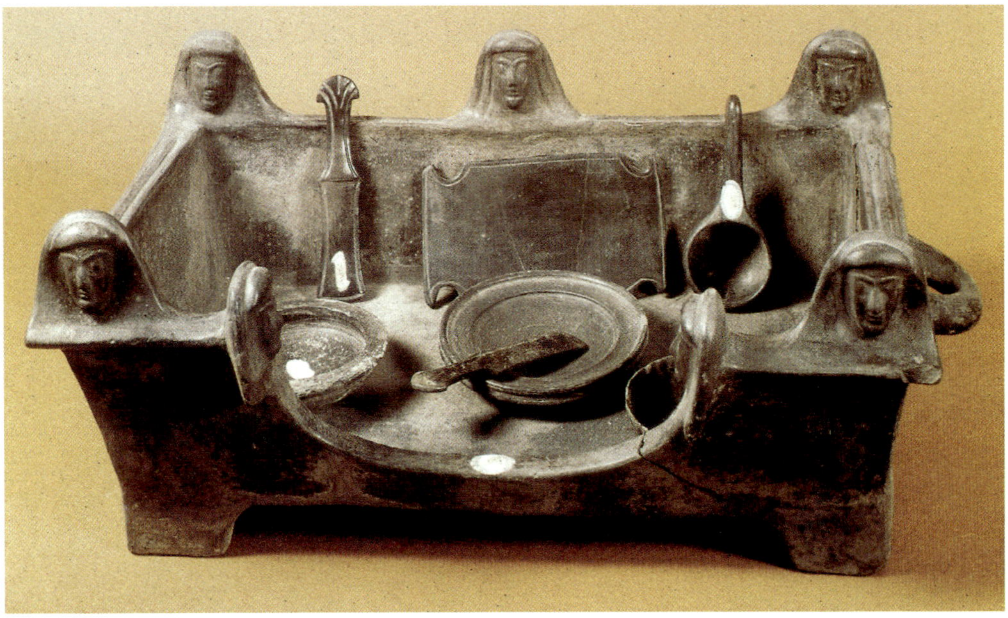

192 Miniature foculo (funerary tray) and accessories

Bucchero pesante
Chiusi
Second half of the 6th century BC

Sets of equipment like this, representing domestic or ritual objects, were made specifically for funerary use. The ten items in the group probably do not all belong to the same set. *SR*

Haynes 2000, 171, fig. 151

(a) Foculo (tray with two handles)

Length 41.7 cm; width 26.0 cm

This was for carrying food.

National Museum of Archaeology, Florence, inv. 3122

(b) Small tray

Length 12.5 cm; width 7.0 cm

National Museum of Archaeology, Florence, inv. 3123

(c) Chalice

Height 8.0 cm

National Museum of Archaeology, Florence, inv. 3124

(d) Small cup

Height 4.0 cm

National Museum of Archaeology, Florence, inv. 3125

(e) Two small plates

Diameters 12.5 cm, 13.0 cm

National Museum of Archaeology, Florence, inv. 3126, 3127

(f) Kyathos (ladle)

Height 4.5 cm

National Museum of Archaeology, Florence, inv. 3128

(g) Pyxis (box)

Height 2.1 cm; diameter 4.7 cm

National Museum of Archaeology, Florence, inv. 3129

(h) Simpulum (ladle)

Length 14.0 cm

National Museum of Archaeology, Florence, inv. 3130

(i) Spoon

Length 13.7 cm

National Museum of Archaeology, Florence, inv. 3131

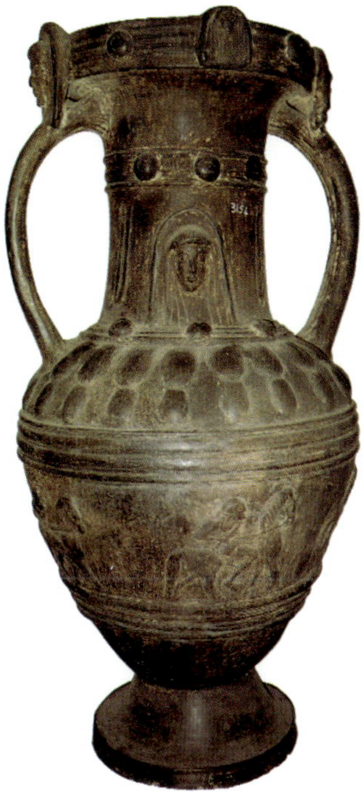

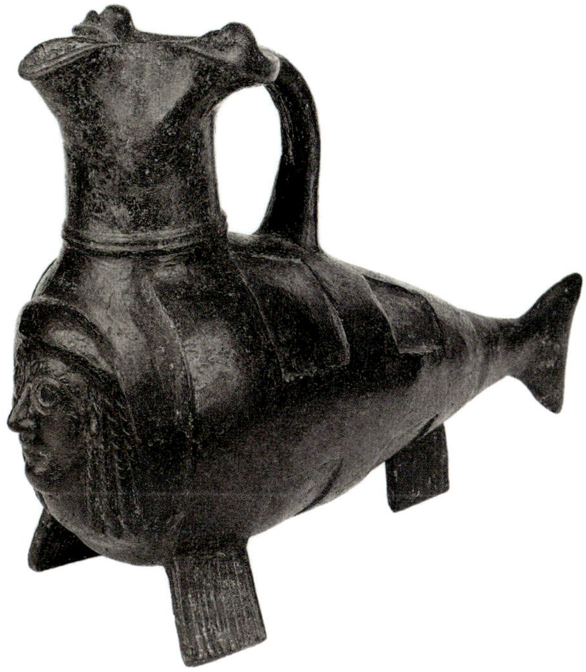

193 **Amphora (container for liquids)**

Bucchero pesante
Chiusi
Second half of the 6th century BC
Height 59.0 cm

The decoration on this tall vessel is derived from metalwork. A procession of horsemen is modelled around the body of the vase. *GCC*

National Museum of Archaeology, Florence, inv. 3154

194 **Askos (jug)**

Bucchero pesante
Chiusi
Second half of the 6th century BC
Height 26.0 cm; length 36.0 cm

This unusual jug with its fish-shaped body and spouted trefoil mouth may have been part of a banqueting set. *GCC*

National Museum of Archaeology, Florence, inv. 3077

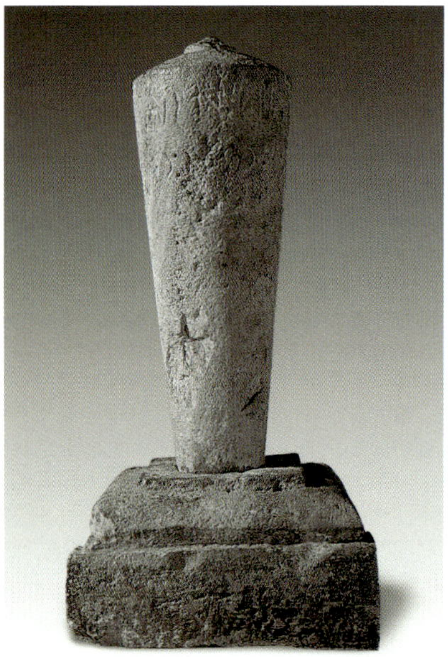

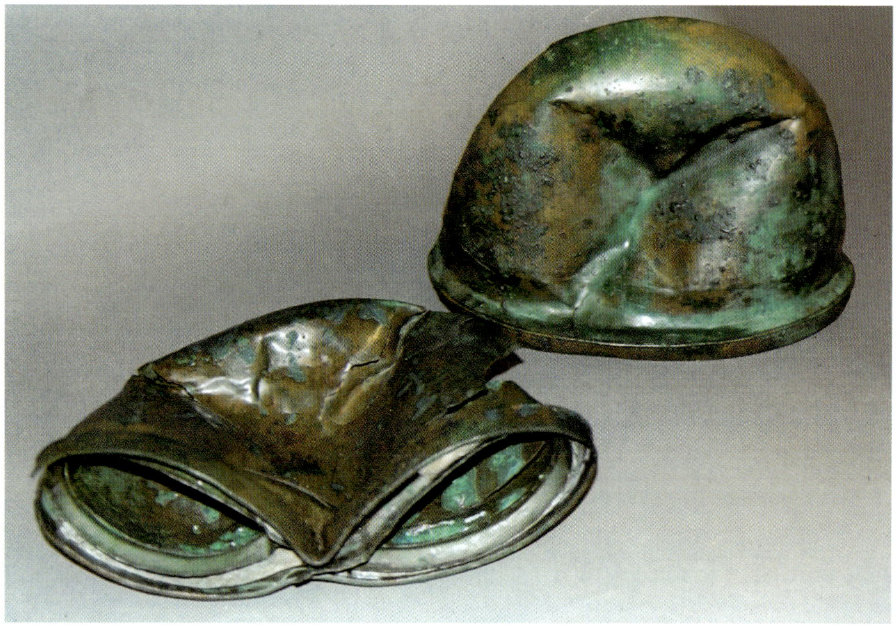

195 Club-shaped cippus (tomb marker)

Travertine
Tomb 18, Casone necropolis, Monteriggioni
5th century BC
Height 70.0 cm

Cippi in the shape of a club have been found in many parts of northern Etruria, especially in the area of Volterra. They were introduced from the start of the 6th century BC, and may imitate earlier examples made from wood. This example has an inscription near the top.

GCC

Guarnacci Museum, Volterra, inv. MG0100

196 Two helmets

Bronze
Vetulonia
Early 5th century BC
Height 21.0 cm

These two helmets of Negau type were among a group of 125 found in a deposit near the walls of the citadel of Vetulonia. They were all deliberately flattened and damaged, ensuring they could not be used, and inscribed with the word 'haspnaś', probably the name of a noble family. The circumstances behind this intriguing deposit may have been connected to Vetulonia's declining fortunes at this time. *GCC/EG*

National Museum of Archaeology, Florence, inv. 8797, 8798
Torelli 2000, 262, 562, cat. no. 70; Haynes 2000, 265

197 Diadem

Gold
Vetulonia
6th to 5th centuries BC
Length 18.2 cm; diameter of plaques 1.8 cm

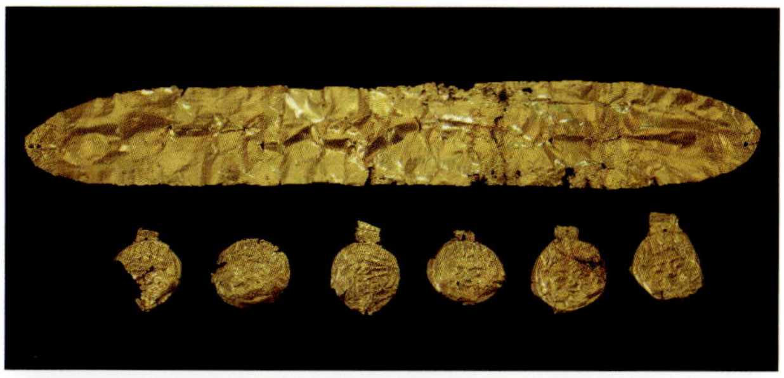

This diadem consists of a rectangular strip of plain gold sheet. It was adorned with six slightly convex pendant plaques, now detached, each decorated with a gorgon's head. The decoration was produced by stamping or rubbing the gold into a matrix. *MCy*

National Museum of Archaeology, Florence, inv. 81094
Gioielli 1988, no. 8; Mágico 1996, 128, no. 57

198 Nine pendant plaques

Gold
Vetulonia
First half of the 5th century BC
Diameter 2.4 cm

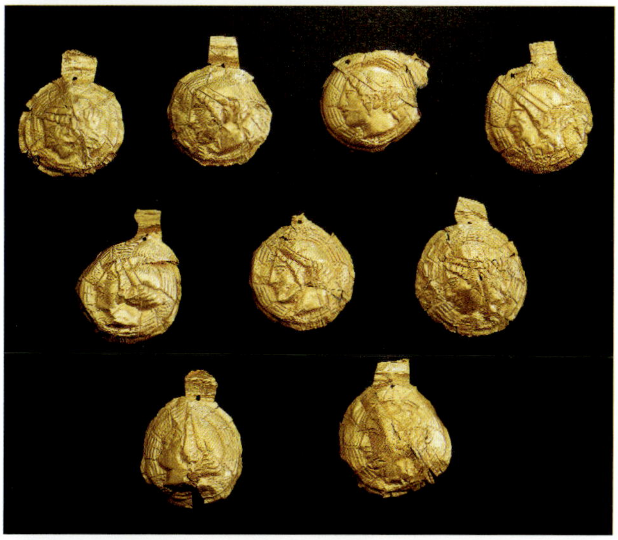

Similar to the pendants attached to number 197, these nine small convex gold plaques are decorated with the profile head of a woman. *MCy*

National Museum of Archaeology, Florence, inv. 81100-81108
Becatti 1955, pl. 315; Gioielli 1988, no. 11; Mágico 1996, 128, no. 58

199 Plaque

Gold
Vetulonia
First half of the 5th century BC
Diameter 4.5 cm

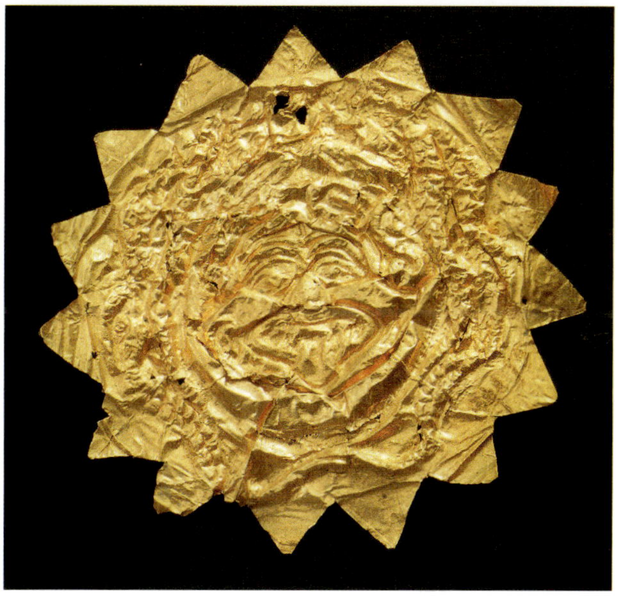

This plaque is decorated with a gorgon's head encircled by a plant motif. *MCy*

National Museum of Archaeology, Florence, inv. 81095
Gioielli 1988, no. 7; Mágico 1996, 128, no. 56

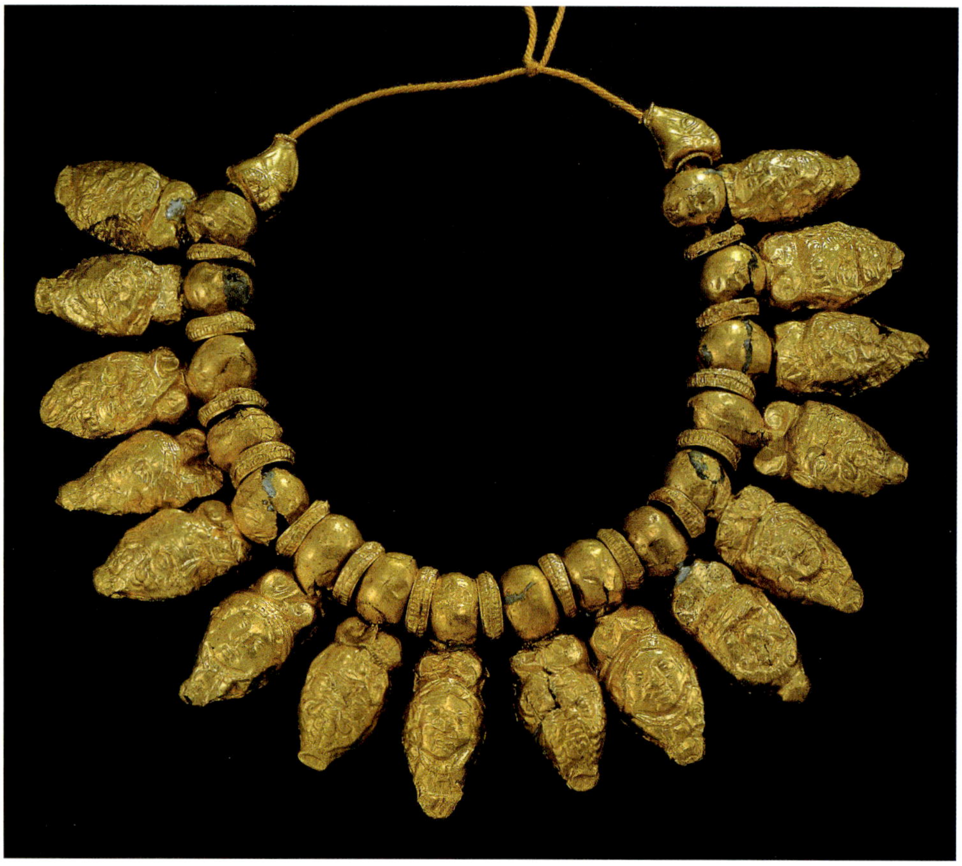

200 **Necklace**

Gold

Volterra, Galuzzi Collection

Third quarter of the 4th century BC

Length 23.5 cm

The 16 pendants of this necklace, made of gold sheet stamped with the heads of maenads and silens, are based on types made in the goldsmiths' workshops of Taras (modern Taranto in South Italy) re-worked to suit local tastes. In mythology the maenads were frenzied women followers of Dionysos, the wine god, and the silens were the drunken sons of Silenus, his elderly companion. The silen's head motif was very popular in the Volterra area, where it was also used on ceramics from the Malacena workshop. The two necklace terminals are in the form of rams' heads. The elements have been re-strung. *MC/EG*

National Museum of Archaeology, Florence, inv. 15951

Civiltà 1985, 146, no. 79; Torelli 2000, 573, cat. no. 95; Cristofani and Martelli 1983, cat. no. 265

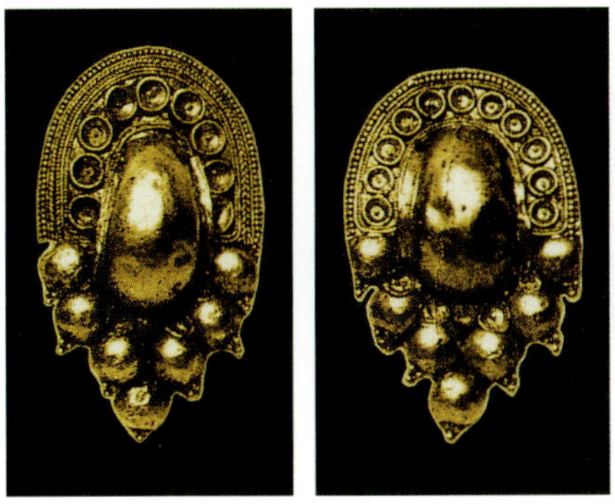

201

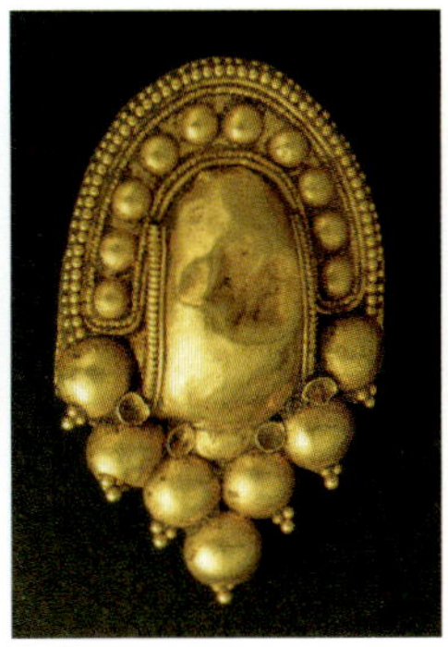

202

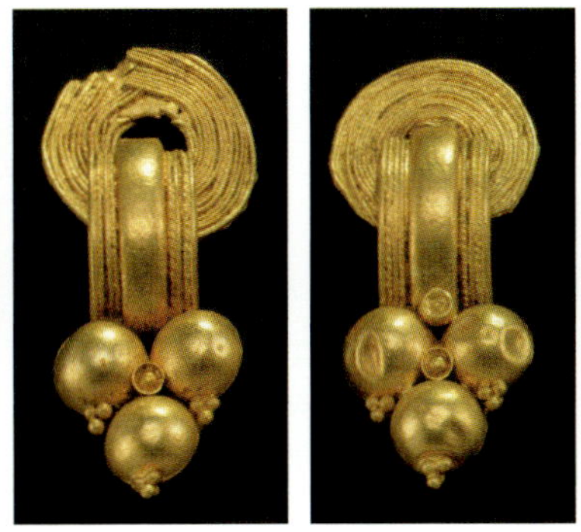

203

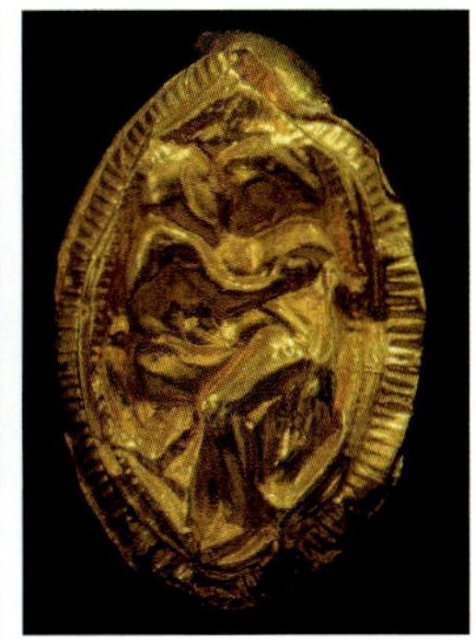

204

201 **Pair of earrings**

Gold
San Cerbone necropolis, Populonia
Second half of the 4th century BC
Height 7.0 cm

National Museum of Archaeology, Florence, inv. 80884, 80885

202 **Earring**

Gold
San Cerbone necropolis, Populonia
Second half of the 4th century BC
Height 3.0 cm

This earring was found out of context, and the tomb in which it had originally been buried is unknown. Other examples of this type of earring (known as 'a grappolo') are known from Populonia (see number 201). The fashion for this style of earring probably began in the last two decades of the 5th century and continued throughout the 4th. The type is often shown being worn in tomb paintings and on sculptures (see number 290). The size of the earrings developed over time, and the decoration became increasingly elaborate, often incorporating figurative and floral elements. *ARo*

National Museum of Archaeology, Florence, inv. 88269
See Cristofani and Martelli 1983, 62-3

203 **Pair of earrings**

Gold
Tomb 16, Peschiera necropolis, Todi
Beginning of the 4th century BC
Height 2.6 cm

Simply decorated with twisted wires and granules, these are amongst the oldest examples of the 'a grappolo' type of earring. Their form developed into earrings like number 202, where the different parts – upper, middle and lower sections – became unified into a single shape, and the lower spheres were replaced by hemispherical elements created out of the same sheet as the body of the earring. *GP*

National Museum of Archaeology, Florence, inv. 74757-1/2

204 **Finger ring**

Gold
Vetulonia
First half of the 4th century BC
Bezel 2.5 × 1.5 cm

This type of ring, which belongs to a series known as the Fortnum group, was made in Etruria from the end of the 5th century BC. It is made from gold sheet. The bezel shows an erotic scene, although other examples have scenes inspired by mythological or heroic subjects. *GCC*

National Museum of Archaeology, Florence, inv. 81113
cf. Boardman 1966, 10ff.; Cristofani and Martelli 1983, 66

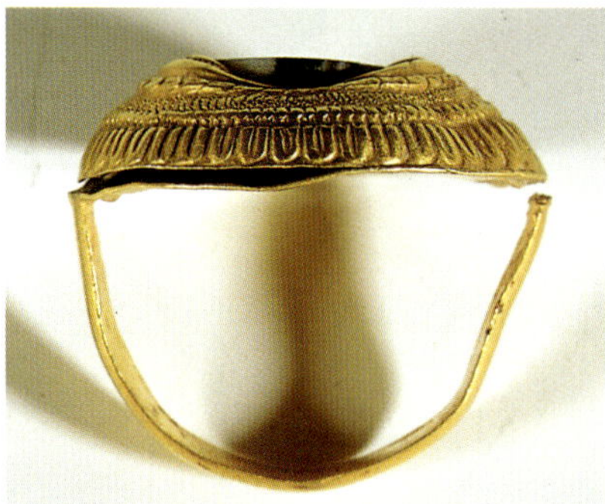

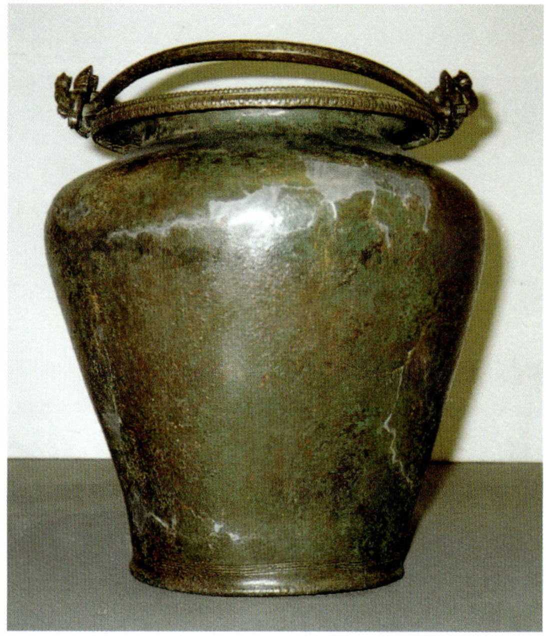

205 Finger ring

Gold, agate
Populonia
Second half of the 4th century BC
Diameter 2.7 cm

The oval gold setting of the ring bezel has been worked from the front and the back. It is set with a banded agate. The type dates from the Late Classical to the Early Hellenistic period. Eye-shaped rings like this one have been found elsewhere in northern Etruria, in Volterra and Chiusi as well as Populonia. *GCC*

National Museum of Archaeology, Florence, inv. P1
Cianferoni 1992, 29, fig. 51, 39-40, no. 102

206 Situla (pail)

Bronze
Populonia
Second half of the 4th century BC
Height 25.0 cm

This would have been used as a wine vessel, forming part of a banqueting set with a ladle and strainer. Situlae of this kind were often deposited in Hellenistic tombs, especially in central and northern Etruria and the Po valley. The type is documented over a long period, from the 5th century to the beginning of the 3rd century BC. This distinctive type, with its double handles, is datable to the second part of the 4th century. *GCC*

National Museum of Archaeology, Florence, inv. 80897
Minto 1922, 204, fig. 60, no. 2; Cianferoni 1992, 145, fig. 1

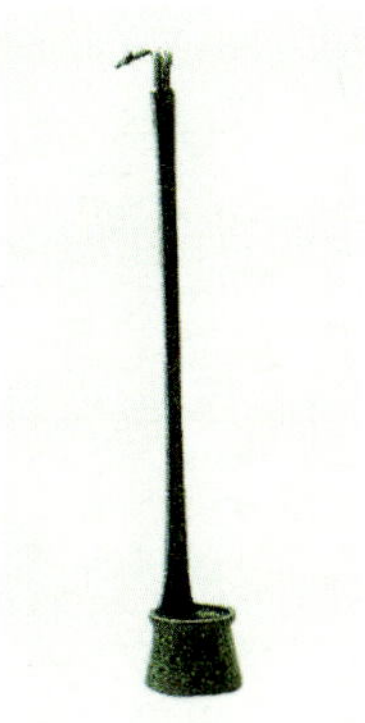

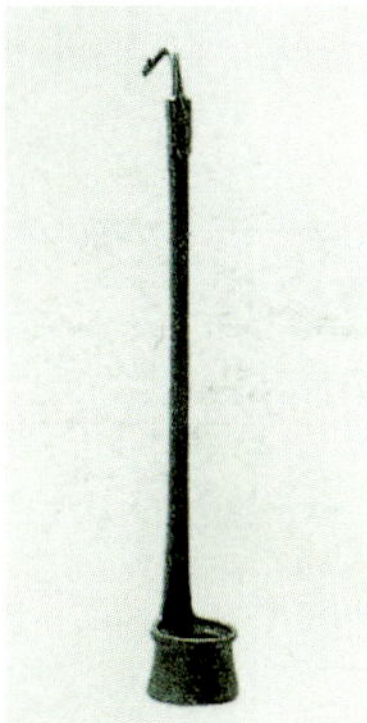

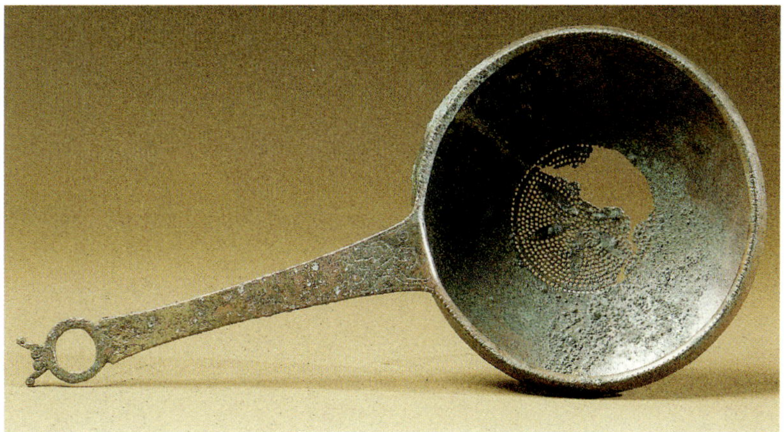

207 **Two simpula (ladles)**

Bronze
Populonia
5th century BC
Lengths 40.0, 37.0 cm

Simpula are always found in pairs. They were used to ladle wine and water out of large vessels and as liquid measures. *GCC/EG*

National Museum of Archaeology, Florence, inv. 77883, 77884
Minto 1922, 200, fig. 59, nos. 1, 2

208 **Colum (strainer)**

Bronze
Populonia
5th century BC
Length 31.0 cm

The colum, part of the banqueting service, was used to strain wine to remove the lees or possibly spices. This type of object was widely used in Italy from the 5th century BC and throughout the Hellenistic period. This example is decorated with a little figure on the handle. *GCC/EG*

National Museum of Archaeology, Florence, inv. 77881
Minto 1922, 200, pl. 59, no. 2

209 **Olpe (jug)**

Bronze
Box tomb 2, La Palazetta necropolis, Bisenzio
Middle of the 5th century BC
Height 17.0 cm

This olpe was found in the same tomb as numbers 210-214. These pieces are typical of the banqueting equipment regularly buried in men's tombs of the 5th and 4th centuries BC.

National Museum of Archaeology, Florence, inv. 74943

210 **Olpe (jug)**

Bronze
Box tomb 2, La Palazetta necropolis, Bisenzio
Middle of the 5th century BC
Height 16.5 cm

National Museum of Archaeology, Florence, inv. 74942

211 **Two simpula (ladles)**

Bronze
Box tomb 2, La Palazetta necropolis, Bisenzio
Middle of the 5th century BC
Lengths 33.0 cm, 50.0 cm

National Museum of Archaeology, Florence, inv. 74931, 74932

212 **Simpulum (ladle)**

Bronze
Box tomb 2, La Palazetta necropolis, Bisenzio
Middle of the 5th century BC
Length 14.8 cm

National Museum of Archaeology, Florence, inv. 74936

213 **Colum (strainer)**

Bronze
Box tomb 2, La Palazetta necropolis, Bisenzio
Middle of the 5th century BC
Length 27.0 cm

National Museum of Archaeology, Florence, inv. 74937

214 **Basin**

Bronze
Box tomb 2, La Palazetta necropolis, Bisenzio
Middle of the 5th century BC
Diameter 54.0 cm

National Museum of Archaeology, Florence, inv. 74933

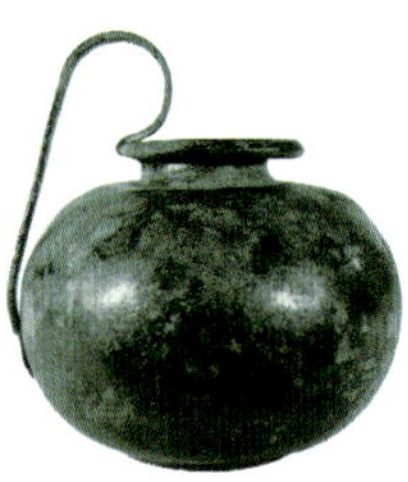
209

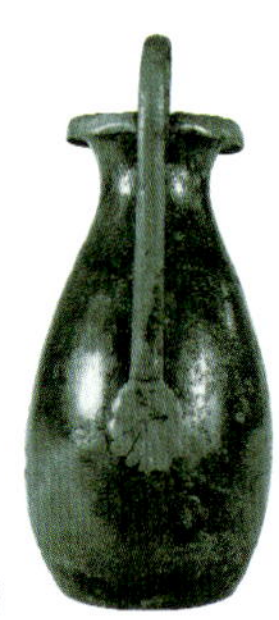
210

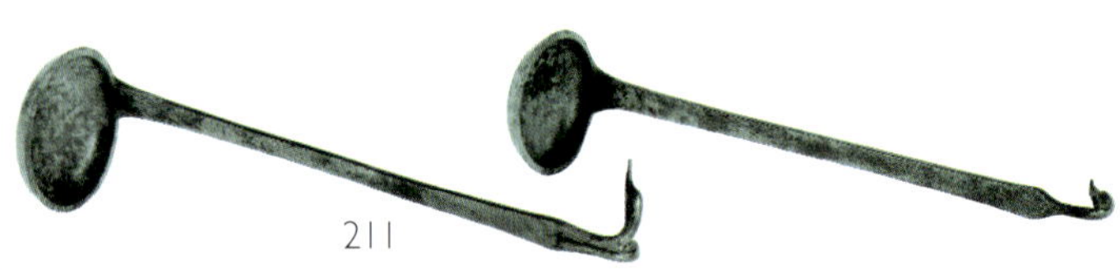
211

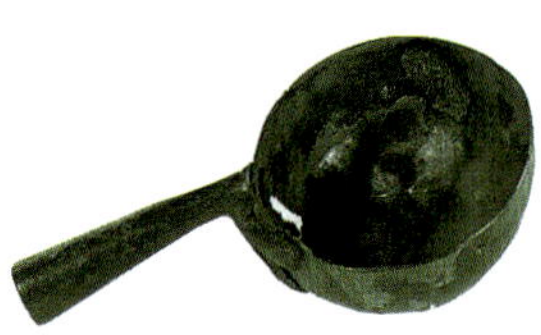
212

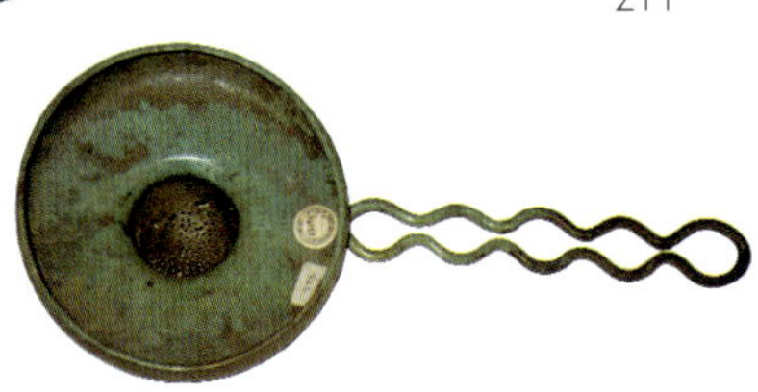
213

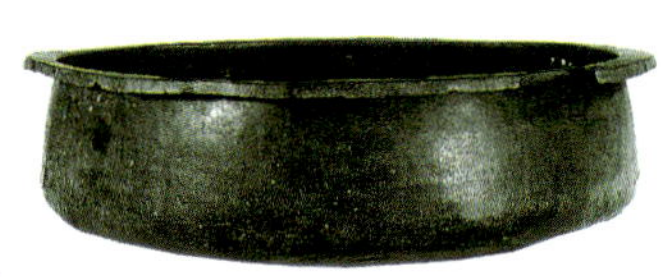
214

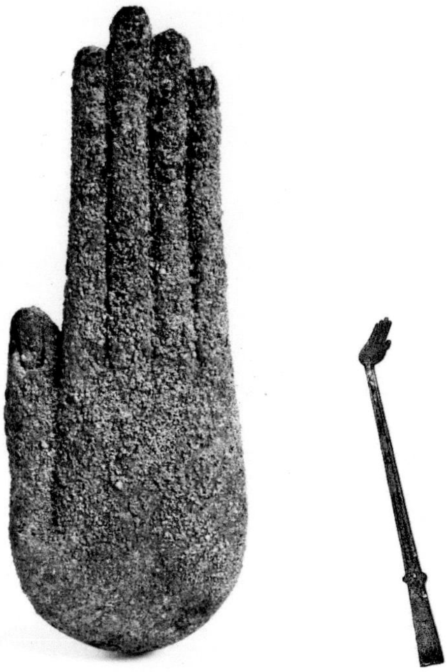

215 **Poker (and detail)**

Bronze
Unknown provenance
5th to 4th centuries BC
Length 36.2 cm

Although pokers have often been found in Etruscan tombs, very few are known with one end in the form of a hand. An important poker was found in an aristocratic woman's grave known as the Tomb of the Hydriai of Meidias in Populonia, which contained many bronzes and jewels. The poker from that tomb was associated with a brazier and other fire-making equipment, suggesting it may have been related to the married woman's social responsibility for the domestic hearth.

GCC

Museum of Archaeology, Siena, inv. 37399
Romualdi 1998, 20

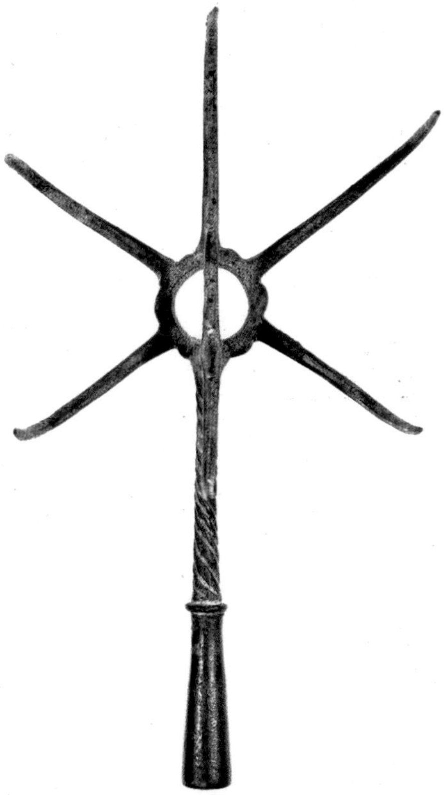

216 **Graffione (possibly a candelabrum)**

Bronze
Unknown provenance
5th to 4th centuries BC
Length 31.5 cm

Many bronze graffioni have been found, mostly dating from the 5th and 4th centuries BC. Their purpose is not certain, but it has been suggested they were used as some kind of candelabrum at banquets. The use of beautifully decorated bronze candelabra is well-documented in Etruria.

GCC/EG

Museum of Archaeology, Siena, inv. 37390

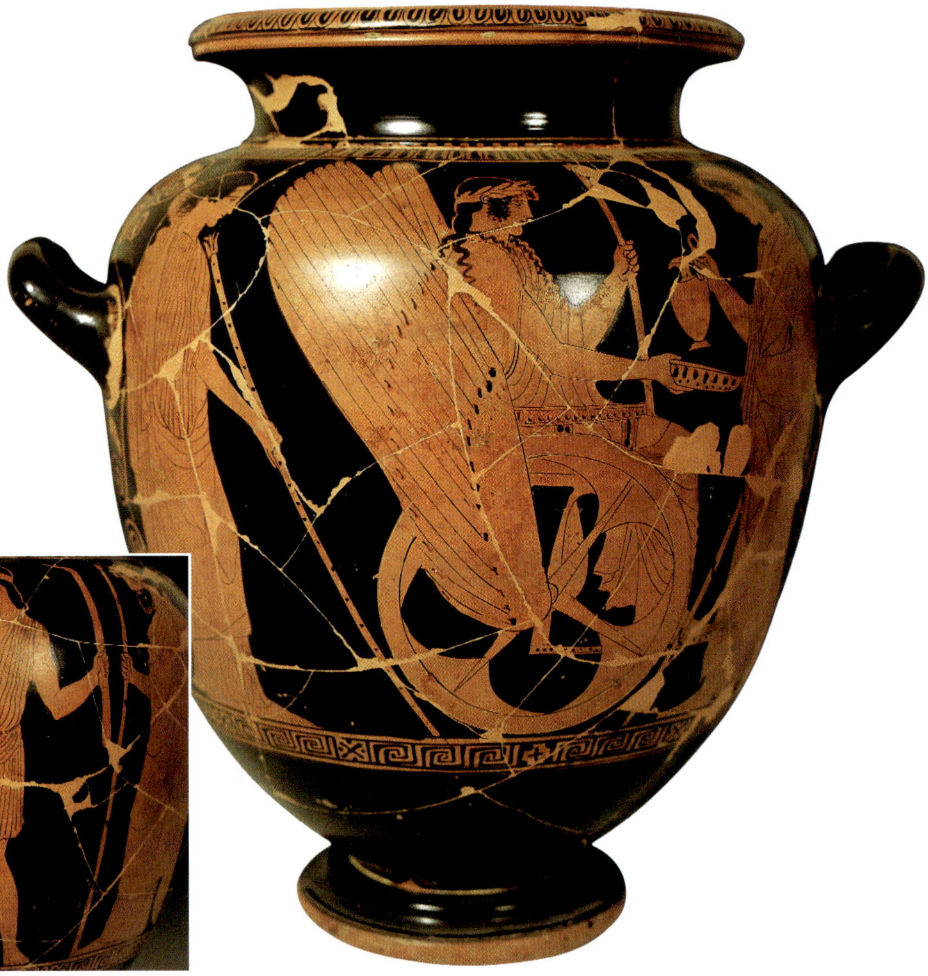

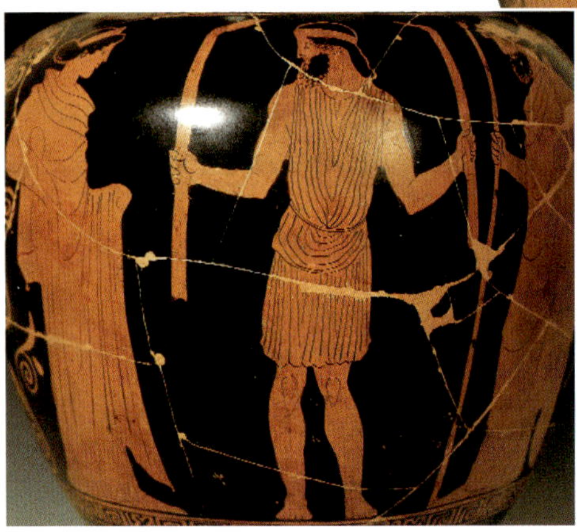

217 **Attic red-figure stamnos (container for liquids) [and detail]**

Painted ceramic

Tomb 3, Crocifisso del Tufo necropolis, Orvieto

Third quarter of the 4th century BC

Height 38.5 cm

In red-figure vase-painting, the lighter-coloured figure decoration was left reserved against a black background. Internal details were indicated using relief lines and brush strokes of diluted clay slip that fired black. This imported stamnos was painted by the Attic red-figure vase-painter Polygnotus. On one side Triptolemos is shown seated between Demeter and Persephone. Triptolemos was a youth chosen by Demeter to bring agriculture and grain to the world. He is usually shown, as here, seated in the winged chariot given to him by the goddess. On the other is a figure of a man with two torches between a king and a woman, probably Hades and Persephone. *GCC/EG*

National Museum of Archaeology, Florence, inv. 75748

Beazley 1963, 1028, no. 1678

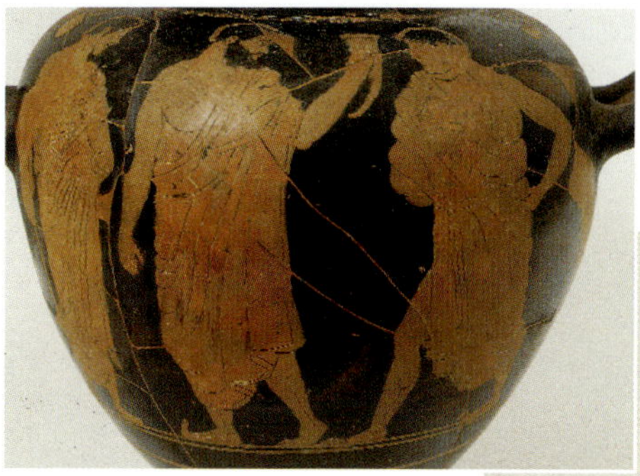

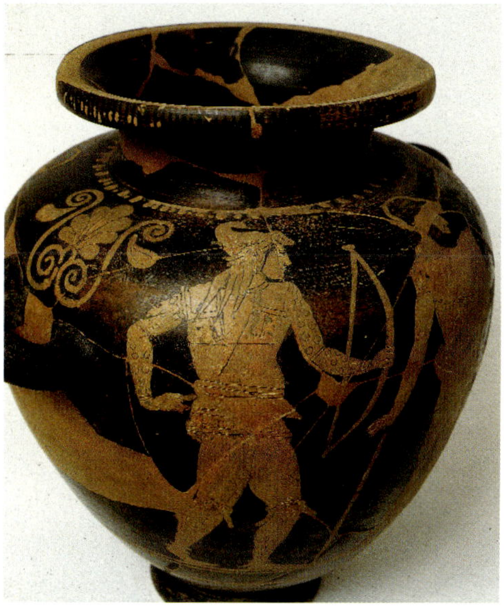

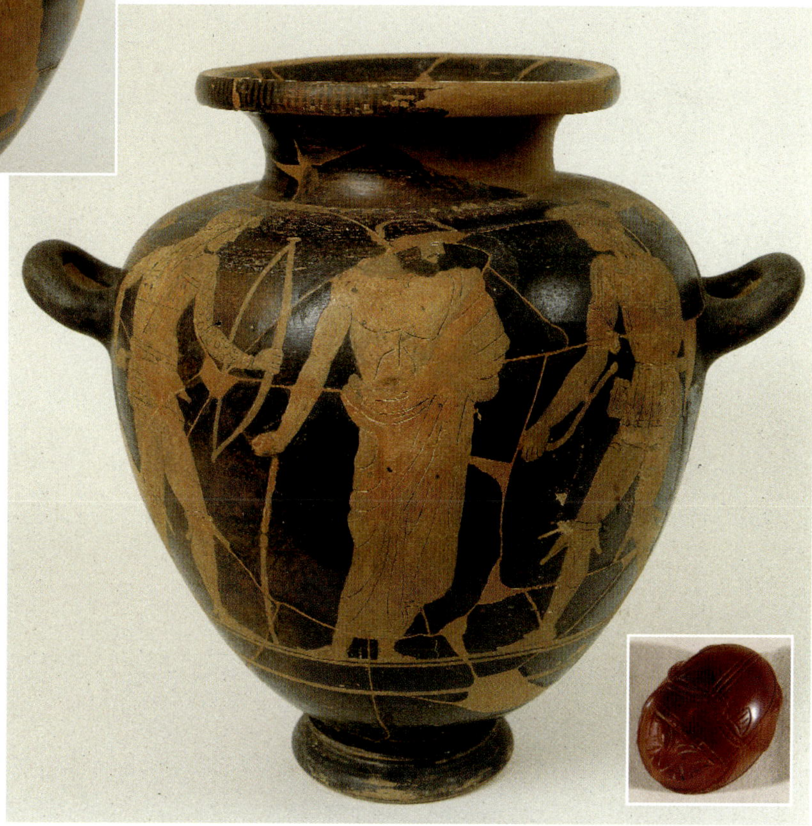

218 Etruscan stamnos (container for liquids) with applied red decoration [and details]

Painted ceramic
San Apollinare necropolis, Sarteano
Middle of the 5th century BC
Height 36.5 cm

This Etruscan stamnos was painted by the vase-painter known as the Bargagli Painter, who worked in Chiusi in the middle of the 5th century BC. It was painted in a style which imitated Attic red-figure vase-painting (see number 217), but the technique is very different. The red areas were painted on top of the black surface and the inner details were then incised through the red paint, exposing the black. This is one of the oldest examples of the applied red technique, developed around 480 BC. It was used in both Vulci and Chiusi, the source of this vase.

The stamnos is decorated with a scene depicting Eurytus, king of Oechalia, and two archers, probably his sons. The scene may refer to the myth that Eurytus held an archery competition, offering his daughter Iole to the man who defeated him and his son Iphitus. The competition was won by Herakles, but the king refused to give up his daughter to him. In one version of the myth, Herakles later killed Eurytus and abducted Iole.

This vase, which was used as a cinerary urn, contained an engraved carnelian scarab. The engraving, which is of the highest quality, shows Theseus armed with a club and a catapult. Etruscan gemstones were produced in great numbers for the domestic market from the late 6th century BC on. *SB/EG*

Museum of Archaeology, Siena, inv. B304
Bruni 1993, 282, fig. 1, pl. 12a-d

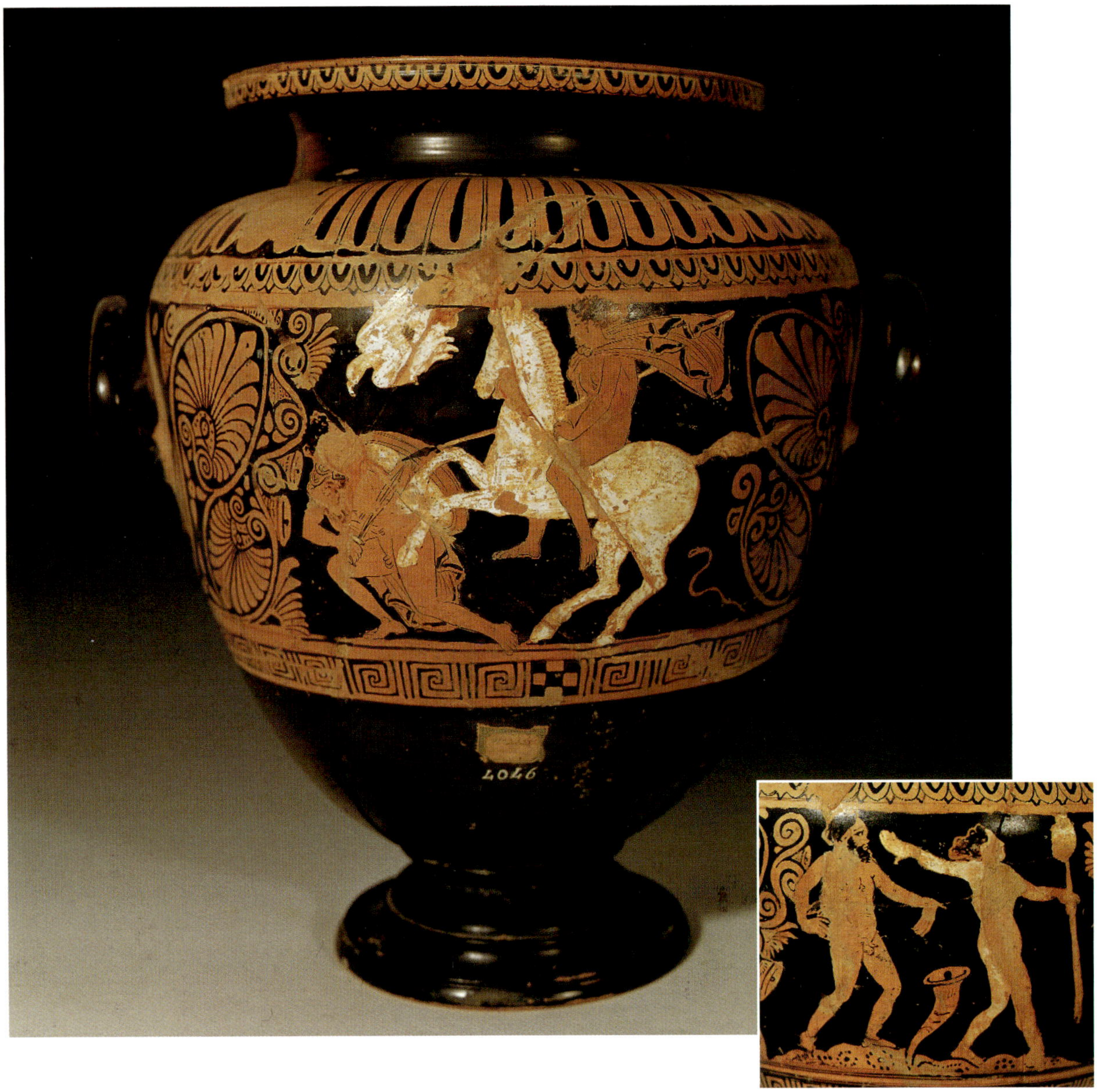

219 Faliscan red-figure stamnos (container for liquids)

Painted ceramic
Unknown provenance
Middle of the 4th century BC
Height 40.0 cm

This red-figure stamnos was made in the Faliscan capital, Falerii Veteres (modern Civita Castellana), and has been attributed to the vase-painter known as the Marconi Painter, one of the most prolific vase-painters of the Faliscan workshops. The supply of imported Attic pottery had almost stopped by the end of the 5th century BC, and new workshops were set up in South Italy and Etruria by immigrant Greek potters and painters to satisfy the continuing demand. Falerii Veteres was an important production centre, making large and medium-sized red-figure vases decorated with mythological scenes from about 380 to 340 BC. Vulci also continued the red-figure tradition and often copied Attic originals from about 400 BC.

One side of this stamnos is decorated with a horseman wielding a spear attacking a warrior crouching in front of his horse. A bird of prey is swooping on the victim. The other side shows a dancing maenad and satyr, revelling followers of the wine god Dionysos. *SB/EG*

National Museum of Archaeology, Florence, inv. 4046
Etruscos 1999, 275-6, no. 450

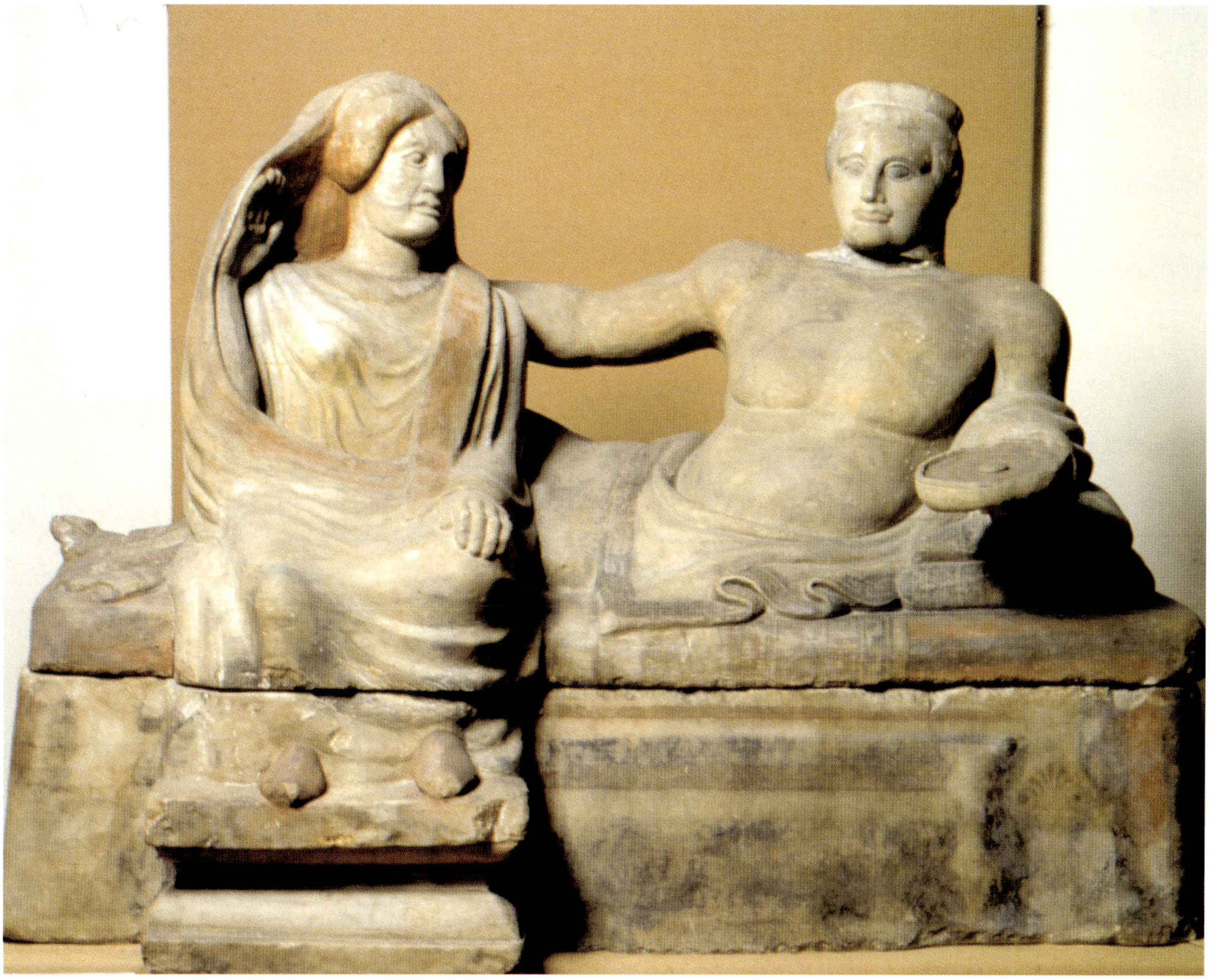

220 **Ash urn**

Painted alabaster
Bottarone, near Città della Pieve (near Chiusi)
Beginning of the 4th century BC
Length 123.0 cm; height 88.0 cm

This ash urn was made in Chiusi. The representation of the wife seated at the feet of her dead husband appears to be unparalleled. She is shown with her head turned slightly towards him, drawing her mantle aside with one hand. The husband is reclining on a banqueting couch, holding a phiale mesomphalos (a dish with a domed centre) in one hand. His other hand rests affectionately on his wife's shoulder. (Doubts about the authenticity of the man's head have led to its removal from the ash urn in the past; it is now thought to be ancient and has been re-joined to the body.) There are extensive traces of paint on the figures' clothing, the couch and the chest of the ash urn. The interior of the chest is divided into two compartments to accommodate a double burial. It contained superb jewellery including gold necklaces, earrings and hair pins. This is apparently the earliest example of the use of alabaster for Chiusine ash urns. Alabaster was used particularly from the second half of the 3rd century BC in Chiusi, replacing the local pietra fetida, a fine-grained limestone smelling strongly of sulphur. *ARo*

National Museum of Archaeology, Florence, inv. 73577
Torelli 2000, 603, cat. no. 194

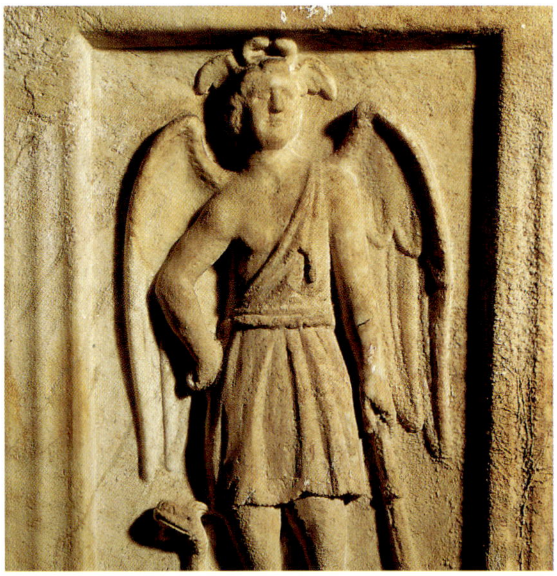

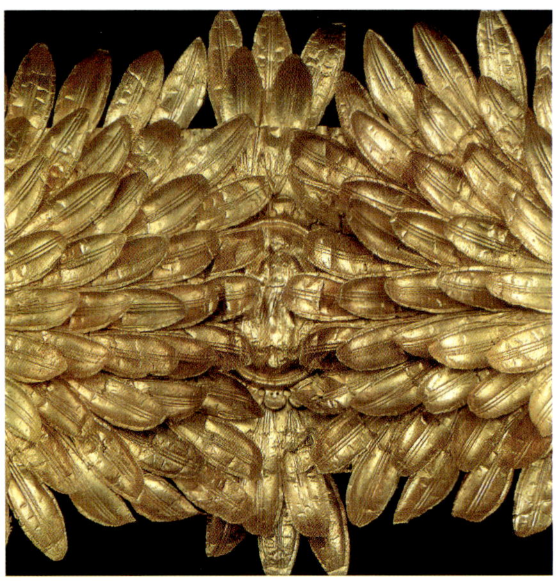

ETRUSCAN DECLINE

About 325–90 BC

It was the rising power of Rome, and its determined ambition for expansion, that led to the protracted but inevitable end of Etruria. Veii, the nearest Etruscan city to Rome, was the first to fall. Although there had been close links between the two in the 6th century BC, these broke down in the 5th. In 406 BC Rome laid siege to Veii, which finally fell ten years later in 396 BC. Veii was sacked and its territories taken over by Roman settlers. For a while there was a period of relative peace as the Etruscans and the Romans faced the advance of the Gauls, who were threatening the territories of both. In 390 BC the Gauls entered Etruria through the Po valley and continued south to Rome. They sacked the city, demanded gold and then withdrew, to be defeated by an army from Cerveteri. The Romans had sent their priests and Vestal Virgins, together with their sacred objects, to Cerveteri for safe-keeping, an indication of the good relationship between the two cities at this time.

The respite was short-lived, however, and the Etruscans soon felt the renewed effects of Rome's aggression as the latter's ambitions to expand led to constant conflict over the subsequent decades. Not long after Rome was defeated by the Gauls, it occupied further cities in southern Etruria. Tarquinian armies faced Rome in a bitter war lasting from 358 to 351 BC, ending in Tarquinia's call for a truce. The Etruscans formed an alliance with the Samnites, Umbrians and Gauls, but this failed to stem the tide, and Rome triumphed at a great battle against the alliance in Umbria in 295 BC. Eventually Rome wore down Etruscan resistance. One by one, Etruscan towns and cities fell into its hands. The last city to fall was Cerveteri (Caere), in 273 BC.

After the fall of Cerveteri, the various Etruscan cities negotiated treaties. Rome consistently gave its support to the aristocracy, the local ruling elites. The Etruscan cities were required to remain loyal to Rome and support its military initiatives. In 225 BC they fought as allies against the Gauls. Twenty years later, in 205 BC, the Etruscans agreed to support Rome's advance into Africa. The Roman historian Livy has recorded fascinating details of the Etruscans' supply of provisions and equipment for Scipio's expedition against Carthage, shedding intriguing light on their economy at the end of the 3rd century BC. Each city, he noted, offered its principal products. Cerveteri supplied grain; Tarquinia supplied cloth for sails; Arezzo provided thousands of weapons and tools as well as wheat; Perusna (Perugia), Chiusi and Roselle provided grain and wood for shipbuilding; Populonia supplied iron, while Volterra gave grain and wood.

Rome's conquest of southern Etruria deprived the local aristocrats of much of their land as the cities lost significant parts of their territories. The turmoil led to the rapid decline of the main cities, which in turn had a severe effect on craft production. In the economic depression that followed defeat, the middle classes, made up of merchants and manufacturers, were impoverished. Alternative means of survival were sought, and many men became professional soldiers. There was also a rise in emigration as many simply left to seek a better future elsewhere. This may account for the fate of a *liber linteus*, a linen book of the 2nd century BC, now in Zagreb. Originally an Etruscan religious calendar written in the Cortona or Perugia area, it somehow reached Egypt, where it was cut up and recycled as part of an Egyptian mummy's funerary wrappings.

By contrast, in northern Etruria the cities continued to enjoy a good standard of living, and the territories that depended upon them thrived. They teemed with settlements and workshops. Agriculture, under the control of the local aristocracy, was intensively practised. A large new social class appeared, made up of freedmen, descended from former slaves, men of modest means who worked in the countryside belonging to the territories of the cities. This class supported the thriving northern Etruscan economy. The strong economic climate enabled the crafts to reach a larger and wider market.

However, standardization and mass-production became the hallmarks of the art of the period. Typical are the terracotta ash urns made in Chiusi, which were mould-made in huge quantities, the stone ash urns of Volterra and Perugia, with their repetitive themes and subjects, and the sarcophagi of Tarquinia and Tuscania. The quality of these products decreased noticeably. Pottery also fell into an artistic decline and vase-painters used a far narrower range of subjects. Narrative compositions were abandoned in favour of isolated, conventionalized figures. The most common images were female heads shown in profile, and simple geometric and floral motifs. A similar decline is apparent in bronze-working, particularly the mirrors, which were decorated simply and with poor quality engraving. Little remains of the artworks which must have adorned the major public buildings. One of the best examples is the great pediment from the 2nd century BC temple at Talamone, south-west of Grosseto, with its terracotta sculptural friezes.

The art of the 3rd to 1st centuries BC traces the integration of Etruria into the sphere of Rome. Although the Etruscan language continued in limited use alongside Latin until the first century AD, the formal end of the Etruscans came with the Augustan settlement of 27 BC, when Etruria became the seventh region of Roman Italy. *SB/EG*

Previous page:
above: detail of an ash urn (no. 223)
below: detail of diadem (no. 234)

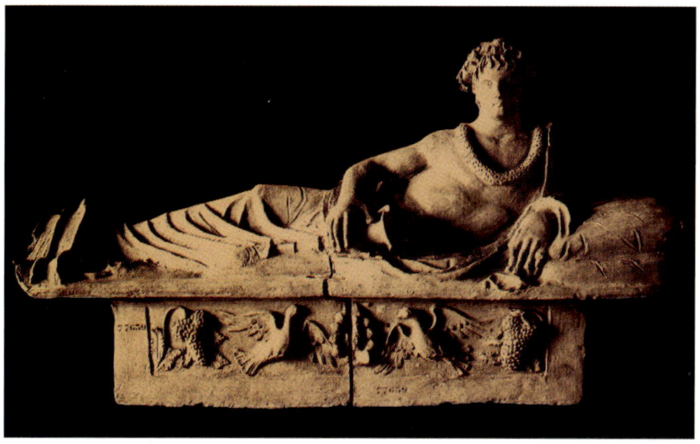

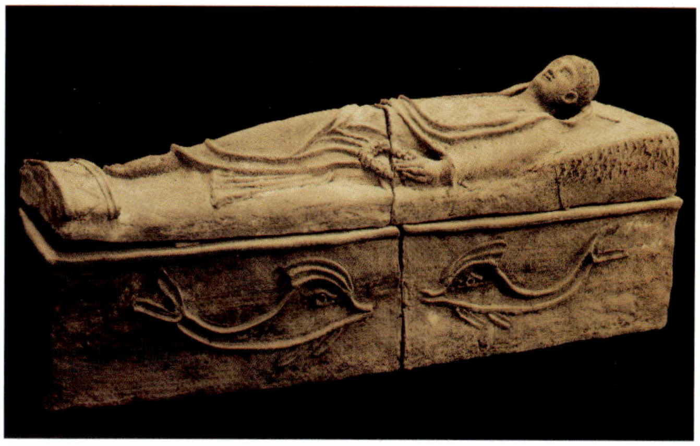

221 Sarcophagus

Terracotta
Unknown provenance
Second half of the 2nd century BC
Maximum length 170.0 cm

The custom of placing the dead in sarcophagi, or coffins, had become standard practice from the 5th century BC, and wealthy family tombs contained large numbers of them. The dead person was shown on the lid, reclining during an eternal banquet. Sarcophagi became increasingly standardized during the 3rd and 2nd centuries, and the rendering of the figures on the lids were more summarily executed. Sarcophagi began to be made in terracotta during the 2nd century BC. They were produced in moulds, with extra detailing added later by hand. *SB/EG*

National Museum of Archaeology, Florence, inv. 77639

222 Sarcophagus

Terracotta
Statlane tomb, Tuscania
End of the 2nd century BC
Maximum length 189.0 cm

This sarcophagus is from a tomb at Tuscania, near Tarquinia, which belonged to one of the local aristocratic families, the Statlane. Sarcophagi like these were intended for wealthy aristocrats, and copy types from the workshops of Tarquinia. Over time, the detailing on the sarcophagi became increasingly simplified. The lid, made in two parts, is sculpted with the representation of a recumbent man wearing a long toga. The man's hair and facial features are carefully defined, although the details of the clothing are more schematic. The chest is decorated with the outlines of dolphins worked in relief, and there are traces of red and white paint. *SB/EG*

National Museum of Archaeology, Florence, inv. 75676 (lid), 75977 (chest)

Etruscos 1999, 266, no. 418

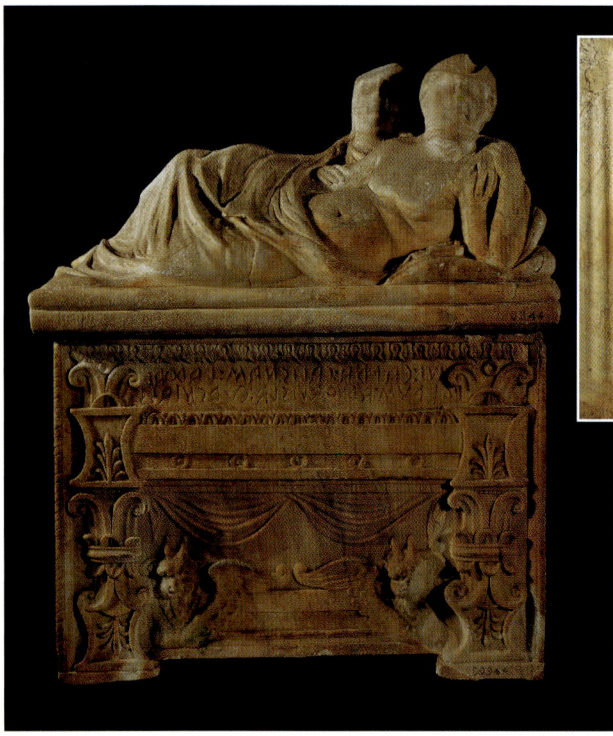

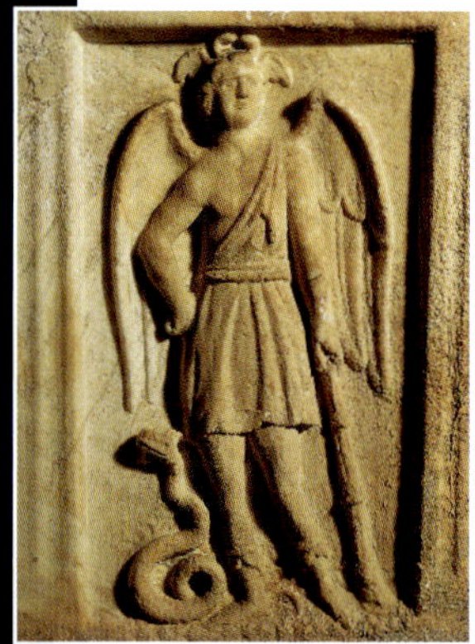

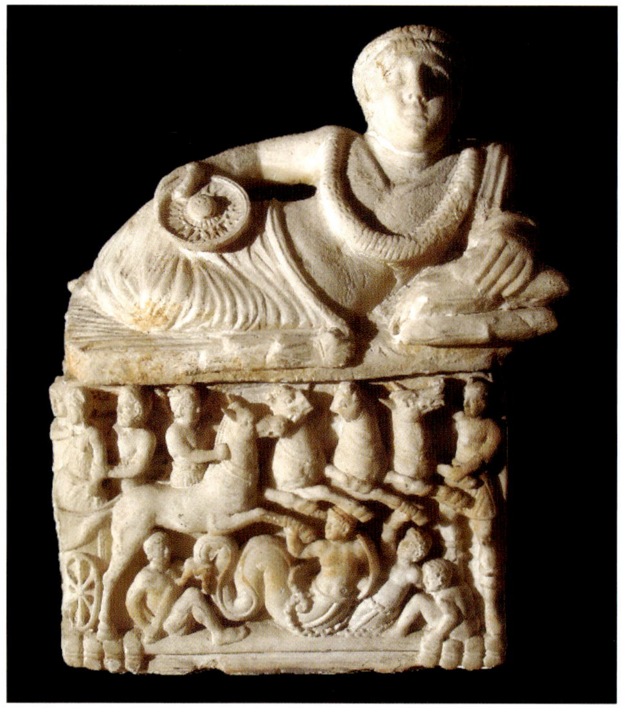

223 Ash urn (and detail)

Alabaster
Caliśna Sepu family tomb, Monteriggioni (Siena)
2nd century BC
Maximum length 87.5 cm; height 105.0 cm

On sarcophagi and ash urns, the dead were shown reclining on a couch at a banquet, either alone or with a spouse. A husband and wife are represented together on the lid of this urn; unlike the Greeks, the Etruscans often showed wives alongside their husbands at banquets. The figures are of an elderly couple, shown lying on cushions. The figures on the lid had been deliberately covered with a large terracotta tile, intended to protect them from water damage. The chest is elaborately decorated and bears an inscription giving the names of the dead. Inside the urn is divided in two and houses the couple's ashes wrapped in cloth. There are traces of gilding on the rings worn by both figures on the ring fingers of their left hands.

The urn was made in Volterra, one of the most important production centres for ash urns from the end of the 3rd century BC. It is unusually large in scale. The urns were usually made of alabaster, like this one, tufa or, more rarely, terracotta. The chests were ornamented with relief scenes or decorative motifs. *GCC*

National Museum of Archaeology, Florence, inv. 80944

224 Ash urn

Alabaster
Barberino Val d'Elsa (Florence)
2nd century BC
Maximum length 69.0 cm; height 91.0 cm

The reclining man shown on the lid wears a garland around his neck and a wreath on his head. He holds a patera (a shallow libation dish) in his right hand. There are traces of red on the cloak draped over his left shoulder. The front of the chest is decorated with elaborately detailed scenes of a four-horse chariot and the rape of Persephone by Hades, king of the Underworld. *GCC*

National Museum of Archaeology, Florence, inv. 92061

225 ## Ash urn

Alabaster
Barberino Val d'Elsa (Florence)
2nd century BC
Maximum length 65.0 cm; height 80.0 cm

The woman on the lid of this urn wears a necklace and bracelet. Her head is supported on her left hand and she holds a fan in her right hand. An inscription is visible along the front edge of the lid. *GCC*

National Museum of Archaeology, Florence, inv. 92054

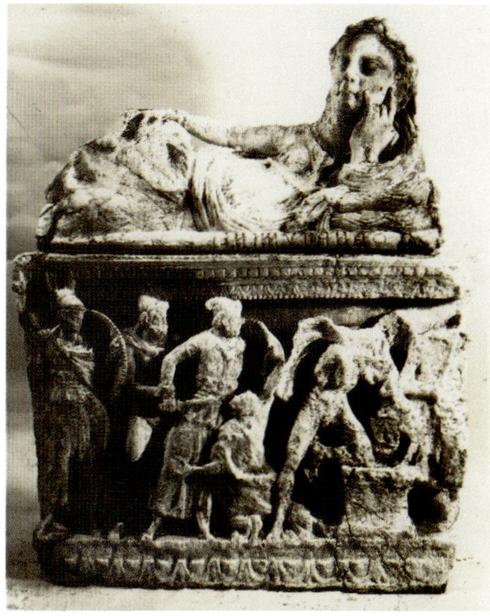

226 ## Ash urn

Travertine
Barberino Val d'Elsa (Florence)
2nd century BC
Maximum length 57.0 cm; height 80.0 cm

The man on the lid holds a patera (a shallow libation dish) in his right hand. The chest is decorated with a pair of lions or griffins to either side of a large amphora. *GCC*

National Museum of Archaeology, Florence, inv. 92056

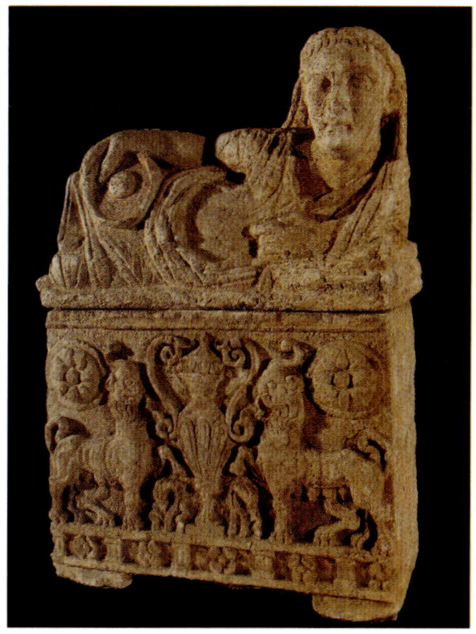

227 ## Ash urn

Travertine
Barberino Val d'Elsa (Florence)
2nd century BC
Maximum length 62.0 cm

The reclining woman on the lid is wearing a diadem decorated with rosettes. Her chiton (tunic) is pinned at the shoulder and belted at the waist. She also wears a necklace. A pomegranate, a symbol of death, rebirth and fertility, is held in her right hand. The chest is decorated with a scene of parting from the dead. *GCC*

National Museum of Archaeology, Florence, inv. 92055

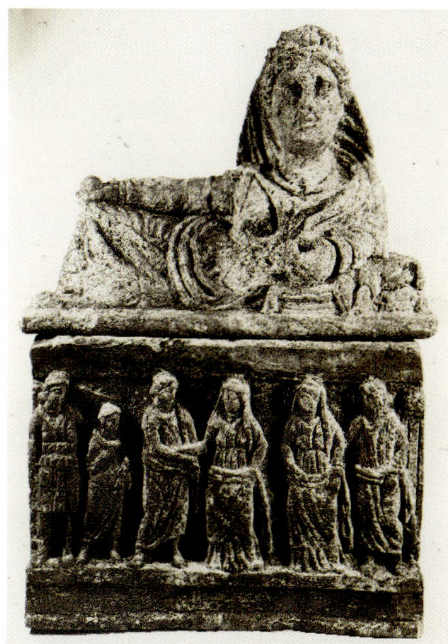

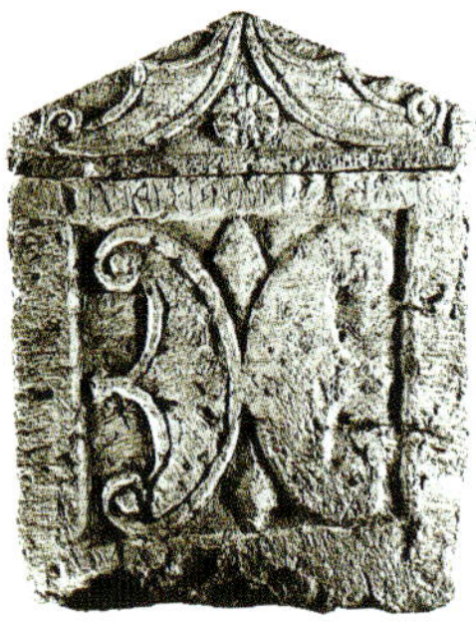

228

Ash urn

Travertine

Monterone, Perusna (Perugia)

2nd century BC

Length 51.0 cm; height 62.0 cm

This type of ash urn, with its lid in the form of a ridge roof, is characteristic of the Perugia area from the late 4th to the middle of the 1st century BC. They were usually made of local travertine stone, and produced in large numbers to suit local taste. They are generally less accomplished than those made in Volterra and Chiusi, and tend to have more generic relief scenes or simple symbolic motifs. This example has an inscription at the top of the chest. *AM*

National Museum of Archaeology, Florence, inv. 86707 (lid); 86728 (chest)

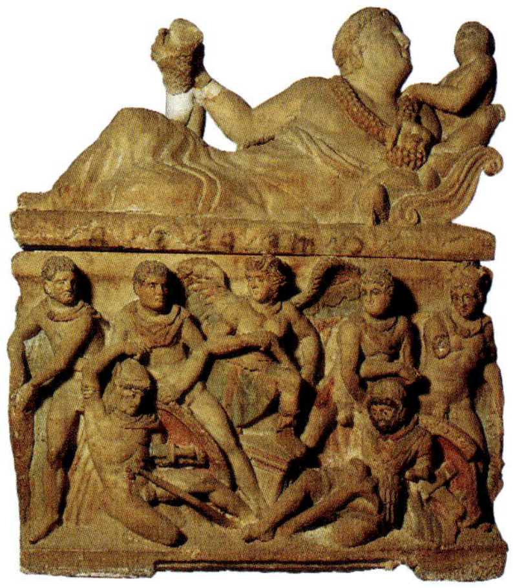

229

Ash urn

Alabaster

Sentinate Cumere tomb, Sarteano

End of the 3rd century BC

Maximum height 100.0 cm; maximum length 82.0 cm

The reclining man on the lid wears a garland around his neck and holds a rhyton (drinking vessel). An inscription on the edge of the lid gives his name: *larth cumeresa*. The scene on the chest shows the battle between Eteokles and Polyneikes, sons of Oedipus, who killed each other in their fight over succession to their father, a popular Chiusine subject. This ash urn is typical of the finest quality alabaster urns from Chiusi. Numerous traces of paint survive on its surface. Alabaster was in great demand for ash urns in Chiusi throughout the 3rd century. By the first decades of the 2nd century, alabaster was superseded by travertine, and by the middle of the 2nd century terracotta urns predominated in Chiusi until the 1st century BC. *IO*

Museum of Archaeology, Siena, inv. B731

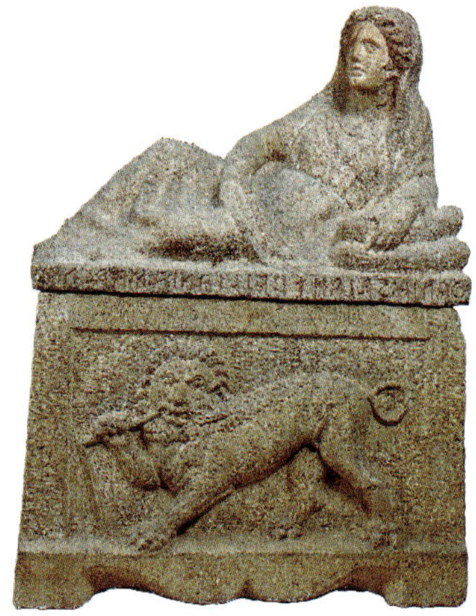

230

Ash urn

Travertine

Sarteano

Second quarter of the 2nd century BC

Maximum height 110.0 cm; maximum length 78.0 cm

The detailing of the reclining woman on the lid illustrates a common surface treatment used in Chiusi. The areas of the woman's skin have been polished, whereas the clothing has been textured with a chisel, creating strong surface contrasts. *AM*

Museum of Archaeology, Siena, inv. B726

Artigianato 1985, 49, no. 27

Some scholars have expressed reservations about the authenticity of the lion carved on the chest. They have also suggested that the lid may not have originally belonged to this chest. *EG*

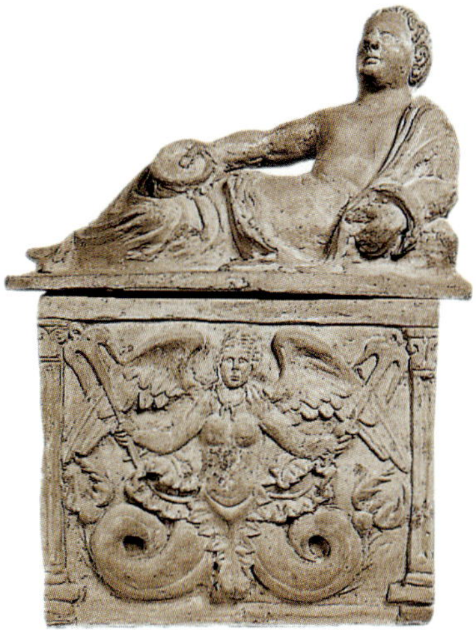

231

Ash urn

Terracotta

Chiusi

First half of the 2nd century BC

Maximum height 62.0 cm; maximum length 46.0 cm

The reclining man on the lid holds a patera (a shallow libation dish). The mythological sea monster Scylla, holding two anchors, is represented on the chest. Scylla is often shown on ash urns, on the earlier alabaster and travertine examples as well as the terracotta ones. *AR/EG*

Museum of Archaeology, Siena, inv. C100

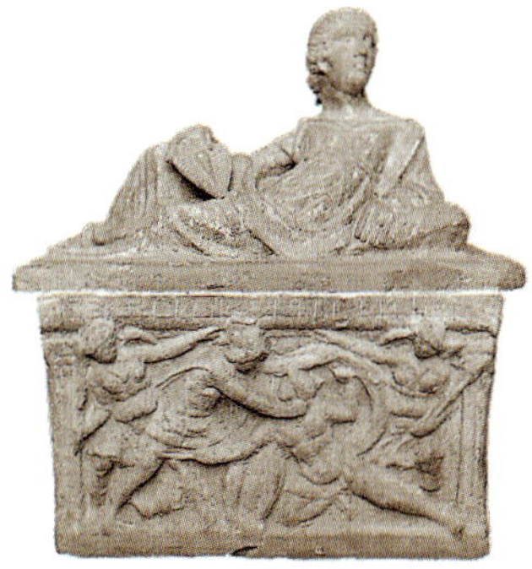

232

Ash urn

Terracotta

Sarteano

2nd century BC

Maximum height 53.0 cm; maximum length 44.5 cm

A reclining woman is shown on the lid. On the chest there is a representation of the fight between Eteokles and Polyneikes in the presence of female demons (see also number 229). This was one of the most popular scenes on the terracotta urns of Chiusi. Hundreds of identical mass-produced examples are known, all taken from a single mould. Urns like these were made for the large class of people of limited means who lived and died in the rural areas around Chiusi. *AR/EG*

Museum of Archaeology, Siena, inv. 68039

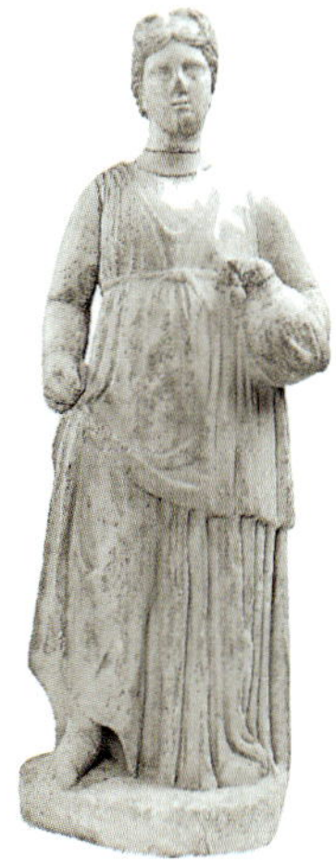

233

Statue of a woman

Marble

Unknown provenance

Last decades of the 3rd century BC

Height 68.0 cm

The woman is dressed in a chiton (a long, sleeveless tunic), girdled high under the breasts. She is holding a dove (a typical offering) in her left hand. The head does not belong to the body and was made by a different, more accomplished sculptor. The statue may be compared with a group of female funerary statuettes from the Volterra area. Such funerary statues are fairly rare, and may have served as tomb markers for women of wealthy families. *GCC/EG*

Museum of Archaeology, Siena, inv. P100

For more information about these funerary statues, see Bonamici in Artigianato 1985, 123ff.

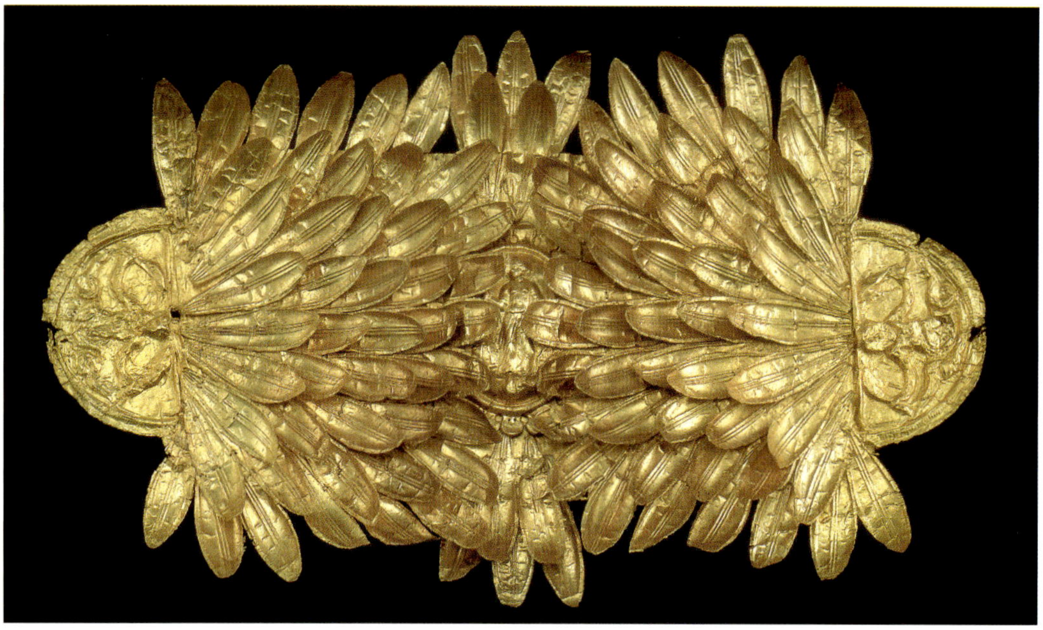

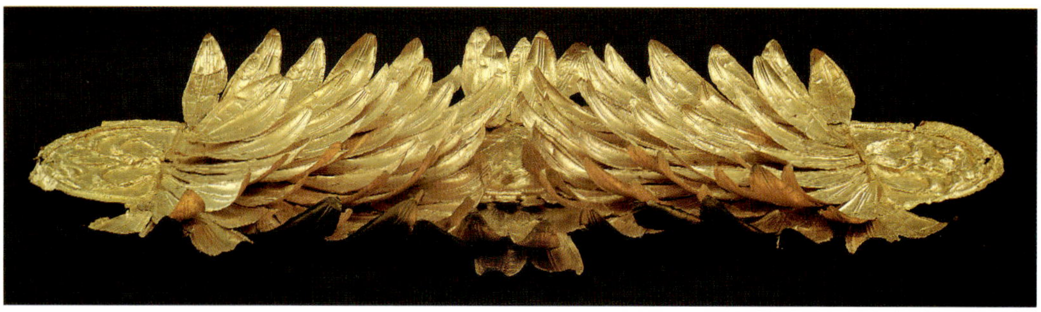

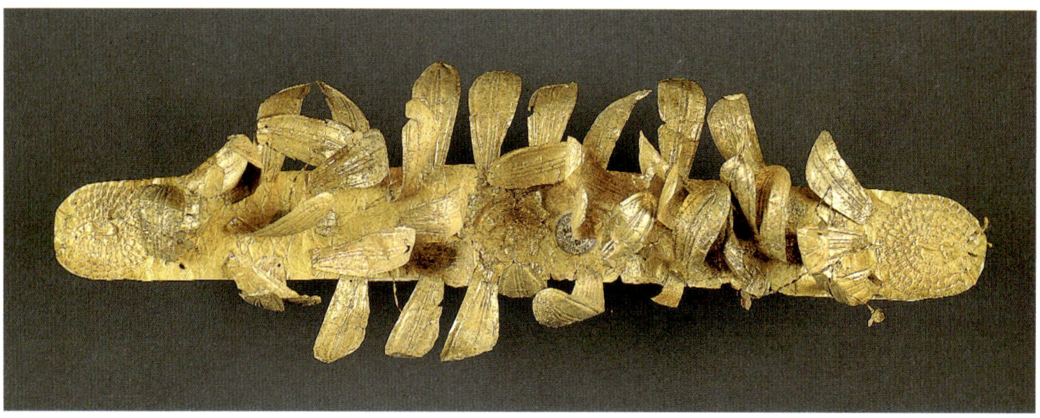

234 **Diadem (two views)**

Gold

Sperandio necropolis, Perugia

End of the 4th century BC

Length 33.0 cm

The Hellenistic diadems of Etruria were made of rectangular gold sheet with rounded ends and decorated with repoussé. The rounded ends of this example are decorated with the monster Typhon holding dolphins. Numerous gold leaves, also in repoussé, were attached to the front through slits. There is a central roundel with a representation of a winged female figure holding a mirror and a perfume jar. Diadems were worn by men and women, in life as well as in death, and were a symbol of honour, prestige and wealth, emphasizing the status and political and economic power of the individual within the community. *GCC/EG*

National Museum of Archaeology, Florence, inv. 84339

Torelli 2000, 574, cat. no. 102

235 **Diadem**

Gold

Chiusi

End of the 4th century BC

Length 30.0 cm

National Museum of Archaeology, Florence, inv. 83374

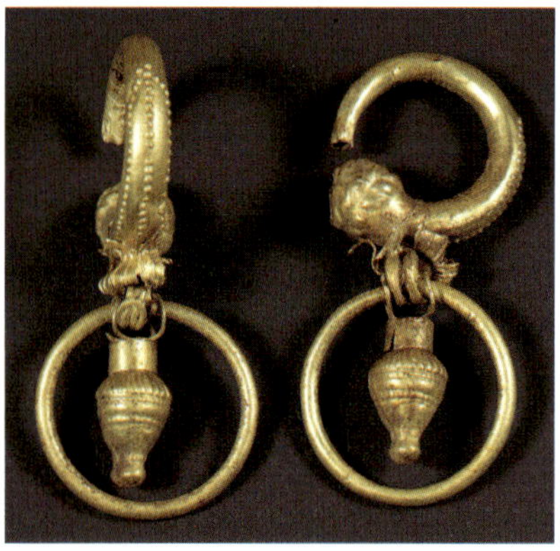

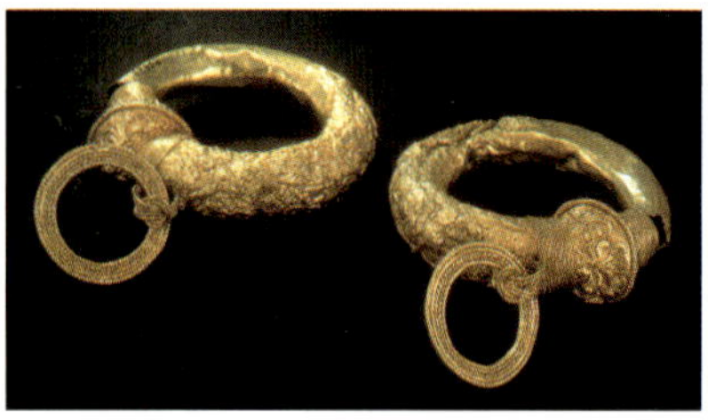

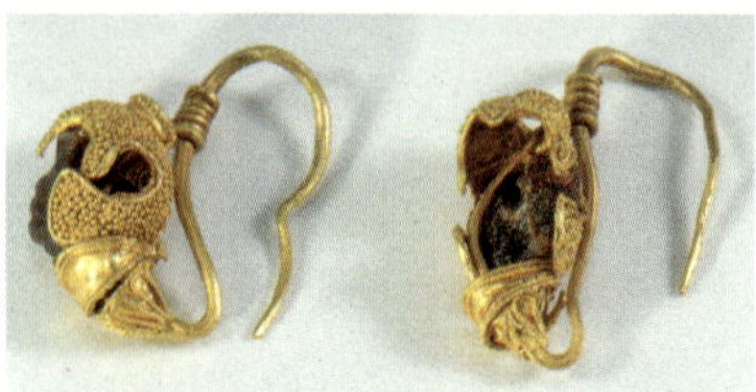

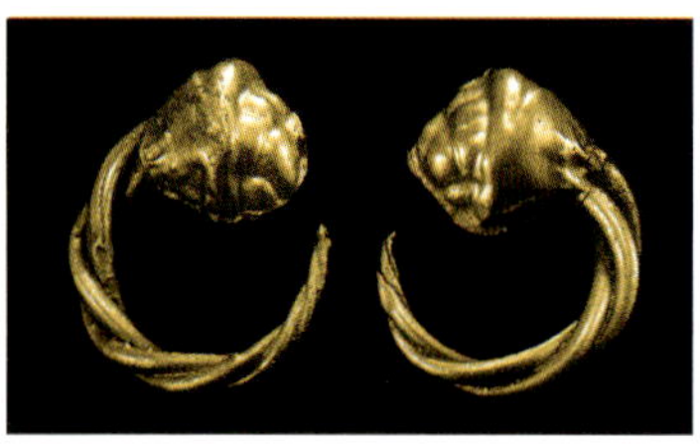

236 **Earrings**

Gold

Tomb 20, Peschiera necropolis, Todi

Middle or third quarter of the 4th century BC

Length 7.3cm

This type of earring has been found in Aleria, Corsica, dating to the second half of the 5th century BC. It spread mainly through the northern part of Etruria during the 4th and 3rd centuries, becoming increasingly more complex. These examples have been elaborated by the addition of a ring and a pendant shaped like a jar. These particular earrings have been dated by their tomb context. *GCC*

National Museum of Archaeology, Florence, inv. 74786-1/2

Mágico 1996, 132, no. 66; for the development of the earring type, see Cristofani and Martelli 1983, 63.

237 **Earrings**

Gold

Unknown provenance

Second half of the 4th to the beginning of the 3rd century BC

Length 7.3 cm

Another, more elaborate example of the type represented by number 236. The sheet gold was richly decorated using a matrix, and embellished with fine filigree and granulated details. *MCy/EG*

National Museum of Archaeology, Florence, inv. 15742, 15824

Gioielli 1988, 150, no. 90

238 **Earrings**

Gold and amber

Bellora (Livorno)

End of the 4th century BC

Length 2.3 cm

This type of earring with an African head was a popular, widespread type in the Hellenistic period. The heads were often made of garnet. Here they are made from amber, capped with gold decorated with skilfully-worked and very fine granulation representing tight curls. Similar examples are known from Taranto in South Italy. *GC/EG*

Guarnacci Archaeological Museum, Volterra, inv. 91

Cristofani and Martelli 1983, 134, no. 256; Mágico 1996, 136, no. 76

239 **Earrings**

Gold

Tomb 9, Peschiera necropolis, Todi

End of the 4th or 3rd century BC

Length 2.0 cm

These earrings came from a woman's cremation burial in a very wealthy tomb. This type of earring with a lion's head terminal is found widely in Etruria and South Italy, especially in Taranto. *GP*

National Museum of Archaeology, Florence, inv. 74717-1/2

Dominici in NSc 1981, 185; Mágico 1996, 137, no. 77

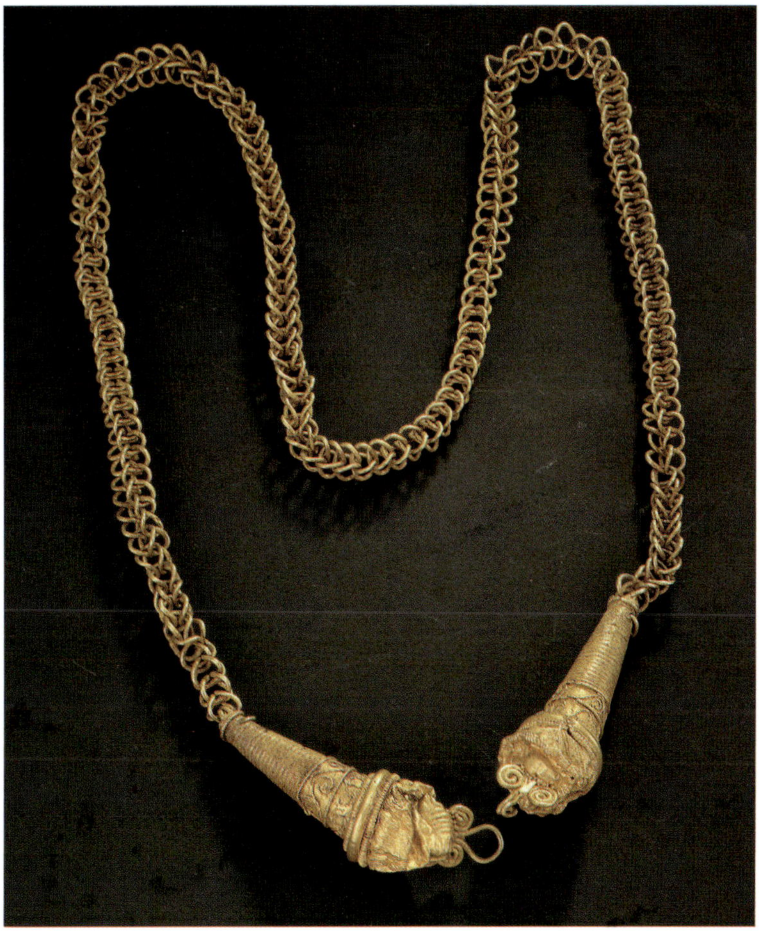

240 **Necklace**

Gold

Tomb 20, Peschiera necropolis, Todi

First half of the 3rd century BC

Length 56.3 cm

The gold chain was made using a typical technique called loop-in-loop. The first ring is formed into an ellipse and folded in half. The next link is similarly shaped, then threaded through the two folded ends of the first and also folded in half. This process is continued until the chain reaches the desired length. The lion's head terminals are also found elsewhere in pre-Roman Italy. These elaborately decorated examples would probably have been worn to the front. *GP/EG*

National Museum of Archaeology, Florence, inv. 74785

Dominici in NSc 1981, 332; Mágico 1996, 138, no. 81

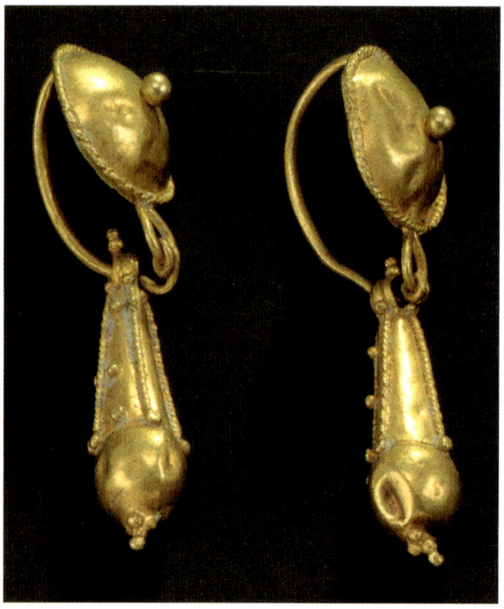

241 ## Earrings

Gold
Chiusi
3rd century BC
Length 4.8 cm

This is another earring type found widely in Etruria and South Italy during the Hellenistic period. The detailing of the discs and pendants could vary greatly. This pair is decorated with simple twisted filigree wires and granules. *SB/EG*

National Museum of Archaeology, Florence, inv. 77552

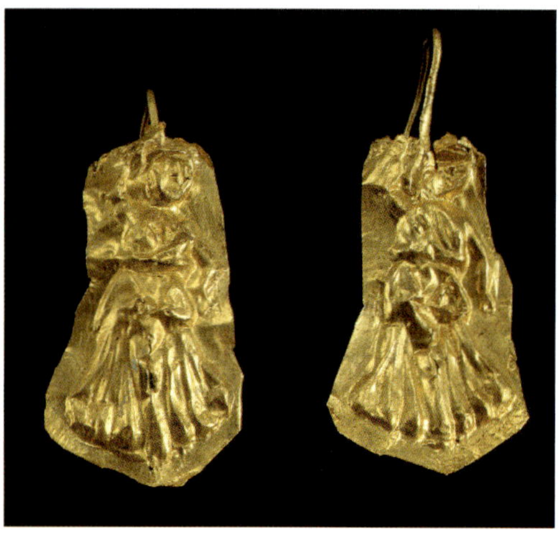

242 ## Earrings

Gold
Tomb 20, Peschiera necropolis, Todi
3rd to 2nd centuries BC
Length 4.7 cm

The sheet gold pendants of these earrings are simply decorated in repoussé with a dancing female figure, her right arm raised above her head. This type of earring with a large gold plaque was apparently characteristic of Volterra in northern Etruria. *GCC*

Guarnacci Archaeological Museum, Volterra, inv. 92
Cristofani and Martelli 1983, 132, no. 246; Mágico 1996, 139, no. 84

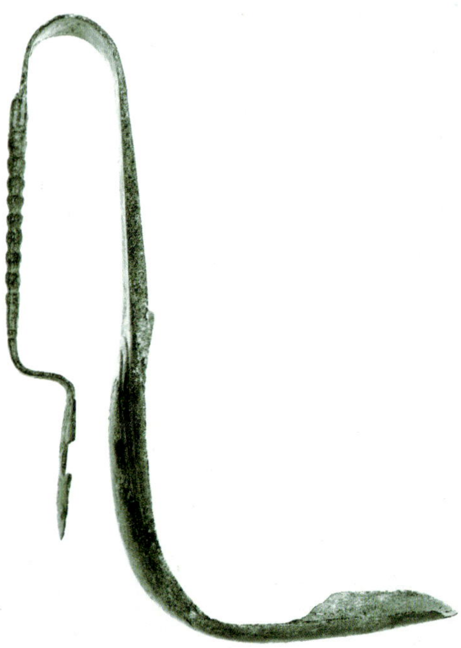

243 ## Strigil

Bronze
Unknown provenance
End of the 4th to the beginning of the 3rd century BC
Length 20.0 cm

Strigils were used to scrape dust and sweat from the body after physical exercise. Athletes rubbed their bodies with oil and pumice before contests, and strigils were used to remove this too. This example has a decorated handle. *GCC*

Museum of Archaeology, Siena, inv. 37509a

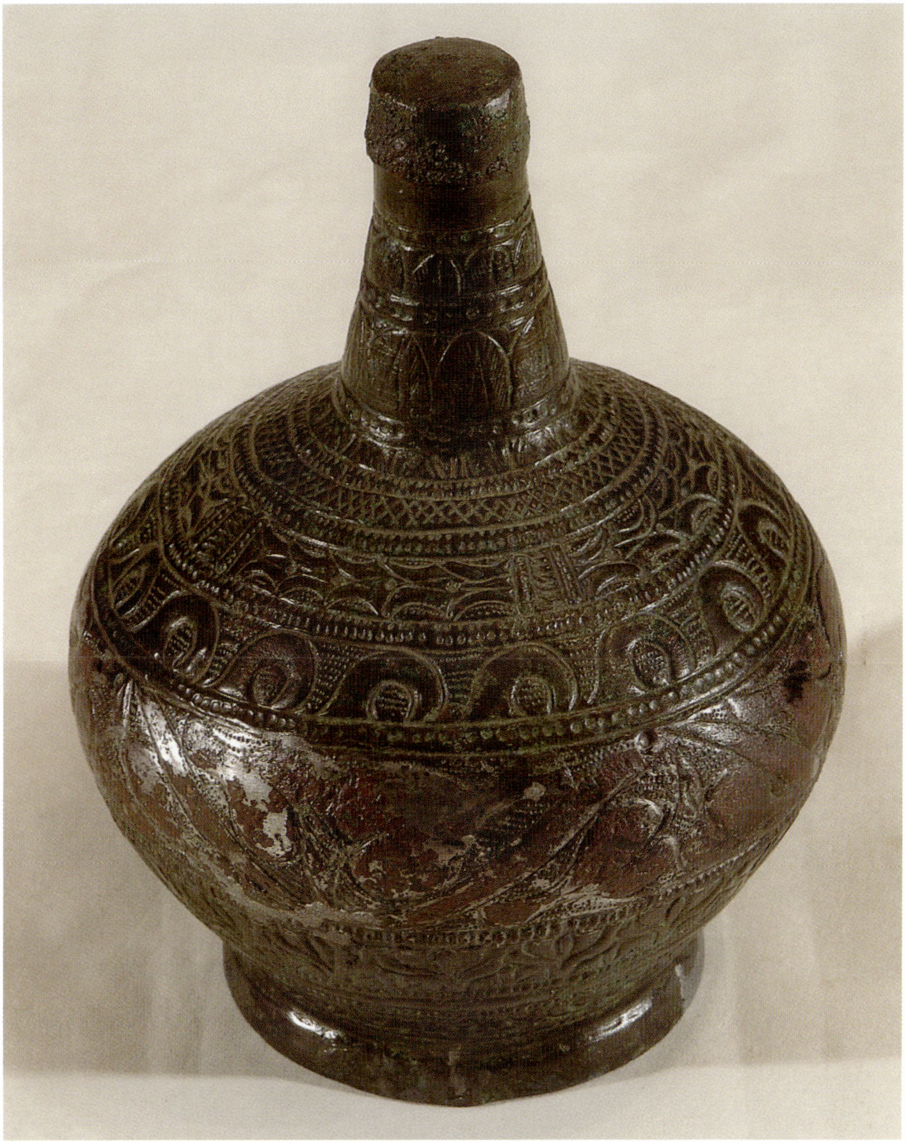

244 Flask

Bronze

Cinigiano

Second half of the 3rd to the beginning of the 2nd century BC

Height 15.0 cm

Bottles like these have often been found associated with strigils, suggesting they may have contained unguents and oils used for cleaning the body. Some examples had stoppers with a ring, from which they hung by a chain. *GCC*

National Museum of Archaeology, Florence, inv. 24034

Artigianato 1995, 148, no. 196

245 **Helmet**

Bronze
Buca di Spoglio, Piano delle Granate, Populonia
Last decades of the 4th to the middle of the 3rd century BC
Height 20.0 cm

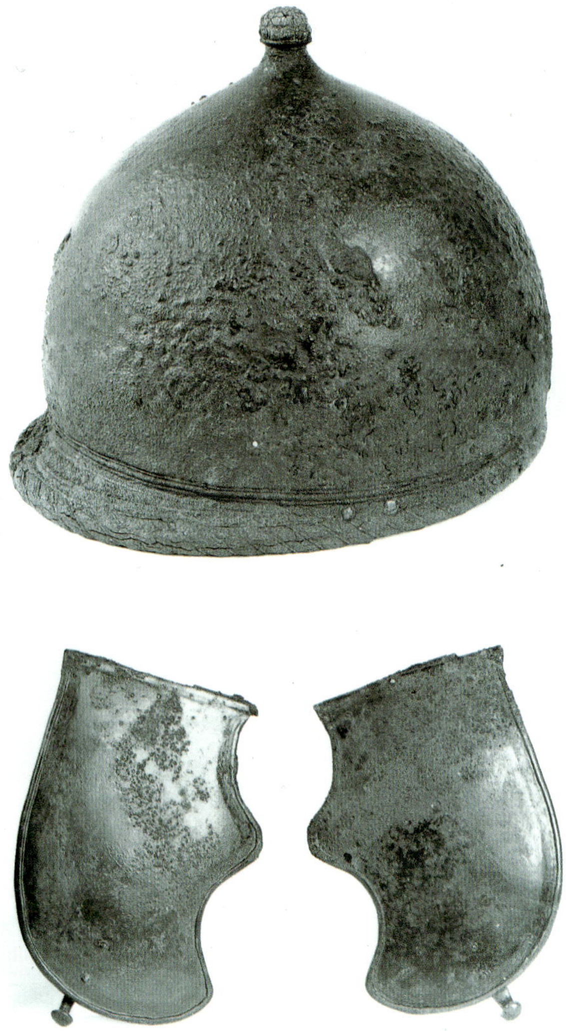

The production of helmets of this type has often been wrongly attributed to Celtic workshops as they were an important part of the battle dress of the Gauls. They were actually made in Etruria and central Italy, from whence they were widely exported. Examples are known from elsewhere in Italy, north and south. This example shows an early stage in the development of the type, with a domed boss on the top, a narrow neckguard and simple hinged cheekpieces. *GCC*

National Museum of Archaeology, Florence, inv. 94404
De Agostino in NSc 1961, 100, no. 5, fig. 40

246 **Kyathos (one of five shown)**

Bronze
Buca di Spoglio, Piano delle Granate, Populonia
End of the 4th to the beginning of the 3rd century BC
Heights 11.0 cm, 9.3 cm, 8.2 cm, 7.7 cm, 7.5 cm

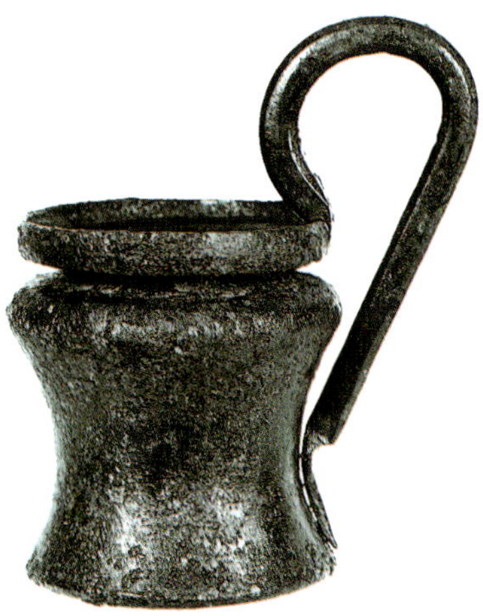

Small cups like this were part of the banqueting service, and were used like ladles to scoop wine out of a larger container. They may also have been units of liquid measure: they are always found in sets, usually of five, each one of a different size and volume. *GCC*

National Museum of Archaeology, Florence, inv. 94406-94410
De Agostino in NSc 1961, 102, nos. 7 and 11, fig. 41

247 ## Colum (strainer)

Bronze
Buca di Spoglio, Piano delle Granate, Populonia
End of the 4th to the beginning of the 3rd century BC
Length 30.0 cm

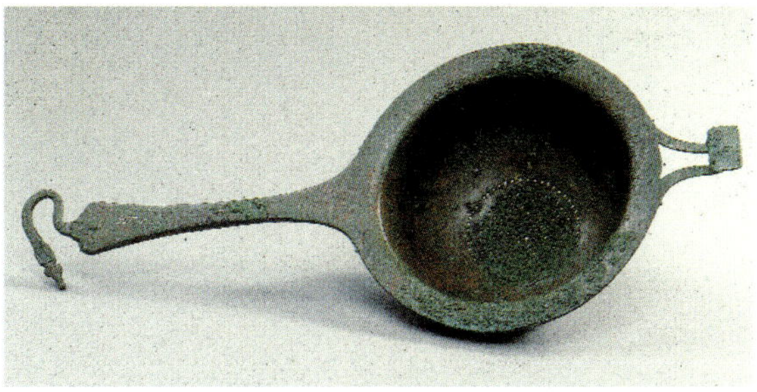

The colum, used for straining wine at banquets, was widely used all over central Italy during the Hellenistic period. This type has been found not only in Etruria but also in the Gallic cemeteries of Il Pieno and in the Po valley throughout the second half of the 4th century and the 3rd century BC. The rectangular tab at the edge of the bowl was used to rest the colum on top of the wine cup. It could be hung up when not in use. *GCC*

National Museum of Archaeology, Florence, inv. 94405
De Agostino in NSc 1961, 102, no. 6, fig. 41

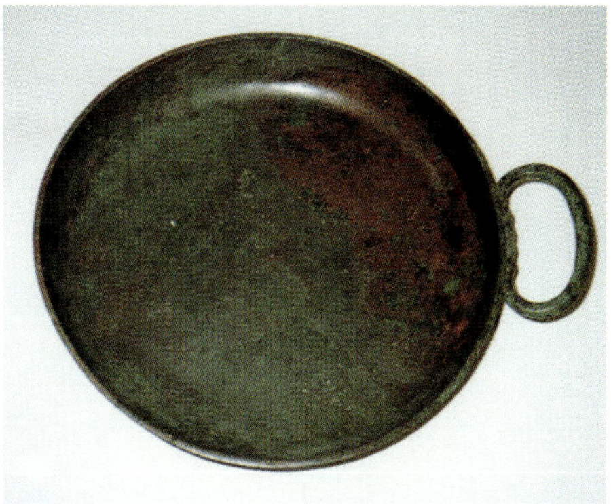

248 ## Tray with handle

Bronze
Populonia
End of the 4th to the beginning of the 3rd century BC
Diameter 30.5 cm

Single-handled trays, generally used to carry wine cups, formed part of the numerous banqueting services found in Etruscan tombs of the Hellenistic period. Most of these sets are from the central and northern parts of Etruria, especially the region around Chiusi and the cities of the coastal area, including Populonia and Talamone, as well as Volterra and Sovana (near Pitigliano). *GCC*

National Museum of Archaeology, Florence, inv. 77891

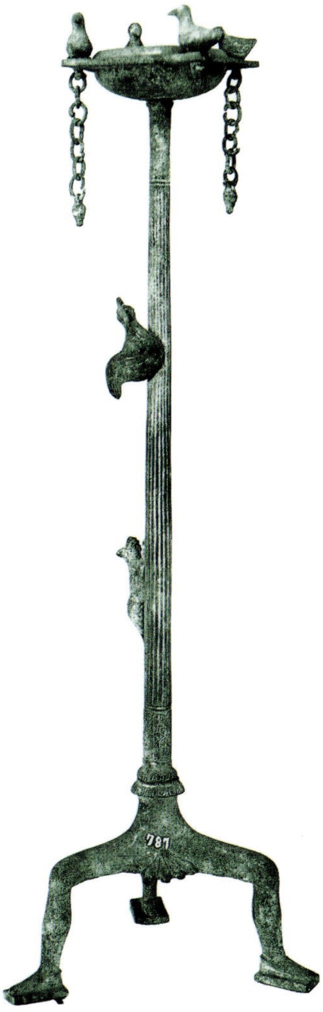

249 ## Thymiaterum (incense burner)

Bronze
Portone necropolis, Volterra
Last decades of the 3rd century BC
Height 40.0 cm

Thymiateria were placed on tables at banquets. This very typical example is supported on three feet in the form of human male legs. The shaft is decorated with a cat stalking a bird. The bowl at the top, used to burn the incense, is ornamented with doves at the rim and bronze pendants hung from chains. *GCC/EG*

National Museum of Archaeology, Florence, inv. 787
For this type of object, see Testa 1989

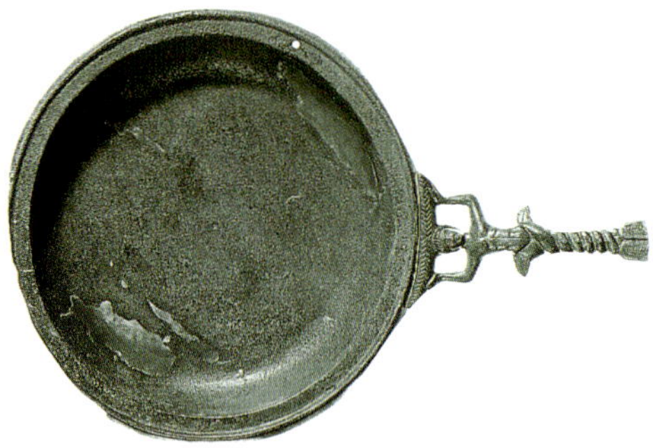

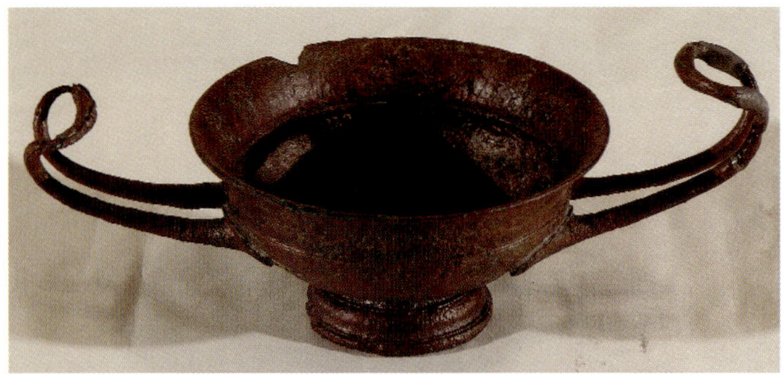

250 **Handled patera (dish)**

Bronze

Portone necropolis, Volterra

Last quarter of the 4th century BC

Diameter of dish 21.5 cm

Paterae like this one, and one-handled trays like number 248, were part of the banqueting service and were used to carry and serve the wine cups. The handle is in the form of a Triton, a sea god.

GCC

National Museum of Archaeology, Florence, inv. 1371

251 **Kylix (drinking cup)**

Silvered bronze

Portone necropolis, Volterra

Last quarter of the 4th century BC

Height 11.3 cm

This metal wine cup had its surface treated to resemble silver. The form was copied in ceramic, especially in what is known as the Malacena workshop at Volterra (see number 261). *GCC*

National Museum of Archaeology, Florence, inv. 1581

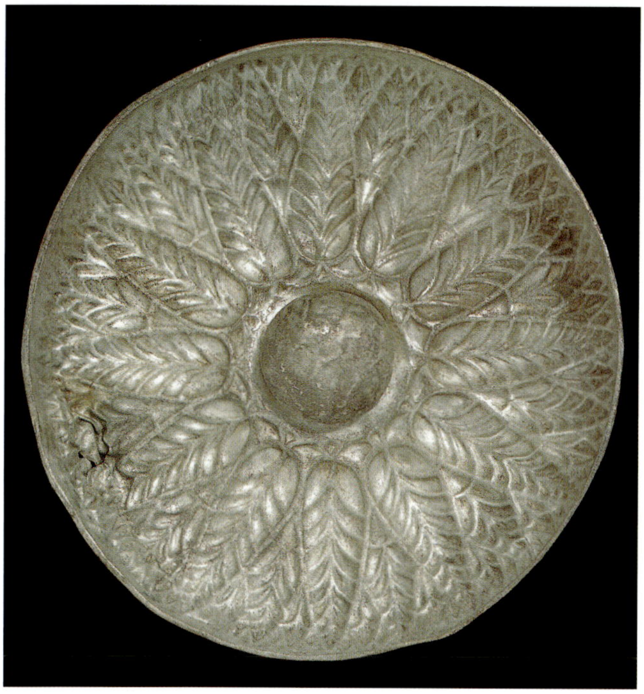

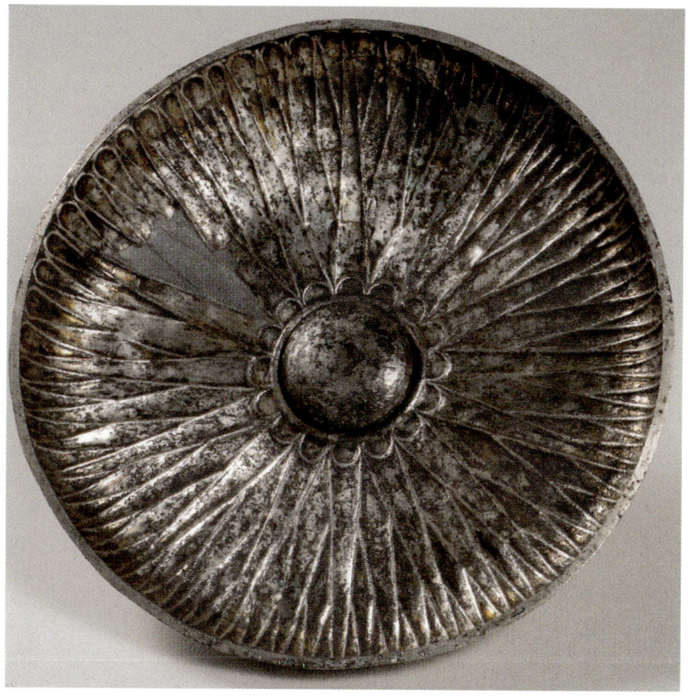

252 **Patera (dish)**

Silver
Unknown provenance
End of the 4th century BC
Diameter 21.0 cm

This dish, once in the Medici collections, is a rare survival of an Etruscan vessel made of precious metal. Such luxurious and costly originals provided the prototypes for black-glazed pottery vessels. The pottery types were made by the Malacena workshop in Volterra at the end of the 4th century, and by potters from Cales in Campania during the 3rd and 2nd centuries.

Prestigious dishes like this were used by the wealthy and powerful throughout the Hellenistic world. Examples have been excavated in the royal tombs of Thrace of the second half of the 4th century. They were probably often included in the banqueting services of the richest families of northern Etruria, especially in Volterra. They are regularly shown held by the reclining men sculpted on the lids of ash urns from 2nd century Volterra. They seem to be characteristic of male burials. The embossed dome in the centre of the dish helped the bearer to hold it more securely. *GCC*

National Museum of Archaeology, Florence, inv. 132265

253 **Patera (dish)**

Silver
Populonia
End of the 4th century BC
Diameter 18.4 cm

Another example of a silver vessel. This example is from Populonia.

National Museum of Archaeology, Florence, inv. 94403

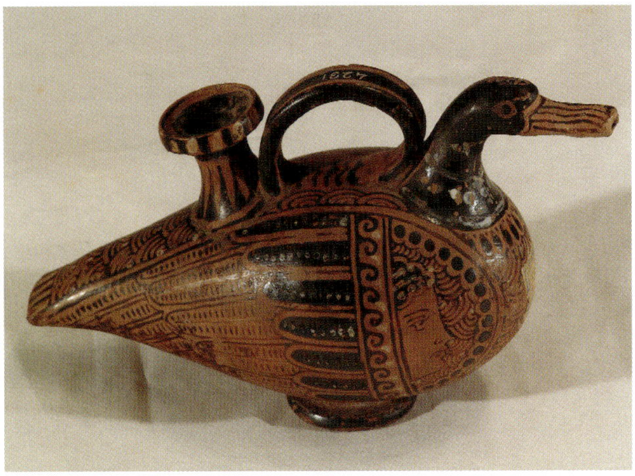

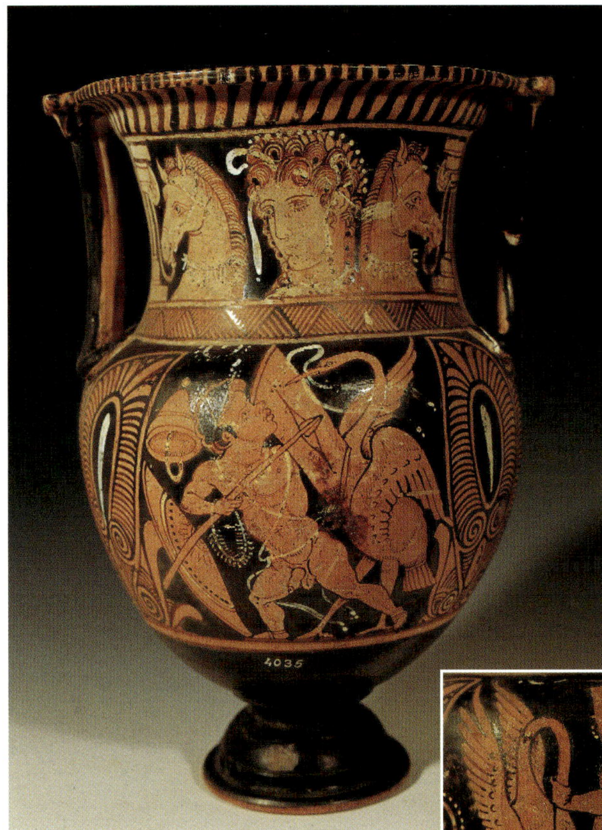

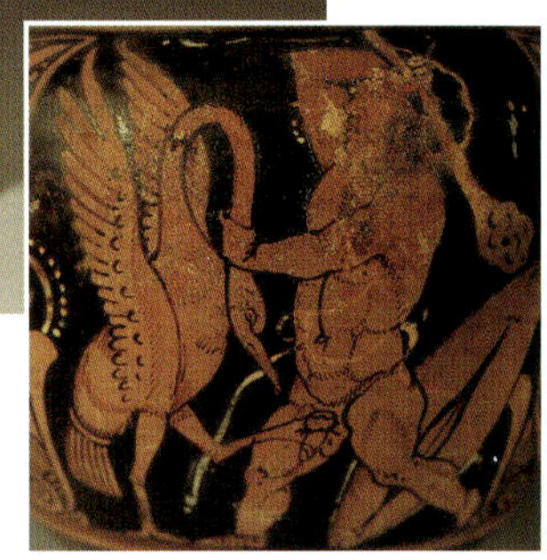

254 **Etruscan red-figure duck askos (container for perfumed oils)**

Painted ceramic
Portone necropolis, Volterra
Last quarter of the 4th century BC
Height 10.8 cm

This duck-shaped vessel was filled through the funnel spout on the duck's back and oil was allowed to drop out through the smaller hole in the beak. The duck's body is partly decorated with the feathers of the wing and tail, and partly with the profile head of a woman. Chiusine potters revived the tradition of duck askoi (an older form) in the 4th century BC, and the tradition was continued by workshops in southern Etruria. This example can be attributed to what is known as the Clusium group, and specifically to the Painter of the Florence Stamnoi. Clusium is the ancient name of the city of Chiusi. *BA/EG*

National Museum of Archaeology, Florence, inv. 4231
Etruscos 1999, 275, no. 449

255 **Etruscan red-figure kelebe**

Painted ceramic
Portone necropolis, Volterra
End of the 4th century BC
Height 42.9 cm

This type of vessel was regularly used as an ash urn. This function is reflected in the decoration: the columns visible on the neck, to which the horses are tied, are part of a tomb. The scene on the body of the vase represents the mythological fight between the Pygmies and the Cranes. Such combat scenes, as well as horses' and women's heads, were frequently used to decorate ash urns and sarcophagi. These kelebai were probably made at Volterra, and were mainly used in that area, but were also popular as funerary vases elsewhere in northern Etruria. *BA*

National Museum of Archaeology, Florence, inv. 4035
Civiltà 1985, 60, no. 128

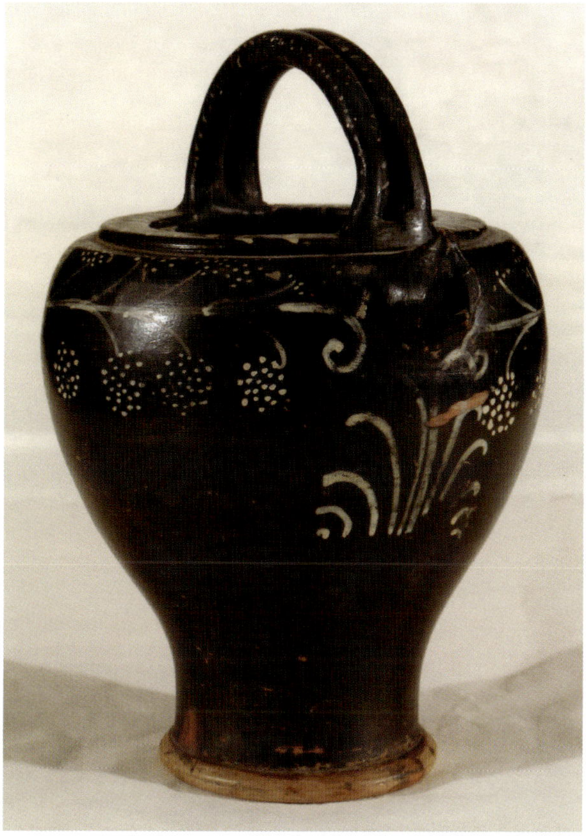

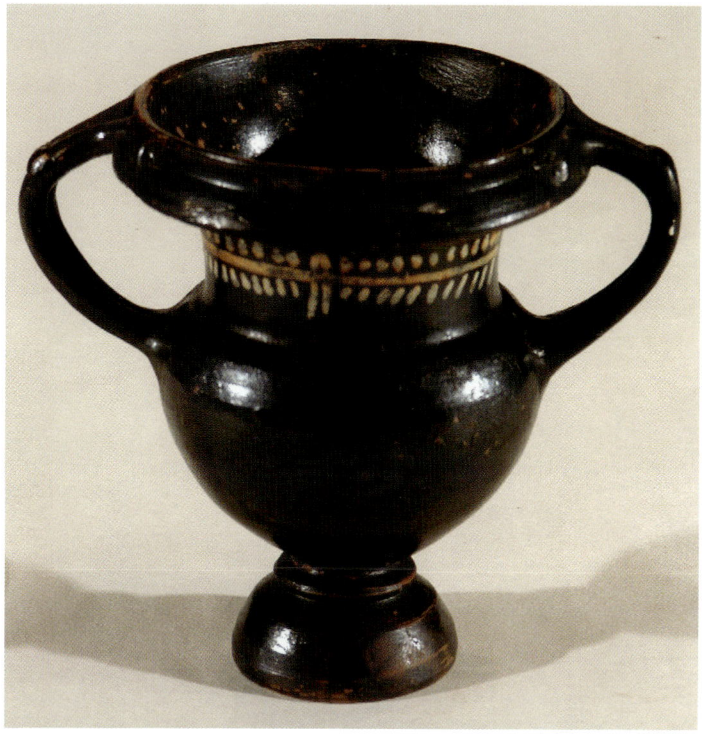

256 **Situla (pail-shaped vessel)**

Black-glazed ceramic
Unknown provenance
Last quarter of the 4th century BC
Height 22.5 cm

This style of pottery, imitating what are known as Gnathian ceramics from Apulia, was made in Etruria in Tarquinia and Cerveteri. The black-painted bodies were decorated with added white. *EM*

Museum of Archaeology, Siena, inv. 38573
Mangani 1991, 79, no. 54

257 **Krateriskos (container for liquids)**

Black-glazed ceramic
Unknown provenance
End of the 4th century BC
Height 11.6 cm

Examples of this kind of vessel have been found principally in Tarquinia, where the workshops that made them were probably located. This example is apparently of Greek origin. *EM*

Museum of Archaeology, Siena, inv. 38571
Mangani 1991, 81, no. 58

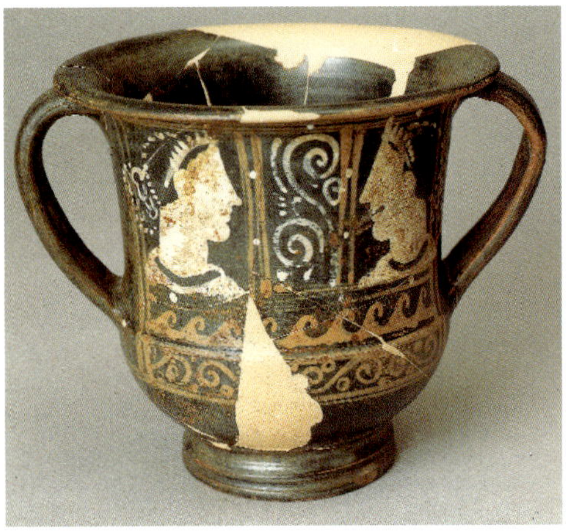

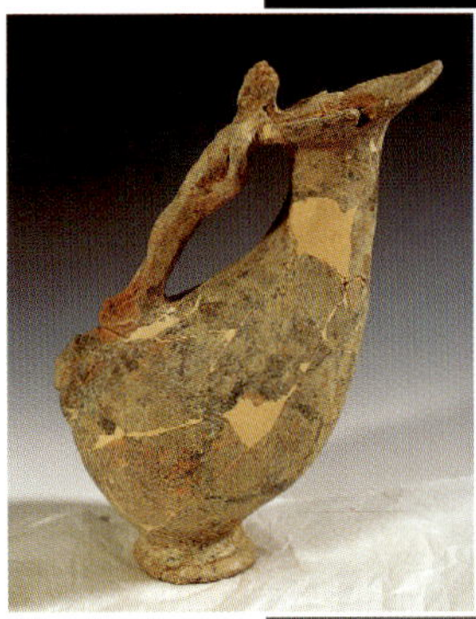

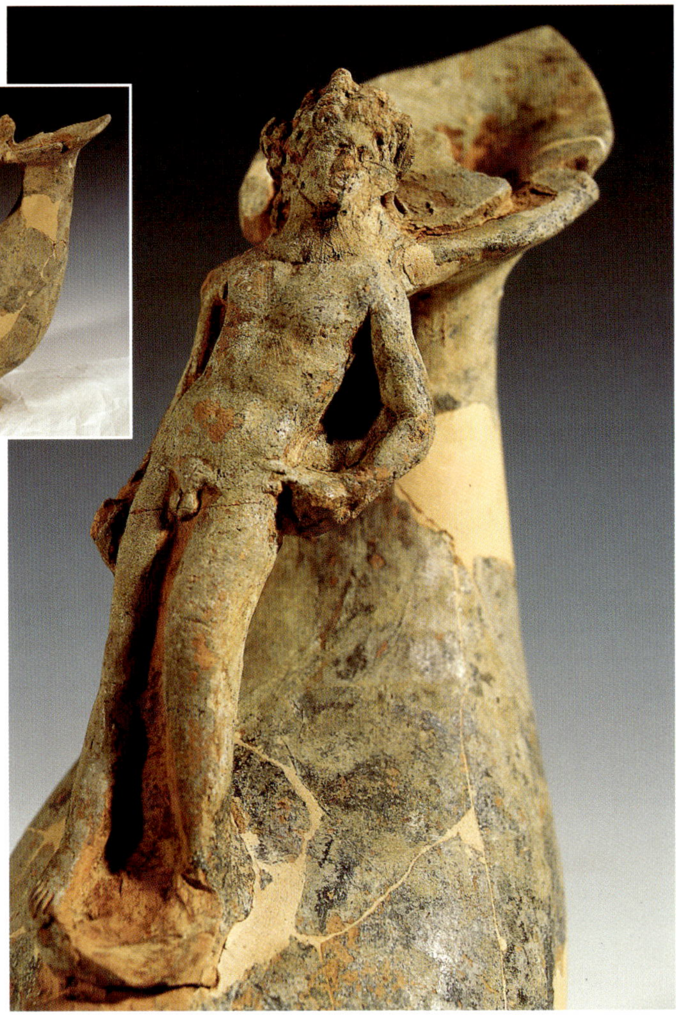

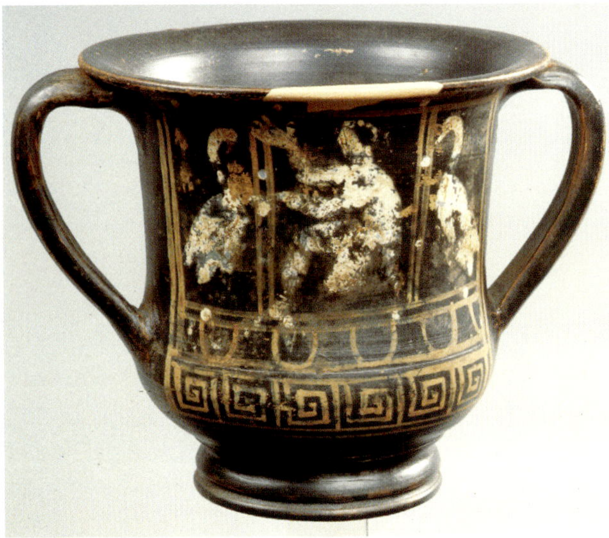

258 **Etruscan red-figure kantharos (drinking cup) [two views]**

Painted ceramic

Populonia

End of the 4th to the beginning of the 3rd century BC

Height 14.9 cm

This cup with overpainted white decoration is well made, but the motifs are characteristically standardized. It has been attributed to a painter close to the Centauromachia Painter who worked in Populonia.

SB

National Museum of Archaeology, Florence, inv. 81910

Bruni 1992, 77, figs. 76-8

259 **Askos (jug)**

'Silvered' ceramic

Tuscania

End of the 4th century BC

Height 25.5 cm

This is an example of a very special type of pottery known as ceramica argentata, made from a lightly coloured refined clay. Vessels were dipped in tin after firing to produce a more economical version of costly silverware. They were made for funerary use, and probably originally had a shiny surface. Ceramics like these are valuable for understanding 4th and 3rd century Etruscan silverware, which has almost disappeared from the archaeological record. This example has an elaborately modelled handle in the form of Dionysus, which must have looked convincingly metallic when the vessel was new. *GCC/EG*

National Museum of Archaeology, Florence, inv. 77646

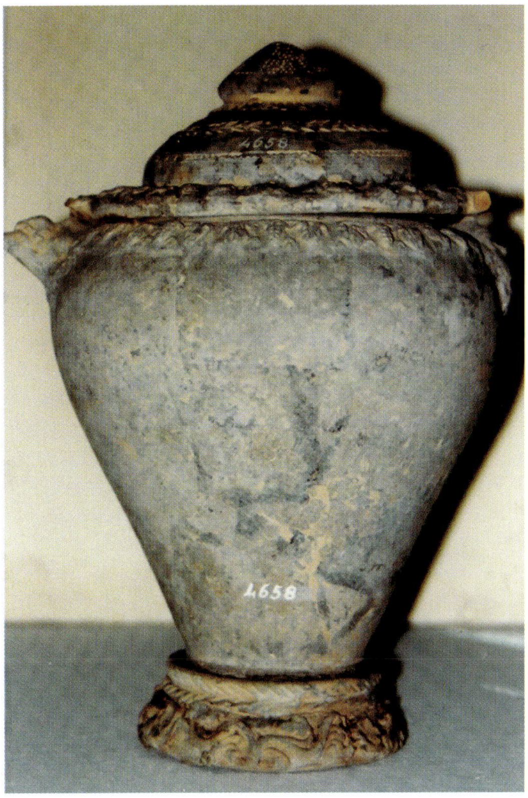

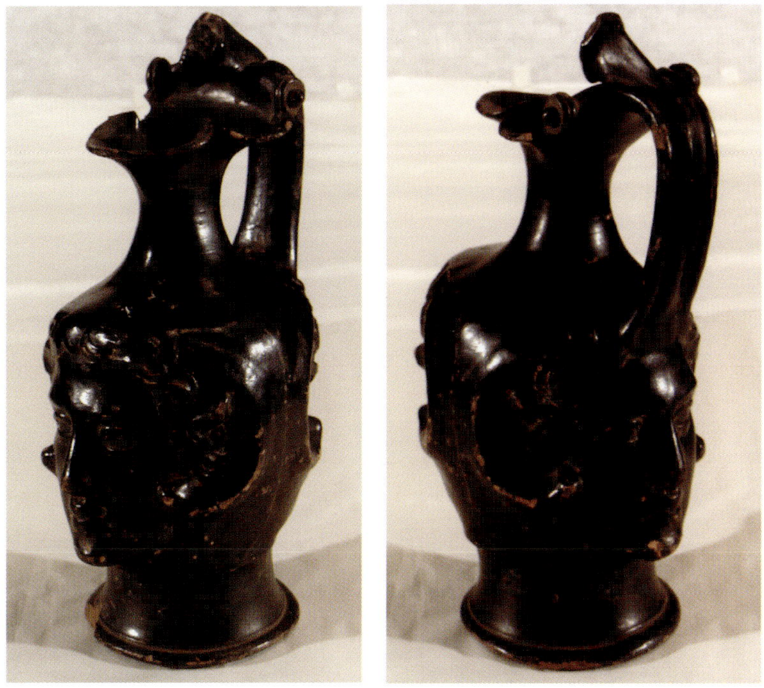

260 **Situla (pail-shaped vessel) and lid**

'Silvered' ceramic
Unknown provenance
End of the 4th century BC
Height 32.0 cm

This spouted vessel is another example of ceramica argentata. Vessels of this shape, including examples in precious metals, have been found in the rich tombs of Thrace and Macedonia in Greece. The lid resembles bronze vessels from inland Etruria, especially from Bolsena, Todi, Chiusi and Viterbo. *GCC*

National Museum of Archaeology, Florence, inv. 4658

261 **Oinochoe (jug)**

Black-glazed ceramic
Unknown provenance
3rd century BC
Height 30.0 cm

This type of very glossy black-painted pottery began to be made in Italy in the 4th century. It was inspired by Greek wares, especially those from Attica. Before long, ceramic workshops in many different centres in Italy were producing this kind of pottery. This finely moulded double-headed jug, and the next three vessels (numbers 262-264), are attributed to the best of these workshops, the so-called Malacena workshop of Volterra. Its name derives from the site of an important family tomb called the Caliśna Sepu tomb in the area of Monteriggioni. The tomb contained a large number of ceramics of this type (see number 263). They were skilfully made and often highly elaborate, and are characterized by a brilliant metallic blue-black glaze imitating metalwork. There was a great demand for these Volterran Malacena ceramics from other Etruscan centres and elsewhere. They would have been luxury items, affordable only by the wealthy. *LP*

National Museum of Archaeology, Florence, inv. 4469

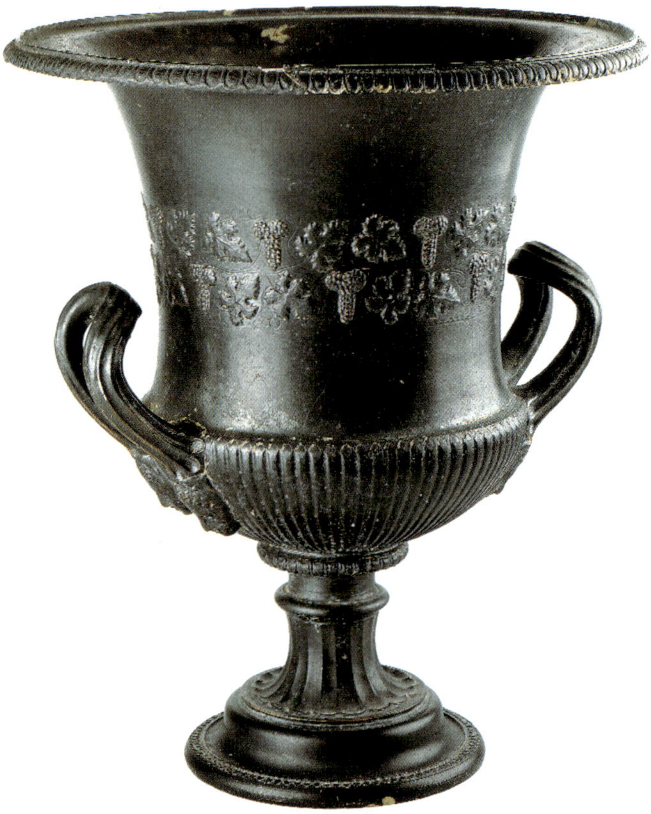

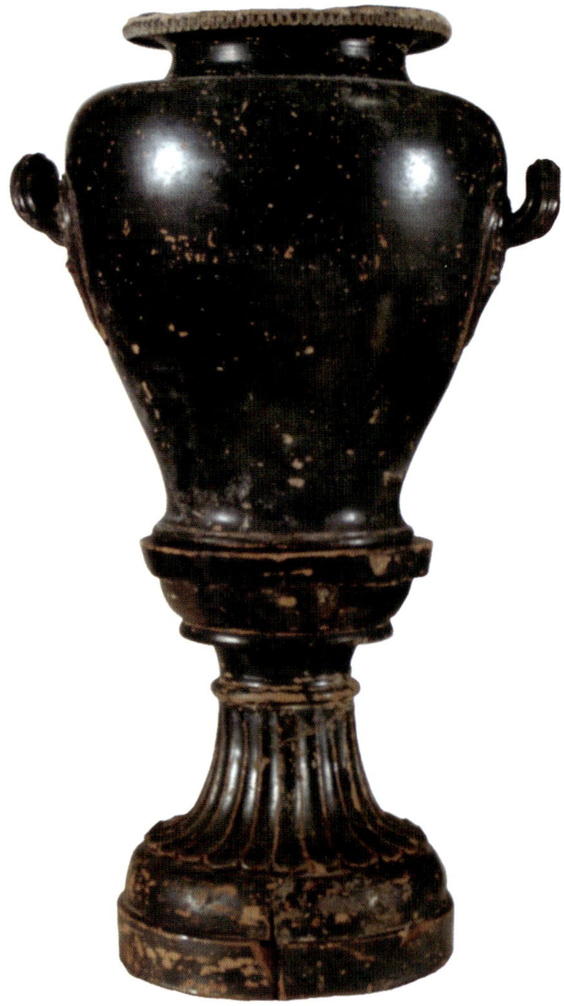

262 **Krater (vessel for mixing wine and water)**

Black-glazed ceramic
Unknown provenance
Last quarter of the 4th century BC
Height 43.3 cm

Large vases like this were amongst the most popular products of the Malacena workshops. It is appropriately decorated with vine leaves and bunches of grapes. *AP/EG*

National Museum of Archaeology, Florence, inv. 4559
Artigianato 1985, 185, no. 247

263 **Stamnos (container for liquids) and stand**

Black-glazed ceramic
Caliśna Sepu tomb, Monteriggioni
Second half of the 4th century BC
Height including stand 65.0 cm

This is another example of the high quality pottery from the accomplished Malacena workshops. Its form is clearly derived from metal prototypes. The handles are decorated with silens' heads. *GCC*

Archaeological Museum, Colle Val d'Elsa, Siena, inv. C144

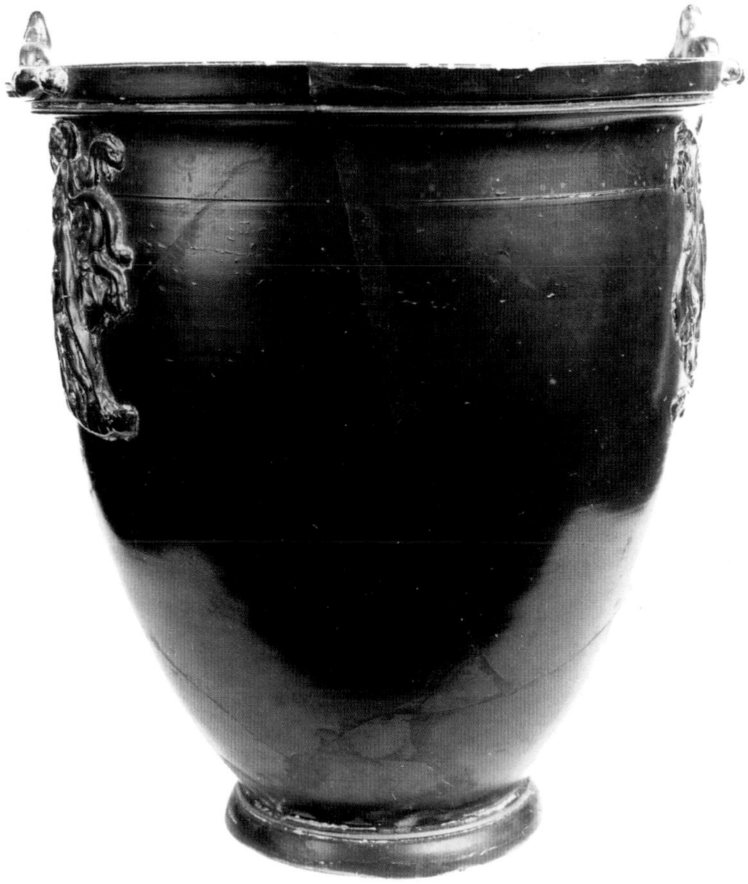

264 Situla (pail-shaped vessel)

Black-glazed ceramic
Unknown provenance
End of the 4th to the beginning of the 3rd centuries BC
Height 28.0 cm

This is another fine example of Malacena ware, clearly derived from metalwork. Many bronze examples of this shape of vessel are known from the Volterra area. There is a particularly fine moulded scene of Dionysiac revels on the two sides of the situla. *GCC/EG*

National Museum of Archaeology, Florence, inv. 75432

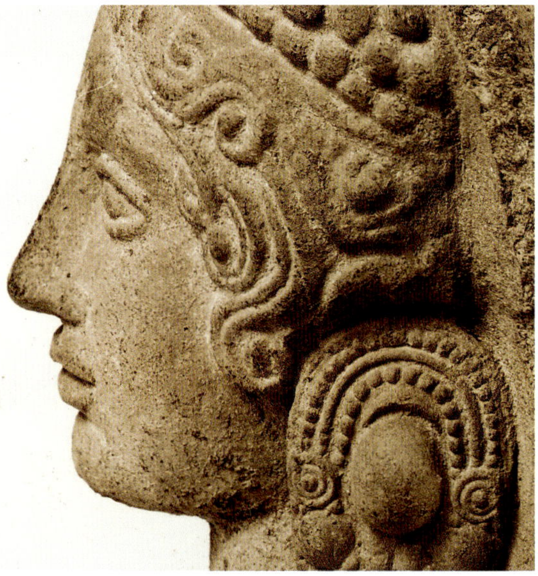

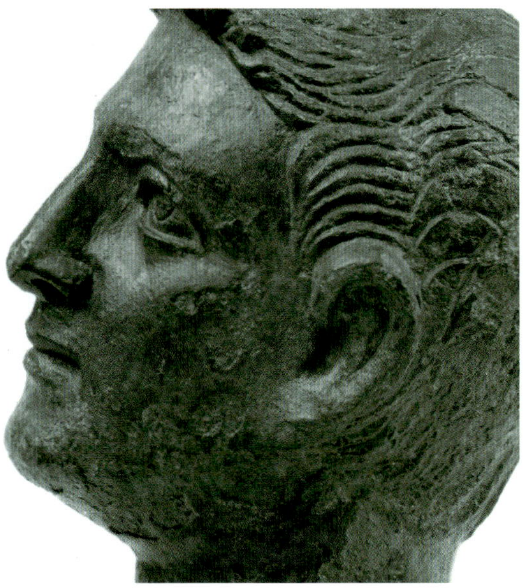

ASPECTS OF ETRUSCAN RELIGION

The Etruscans were well known in antiquity for their religious observance. The Roman writer and orator Seneca wrote, 'This is the difference between us and the Etruscans … we think that because clouds collide, lightning is produced; while they think clouds collide so lightning can be produced. As they believe everything is attributable to the gods, they think that things do not foretell the future because they have happened, but that they happen because they are intended to foretell the future.' Among their contemporaries, and especially the Romans, the Etruscans were known not only for their respect for divine guidance, but also for their skill in interpreting this guidance through highly developed techniques of divination (the art of observing portents and using them to understand divine will). The Etruscan priests concerned with divination, the 'haruspices', were so highly respected that the Romans were willing to consult them at moments of crisis. The principal divination techniques were based on observing details of signs such as lightning, the appearance of the intestines of sacrificed animals, and the flights of birds.

The Etruscans were particularly diligent regarding the proper performance of religious rites. Although very few Etruscan religious texts survive, even as fragments, it is known from Roman sources that the entire canon of Etruscan belief and practice was fully recorded in their Sacred Books. The *libri haruspicini* set out in detail the information needed to study and interpret the internal organs of sacrificial animals to foretell the future. The liver was especially important, and scenes on engraved mirrors show Etruscan priests inspecting this organ. Models of livers in clay and bronze also survive. The most important is a full-size bronze model of a sheep's liver of 2nd century BC date, which was found near Piacenza. It was probably used for teaching. Its surface is divided into 16 sections, sub-divided into a further 24, with each section inscribed with the name of its associated deity. All the names are of Etruscan or Italic gods. Another very important branch of divination involved the observation of signs from the sky, which was similarly divided into sections. The *libri fulgurales* dealt with the study and interpretation of lightning and thunderbolts.

The Etruscans worshipped many gods, whose names offer important clues to their origins. Some are obviously derived from the names of Greek gods: Aplu (Apollo), Artumes (Artemis), Aita (Hades), Phersipnai (Persephone) and Hercle (Herakles). Other names came from the Italic world: Uni (Juno), Menerva (Minerva), Selvans (Silvanus), Nethuns (Neptune) and Satre (Saturn). Some names – Tinia, Turan, Turms and Laran – seem to be entirely local in origin. Representations of these deities suggest they can also be identified with Greek gods. Tinia may be partially equated with Zeus, Turan with Aphrodite, Turms with Hermes and Laran with Ares. There were also other uniquely Etruscan divinities, such as the goddesses Nortia and Thufltha.

The principal gods of the Etruscans were Tinia, Uni and Menerva, who were sometimes worshipped in the same temple. Tinia was the supreme god, ruler of the universe and the lord of destiny, whose identifying attribute was the thunderbolt. His wife, Uni, was the principal female deity, who protected women in childbirth. Menerva's attributes were the helmet, the spear and the owl. A healing goddess and guardian of fertility, anatomical *ex-votos* (models presented as ritual gifts) were commonly offered to her at her sanctuaries. Other important deities were Laran, the god of war; Turan, the goddess of love and beauty; Aplu, the Greek Apollo, and his sister Artumes, the Greek Artemis; Fufluns, the god of wine, who protected grape cultivation; and Nethuns, god of the sea.

In the absence of texts, the archaeological evidence from temples and sanctuaries is particularly important. In the Etruscan world a temple was not simply a place to pray and make offerings, but also served as a communal place to meet and socialize. Temples were built within the cities and outside in the countryside. Rural sanctuaries were often dedicated to gods associated with healing. Sanctuaries were also located within cemeteries and in important commercial centres such as Pyrgi, a port near Cerveteri, and Gravisca, the harbour of Tarquinia.

According to Vitruvius, the Roman architect and writer on architecture and engineering, the 'Tuscan' temple had a roughly square plan and was divided lengthwise into two parts. Behind the façade, the open front part (the 'pronaos') was a deep porch which gave access to the interior of the building, the 'cella'. There were up to three cellae, which housed the cult statues of the gods worshipped there. The walls were constructed of wood, stone blocks and mud brick on a high stone podium, and the wooden ceiling beams supported a tiled roof. The ends of the wooden beams exposed to the elements were protected by terracotta plaques and facing slabs, which were attached with nails. The open pediments were adorned with terracotta figures in high relief, and statues were placed on the main roof beam (the 'columen'). The altar, which could be of substantial size, was placed outside in front of the building. Usually only the foundations and the architectural ornaments of temple buildings survive.

The deity to whom a temple was dedicated can often be identified from inscriptions or the votive offerings found at the site. Such offerings were made to ensure divine favour or to give thanks. They were stored permanently at the sanctuaries in huge numbers, and were often carefully buried when the site was abandoned. The votives sometimes represent the deity but, more often, the offerers themselves or the favour desired. They generally took the form of ceramic or bronze human and animal figurines, models, pottery, various kinds of metalwork, pre-monetary currency or even coinage, and reflect the relative affluence and status of their donors. The name of the god or the worshipper was sometimes inscribed on them. Objects like these provide a vast resource for interpreting Etruscan beliefs and practice. The number of offerings increased significantly in the late Classical and Hellenistic periods, a time when a new type of anatomical votive offering appeared in the form of models of different parts of the body: heads, legs, hands, feet and internal organs. Related to healing and fertility, these largely reflect the religious beliefs of the lower social classes and provide a poignant testimony to the needs and religious devotions of Etruscan worshippers.

GCC/EG

Previous page:
above: detail of a votive head of a woman (no. 290)
below: detail of a votive head of a man (no. 295)

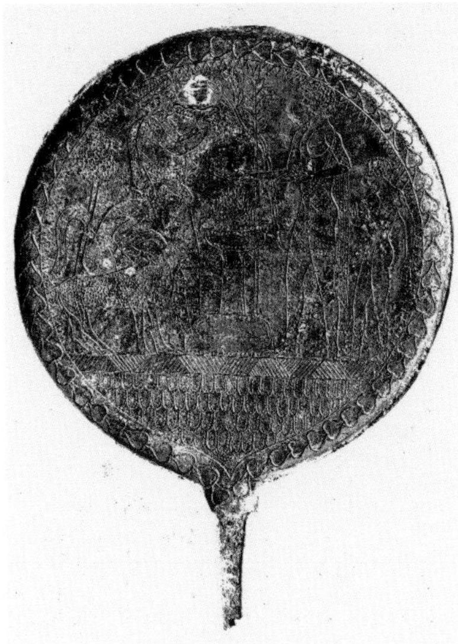

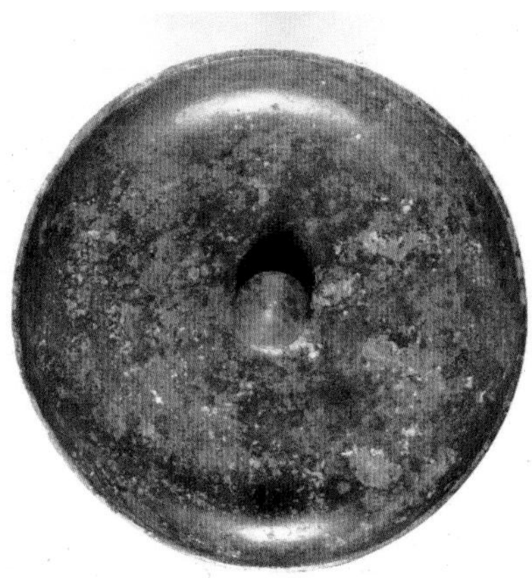

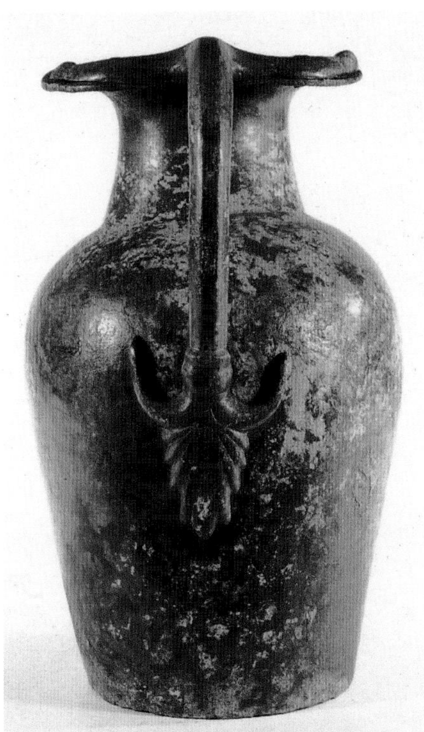

265 Mirror

Bronze
Palestrina
5th century BC
Diameter 6.5 cm

Bronze mirrors were popular possessions for wealthy women from the end of the 6th century BC. Several thousand examples have survived ranging in date from the 6th to the 3rd centuries BC. They were produced in many Etruscan cities, and were probably often given as wedding presents. From the end of the 5th century they were made of bronze with a high tin content which improved the reflective qualities of the metal and made it stronger. Examples with a tang (a protruding metal section) like this one would originally have had a handle made of wood, bone or ivory. Mirrors were often decorated on the back with mythological or domestic scenes, usually relevant to women's lives. This example is decorated with a scene of a sacrifice. The altar is in the middle. To one side stands a bearded man, holding an object (perhaps a bunch of grapes), with a youth watching beside him. To the other side of the altar is a woman playing a double pipe. Beside her crouches a satyr holding a goat, the intended sacrifice. *AM/EG*

National Museum of Archaeology, Florence, inv. 646
Mayer-Prokop 1967, 21, no. 19

266 Patera (shallow libation dish) and jug

Bronze
Box tomb 2, Palazzetta necropolis, Bisenzio
Middle of the 5th century BC
Diameter of patera 14.7 cm; height of jug 29.0 cm

These two objects, which were found together, were used for making libations (liquid offerings) during religious ceremonies. *GCC*

National Museum of Archaeology, Florence, inv. 74934, 74930

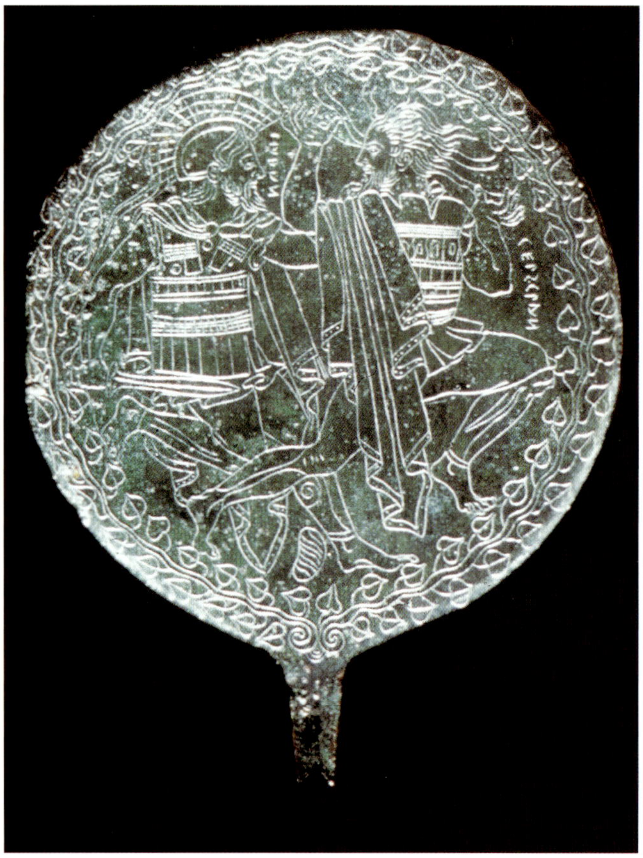

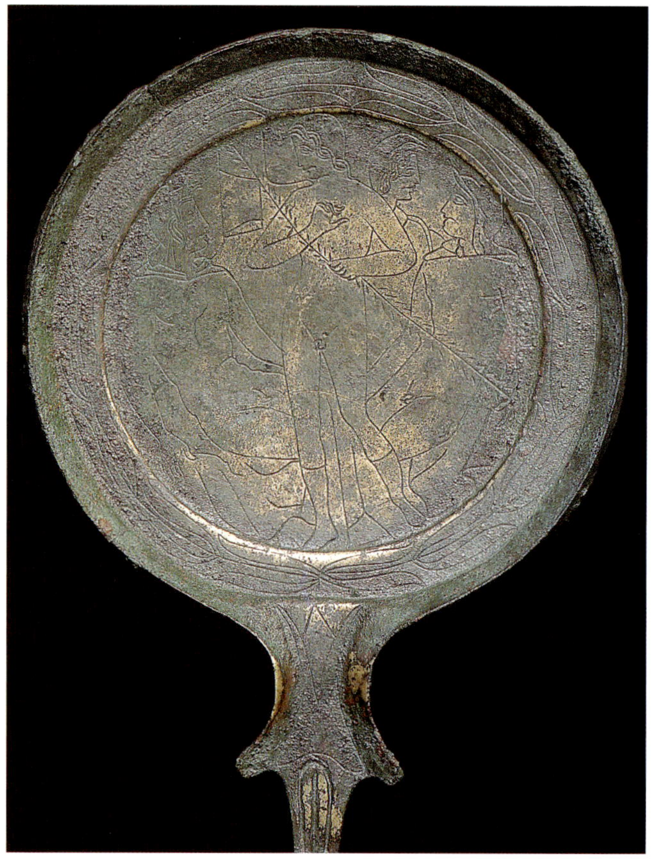

267 **Mirror**

Bronze
Populonia
5th century BC
Diameter 16.3 cm

The scene on the back of this mirror is from the battle between the gods and the giants (called the 'Giganto-machia'). The combatants are named in the inscriptions engraved beside them. One figure is Laran (the Greek god Ares), the other Celsclan, the son of Cel. Cel was the Etruscan mother or earth goddess equivalent to the Greek Ge or Gaia and the Roman Tellus. Scenes of two combatants, which appear on a number of mirrors of the second half of the 5th century BC, may be inspired by similar scenes on the inner surfaces of red-figure Attic cups of the same period. Celsclan's body is shown full-face, while his head and legs are in profile. *GCC*

National Museum of Archaeology, Florence, inv. 79283
Etruscos 1999, 274, no. 446

268 **Mirror**

Bronze
Tuscania
3rd century BC
Height including handle 26.0 cm

The back of this mirror is decorated with the Dioscuri (the Etruscan Tinas Clenar), Castor and Polydeuces (Latinized as Pollux), the half-divine sons of Zeus and Leda. They can be recognized by their characteristic close-fitting hats. The other two figures, in the centre, are Minerva (the Etruscan Menerva) and Helen, the sister of the Dioscuri. By the 3rd century, the form and decoration of mirrors had become very standardized. Designs were executed rather carelessly and apparently without much understanding of their original meaning.

EM/EG

National Museum of Archaeology, Florence, inv. 77760

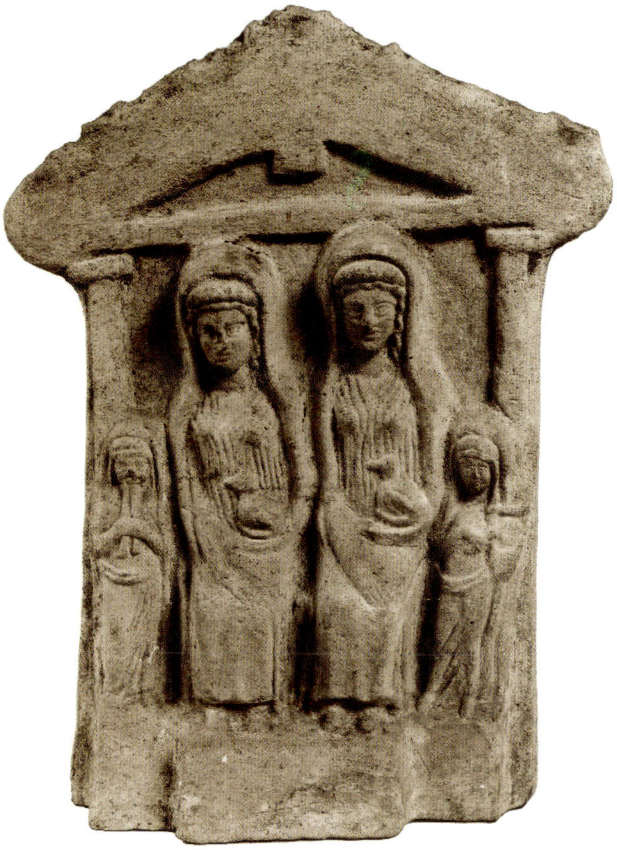

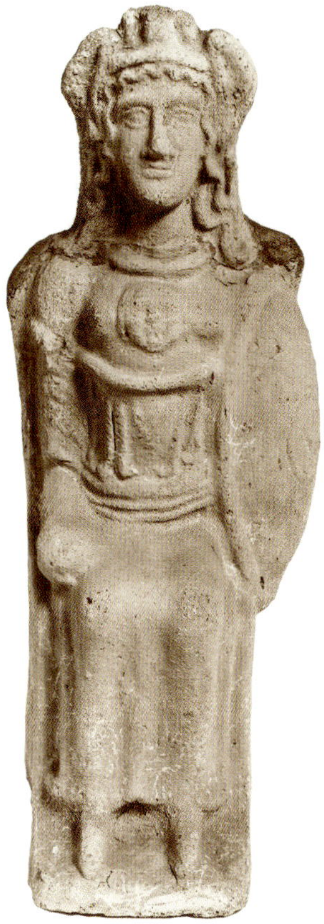

269 **Votive model**

Terracotta
Cerveteri
4th century BC
Height 39.0 cm

This votive offering was found at a temple in Cerveteri dedicated to Uni (the Greek Hera, Roman Juno). It shows a temple building within which are seated two goddesses. Both wear diadems and hold doves in their left hands. Women musicians to either side of them play a double pipe and a lyre. The goddesses on similar votives are usually identified as Vei (Demeter/Ceres) and her daughter Phersipnai (Persephone/Proserpina), but here they could be Uni (to whom the temple was dedicated) and another goddess, perhaps Turan (Aphrodite/Venus), who was worshipped at Gravisca, the harbour of Tarquinia. *AR/EG*

Museum of Archaeology, Siena, inv. 37850

270 **Votive figurine**

Terracotta
Cerveteri
4th century BC
Height 28.7 cm

Found in the same temple as number 269, this figurine represents Menerva (the Greek Athena, the Roman Minerva). Although she was a local Etruscan goddess, who was venerated before her assimilation with Athena, she shares many of Athena's characteristic features. She wears an aegis (medallic shield) decorated with a Gorgon's head on her chest, a helmet, and carries a large shield over her arm. *AR*

Museum of Archaeology, Siena, inv. 37853

271 Seven antefixes (architectural ornaments)

Terracotta
Bolsena
First half of the 2nd century BC

The following seven objects, part of a larger group, were found near Bolsena. The discovery of the ornaments was first revealed in 1862, but their findspot remains unknown. It has been suggested that they came from a sanctuary of the goddess Nortia. According to Roman sources the Etruscan goddess Nortia had a sanctuary at Volsinii, although its location has not yet been identified. She was apparently a goddess of destiny, and the principal deity of Bolsena. Each of the reliefs has a number on the back, suggesting the full set may have comprised 13 ornaments, and some bear an identifying inscription. The group's subject matter used to be understood as a representation of the Greek myth of Perseus and Medusa. More recent studies have suggested alternative interpretations, although all agree the various motifs are linked by a unifying theme. One suggestion is that the theme is the Etruscan myth of Olta, the monster killed by Porsenna. Another sees the subject matter as a representation of the human life cycle, from birth to death, with an emphasis on the structure of Etruscan society with its well-defined stages through public life (the *cursus honorum*), and its class hierarchies. This interpretation explains the presence of individual deities or semi-divine beings through their association with each life event.

GCC

(a)

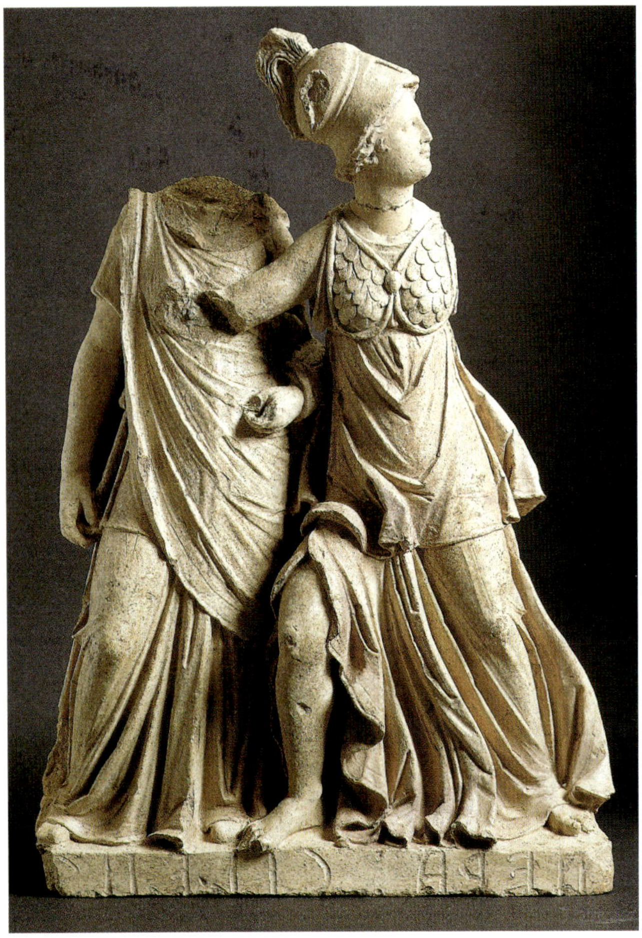

(b)

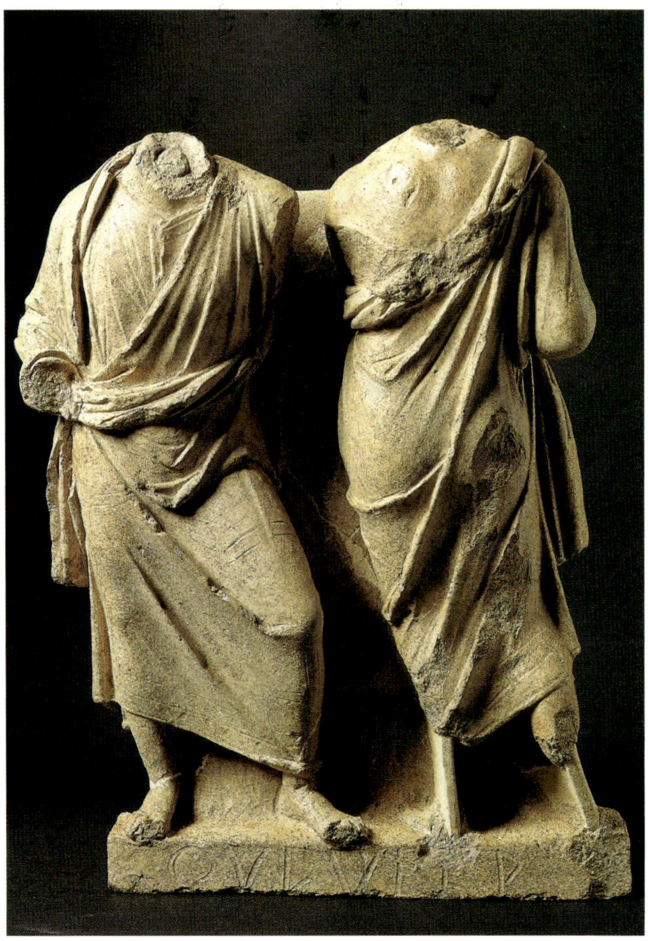

(a) Height 45.0 cm

This fine relief sculpture shows the helmeted goddess Menerva beside Cilens, the Etruscan goddess of the night, who is sometimes associated with Fortuna. There is an identifying inscription on the base.

National Museum of Archaeology, Florence, inv. 79074
Santuari 1985, 380, no. 16, 3, 2

(b) Height 52.0 cm

This shows two draped male figures. There is an inscription along the base.

National Museum of Archaeology, Florence, inv. 79075

(c) Height 52.0 cm

This shows a headless semi-draped female figure.

National Museum of Archaeology, Florence, inv. 79253

(d) Height 41.0 cm

This shows a bearded, naked male figure.

National Museum of Archaeology, Florence, inv. 80884

(c)

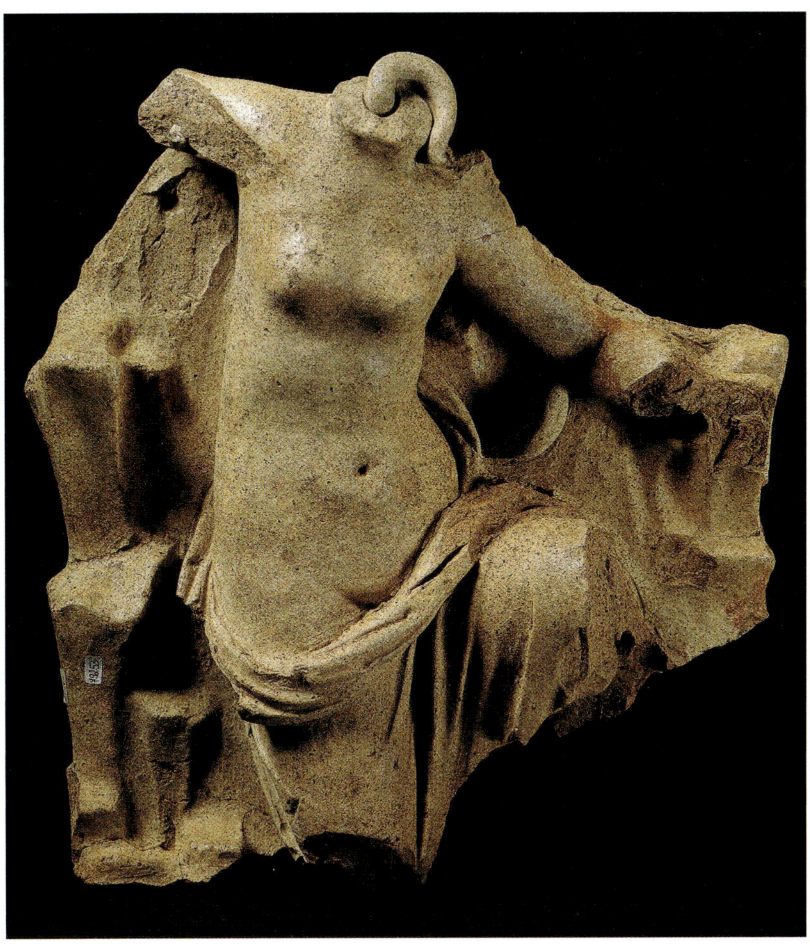

(d)

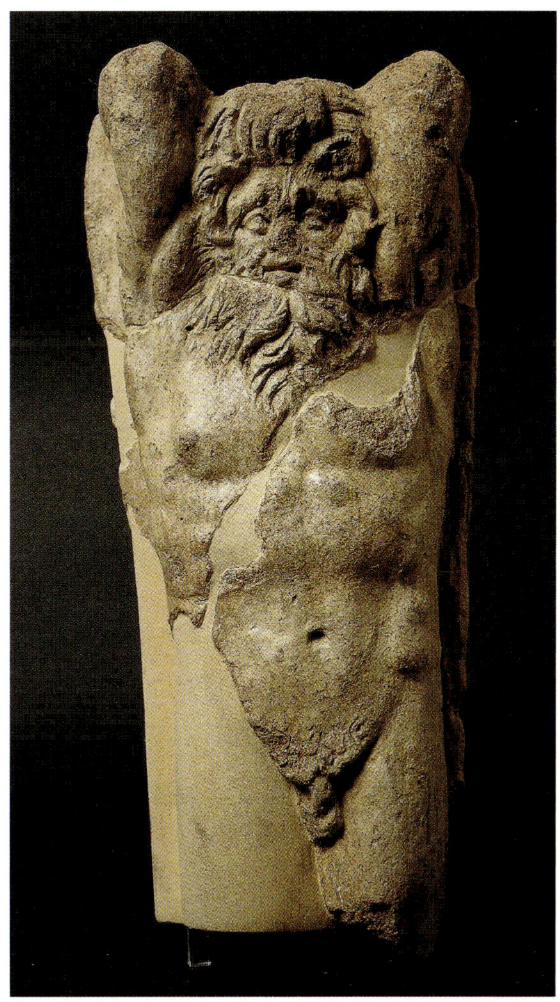

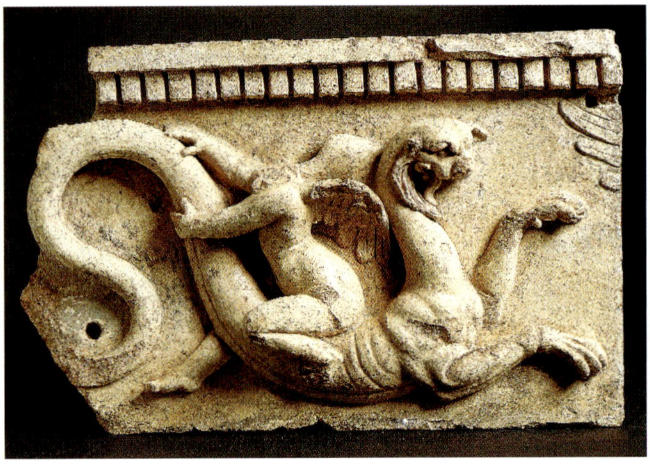

(e)

(e) Length 44.0 cm

This shows a panther-headed sea monster ridden by a small winged figure. There are traces of a wing at the right edge.

National Museum of Archaeology, Florence, inv. 80486b

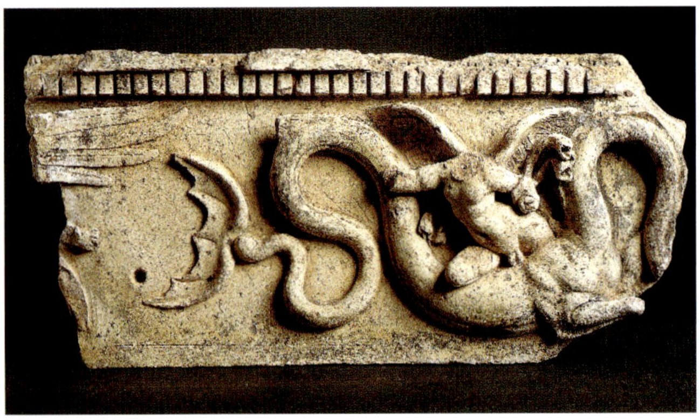

(f)

(f) Length 61.0 cm

This shows a sea monster ridden by a male winged figure. The monster's head is missing, but the fish's tail survives. There are traces of a wing at the left edge.

National Museum of Archaeology, Florence, inv. 80486a

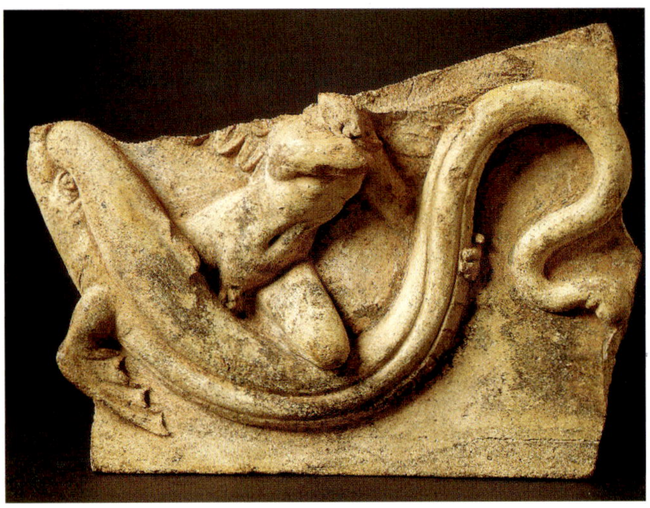

(g)

(g) Length 57.0 cm

This shows a sea monster ridden by a male winged figure.

National Museum of Archaeology, Florence, inv. 80486c

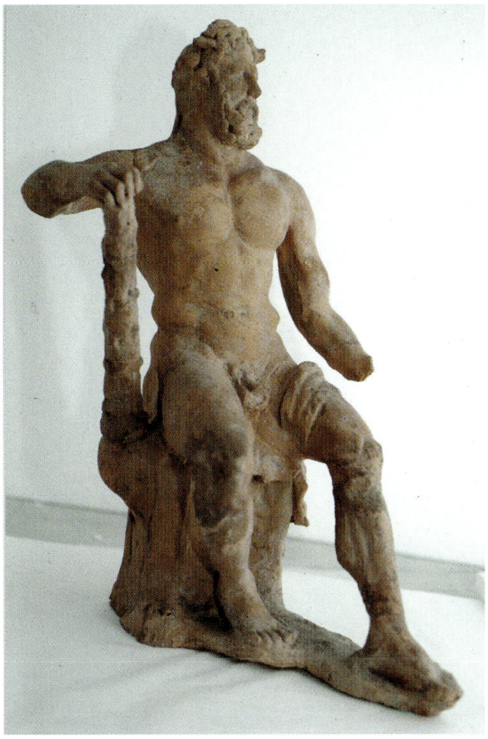

272 **Statuette of Herakles**

Terracotta
Sinalunga (Siena)
3rd century BC
Height 47.0 cm

The Etruscan Hercle was worshipped as a god in Italy, unlike his Greek counterpart, Herakles, who was venerated as a hero. Hercle was very popular in Italy, where he probably had even more places of worship than in Greece. This statuette shows him seated on a rock, with one hand resting on the club which is one of his characteristic attributes. The representation is based on Greek 4th-century BC sculpture.

GCC

National Museum of Archaeology, Florence, inv. 87397

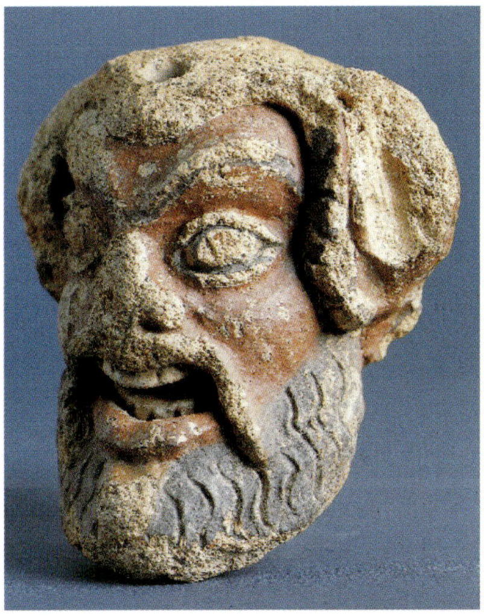

273 **Head of a bearded man**

Terracotta
Volsinii (Orvieto)
About 460 BC
Height 11.0 cm

There were several temples at Orvieto, including one dedicated to Tinia (Zeus/Jupiter). This terracotta head, and number 274, were amongst a group of full-size figured panels in high relief that adorned the roof. The figures apparently represent deities and mythological figures. The bearded head is probably of Silenus, companion of the wine-god Dionysus, usually shown as a drunken and jovial old man. The holes around the head were for iron pegs which originally held a wreath in place. The identity of number 274 is unknown. Both heads retain extensive traces of paint. *GCC/EG*

National Museum of Archaeology, Florence, inv. 71210
Santuari 1985, 80, no. 4.6

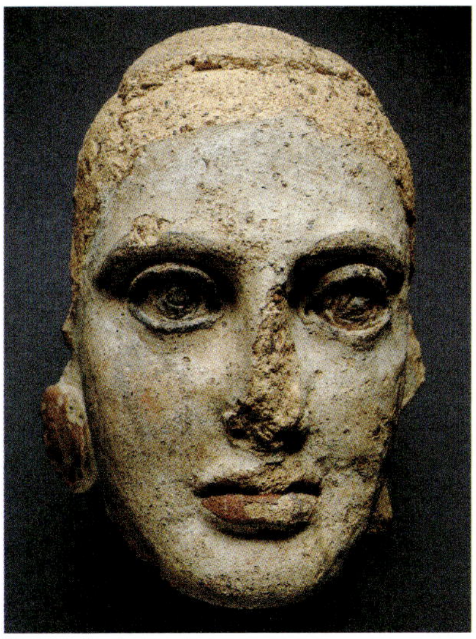

274 **Head of a woman**

Terracotta
Volsinii (Orvieto)
About 460 BC
Height 11.0 cm

National Museum of Archaeology, Florence, inv. 80160

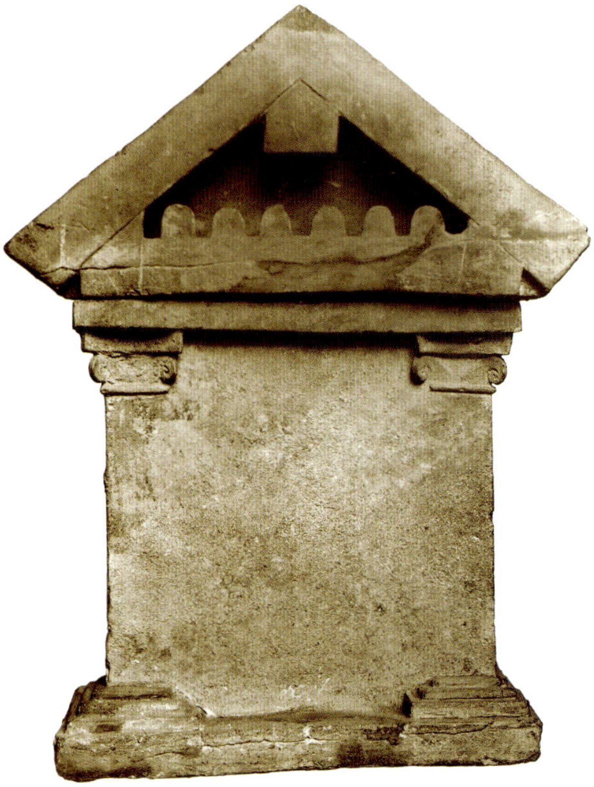

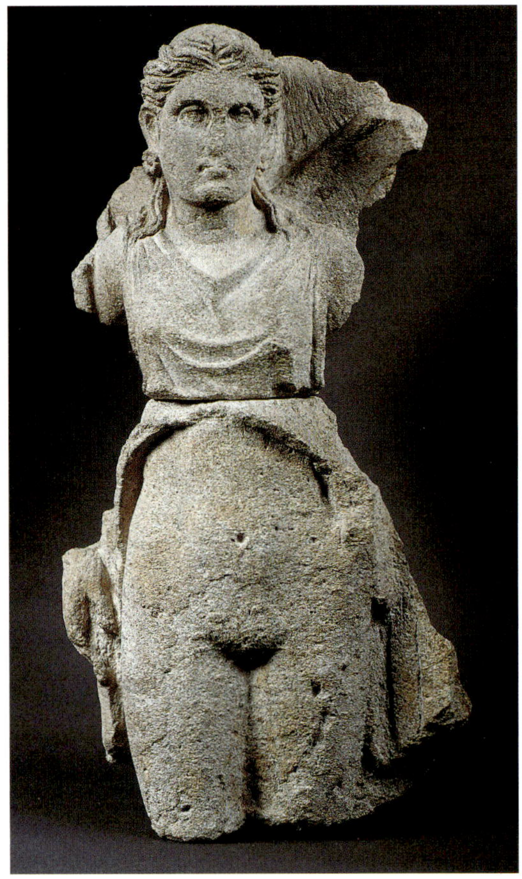

275 Ash urn

Terracotta
Volterra region (Riparbella)
3rd century BC
Height 48.0 cm

This ash urn is in the form of a small rectangular temple building with a pitched roof. There are simplified representations of the antefixes along the lower edge of the roof and cornice, with more detailed modelling of the four Ionic capitals and column bases. *GCC*

National Museum of Archaeology, Florence, inv. 148171
Borelli and Targio 2003, 77

276 Architectural relief

Nenfro
Tomb of the Vipinana family, Carcarella necropolis, Tuscania
End of the 4th to the beginning of the 3rd century BC
Height 94.0 cm

The monumental rock-cut tomb of the aristocratic Vipinana family in Tuscania was ornamented with a façade of ashlar blocks and sculpted decoration. This high relief may have formed part of the façade of this tomb, perhaps originally placed to one side of a door, with another statue on the other side. The relief may represent a winged female spirit called Vanth, who escorted the dead. Traces of a long object, perhaps a torch, are visible in her right hand. Vanth has been recorded beside the entrances to tombs at the end of the 4th century and beginning of the 3rd. *SB/EG*

National Museum of Archaeology, Florence, inv. 75842
Etruscos 1999, 209, no. 3; see also Haynes 2000, 348-9 for an alternative identification of the figure as a siren

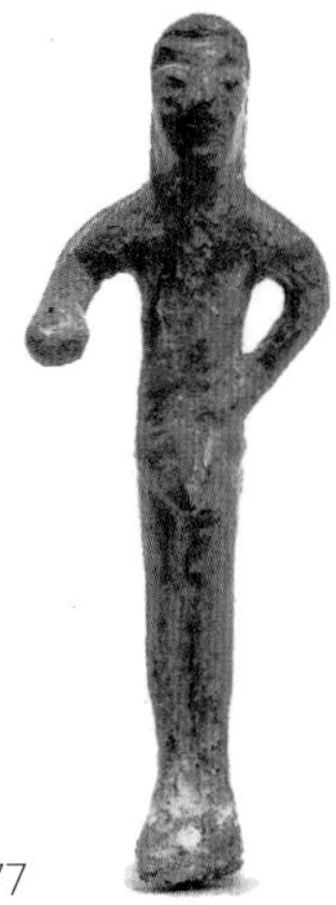

277

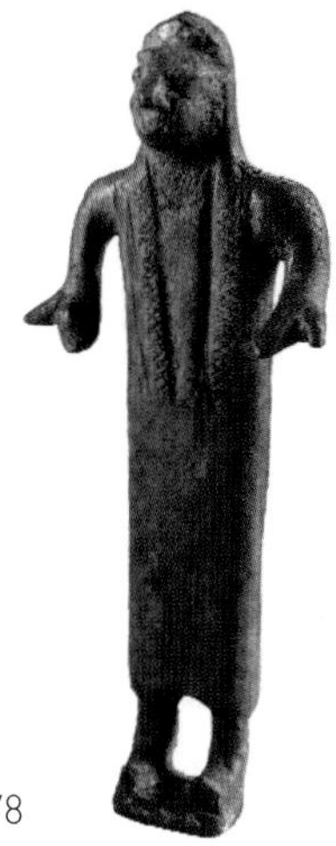

278

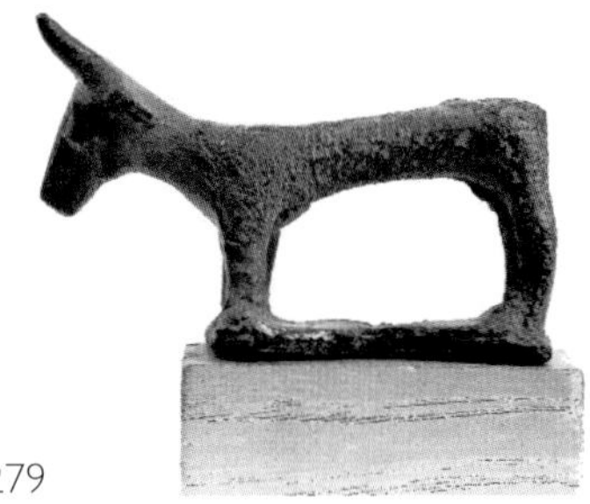

279

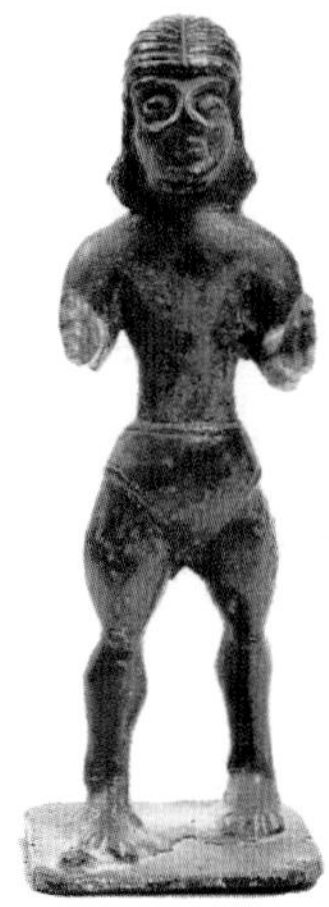

280

277 Votive figurine of a warrior

Bronze

Volterra

Last quarter of the 7th century BC

Height 9.2 cm

This figurine probably once held a spear in its outstretched hand. It belongs to a large group of votive bronzes representing men, women and animals from sanctuaries associated with healing cults. They may represent family groups. Figurines like these have been found over a wide geographical area including northern Etruria, especially in Volterra, Arezzo and Lake Trasimene, the Po valley, and as far afield as southern France. The distribution of these small bronzes throughout Europe reflects the importance of trade routes along the rivers. *GC*

Guarnacci Archaeological Museum, Volterra, inv. MG15

Cristofani 1978, 129; Magnificenza 1998, 94, no. 129

278 Votive figurine of a woman

Bronze

Volterra

Last quarter of the 7th century BC

Height 10.6 cm

This figurine of a female offerer is holding a rounded object, probably a pomegranate or an egg, symbols of fertility and renewal. The figurine belongs to a large group and was probably produced locally in Volterra at the end of the 7th century. *GC*

Guarnacci Archaeological Museum, Volterra, inv. MG65

L'Etruria mineraria 1985, 81, no. 290; Magnificenza 1998, 94, no. 128

279 Votive figurine of an ox

Bronze

Volterra

End of the 7th century BC

Height 4.3 cm

Guarnacci Archaeological Museum, Volterra, inv. MG135

L'Etruria mineraria 1985, 295, no. 291; Magnificenza 1998, 95, no. 130

280 Votive figurine of a warrior

Bronze

Volterra

End of the 7th to the beginning of the 6th century BC

Height 8.5 cm

This male figurine, which is wearing the loincloth known as a 'perizoma', may once have held a sword. It was probably made locally. *GC*

Guarnacci Archaeological Museum, Volterra, inv. MG26

L'Etruria mineraria 1985, 82, no. 292; Magnificenza 1998, 95, no. 131

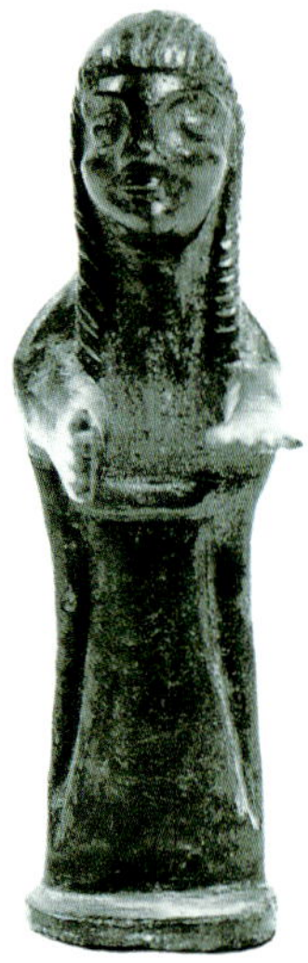

281 **Votive figurine of a woman**

Bronze

Volterra

End of the 7th to the beginning of the 6th century BC

Height 6.1 cm

Guarnacci Archaeological Museum, Volterra, inv. MG91

L'Etruria mineraria 1985, 82, no. 293; Magnificenza 1998, 95, no. 132

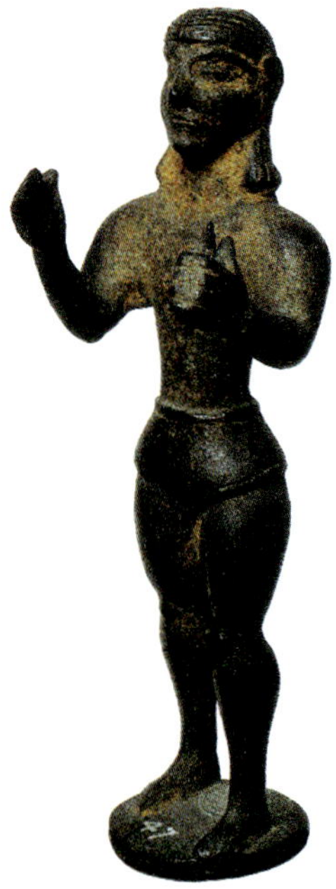

282 **Votive figurine of a warrior**

Bronze

Unknown provenance

Last quarter of the 7th century BC

Height 12.0 cm

This warrior is wearing a perizoma (loincloth) of a kind typically found on bronze figurines from northern Etruria at this date. *GCC*

National Museum of Archaeology, Florence, inv. 47

Cristofani 1985, 261, no. 11; Magnificenza 1998, 96, no. 133

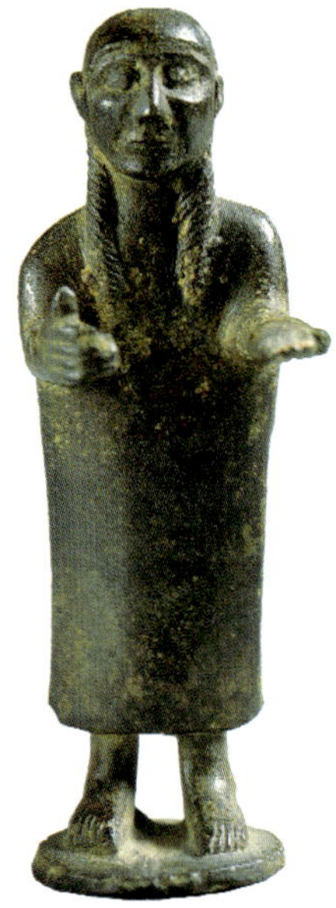

283 **Votive figurine of a woman**

Bronze

Unknown provenance

Last quarter of the 7th century BC

Height 9.0 cm

This figurine of a female offerer was made in inland northern Etruria. The style of the face and the truncated body are reminiscent of bronze figurines from Vetulonia. *GCC*

National Museum of Archaeology, Florence, inv. 221

Cristofani 1985, 261, no. 8; Magnificenza 1998, 96, no. 134

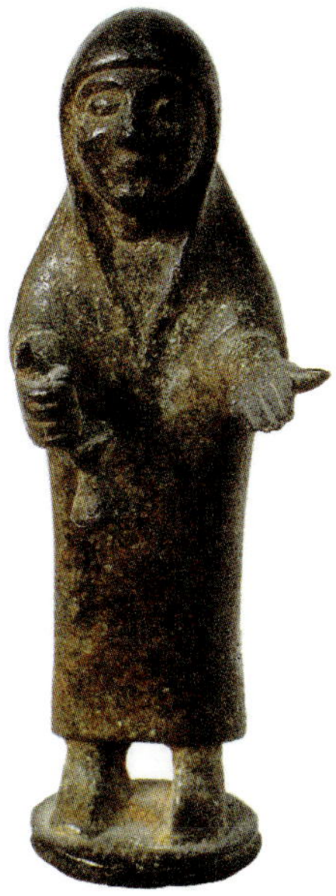

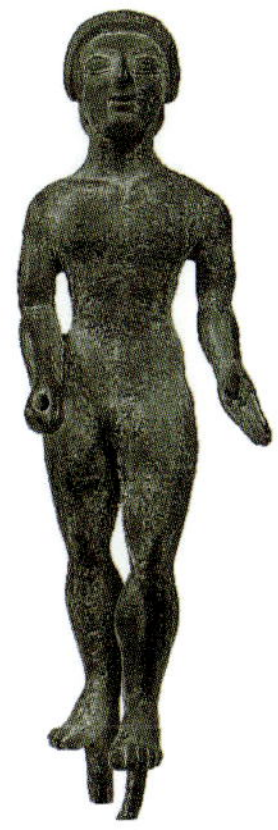

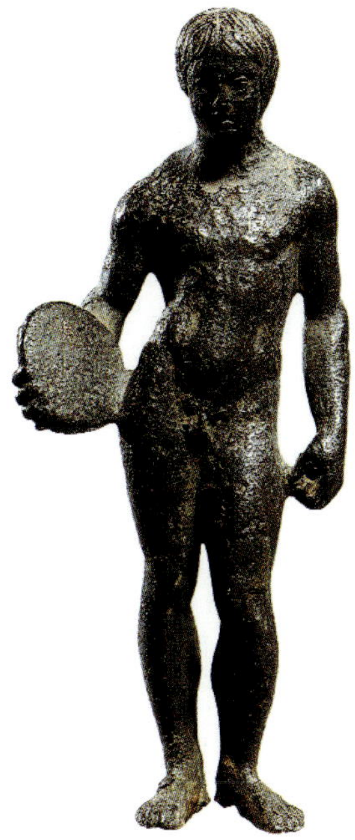

284 Votive figurine of a woman

Bronze
Unknown provenance
Last quarter of the 7th century BC
Height 9.5 cm

This figurine of a female offerer is holding a kyathos (ladle). The style of the cloak is typical of the second half of the 7th and the first half of the 6th century BC, and the form of the kyathos similarly suggests a date in the second half of the 7th century. Comparable examples are known from Vetulonia, Populonia, Volterra and Monteriggioni. *GCC*

National Museum of Archaeology, Florence, inv. 225

Cristofani 1985, 261, no. 10;
Magnificenza 1998, 96, no. 135

285 Figurine of a youth

Bronze
Castellina in Chianti
First half of the 5th century BC
Height 17.0 cm

The workshop that produced this figurine of a kouros, or naked youth, also made figurines of athletes, augurs (priests), and, later, groups of Herakles and the Nemean lion. It was probably located in Volterra. *GCC*

National Museum of Archaeology, Florence, inv. C200

286 Figurine of a discus thrower

Bronze
Unknown provenance
Second quarter of the 5th century BC
Height 13.5 cm

This figurine was inspired by a sculpture made by the famous Greek sculptor Polyclitus in the 5th century BC and which is known through copies made in the Roman period. Throwing the discus, one of the most ancient sports of the Olympic games, was very popular in Etruria. *GCC*

National Museum of Archaeology, Florence, inv. 18

Sport 1988, 101, no. 47

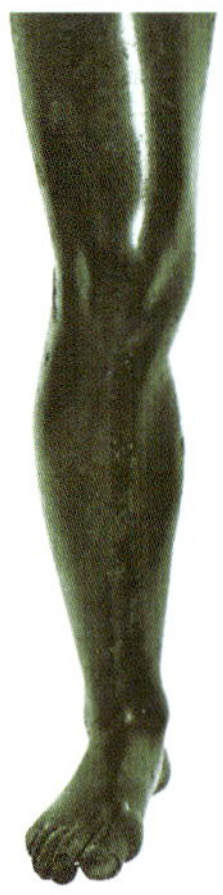

287 Votive model of a leg

Bronze
Castellina in Chianti
Middle of the 5th century BC
Height 6.0 cm

This is a skilfully-made model of a leg and foot. The practice of offering anatomical votives (*ex-votos*) at the sanctuaries of gods associated with healing increased in popularity from the 5th century BC onwards. Although fairly rare at this early date, they became much more common during the Hellenistic period, especially in terracotta, when they represent the offerings made by ordinary people from the lower social classes. *GCC*

National Museum of Archaeology, Florence, inv. CS100

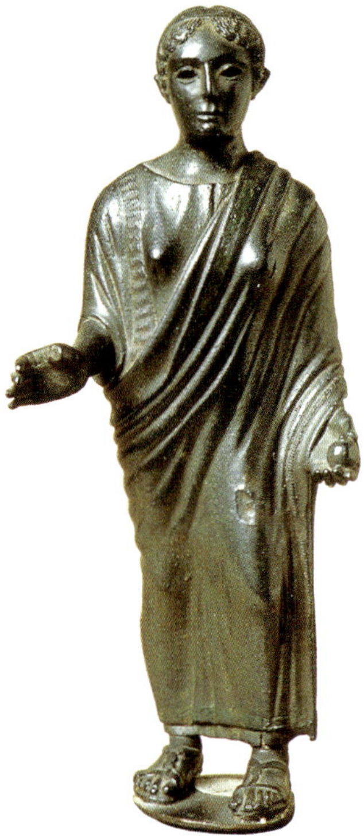

288 Votive figurine of a woman

Bronze
Unknown provenance
Third quarter of the 5th century BC
Height 16.5 cm

This figurine represents a woman offerer wearing carefully detailed clothing and sandals, and holding a pomegranate. It shows a style of art which was beginning to move away from severe formality. The figurine was made in inland northern Etruria. *GCC*

National Museum of Archaeology, Florence, inv. 280
Cristofani 1985, 269, no. 50

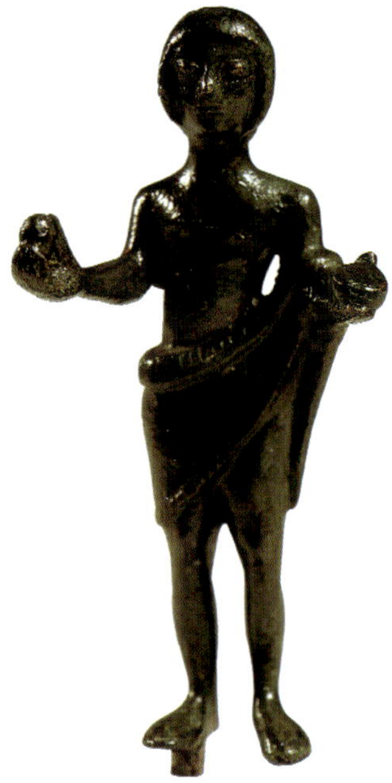

289 Votive figurine of a man

Bronze
Castellina in Chianti
4th century BC
Height 9.4 cm

Arms outstretched in a typical gesture of offering, this figurine of a votary is shown wearing a mantle draped around his hips, and holding a cup and a spherical object. The figurine is one of a series of such offerers made from the beginning of the 5th century, with examples of varying quality produced throughout the 4th and 3rd centuries. *AMi*

Museum of Archaeology, Siena, inv. 39497

290 ## Votive head of a woman

Terracotta
Unknown provenance
4th century BC
Height 28.5 cm

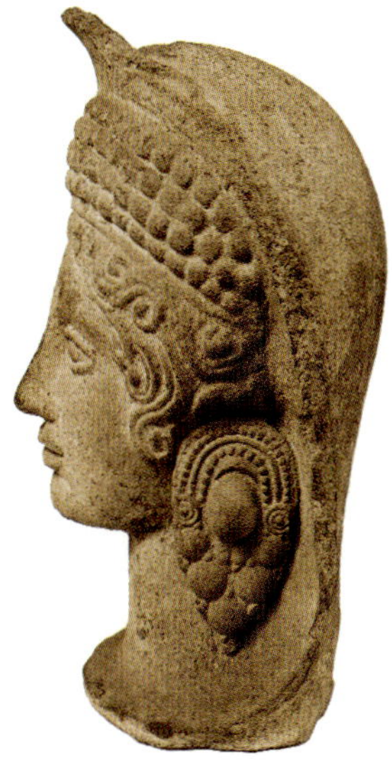

This woman's hair is dressed in an elaborate style, with a tall diadem and veil. She wears large earrings of a style characteristic of the period (see number 202). The richness of her adornment suggests that she represents a wealthy 4th-century BC Etruscan woman. The head was made in a mould, and has a plain back. *GCC/EG*

Museum of Archaeology, Siena, inv. 37818

291 ## Votive head of a young man

Terracotta
Unknown provenance
4th century BC
Height 31.0 cm

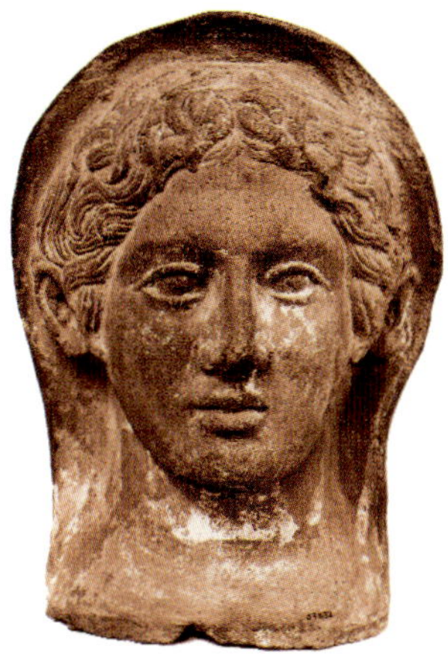

This is a type found in Etruria and Lazio in the second half of the 4th century BC. The man wears a cloak covering his head, as was usual during worship. *GCC*

Museum of Archaeology, Siena, inv. 37833

292 ## Votive head of a woman

Terracotta
Ponterotto temple, Vulci
End of the 4th to the 3rd century BC
Height 24.5 cm

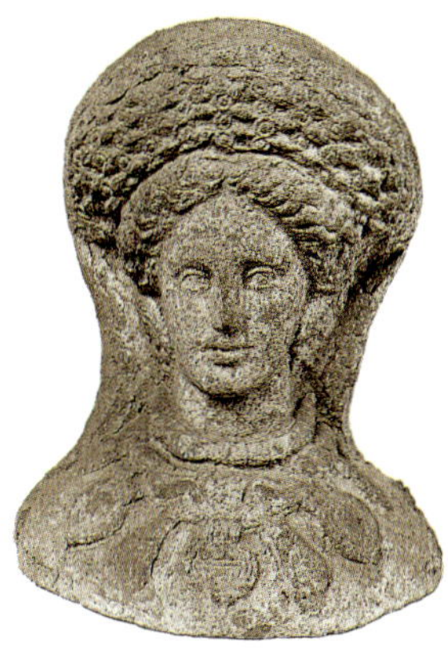

This head represents an Etruscan woman of high status. She is shown wearing a tall, richly decorated diadem, a veil and large earrings in the form of grape clusters. She also wears necklaces including the large pendant amulets known as bullae. *GCC*

Museum of Archaeology, Siena, inv. 37821

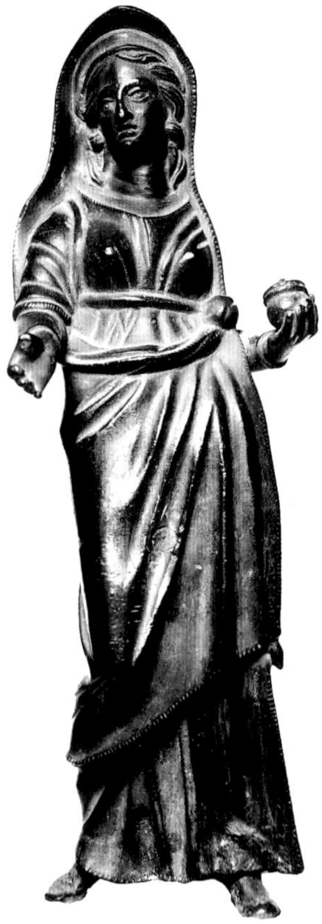

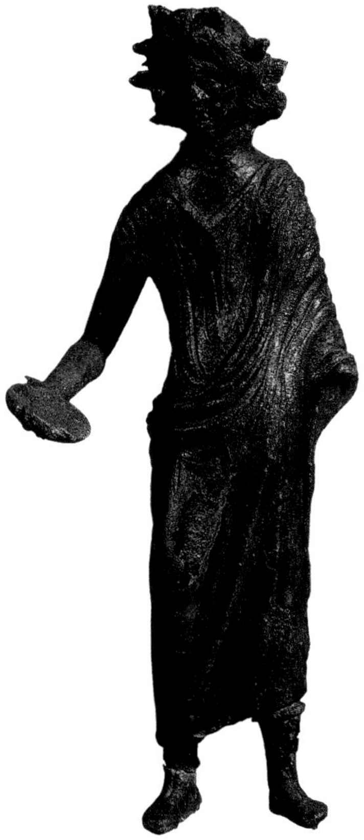

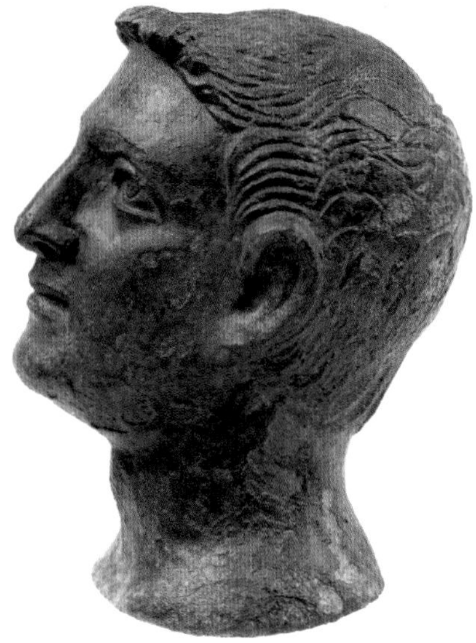

295 **Votive head of a man**

Bronze
Pozzarello sanctuary, Volsinii (Bolsena)
2nd century BC
Height 13.0 cm

This votive head and numbers 296-300 come from a sanctuary established during the 3rd century in association with the founding of the new city of Volsinii at Bolsena, following the destruction of the old city (at Orvieto) by the Romans. The cults of Volsinii were those of the Etruscan deity Selvans (god of boundaries and fields, related to the Roman Silvanus) and the Roman deities Ceres and the Bona Dea. Most of the votives from the sanctuary deposits were related to the latter two deities, who were associated with healing, the underworld and fertility. Objects like the knife are related to blood sacrifices and offerings, and the surgical tweezers, the eyes and the faces to healing cults. *PT/GCC*

National Museum of Archaeology, Florence, inv. 82956

Civiltà 1985, 388; Santuari 1985, 84-5, nos. 4, 8

293 **Votive figurine of a young woman**

Bronze
Unknown provenance
3rd century BC
Height 26.0 cm

This fine votive bronze shows a young woman wearing a high-girdled chiton and a short mantle covering her head and the lower part of her body. The locks of her hair are swept back to either side of her forehead, under a diadem. She holds an offering in the form of a pyxis (box). *GCC*

National Museum of Archaeology, Florence, inv. 549

294 **Votive figurine of a man**

Bronze
Vetulonia
3rd to 2nd centuries BC
Height 30.0 cm

This male figure of an offerer, dressed in a tunic and mantle, is wearing a wreath of vine leaves identifying him as a worshipper of Dionysus. He is holding a patera (dish) in his right hand. This type of votive figure, which has been found over a very wide area, is one of the most common from Etruria and Lazio. *GCC*

National Museum of Archaeology, Florence, inv. 6434

Cristofani 1985, 275, no. 76

296 Votive figurine of a youth

Bronze

Pozzarello sanctuary,
Volsinii (Bolsena)

2nd century BC

Height 16.5 cm

This type of votive of a young man wearing a toga was also common in Lazio. It is associated with the rite of passage to manhood, when youths first assumed the toga as part of the *Liberalia* festival, celebrated on 17 March.

PT/GCC/EG

National Museum of Archaeology,
Florence, inv. 82847

297 Votive figurine of a youth

Bronze

Pozzarello sanctuary,
Volsinii (Bolsena)

2nd century BC

Height 14.8 cm

National Museum of Archaeology,
Florence, inv. 82951

298 Three plaques with representations of eyes

Gold

Pozzarello sanctuary,
Volsinii (Bolsena)

2nd century BC

Length 2.0-6.0 cm

National Museum of Archaeology,
Florence, inv. 82957a-c

299 Miniature surgical tweezers

Silvered bronze

Pozzarello sanctuary,
Volsinii (Bolsena)

2nd century BC

Length 14.0 cm

National Museum of Archaeology,
Florence, inv. 13931a

300 Miniature knife

Bronze

Pozzarello sanctuary,
Volsinii (Bolsena)

2nd century BC

Length 10.0 cm

National Museum of Archaeology,
Florence, inv. 13932c

301 Axe

Iron

Fucoli sacred area,
Chianciano Terme

2nd century BC

Length 88.0 cm

This sacrificial axe was found at the site of a sacred building and may have been used as an item of insignia during religious ceremonies. It has a blade inlaid in copper with the shape of a knife and a long, elegantly shaped handle with a stylized ram's head terminal.

Archaeological Museum,
Chianciano Terme, inv. 174307

Torelli 2000, 620, cat. no. 265

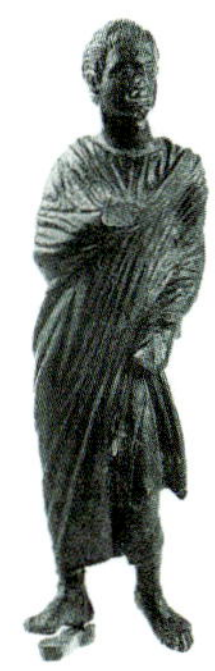

296

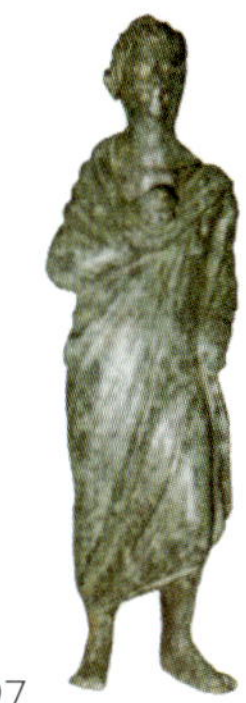

297

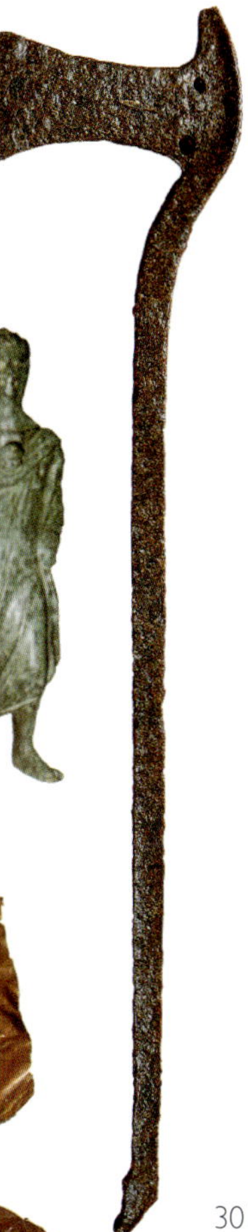

301

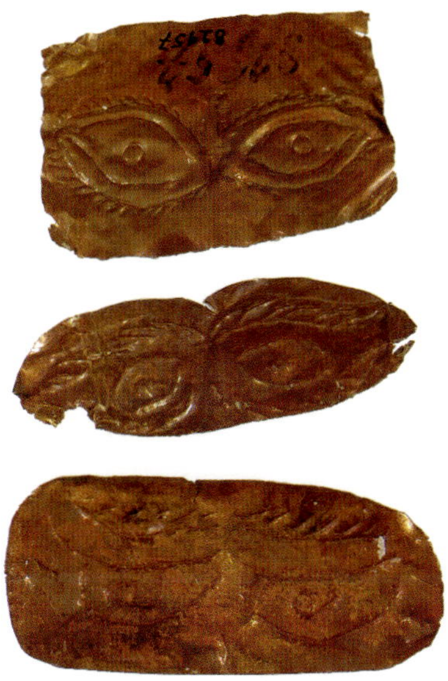

298

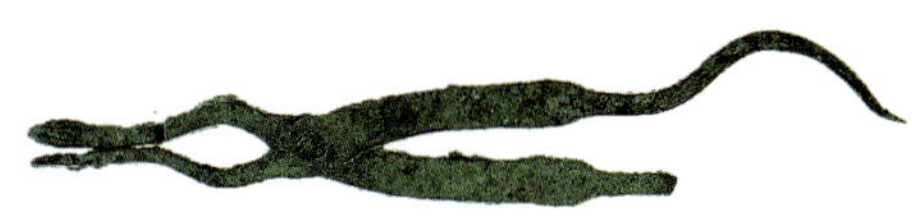

299

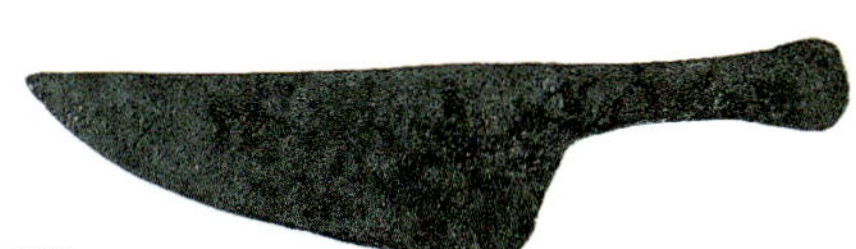

300

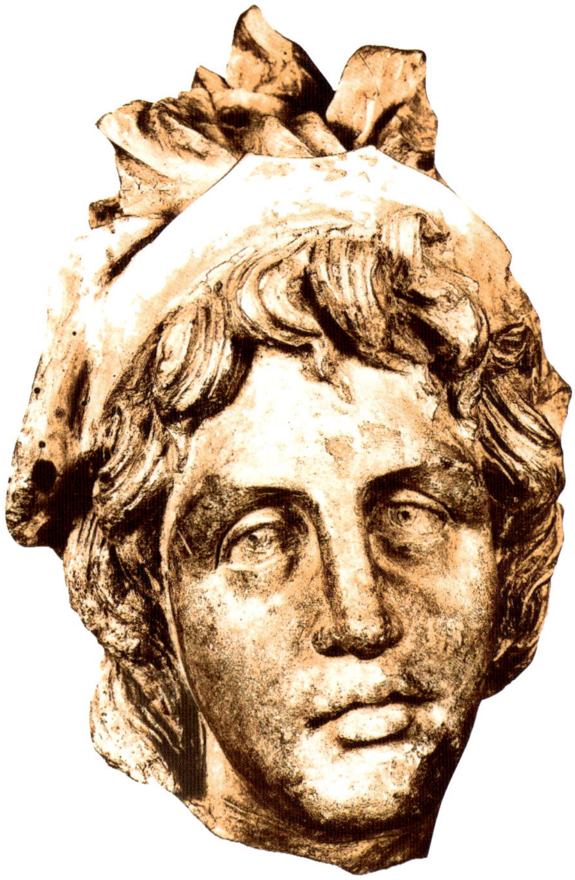

302 Head of a youth

Terracotta
La Catona, Arezzo
Middle of the 2nd century BC
Height 18.5 cm

This fine head of a young man wearing a Phrygian cap is part of a temple sculpture in high relief. Several areas were left unworked. There is well-preserved red paint on the head and cap. The head is shown in three-quarter view, tilted and turned slightly to the left. Long wavy locks of hair frame the face. The sculptor has succeeded in conveying in clay the softness of the Phrygian cap and the separately-worked ribbon around the head. The youth's intense, rather melancholy expression is typically Hellenistic. It has been suggested the head represents Paris, abductor of Helen.

Archaeological Museum, Arezzo, inv. 87667
Cristofani 1985, 381, 16.6.10; Torelli 2000, 635, cat. no. 318.2

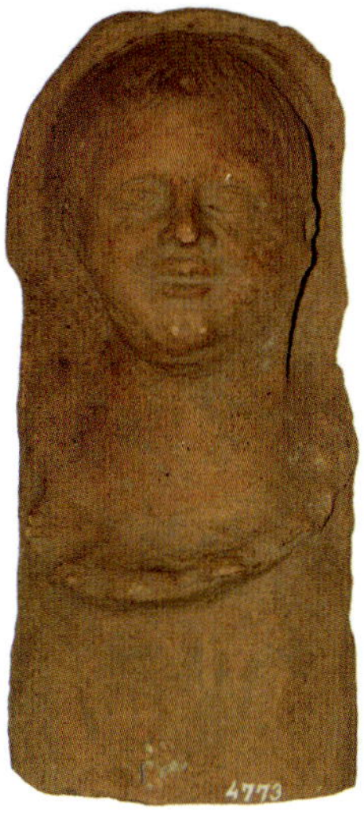

303

Votive model of a baby

Terracotta
Unknown provenance
3rd or 2nd century BC
Height 31.0 cm

Votive models (*ex-votos*) of body parts (see numbers 304-310) were frequently offered to the deities of healing and fertility in the sanctuaries of central Italy in the late Classical and Hellenistic periods. Votives of male and female genital organs and of swaddled babies represent concerns about safeguarding or promoting fertility, and health, especially of vulnerable infants.

National Museum of Archaeology, Florence, inv. 4773

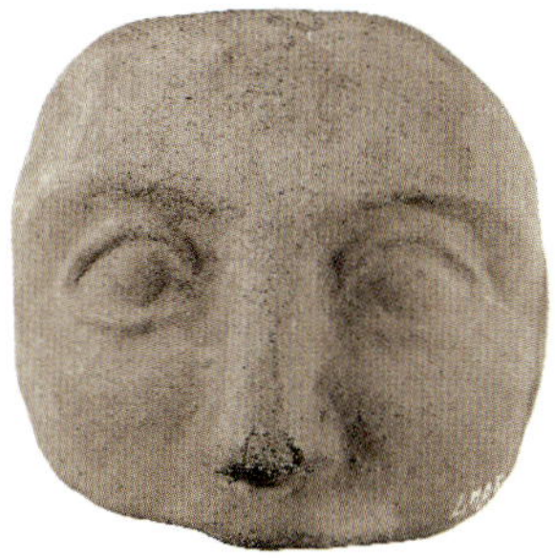

304

Votive head

Terracotta
Unknown provenance
3rd or 2nd century BC
Height 9.0 cm

Only the upper head, eyes and nose are represented.

National Museum of Archaeology, Florence, inv. 4785

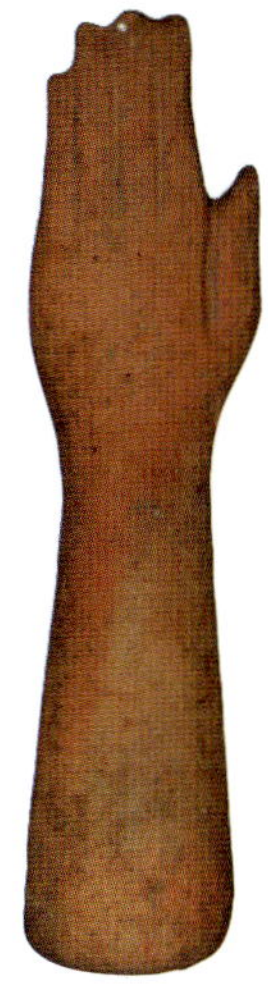

305

Votive model of a hand

Terracotta
Unknown provenance
3rd or 2nd century BC
Length 37.0 cm

National Museum of Archaeology, Florence, inv. 4777

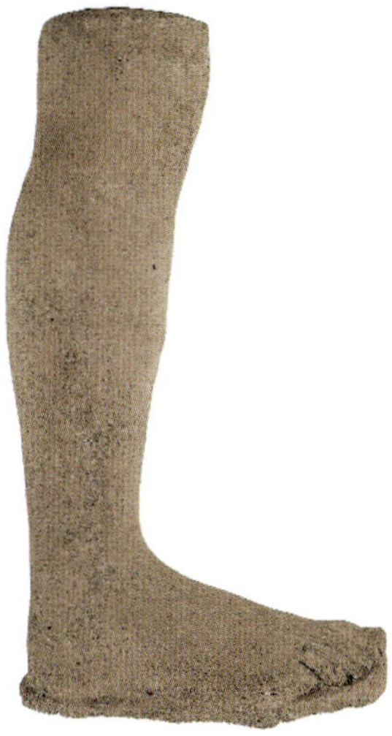

306

Votive model of a leg

Terracotta
Unknown provenance
3rd or 2nd century BC
Height 51.0 cm

National Museum of Archaeology, Florence, inv. 4796

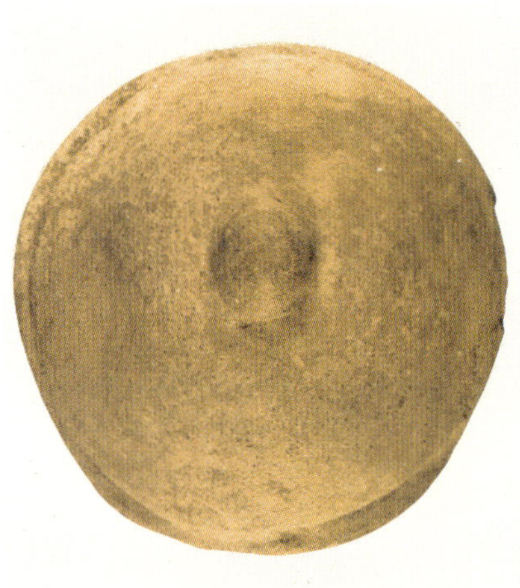

307

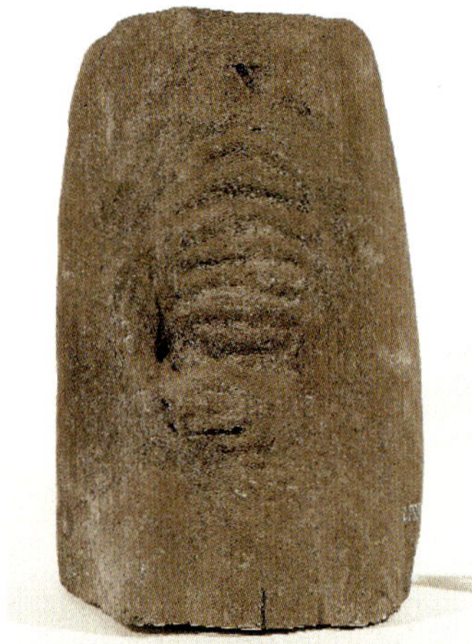

309

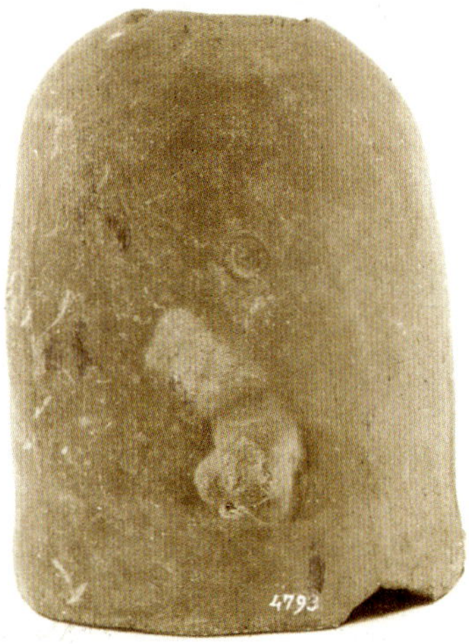

308

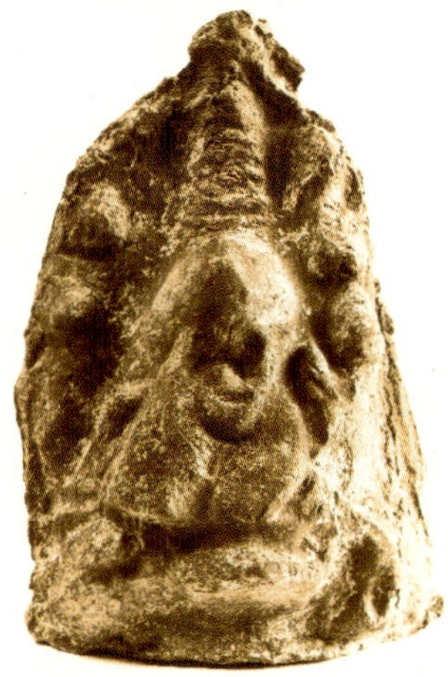

310

307 **Votive model of a breast**

Terracotta
Unknown provenance
3rd or 2nd century BC
Diameter 10.6 cm

National Museum of Archaeology, Florence, inv. 4787

308 **Votive model of a phallus**

Terracotta
Unknown provenance
3rd or 2nd century BC
Height 28.0 cm

National Museum of Archaeology, Florence, inv. 4793

309 **Votive model of a womb**

Terracotta
Unknown provenance
3rd or 2nd century BC
Height 26.5 cm

National Museum of Archaeology, Florence, inv. 4775

310 **Votive model of internal organs**

Terracotta
Unknown provenance
3rd or 2nd century BC
Height 24.0 cm

National Museum of Archaeology, Florence, inv. 80757

311 Votive figurine of a pig or boar

Terracotta
Veii
3rd or 2nd century BC
Length 16.3 cm

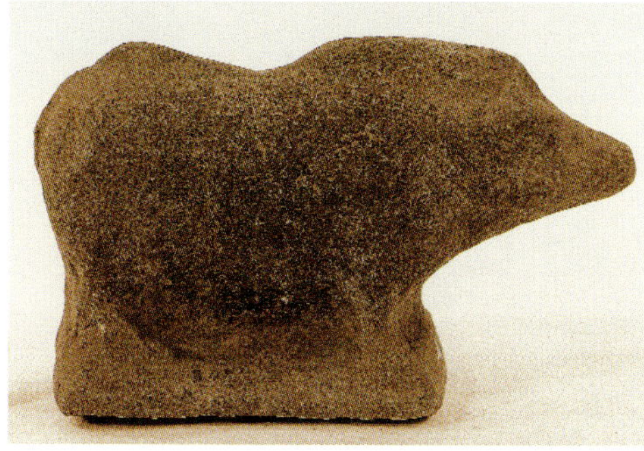

This *ex-voto*, and numbers 312-313, are from a sanctuary deposit found some centuries ago. There is some uncertainty about their provenance. Bronze and terracotta animals were common offerings, probably as cheaper substitutes for animal sacrifices. Animal figurines are most numerous in the inland agricultural areas of Etruria, but were also widely offered elsewhere.

National Museum of Archaeology, Florence, inv. 4819
Santuari 1985, 34, no. 1, 18

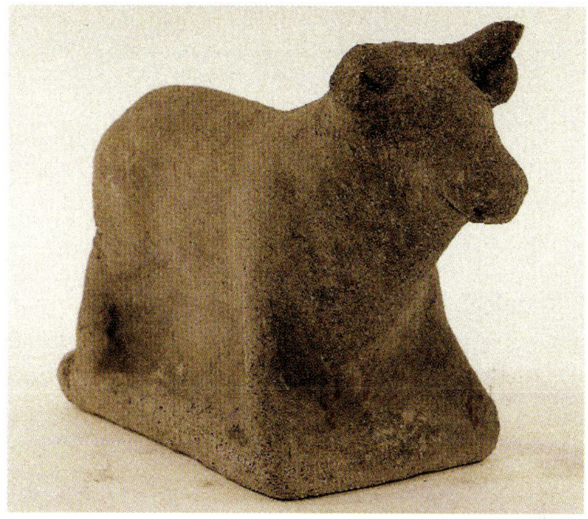

312 Votive figurine of a bull

Terracotta
Veii
3rd or 2nd century BC
Length 16.3 cm

National Museum of Archaeology, Florence, inv. 4822

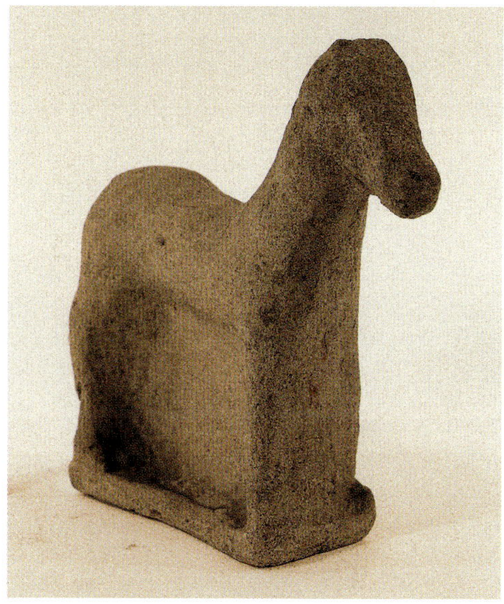

313 Votive figurine of a horse

Terracotta
Veii
3rd or 2nd century BC
Length 16.0 cm

National Museum of Archaeology, Florence, inv. 4831

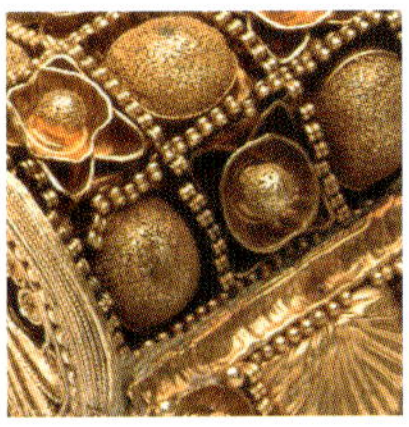
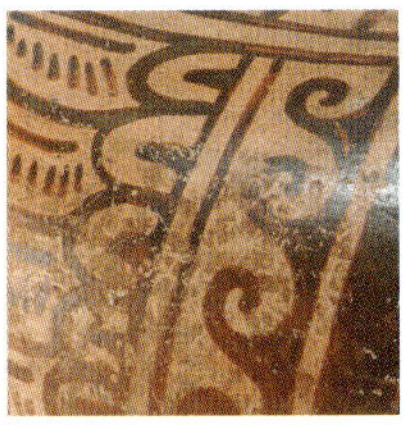
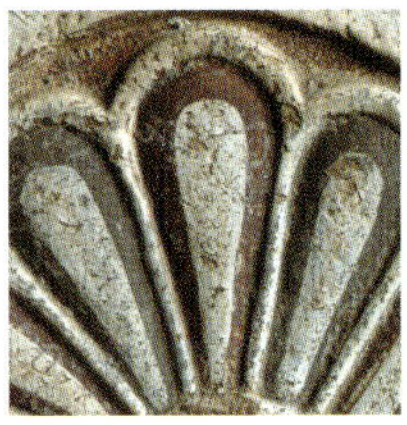

APPENDIX I

A SELECTION OF ETRUSCAN OBJECTS FROM THE NATIONAL MUSEUMS OF SCOTLAND

Elizabeth Goring

These objects are selected from the National Museums of Scotland's own collections. Most of the items were acquired from Alessandro Castellani in 1872, or presented to the museum by Sir Hugh Hume-Campbell in 1887.

The Castellani family were famous 19th-century Roman jewellers renowned for their work in the archaeological style. They took their inspiration from Etruscan metalworking techniques and in doing so assembled a large collection of antiquities. In the 1860s Alessandro Castellani opened branches of the family business in Paris and London.

Sir Hugh Hume-Campbell collected Greek, Etruscan and Roman artefacts in Florence, Rome, Volterra and Naples in the winter of 1843-4. From the 17th century it was customary for the sons of the British aristocracy to visit the major European cities to study language, geography, architecture and culture. This Grand Tour included Italy, and Italian art became a passion. The artistic, technical and political ideas of antiquity were thought to be worth re-exploring. This led to a classical revival that eventually affected all aspects of art and design from architecture to ceramics. *RW*

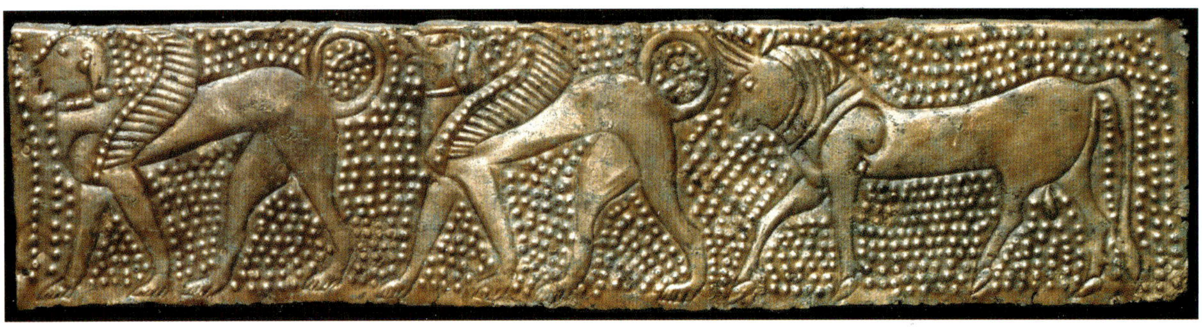

NMS 1

Relief plaque

Bronze
Unknown provenance
7th century BC
Length 44.5 cm

This unusual large plaque was probably a mounting from a piece of furniture. Smaller plaques were more likely to have been mounted on boxes. The three creatures – from left to right a sphinx, a griffin and a bull – are drawn from Near Eastern art.

National Museums of Scotland, inv. A.1887.242
Hume-Campbell 1887, 19, no. 45, pl. 4; Johnstone 1937, 400

NMS 2

Etrusco-Corinthian oinochoe

Painted ceramic

Said to have been found at Canino;
bought from Alessandro Castellani in Rome

Last quarter of the 7th century BC

Height 23.9 cm

This jug is decorated with a row of four hares.

National Museums of Scotland, inv. A.1872.23.35

CVA Edinburgh 1989, 47, pl. 54, 6-8

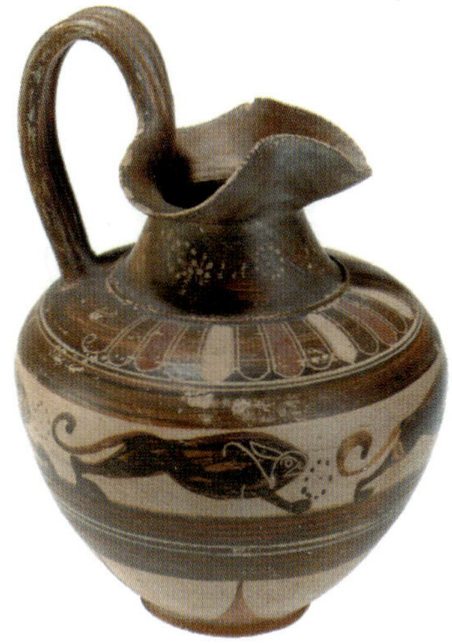

NMS 3

Etrusco-Corinthian amphora (container for liquids)

Painted ceramic

Unknown provenance

First half of the 6th century BC

Height 49.0 cm

The body of this wine vessel is decorated with large incised animals. On one side a lion is attacking an oblivious grazing stag; on the other side is a horse.

National Museums of Scotland, inv. A.1964.18

CVA Edinburgh 1989, 47, pl. 55, 4-7

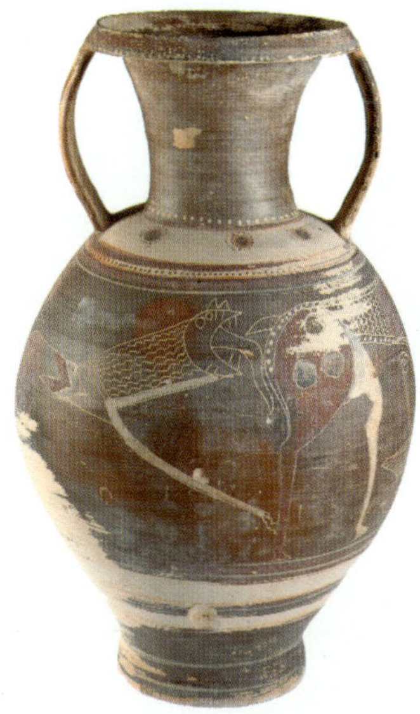

NMS 4

Oinochoe (wine jug)

Bucchero

Unknown provenance; given by Sir Hugh Hume-Campbell of Marchmont

Late 7th century BC

Height 27.5 cm

There is a frieze of incised animals around the body of the jug: two horses, three lions, two sphinxes and two goats.

National Museums of Scotland, inv. A.1887.206

CVA Edinburgh 1989, 50, pl. 58, 5-8; Hume-Campbell 1887, 15, no. 10; Johnstone 1937, 387

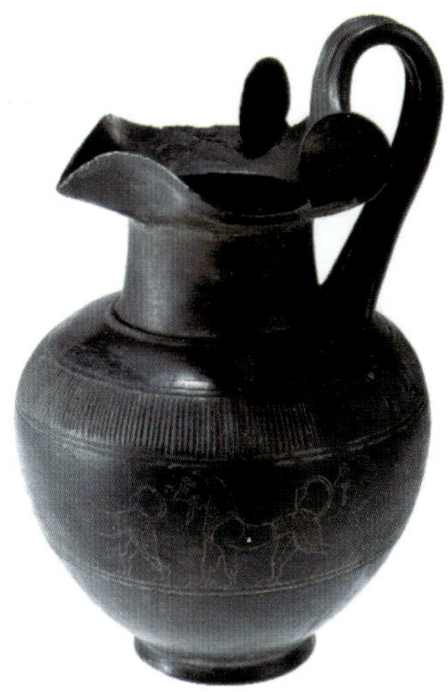

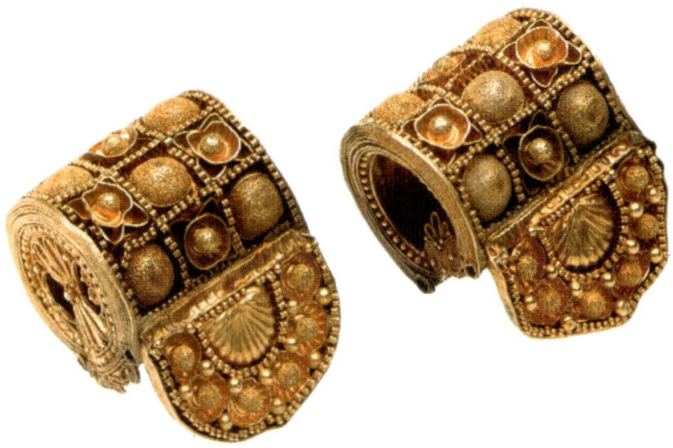

NMS 5

Pair of earrings

Gold

Said to have been found at Pompeii; from the collection of General Ramsay

Second half of the 6th century BC

Height 2.0 cm

This pair of earrings is an example of the 'a bauletto' type (see numbers 233 and 234). These particularly fine earrings are decorated with powder granulation, which uses minute grains of gold for decorative effect.

National Museums of Scotland, inv. A.1956.381 and A-C

Johnstone 1937, 405

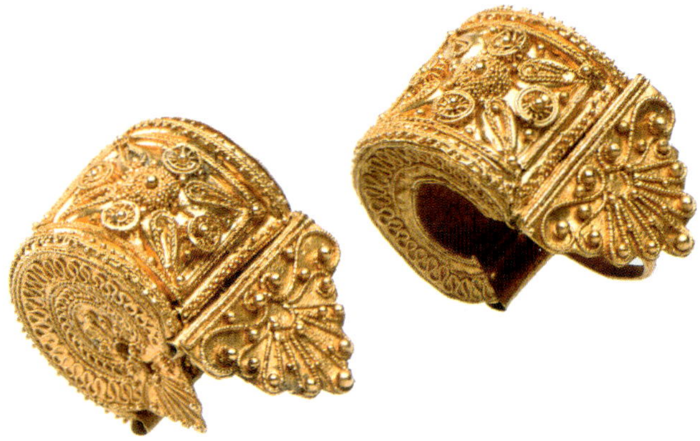

NMS 6

Pair of earrings

Gold

Unknown provenance

Last quarter of the 6th century BC

Height 1.8 cm

Scanning electron microscope study has revealed the Etruscan maker's precision and the control of the elaborate wire and granule decoration (filigree and granulation).

National Museums of Scotland, inv. K.2004.40.1 and 2

Johnstone 1937, 402

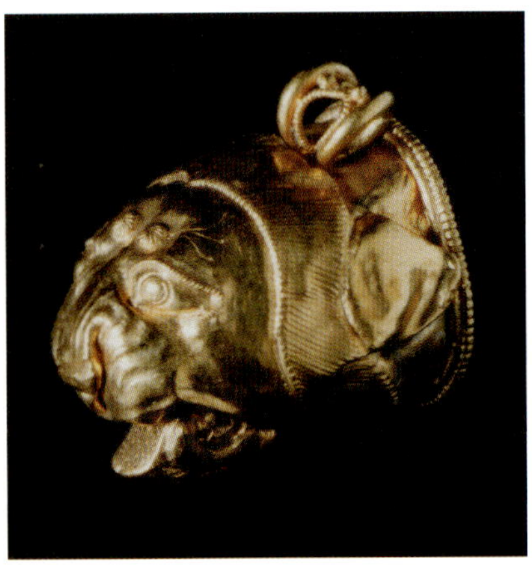

NMS 7

Mount or pendant

Gold

Said to have been found at Pompeii; from the collection of General Ramsay

Third quarter of the 6th century BC

Length 2.2 cm

This element in the form of a lion's head may have been part of a bracelet or necklace. It has a large round opening at the back. There is a double suspension ring behind the lion's mane and a small hole at the bottom end of the opening. This small, raised gold object was ornamented with beaded wires and granules, and details were meticulously added using delicate chasing and repoussé work. Even the lion's tongue has been carefully textured.

National Museums of Scotland, inv. A.1956.382

cf. Cristofani and Martelli 1983, cat. no. 157; Johnstone 1937, 406

NMS 8

Kyathos (ladle)

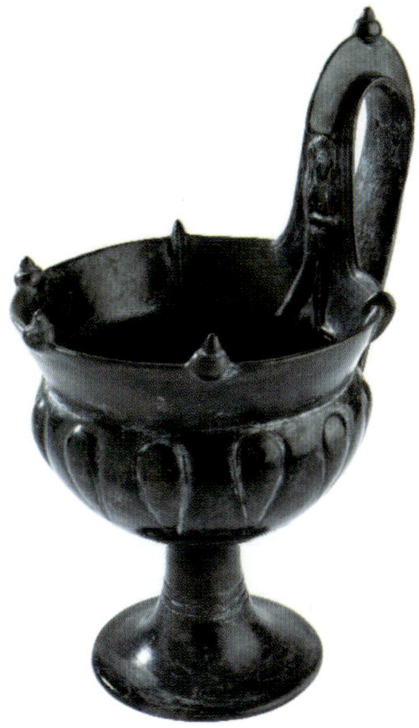

Bucchero
Uncertain provenance; given by Sir Hugh Hume-Campbell of Marchmont
Middle of the 6th century BC
Height 23.9 cm

This high-handled cup is based on a metal prototype. There is a male figure in relief on the inner face of the handle.

National Museums of Scotland, inv. A.1887.202
CVA Edinburgh 1989, 50, pl. 57, 11-12; Hume-Campbell 1887, 14, no. 1; Johnstone 1937, 389

NMS 9

Oinochoe

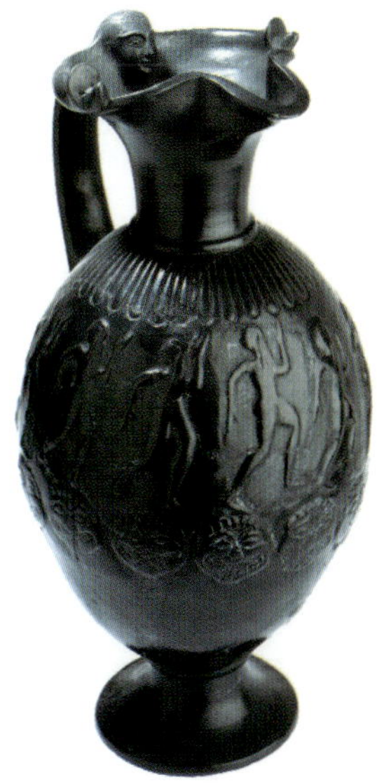

Bucchero
Unknown provenance; given by Sir Hugh Hume-Campbell of Marchmont
Middle of the 6th century BC
Height 52.0 cm

Around the body of this tall vessel is a row of dancing figures created from a matrix. Below them is a row of gorgon's heads.

National Museums of Scotland, inv. A.1887.197
CVA Edinburgh, pl. 60, 1-3

NMS 10

Amphora (wine vessel)

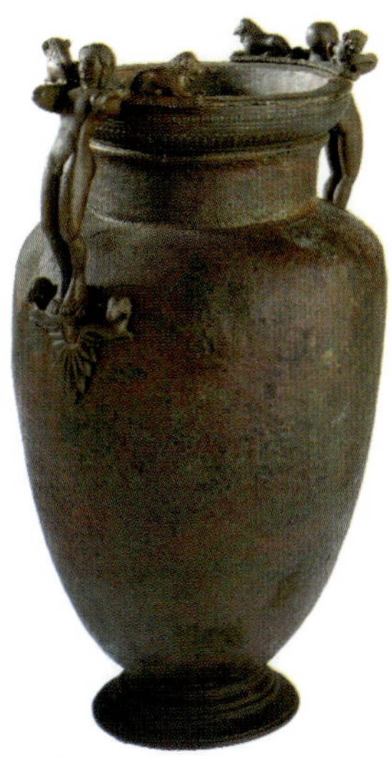

Bronze
Said to have been found at Volterra in 1843
End of the 6th century BC
Height 35.6 cm

This fine vessel, part of a banqueting set, was probably made locally. The elegant handles are in the form of nude male figures standing on palmettes and rams. There are crouching lions on the rim.

National Museums of Scotland, inv. A.1887.251
Hume-Campbell 1887, 19, no. 54 and pls. 6, 7; Johnstone 1937, 399

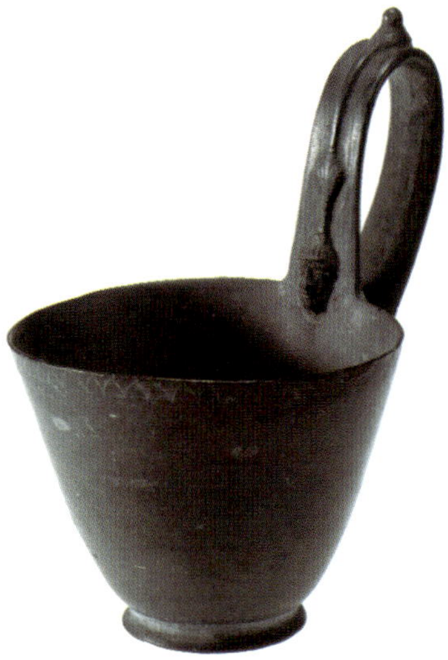

NMS 11

Kyathos (ladle)

Bucchero
Unknown provenance; given by Sir Hugh Hume-Campbell of Marchmont
Second half of the 6th century BC
Height 12.7 cm

This cup of fine bucchero pottery ('bucchero sottile') may have been made in Vulci. There is a human head modelled in relief on the inner face of the handle.

National Museums of Scotland, inv. A.1887.205
CVA Edinburgh 1989, 49, pl. 57, 9-10; Hume-Campbell 1887, 15, no. 9; Johnstone 1937, 389

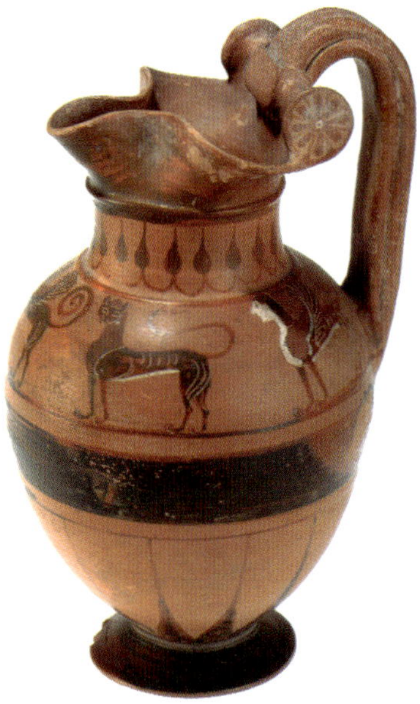

NMS 12

Pontic oinochoe (wine jug)

Painted ceramic
Said to have been found at Chiusi; bought from Alessandro Castellani in Rome
About 540 BC
Height 23.0 cm

This fine jug is decorated on the shoulder with a frieze of alternating panthers and sphinxes. The so-called Pontic vases are the earliest type of Etruscan black-figure pottery, influenced by the East Greek style of vase-painting.

National Museums of Scotland, inv. A.1872.23.6
CVA Edinburgh 1989, 47, pl. 56, 1-3

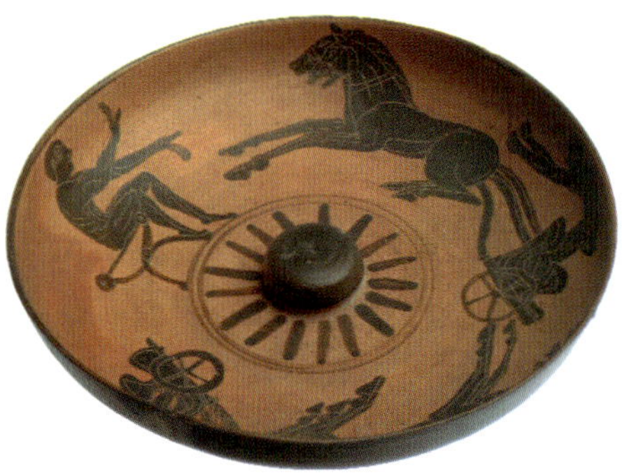

NMS 13

Etruscan black-figure phiale mesomphalos

Painted ceramic
Unknown provenance; given by Sir Hugh Hume-Campbell of Marchmont
First half of the 5th century BC
Diameter 19.6 cm

On the inner face of this dish there is a lively illustration of a chariot race. Two charioteers are driving 'bigae' (chariots drawn by two horses) around a track at full gallop. The man seated on the folding stool is the judge.

National Museums of Scotland, inv. A.1887.209
CVA Edinburgh 1989, 48, pl. 56, 4; Hume-Campbell 1887, 15, no. 13, pl. 1.1; Johnstone 1937, 402

NMS 14

Cista (container for toilet instruments)

Bronze

Probably from Palestrina (Praeneste) in the northern part of Lazio; given by the Earl of Moray

Second half of the 4th century BC

Height 39.4 cm

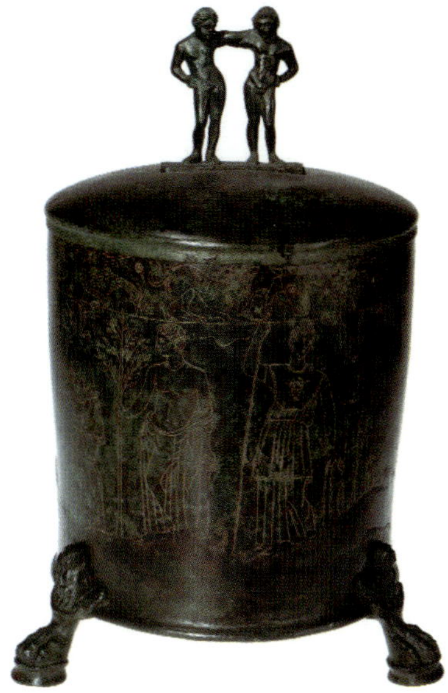

This container was probably used for holding cosmetic or toilet implements – pigments, spoons, combs. It was made in the important metalworking area of northern Lazio by Etruscan craftsmen or under Etruscan influence. This is an important and very typical 4th-century BC vessel, but it may have been re-engraved, and the cast bronze figures on the lid may be problematic.

National Museums of Scotland, inv. A.1922.74 and A

Johnstone 1937, 396-8

NMS 15

Handled patera (dish)

Bronze

Said to have been found at Volterra in 1843

First half of the 3rd century BC

Length 41.9 cm

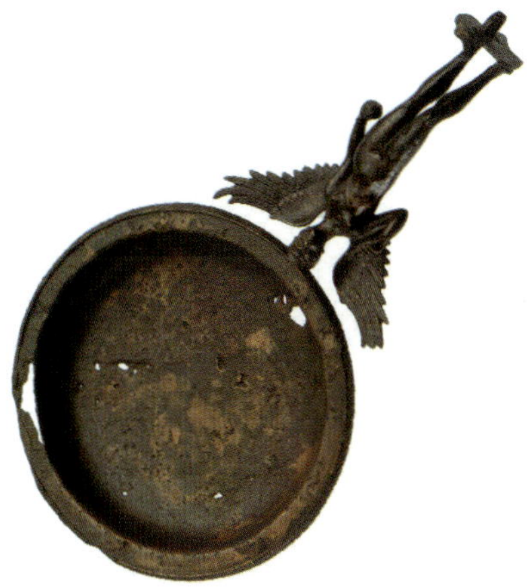

This dish, with its handle in the form of a winged female figure, is a typical product of Volterra. There is a ring at the end of the handle for suspending the dish.

National Museums of Scotland, inv. A.1887.252

Hume-Campbell 1887, 19, no. 55; Johnstone 1937, 392

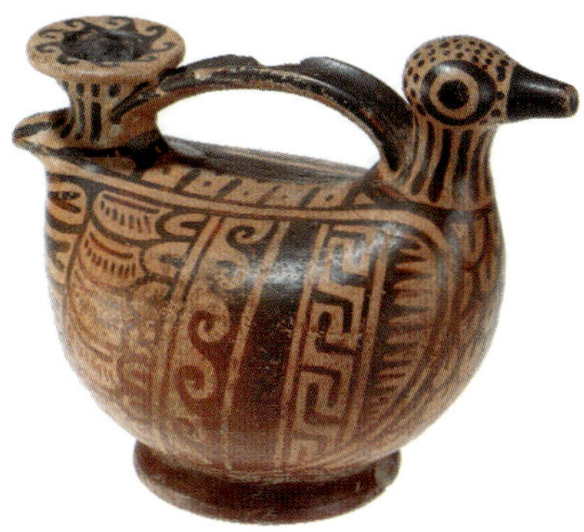

NMS 16

Etruscan red-figure duck askos (container for perfumed oil)

Painted ceramic

Said to have been found at Tarquinia; purchased from Alessandro Castellani in Rome

4th century BC

Height 17.5 cm

This askos is similar to number 254.

National Museums of Scotland, inv. A.1872.23.19

CVA Edinburgh 1989, 48, pl. 56, 11-15

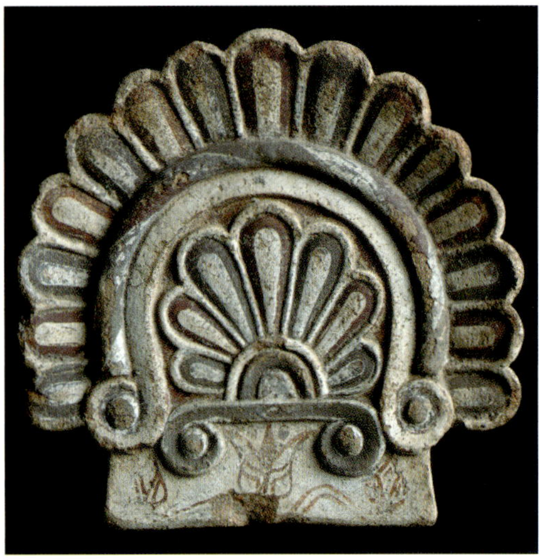

NMS 17

Antefix

Painted terracotta
Said to be from Capua; from the collection of Alessandro Castellani
About 550 BC
Height 26.0 cm

Antefixes of this kind (see also numbers 18 to 22) were generally attached to religious buildings, especially temples, although examples are now also known from domestic buildings. They were used to mask the open ends of the semi-circular roof tiles, above the eaves along the sides of the roof. They were both decorative and functional, protecting the wooden structure of the buildings from the elements. This example has particularly well-preserved painted decoration, and is unusual in having painted lotuses along its lower edge.

National Museums of Scotland, inv. A.1877.21.7
Johnstone 1937, 405

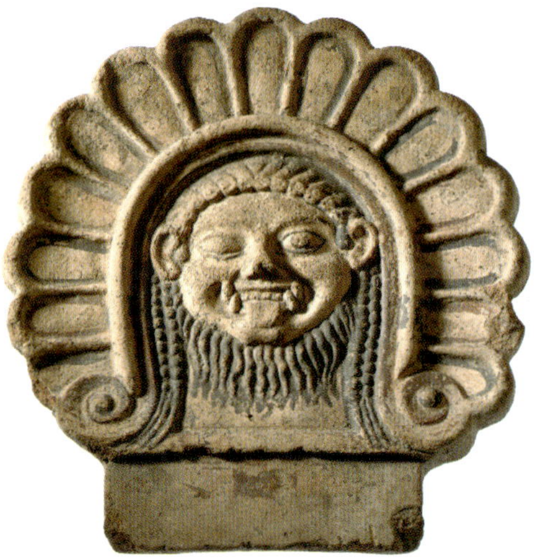

NMS 18

Antefix

Painted terracotta
Said to be from Capua; from the collection of Alessandro Castellani
About 550 BC
Height 37.5 cm

This antefix has a fine representation of a gorgon's head. There are extensive traces of red and black paint.

National Museums of Scotland, inv. A.1877.21.3
Johnstone 1937, 404

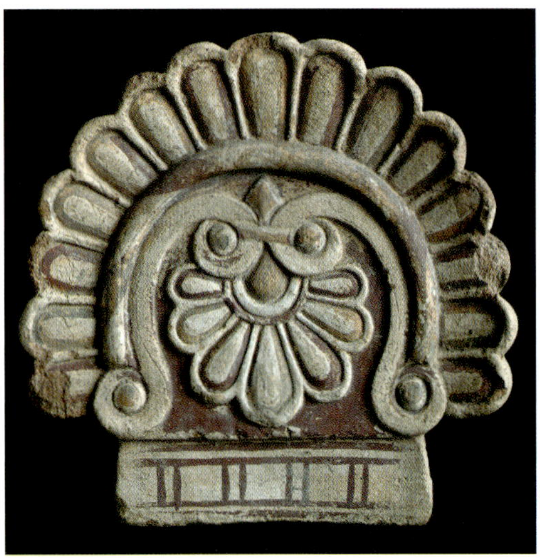

NMS 19

Antefix

Painted terracotta
Said to be from Capua; from the collection of Alessandro Castellani
About 550 BC
Height 25.5 cm

This antefix with a palmette design has exceptionally well-preserved painted decoration.

National Museums of Scotland, inv. A.1877.21.9
Johnstone 1937, 405

NMS 20

Antefix

Painted terracotta
Said to be from Capua; from the collection of Alessandro Castellani
Second half of the 5th century BC
Height 23.5 cm

This antefix is decorated with the head of a woman with long flowing locks. She is wearing a 'bulla', a typical Etruscan pendant charm, suspended from a necklace. She is also wearing a helmet, suggesting she may be the Etruscan deity Menerva (the equivalent of the Greek Athena, the Roman Minerva).

National Museums of Scotland, inv. A.1877.21.6
Johnstone 1937, 405

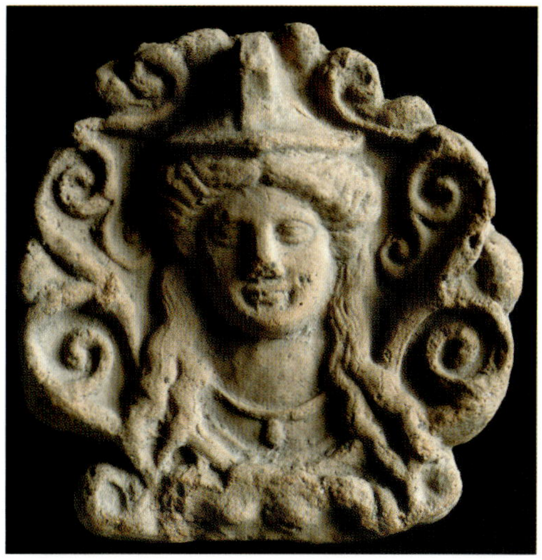

NMS 21

Antefix

Painted terracotta
Said to be from Capua; from the collection of Alessandro Castellani
Third quarter of the 6th century BC
Height 34.5 cm

This antefix is decorated with the head of a woman, set between stylized lotus ornaments and roundels. She wears a high diadem and her hair is dressed in long braids. There are traces of red and black paint.

National Museums of Scotland, inv. A.1877.21.4
Johnstone 1937, 404

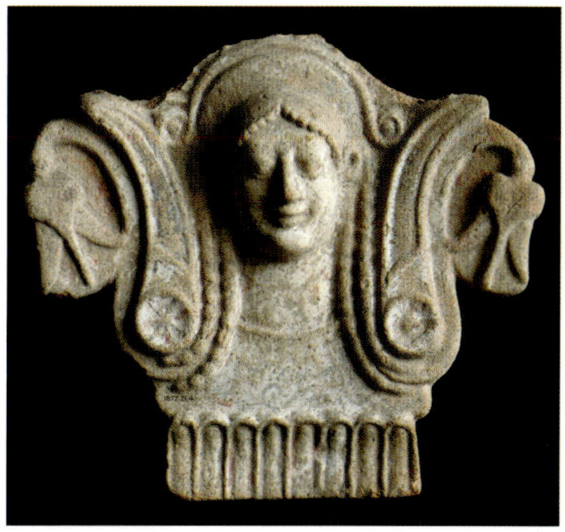

NMS 22

Antefix

Painted terracotta
Said to be from Capua; from the collection of Alessandro Castellani
First quarter of the 5th century BC
Height 27.5 cm

This antefix is decorated with the figure of a horseman, presumably a warrior, wearing a short tunic and cloak.

National Museums of Scotland, inv. A.1877.21.2
Johnstone 1937, 404

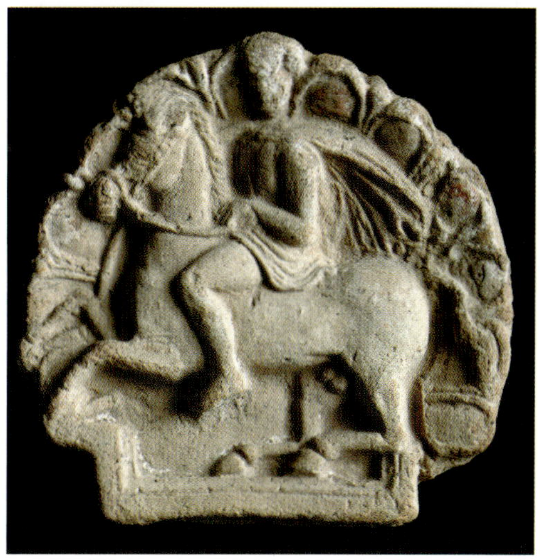

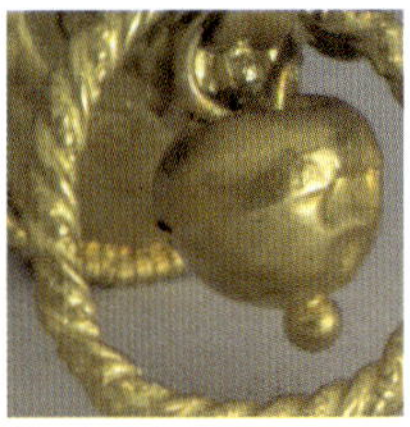 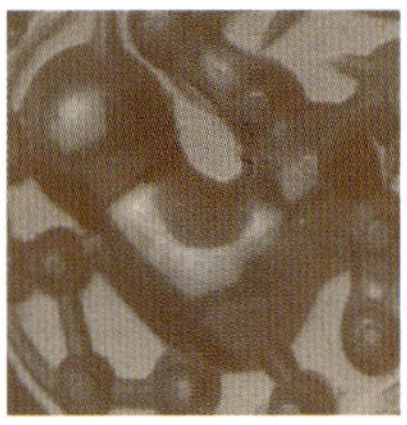 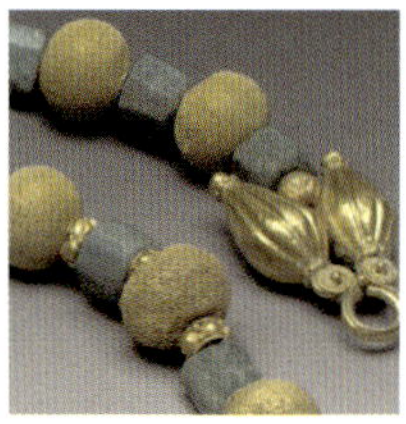

APPENDIX II
A SELECTION OF ETRUSCAN OBJECTS FROM THE BRITISH MUSEUM

Judith Swaddling

The British Museum lent a selection of gold jewellery and engraved gemstones to the exhibition drawn from their extensive and important Etruscan collections.

BM 1

Finger ring

Gold

Unknown provenance; formerly in the collection of Richard Cornwallis Neville, 4th Baron Braybrooke

Bequeathed by Sir Augustus Wollaston Franks

Second half of the 6th century BC

Diameter 2.1 cm; diameter (inner) 1.7 cm; length (bezel) 2.0 cm; weight 3.11 g

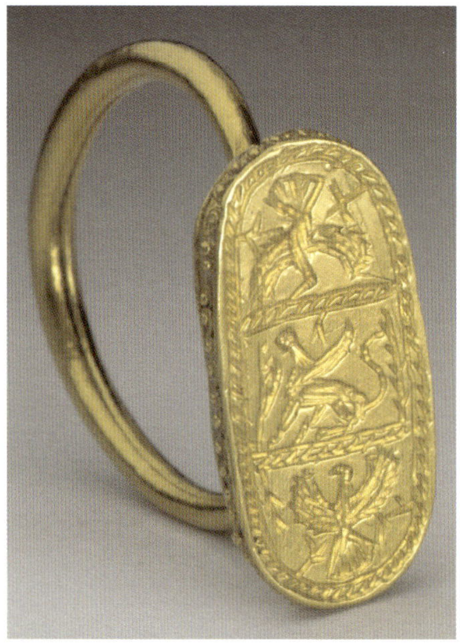

This Ionian style ring was probably made in Etruria. The bezel is engraved with a sphinx between eagles in flight, within hatched borders.

British Museum, inv. GR.1917.5-1.21

Marshall 1907, no. 21; for the type, see Cristofani and Martelli 1983, nos. 175-9

BM 2

Finger ring

Gold

Unknown provenance; formerly in the Campanari collection

5th to 4th centuries BC

Diameter 2.4 cm; diameter (inner) 2.1 cm; length (bezel) 2.3 cm; weight 11.01 g

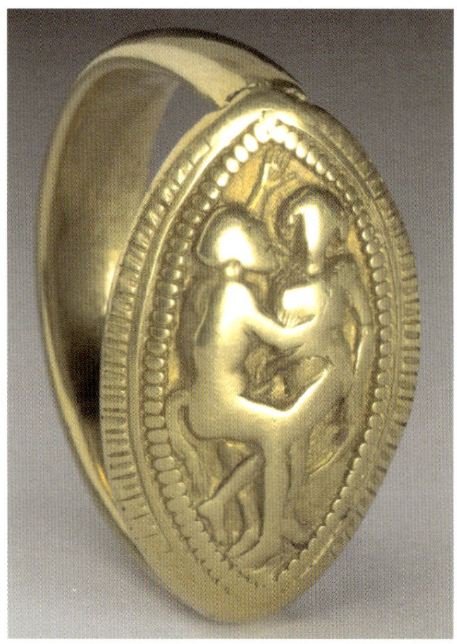

The well-worn bezel of this Etruscan ring is decorated in relief with an erotic scene of a satyr and a nymph. The ring belongs to the so-called Fortnum type.

British Museum, inv. GR.1846.6-29.17

Marshall 1907, no. 214; Fortnum 1873, 360 note

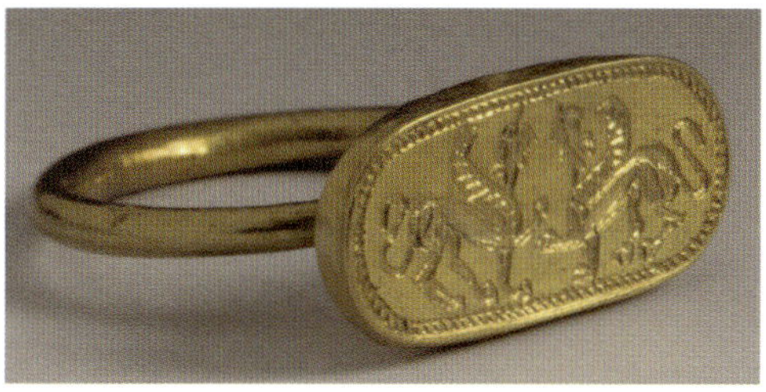

BM 3

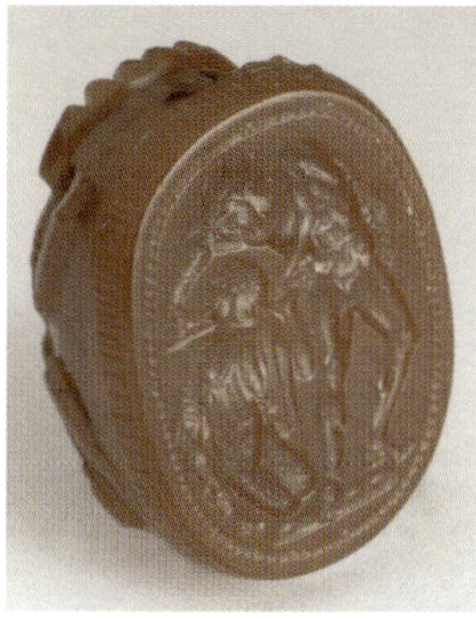

BM 4

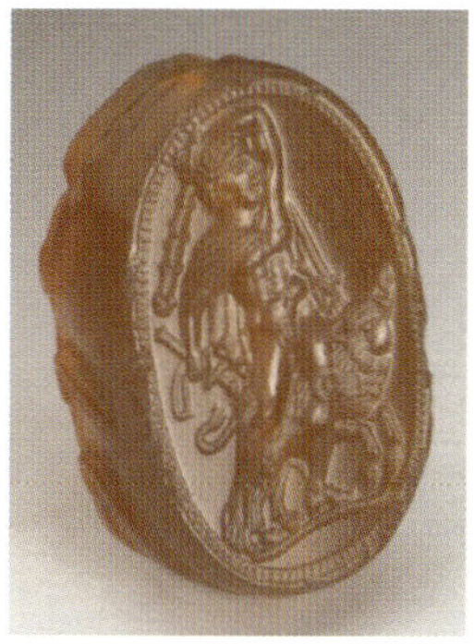

BM 5

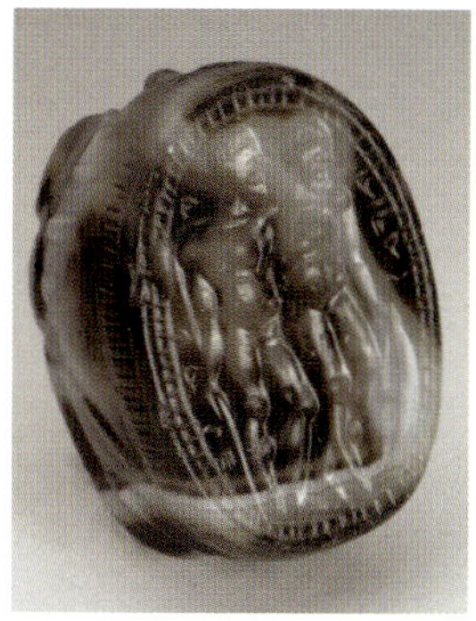

BM 6

BM 3

Finger ring

Gold

Unknown provenance; formerly in the Campanari collection

Second half of the 6th century BC

Diameter 2.2 cm; diameter (inner) 1.8 cm; length (bezel) 2.0 cm; weight 3.36 g

This Ionian-style finger ring was made in Etruria. It has an engraved design of two opposed sphinxes each with a raised front paw, within a hatched border.

British Museum, inv. GR.1846.6-29.19

Marshall 1907, no. 24; for the type, see Cristofani and Martelli 1983, nos. 175-9.

BM 4

Engraved gem

Carnelian

Cortona; formerly in the Castellani collection

6th century BC

Length (bezel) 1.6 cm; width 1.3 cm

This Etruscan gemstone in the form of a scarab is engraved with Perseus cutting off Medusa's head with a curved blade. She grasps at the sword, clutching a snake in her right hand. The representation contrasts with Greek versions where she has snake-like hair and a grotesque face with protruding tongue.

British Museum, inv. GR.1865.7-12.97

Walters 1906, no. 623; Richter 1968, no. 854; Zazoff 1968, no. 55; LIMC IV, 1, p. 338, no. 99

BM 5

Engraved gem

Carnelian

Chiusi; formerly in the Fanelli and Castellani collections

Late 5th to early 4th centuries BC

Length (bezel) 1.8 cm; width 1.2 cm

This Etruscan scarab is engraved with Theseus or Herakles and a boar.

British Museum, inv. GR.1872-4.1140

Walters 1906, no. 668; Richter 1968, no. 795; Zazoff 1968, no. 115

BM 6

Engraved gem

Banded agate

Unknown provenance; formerly in the Santangelo and Castellani collections

5th century BC

Length 1.8 cm (bezel); width 1.4 cm

This Etruscan scarab is engraved with Achilles holding a spear and Ajax holding a shield. Both are nude and their names are inscribed beside them (the Etruscan versions being Achale and Aifas).

British Museum, inv. GR.1872.6-4.1142

Walters 1906, no. 670; Richter 1968, no. 823; Zazoff 1968, no. 332

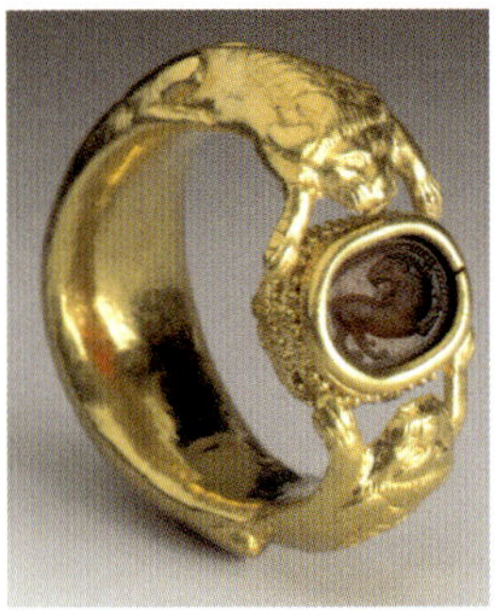

BM 7

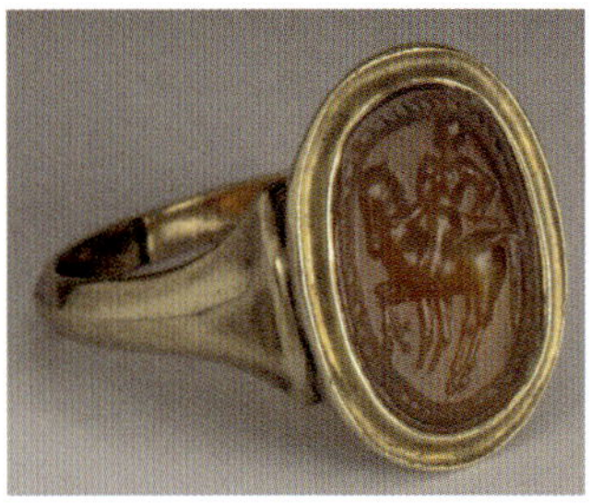

BM 8

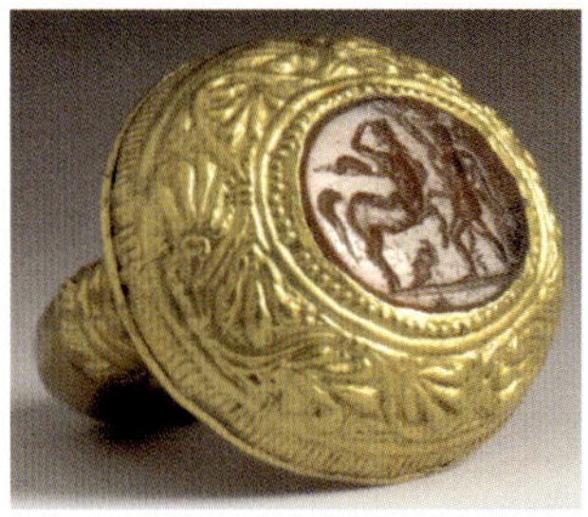

BM 9

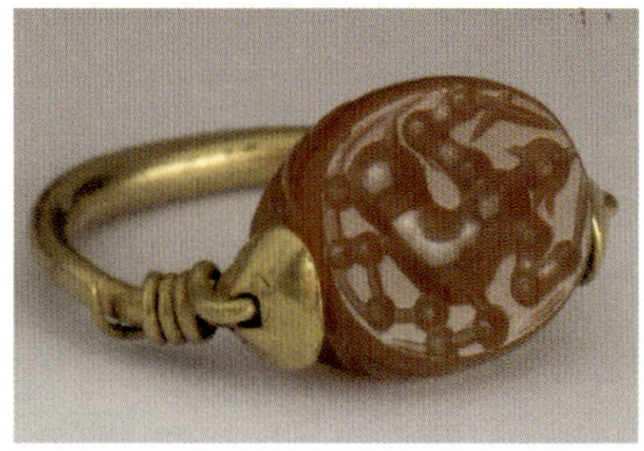

BM 10

BM 7

Finger ring

Gold, sard

Unknown provenance; formerly in the Féjerváry collection

Early 5th century BC

Diameter 2.9 cm; diameter (inner) 2.1 cm; length (bezel) 1.3 cm; weight 15.55 g

This Etruscan finger ring has a broad hoop, ending on either side with a crouching lion in relief. The forepaws of the lions are outstretched and support a sard scarab in a gold band-setting ornamented with filigree and granules. The engraved design shows a lion with its head turned back.

British Museum, inv. GR.1856.6-25.18

Marshall 1907, no. 300; Walters 1906, no. 700; J. Boardman 1968, no. 417; Zazoff 1968, no. 1430; Cristofani and Martelli 1983, no. 189

BM 8

Engraved gem

Gold, sard

Unknown provenance; formerly in the Sir William Hamilton collection

4th century BC

Length 1.5 cm; width 1.2 cm

This Etruscan gemstone, engraved with a nude horseman dismounting, is set in a modern ring of 18th-century date. The horseman may simply be a rider or alternatively could be a contestant in the 'anabates' race, where the horseman dismounted and ran beside his horse for the last stretch. This event was included in the ancient Olympic Games. The lids of some bronze vessels from Campania are decorated with similar figures in bronze.

British Museum, inv. GR.1772.3-14.49

Walters 1906, no. 779; Zazoff 1968, no. 1219

BM 9

Finger ring

Gold, sard

Said to have been found at Bolsena; formerly in the Castellani collection

4th century BC

Diameter 3.7 cm; diameter (inner) 2.0 cm; length (bezel) 1.9 cm; weight 19.37 g

This finger ring has a hollow semi-circular hoop and a large oval setting containing a sard intaglio. The engraved design shows a combat between a Centaur and a Lapith (from Thessaly) holding a torch. There is a crested helmet on the ground.

British Museum, inv. GR.1872.6-4.149

Walters 1906, no. 789; Marshall 1907, no. 357; for the type, see Cristofani and Martelli 1983, 244

There is some doubt as to whether the gem and also the ring may be of 19th-century origin, but the type is Etruscan, of about the 3rd century BC

BM 10

Finger ring

Gold, sard

Unknown provenance; formerly in the Castellani collection

4th to 3rd centuries BC

Diameter 1.8 cm; diameter (inner) 1.6 cm; length (bezel) 1.0 cm; weight 2.91 g

This Etruscan swivel ring is set with a sard scarab engraved with a Centaur, perhaps holding branches. The design was cut using the rounded or 'a globolo' style, achieved almost entirely with a drill.

British Museum, inv. GR.1872.6-4.15

Walters 1906, no. 839; Marshall 1907, no. 321; Zazoff 1968, no. 897; for the style and subject matter, cf. M. Henig 1994, no. 111 and Richter 1968, nos. 875-6.

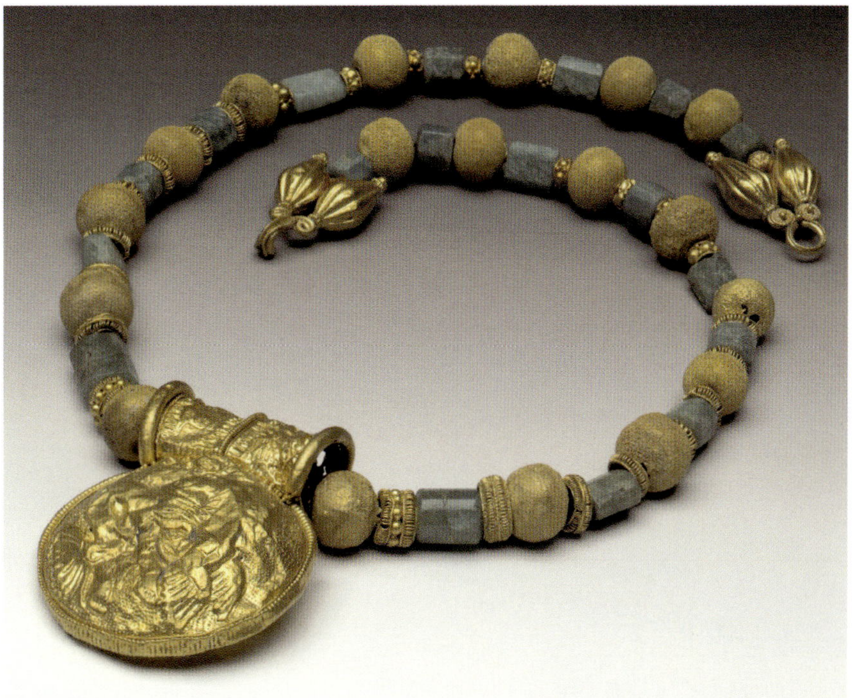

BM 11

Necklace

Gold, plasma

Unknown provenance; acquired before 1911, and probably put together in modern times from ancient beads

5th to 2nd centuries BC

Length 46.4 cm; weight 1102.0 g

This necklace is composed of a variety of gold and plasma beads and rings and a central hollow 'bulla' embossed with a Nereid (sea nymph) on a winged sea-horse. She is holding what may be a shell in her right hand. The bulla is suspended from a gold cylinder stamped with a leaf pattern. At each end of the necklace is a clasp (probably not belonging) formed of amphora-shaped beads.

Bullas were characteristically worn by the Etruscans, both people and animals, apparently as amulets. Some, like this one, appear to have contained a resin-like substance, perhaps perfumed, and holes in the surface of the bulla (here at the back) may have encouraged the fragrance to be released on contact with the skin. In Roman times the custom of wearing the bulla was preserved in that babies were given one on the day of birth. These were made of gold in the case of the wealthy and leather for the poor. A boy removed his bulla only after he received his adult toga, signifying his Roman citizenship, while a girl only removed hers on her wedding day.

British Museum, inv. GR.1980.2-1.97

Marshall 1911, no. 2284; for similar bullas, see Cristofani and Martelli 1983, nos. 260-4

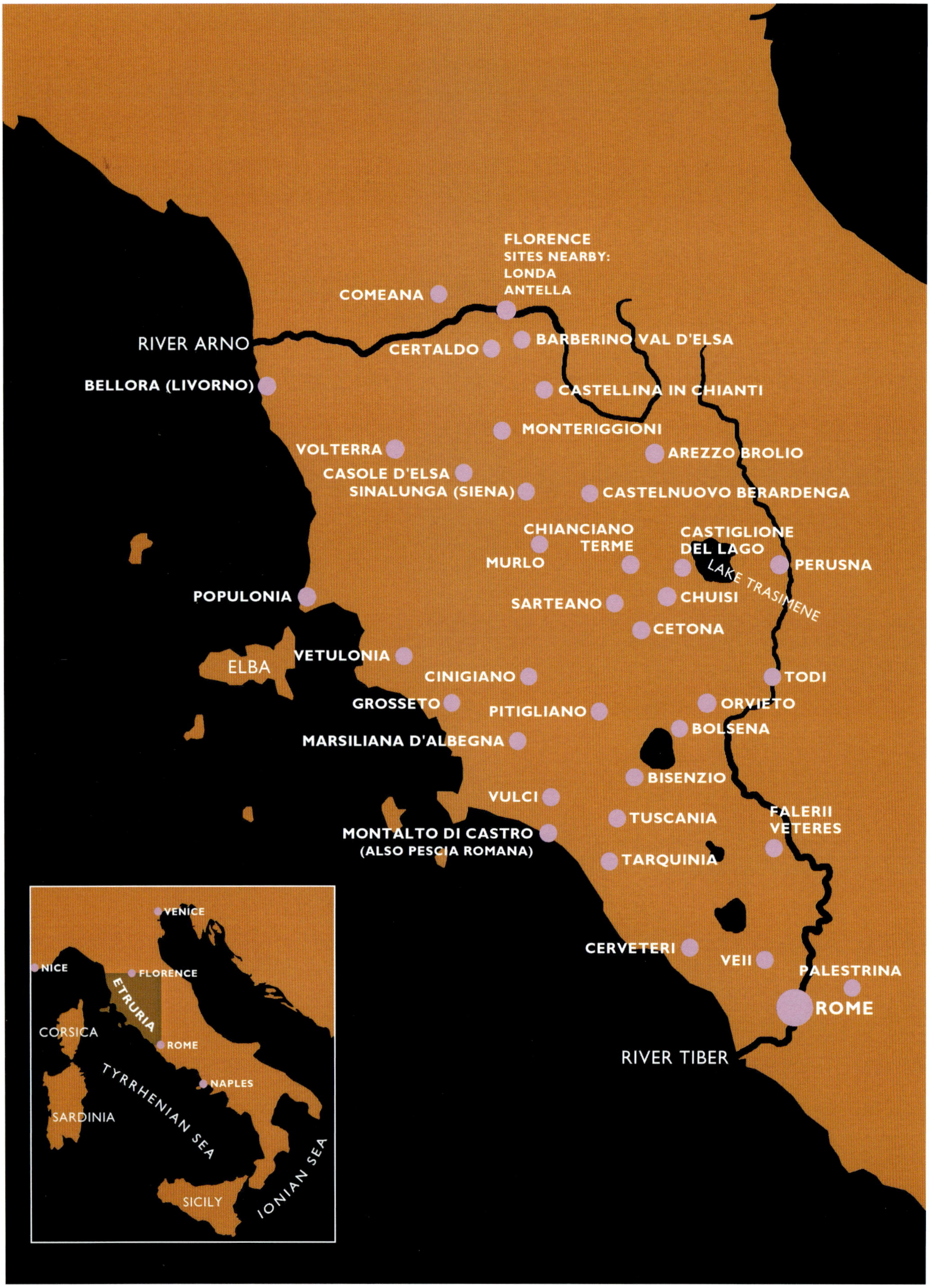
FLORENCE
SITES NEARBY:
LONDA
ANTELLA
COMEANA
RIVER ARNO
CERTALDO
BARBERINO VAL D'ELSA
BELLORA (LIVORNO)
CASTELLINA IN CHIANTI
MONTERIGGIONI
VOLTERRA
AREZZO BROLIO
CASOLE D'ELSA
SINALUNGA (SIENA)
CASTELNUOVO BERARDENGA
CHIANCIANO
TERME
CASTIGLIONE
DEL LAGO
MURLO
PERUSNA
LAKE TRASIMENE
POPULONIA
SARTEANO
CHUISI
CETONA
ELBA
VETULONIA
CINIGIANO
TODI
GROSSETO
PITIGLIANO
ORVIETO
BOLSENA
MARSILIANA D'ALBEGNA
BISENZIO
VULCI
TUSCANIA
FALERII
VETERES
MONTALTO DI CASTRO
(ALSO PESCIA ROMANA)
TARQUINIA
CERVETERI
VEII
PALESTRINA
ROME
RIVER TIBER
VENICE
NICE
FLORENCE
ETRURIA
CORSICA
ROME
NAPLES
TYRRHENIAN SEA
SARDINIA
SICILY
IONIAN SEA

ETRURIA		REST OF EUROPE, NEAR EAST AND AFRICA
	2000 BC	[c.2000] Building of the inner circle of Stonehenge
	1900	
	1800	
[c.1700–1300] Middle Bronze Age – Development of settlement sites in lowland Etruria	1700	[c.1650] Formation of the Kingdom of the Hittites
	1600	[c.1630] End of the Middle Kingdom and division of Egypt
	1500	[c.1550] Beginning of the Mycenaean period in Greece; [c.1539] Beginning of the New Kingdom in Egypt
	1400	
[c.1300–900] Late Bronze Age – Transition from village to state societies	1300	[c.1322] Burial of King Tutankhamun in the Valley of the Kings in Egypt
	1200	[c.1250] Date of the 'Fall of Troy' according to Greek myth
	1100	[c.1150] Fall of Mycenaean Greece – palaces and towns abandoned, beginning of the Dark Ages in Greece
	1000	[c.950] Beginning of the Assyrian Empire
[900–725] **The Rise of the Etruscans** – Earliest evidence of the settlements of the Villanovan civilization marking the beginnings of the Etruscan civilization	900	[c.900] End of Greek Dark Ages, beginning of the Geometric Period
	800	[c.800] Start of Celtic Iron Age (Hallstatt); [c.776] First Olympic Games held; [c.750] Evidence of iron-working in Britain
[725–580] **Wealth and Power** – The Orientalizing period	700	
[580–480] **Urban Society** – The Archaic period	600	[c.612] Fall of the Assyrian Empire
	500	[c.490] Battle between the Greeks and the Persians at Marathon
	400	[c.432] The Parthenon in Greece built
The decline of Etruscan culture and the expansion of Rome into Etruscan territory	300	[332] Egypt conquered by Alexander the Great
Etruscans receive Roman citizenship in 90BC	200	[c.218] The Carthaginian commander Hannibal and his army cross the Alps on elephants during the 2nd Punic War against Rome
[325–90] **Etruscan Decline** – Etruria eventually absorbed into the Roman Empire	100	
	AD 1	[30] Queen Cleopatra defeated by Augustus Caesar. Egypt absorbed into the Roman Empire

BIBLIOGRAPHY

[* denotes the abbreviation that has been used in the text]

Artigianato 1985*

Artigianato artistico: L'Etruria settentrionale interna in età ellenistica. Volterra and Chiusi exhibition. Milan 1985

Beazley 1956*

J D Beazley, *Attic black-figure vase-painters.* Oxford 1956

Beazley 1963*

J D Beazley, *Attic red-figure vase-painters.* Oxford 1963

Becatti 1955*

G Becatti, *Oreficerie antiche delle minoiche alle barbariche.* Rome 1955

Boardman 1966*

J Boardman, 'Etruscan and South Italian rings in Oxford', Papers of the British School at Rome 34, 1966

Boardman 1968*

J Boardman, *Archaic Greek Gem.* London 1968

Borelli and Targio 2003*

F Borelli and M C Targio, *The Etruscans: art, architecture and history.* London 2003

Bruni 1992*

S Bruni in *Populonia in età ellenistica: i materiali dalle necropoli. Atti del seminario, Florence, June 1986.* Florence 1992

Bruni 1993*

S Bruni, 'La Civiltà di Chuisi e del suo territorio', in Proceedings of the 17th Congress of Etruscan and Italic Studies (Chianciano Terme, 1989). Florence 1993

Camporeale 1969*

G Camporeale, *I commerci di Vetulonia in età orientalizzante.* Florence 1969

Camporeale 1984*

G Camporeale, *La caccia in Etruria.* Rome 1984

Cento Preziosi 1984*

Cento Preziosi Etruschi. Arezzo exhibition. Florence 1984

Cianferoni 1992*

G C Cianferoni in *Populonia in età ellenistica: i materiali dalle necropoli. Atti del seminario, Florence, June 1986.* Florence 1992.

Civiltà 1985*

Civiltà degli etruschi. Florence exhibition. Milan 1985

Cristofani 1978*

M Cristofani, *L'arte degli etruschi.* Turin 1978

Cristofani 1979*

M Cristofani, *The Etruscans: a new investigation.* London 1979

Cristofani 1985*

M Cristofani, *I bronzi degli etruschi.* Novara 1985

Cristofani and Martelli 1983*

M Cristofani and M Martelli (eds), *L'oro degli etruschi.* Novara 1983

CVA Edinburgh 1989*

E Moignard, *Corpus Vasorum Antiquorum, National Museums of Scotland, Edinburgh.* Edinburgh 1989

Etruscos 1999*

Los Etruscos. Mexico City exhibition. Milan 1999

Etrusker 1987*

Etrusker in der Toskana: Etruskische gräber der frühzeit. Hamburg and Malmö exhibition. Florence 1987

Falchi 1891*

I Falchi, *Vetulonia e la sua necropoli antichissima.* Florence 1891

Fortnum 1873*

C D E Fortnum, 'On some antique gold and other finger rings found at Palestrina', *Archaeologia* 44, 1873, 353-62

Gioielli 1988*

Gioielli e ornamenti dagli egizi all'alto medioevo. Arezzo exhibition. Florence 1988

Haynes 2000*

S Haynes, *Etruscan civilization: a cultural history.* London 2000

Henig 1994*

M Henig, *Classical Gems, Ancient and Modern Intaglios in the Fitzwilliam Museum, Cambridge.* Cambridge 1994

Higgins 1980*

R A Higgins, *Greek and Roman Jewellery.* 2nd edition, London 1980

Hume-Campbell 1887*

Catalogue of a collection of Greek, Etruscan, and Roman bronzes, fictile ware, and glass presented to the Edinburgh Museum of Science and Art by Sir Hugh Hume-Campbell of Marchmont, Bt. Edinburgh 1887

Johnstone 1937*

M A Johnstone, 'Etruscan collections in the Royal Scottish Museum, Edinburgh, and the National Museum of Antiquities of Scotland, Edinburgh', *Studi Etruschi* 11, 1937, 387-406

Jucker 1991*

I Jucker, *Italy of the Etruscans.* Jerusalem 1991

L'Etruria mineraria 1985*

L'Etruria mineraria. Portoferraio, Massa Marittima and Populonia exhibition. Florence and Milan 1985

LIMC*

Lexicon Iconographicum Mythologicae Classicae. Munich and Zurich 1981, continuing

Mágico 1996*

El mágico oro. Italia tesoro de la antigüedad. Seville exhibition. Florence 1996

Magnificenza 1998*

La magnificenza dei prinicipi etruschi. Sao Paolo exhibition. Florence 1998

Mangani 1991*

E Mangani, M Cygielman, *La collezione Chigi-Zondadari.* Rome 1991

Marshall 1907*

F H Marshall, *Catalogue of the Finger Rings, Greek, Etruscan and Roman, in the Departments of Antiquities, British Museum.* London 1907

Marshall 1911*

F H Marshall, *Catalogue of the Jewellery, Greek, Etruscan and Roman, in the Departments of Antiquities, British Museum.* London 1911

Martelli 1978*

M Martelli, 'La ceramica greco-orientale in Etruria', in *Les céramiques de la Grèce de L'Est et leur diffusion en Occident,* Proceedings of the meeting, Naples, 1976. Paris 1978

Mayer-Prokop 1967*

I Mayer-Prokop, *Die gravierten etruskischen Griffspiegel archaischen Stils.* Mitteilungen des Deutschen Archäologischen Instituts, Römische abteilung, Ergänzungsheft 13. Heidelberg 1967

Minto 1921*

A Minto, *Marsiliana d'Albegna.* Florence 1921

Minto 1922*

A Minto, *Populonia: la necropoli arcaica.* Florence 1922

Minto 1932*

A Minto, 'Le ultime scoperte archeologiche di Populonia (1927-1931)', *MonAnt* 34, 1932

MonAnt*

Monumenti antichi publicati percura della Accademia Nazionale dei Lincei

Neeft 1983*

C F Neeft, *Protocorinthian subgeometric aryballoi.* Amsterdam 1983

NSc*

Notizie degli scavi di antichità

Payne 1931*

H Payne, *Necrocorinthia.* Oxford 1931

Richter 1968*

G M A Richter, *The Engraved Gems of the Greeks, Etruscans and Romans, Part I, The Engraved Gems of the Greeks and Etruscans. A History of Greek art in Miniature.* London 1968

Ridgway 1997*

D Ridgway, 'Nestor's cup and the Etruscans', *Oxford Journal of Archaeology* 16, 3 (1997), 334-5

Ridout Sharpe 1991*

J S Ridout Sharpe, 'The mollusca' in E Peltenburg, *Lemba Archaeological Project II.2, A Ceremonial Area at Kissonerga,* 75-84. Göteborg 1991

Rieu 1966*

E V Rieu (trans), Homer, *The Iliad.* Harmondsworth 1966

Romualdi 1998*

A Romualdi in *Una donna di rango a Populonia: tra la fine del quinto e gli inizi del quarto secolo a.C.* Florence exhibition. Florence 1998

Santuari 1985*

Santuari d'Etruria. Arezzo exhibition. Milan 1985

Shefton 1979*

B Shefton, *Die 'rhodischen' bronzekannen.* Mainz 1979

Sport 1988*

Lo sport nell'antichità. Florence exhibition. Florence 1988

StEtr*

Studi Etruschi

Sundwall 1943*

J Sundwall, *Die älteren italischen fibeln.* Berlin 1943

Szilágyi 1967*

J G Szilágyi in *Wissenschaft zeitschrift der universität Rostock.* 1967

Testa 1989*

A Testa, *Candelabri e tymiateria.* Rome 1989

Torelli 2000*

M Torelli, *The Etruscans.* Venice 2000

von Hase 1971*

F W von Hase, 'Gürtelschliessen des 7 und 6 jahrhunderts v. chr. in mittelitalien', *Jahrbuch des Deutschen Archäologischen Instituts* 86, 1971

Walters 1906*

H B Walters, *Catalogue of the Engraved Gems and Cameos, Greek Etruscan and Roman, in the British Museum,* London 1906

Walters 1926*

H B Walters, *Catalogue of the Engraved Gems in the British Museum.* London 1926

Zazoff 1968*

P Zazoff, *Etruskische Skarabäen.* Mainz-am-Rhein 1968

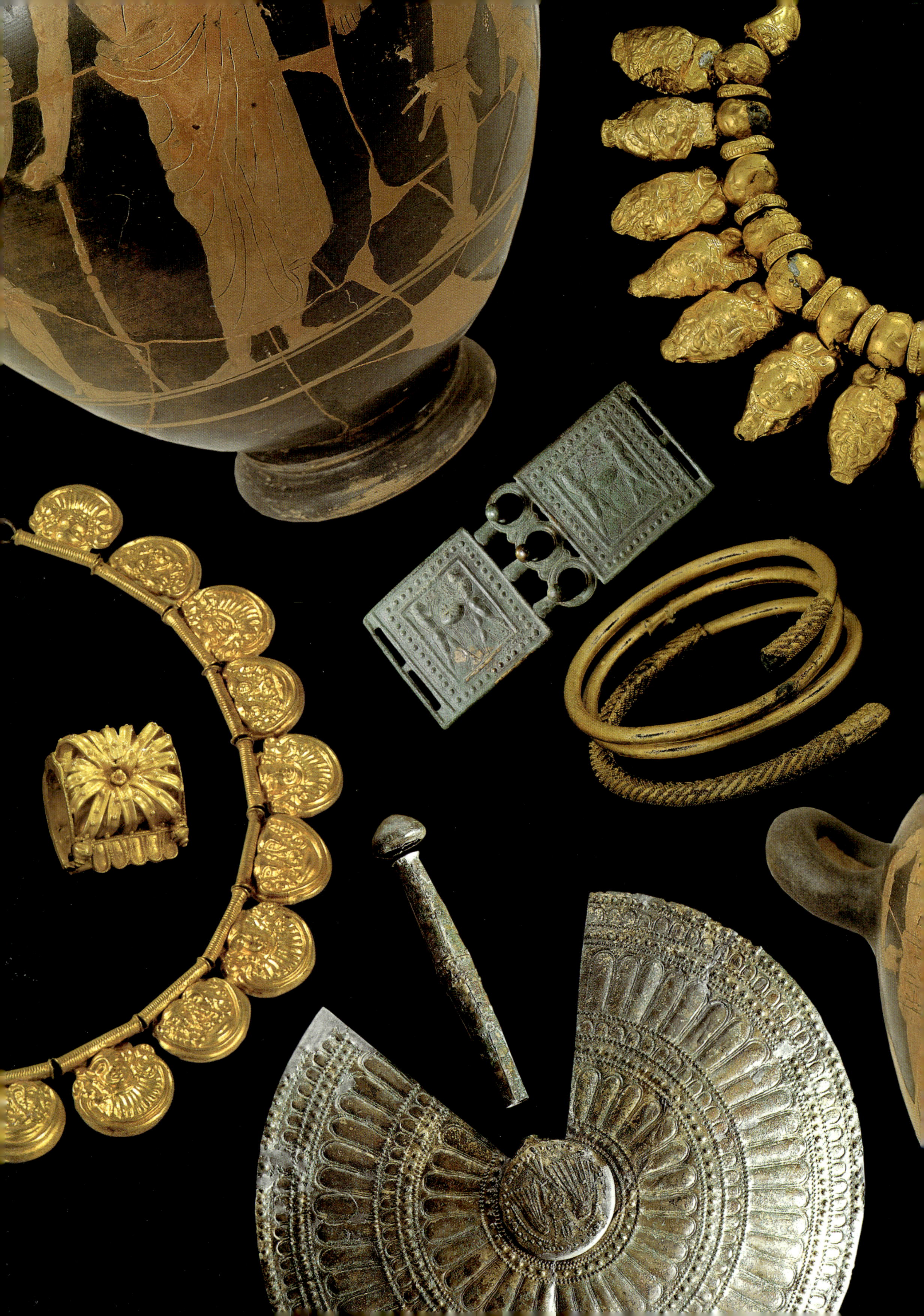